THE ATLANTIC CROSSING GUIDE

RCC PILOTAGE FOUNDATION

THE ATLANTIC CROSSING GUIDE

PREPARATION, PASSAGES AND ASSOCIATED CRUISING GROUNDS

6TH EDITION

Jane Russell

Previous editions revised and updated by
John Lawson, Anne Hammick and Gavin McLaren

Original edition by
Philip Allen

ADLARD COLES NAUTICAL
LONDON

Published by Adlard Coles Nautical
an imprint of A & C Black (Publishers) Ltd
36 Soho Square, London W1D 3QY
www.adlardcoles.com

Copyright © RCC Pilotage Foundation 1983, 1988, 1992, 1998, 2003, 2010

First published in Great Britain by Adlard Coles 1983
Reprinted with amendments 1984, 1985
Second edition 1988
Revised reprint 1989
Third edition published by Adlard Coles Nautical 1992
Reprinted with amendments 1994
Reprinted 1996
Fourth edition 1998
Fifth edition 2003
Sixth edition 2010

ISBN 978-1-4081-1380-6

All rights reserved. No part of this publication may be reproduced in any form or by any means – graphic, electronic or mechanical, including photocopying, recording, taping or information storage and retrieval systems – without the prior permission in writing of the publishers.

A CIP catalogue record for this book is available from the British Library.

This book is produced using paper that is made from wood grown in managed, sustainable forests. It is natural, renewable and recyclable. The logging and manufacturing processes conform to the environmental regulations of the country of origin.

Designed by Suchinda Thompson
Typeset in ACaslon 10/13pt

Printed and bound in Barcelona, Spain by GRAFOS, SA
Arte sobre papel

Some of the plans included have been based, with permission, on British Admiralty Charts and Publications.

CAUTION

Whilst the RCC Pilotage Foundation, the author and the Publisher have used reasonable endeavours to ensure the accuracy of the content of this book, it contains selected information and thus is not definitive. It does not contain all known information on the subject in hand and should not be relied on alone for navigational use; it should only be used in conjunction with official hydrographic data. This is particularly relevant to the plans, which should not be used for navigation.

The RCC Pilotage Foundation, the author and the Publisher believe that the information that they have included is a useful aid to prudent navigation. But the safety of a vessel depends ultimately on the judgement of the skipper, who should assess all information, published or unpublished.

The information provided in this book may be out of date and may be changed or updated without notice. The RCC Pilotage Foundation cannot accept any liability for any error, omission or failure to update such information.

To the extent permitted by law, the RCC Pilotage Foundation, the author and the Publishers do not accept liability for any loss, and/or damage howsoever caused that may arise from reliance on information contained in these pages.

Additional information

Additional or updated information for this book can be found on the Publications page on the RCC Pilotage Foundation website www.rccpf.org.uk

This site also includes a considerable amount of pilotage information which may be of interest to readers of this book.

Cover illustrations:
Heading up the Caribbean island chain to a landfall at St Lucia. Photo: Mike Robinson
A typical San Blas village, Western Caribbean. Photo: Richard Woods
The dinghy dock at New Plymouth, Green Turtle Cay, Bahamas. Photo: Richard Woods
A Greenland iceberg. Photo: Mark Hillmann

Page ii: An anchorage in the San Blas group of islands, Panama, Western Caribbean. Photo: Richard Woods

Contents

Foreword to sixth edition	vii
The RCC Pilotage Foundation	vii
Preface	viii
Acknowledgements	viii
Index of Plans	xii
Introduction	1

I PREPARATIONS — 2

1 Thinking it through — 2
- Asking the right questions — 2
- Being self-sufficient — 2
- Joining a rally — 3

2 Preparing the boat — 5
- Hull, deck and through fittings — 5
- The rig — 7
- Sails — 9
- Ground tackle — 12
- Fendering — 15
- Automatic steering — 15
- The engine, electrical system and electronics — 16
- Alternative power generation — 19
- Dinghies and outboard engines — 20
- Maintenance and spares — 21

3 Creating a home from home — 23
- Awnings and screens — 23
- Below decks — 25
- Food and water — 32

4 The crew — 38
- Crew dynamics — 38
- Onboard routine — 39
- Keeping healthy — 43

5 Navigation and communication — 46
- Ship's log — 46
- Navigation equipment — 46
- Communication — 50

6 Protocol, paperwork and procedures — 53
- Formalities — 53
- CITES — 53
- Documentation — 54
- Entry procedures — 55
- Money — 56
- Duty-free imports — 56
- Insurance — 56
- Traffic Separation Schemes — 57

7 Dealing with risk — 58
- Falling overboard — 58
- Gales, hurricanes and line squalls — 59
- Lightning — 60
- Emergency steering — 60
- Collisions — 61
- Fire — 61
- Liferafts and grab bags — 61
- Flares — 62
- EPIRBs — 62
- SARTs — 63
- Security and firearms — 63
- Pests — 63
- Other risks — 63

8 Contribution to science — 64

II PASSAGES AND LANDFALLS 66

Overview of the North Atlantic 66
    Route timing 67
    Weather forecast transmissions 71
    Port information 74

9 The Atlantic Coast of Europe 75
1	Crosshaven, Cork, Ireland	78
2	Falmouth, United Kingdom	82
3	Brest, France	86
4	La Coruña, Spain	89
5	Baiona (Bayona), Spain	92
6	Cascais, Lisbon, Portugal	95

10 Strait of Gibraltar and the Atlantic Coast of Morocco to Madeira and The Canaries 97

Harbours in the Strait of Gibraltar 101
7	Gibraltar	101
8	La Linea, Spain	104
9	Ceuta (Spanish enclave on the Moroccan coast)	106

Harbours on the Atlantic coast of Morocco 108
10	Mohammedia	109
11	Agadir	111

Harbours in Madeira 113
12	Porto Santo	115
13	Quinta do Lorde	117

Harbours in The Canaries 119
14	Las Palmas de Gran Canaria	122
15	Santa Cruz de Tenerife	125

11 Cape Verdes, Senegal and The Gambia 127
16	Porto Grande, Mindelo, Cape Verdes	130

12 Atlantic Ocean – Trade Wind Routes 135

13 Landfalls in the Caribbean 139
17	Bridgetown/Port St Charles, Barbados	149
18	Chaguaramas Bay, Trinidad	153
19	Rodney Bay, St Lucia	157
20	English Harbour/Falmouth Harbour, Antigua	160
21	British Virgin Islands	164

14 Routes across the Caribbean and landfall in Panama 168
22	Colón, Panama	173

15 The Caribbean Islands to Florida 176
23	Luperon, Dominican Republic	179
24	Providenciales, Turks and Caicos	182
25	Georgetown, Great Exuma, Bahamas	184
26	Marsh Harbour, Abacos, Bahamas	186
27	Fort Lauderdale, Florida, USA	188

16 Landfalls on the Atlantic coast of the USA including entrances into the Intracoastal Waterway 191
28	Beaufort/Morehead City, North Carolina	202
29	Norfolk, Virginia	205
30	Annapolis, Maryland	209
31	New York, New York	213
32	Newport, Rhode Island	218
33	Portland, Maine	221

17 Passages in the middle latitudes of the North Atlantic including landfalls in Bermuda and the Azores 224
34	St George's, Bermuda	230
35	Porto das Lajes, Flores, Azores	237
36	Horta, Faial, Azores	239
37	Ponta Delgada, Sao Miguel, Azores	242

18 Passages and landfalls in the high latitudes of the North Atlantic 245
38	Halifax, Nova Scotia, Canada	250
39	St Johns, Newfoundland, Canada	254
40	Stornoway, Isle of Lewis, Scotland, UK	257

Appendix A Charts 260
Appendix B The Atlantic Hurricane Season 264
Appendix C Glossary of Meteorological Terms 267
Appendix D Weather Forecast Areas 270
Appendix E Weights, Measures and Conversions 272
Appendix F Coping with Complete Electronic Failure 273

Index 275

Foreword to the sixth edition

Much has changed in the sailing world since this book was first published in 1983. Boats tend to be larger and rigs and gear have become easier to handle, GPS has simplified ocean navigation and communication is much simpler. However, the ocean itself is unchanging and skippers still remain as responsible for vessel and crew as ever before. Weather may be unkind, equipment may fail and a glorious daytime trade wind sail may be followed by challenging conditions that night.

This book is a guide to help crews to prepare their boats and themselves so that their later memories of the crossing are all good ones. Preparation is the key, along with an understanding of the need for self sufficiency.

As sailing horizons have extended in the past decade, so the Atlantic Crossing Guide now builds on its original core details about the Atlantic Circuit and adds in links to the numerous cruising areas where sailors may leave or join the traditional circuit. The scope of the book may be readily seen on the plan on pages x/xi. As a circumnavigator, Jane Russell has had ample experience and contacts to draw on whilst updating every aspect of this book. Preparing the book has been a major project and the Pilotage Foundation is grateful to Jane for all her research and preparation and to Janet Murphy and her team at Adlard Coles Nautical for the presentation of this work.

The Pilotage Foundation welcomes feedback – text or photographs, e-mail or hard copy – from those sailing these waters. Where appropriate, updated material will be published on our website which also gives details of all our other publications, many of which are available for free download.

Martin Walker
Hon Director
RCC Pilotage Foundation

The RCC Pilotage Foundation

In 1976 an American member of the Royal Cruising Club, Dr Fred Ellis, indicated that he wished to make a gift to the Club in memory of his father, the late Robert E. Ellis, of his friends Peter Pye and John Ives and as a mark of esteem for Roger Pinckney. An independent charity known as the RCC Pilotage Foundation was formed and Dr Ellis added his house to his already generous gift of money to form the Foundation's permanent endowment. The Foundation's charitable objective is 'to advance the education of the public in the science and practice of navigation' which is at present achieved through the writing and updating of pilot books covering many different parts of the world.

The Foundation is extremely grateful and privileged to have been given the copyrights to books written by a number of distinguished authors and yachtsmen including the late Adlard Coles, Robin Brandon and Malcolm Robson. In return the Foundation has willingly accepted the task of keeping the original books up to date and many yachtsmen and women have helped (and are helping) the Foundation fulfill this commitment. In addition to the titles donated to the Foundation, several new books have been created and developed under the auspices of the Foundation. The Foundation works in close collaboration with three publishers – Imray Laurie Norie and Wilson, Adlard Coles Nautical and On Board Publications – and in addition publishes in its own name short run guides and pilot books for areas where limited demand does not justify large print runs. Several of the Foundation's books have been translated into French, Spanish, Italian and German.

The Foundation runs its own website at www.rccpf.org.uk which not only lists all the publications but also contains free downloadable pilotage information.

The overall management of the Foundation is entrusted to Trustees appointed by the Royal Cruising Club, with day to day operations being controlled by the Director. All these appointments are unpaid. In line with its charitable status, the Foundation distributes no profits, which are used to finance new books and developments and to subsidise those covering areas of low demand.

Preface

The trade wind route across the Atlantic was my first long ocean passage. Although I subsequently continued on across the Pacific and Indian Oceans, my memories of how it felt to be in that first phase of adventure remain strong. When I set off from Penarth with my husband, the longest passage either of us had been at sea was 48 hours. We were in our late 20s and sailing on a tight budget, determined to cast off before the norms of land life held us in their grip. Not entirely unexpectedly, I spent 8 days being seasick as we crossed Biscay, so we were eternally grateful to our two good sailing friends, Dominic Preston and Verity Spence, who came with us to Spain and helped us to get over that first hurdle. We had studied every possible book and magazine article, including the *Atlantic Crossing Guide*. We had also loaded ourselves up with a ludicrous amount of provisions, as well as every conceivable piece of spare equipment. Looking back it is a wonder that we didn't sink under the sheer weight of it all!

Despite all the advice and preparation, as we cast off I remember feeling that I was embarking on a personal journey into the unknown. I'm sure that is true for everyone who first sets out to cross an ocean, which is why it still remains a challenge and why the rewards are many and varied, and sometimes unexpected. Living under a light-polluted sky, I had no idea how completely out of touch I was with the rhythms of the moon and the stars. To be alone on night watch in the middle of the Atlantic and see the full night sky laid out above me from horizon to horizon, with the occasional shooting star triggering a flash of pure joy, is an experience burned into my soul. So too is the incredible intensity of phosphorescence as a display team of dolphins surfed and raced alongside in the ocean swell. I remember a frequent feeling of surprise – there were so many 'firsts' and there was so much to learn about the ocean and about all the places and people I encountered.

It was a great privilege to be given the task of creating a new edition of the *Atlantic Crossing Guide*. The combined wisdom and experience of the previous five editions was a very firm foundation on which to work, in fact rather dauntingly so. It seemed quite a challenge to shape something new whilst trying to maintain the quality and character of what has gone before, and I have been glad of my scientific training as well as my cruising experience. I hope that I have done the subject justice.

Corrections and amendments from anyone currently cruising the Atlantic are very welcome – as text or photographs, e-mail or hard copy via the 'feedback' area on the RCCPF website www.rccpf.org.uk. Any navigationally essential updates during the life of this book will be published on that site.

Jane Russell

Acknowledgements

In many ways the fundamentals of ocean cruising remain timeless. At their core is a philosophy of self-reliance and an ability to adapt and deal with unfamiliar conditions, both at sea and on the land. Those threads continue to run through this latest edition. But the *Atlantic Crossing Guide* has also evolved over time to keep pace with all the various technological advances and the consequent changes to accepted wisdom and practice. I have endeavoured to continue that trend in this edition and have been very fortunate to have been helped in the task by a number of contributors, many but not all of whom are RCC members.

I am extremely grateful for all the lovely photographs which are acknowledged in each caption. The plans form an important part of the book and I would like to say a particularly heartfelt thank you to the cartographers, Alan Whitaker and Christine Holley, who patiently deciphered all of my preliminary plans and converted them into professional graphics. Enormous thanks also go to the following people who, in no particular order, have helped me in various ways – I would not have got very far without them: Graham Adam has provided photographs as well as advice in several areas including aspects of joining a rally. Andrew Bishop (World Cruising Club) also contributed to the discussion on rallies. Jill Dickin Schinas is an inspiration to anyone who may have doubts about cruising with children and I tackled this subject with her guidance. Paul Rose, familiar to many from the BBC series *Oceans*, gave me encouraging feedback on my chapter 'Contributions to Science'. Denis Webster (*Tiger Lilly 2*) has been my weather guru. He has contributed a vast amount of information about weather on the trade wind route and throughout the Caribbean as well as putting together the more detailed text on tropical storms in Appendix B.

Barrie Waugh and Edward Mason (CCC), Hilary Keatinge and Jeremy Parkinson have all helped with aspects of the European coastline. Graham Hutt and John Marchment guided me through the Strait of Gibraltar and down the coast of Morocco. Anne Hammick has given great support throughout with advice, information, photographs and further connections to other contributors. Andy O'Grady provided photographs and much of the information about the Cape Verdes and passages to Brazil. Ed Wheeler and Penny Scott-Bayfield helped to shape the section on West Africa. Mike and Devala Robinson (*Sea Rover*) have provided many photographs as well as sharing some very useful information and suggestions as they made their own voyage from the UK to the Caribbean, Panama and beyond. David and Annette Ridout (*Nordlys*) have also contributed several photographs and updates as they voyaged from the South Atlantic, through the Caribbean and back to Europe via Bermuda and the Azores.

John Lytle (*Oriole*) has updated some of the Caribbean port information as well as putting me in touch with other major contributors. Sergio Mauri gave me updates on Jamaica and routes through the Caribbean. John Franklin (OCC, CCA) (*Al Shaheen*) was extraordinarily generous with his time in providing me with a huge amount of the information necessary to update and expand the chapters covering passages and landfalls between the Caribbean and the USA as well as creating the appendix on storm shelters, helping to update the weather forecast section and connecting me to other contributors. The sections on the Bahamas and the Intracoastal Waterway have greatly benefitted from all the input from Richard Woods who has also given a great deal of wise guidance on many other aspects of the book. Photographs and information from Carla Cook, Portos dos Açores, and Cátia Carvalho, Marina Quinta do Lorde, helped to expand and update the Azores and Madeira sections. Willy Ker (*Assent*) was tirelessly patient with me as I strove to do justice to the more northern routes. Bob Shepton and Mark Hillmann (*Milly Brown*) gave further advice and inspiration about these icy waters.

Dan Darwall (*St Anna*) has been a very supportive sounding board throughout and, together with Clive Ellis (*Walkabout*), helped to create Appendix F. *Yacht Scene* of Gibraltar provided the tidal plans for the Strait of Gibraltar via Imray. Elinor Cole at Imray and Josephine Washington and Tamsin Wenham at the United Kingdom Hydrographic Office produced the pictorial chart catalogues.

I am very grateful to Janet Murphy at Adlard Coles for all her encouragement and guidance, and to Carole Edwards and the other staff who have turned my basic text into such an attractive and well laid out book. Several RCCPF workers have already been mentioned but I also owe a great deal to Ros Hogbin who involved me initially, and who has provided invaluable support through the whole process; I would have stumbled much more without her. Thanks also to Penny Scott-Bayfield and Hugh Clay for proof reading and to Martin Walker, the director of the Pilotage Foundation, who gave me this project, and contributed to several aspects of the book. Martin has kept a supportive, calm and steady hand on the helm throughout; he is one of several people who volunteer an unbelievable amount of time and effort towards meeting the aims of the Pilotage Foundation.

Finally, I would like to thank my husband, David, and *Tinfish* – it wouldn't have happened without them!

Jane Russell

Plan 1 An overview of the North Atlantic showing common passage routes and route feeds covered in Part II.

Iceland

Norway Sweden

United Kingdom

Germany

France

indicates French Canals

Portugal Spain

Italy

Azores

Tunisia

Algeria

Libya

Madeira

Morocco

Canary Is

Western Sahara

Mauritania

Cape Verde Is

Senegal

Guinea

Ivory Coast Ghana Nigeria

Cameroon

40° 30° 20° 10° 0° 10°

INDEX OF PLANS

Plan 1 An overview of the North Atlantic showing common routes and route feeds covered in Part II ... x
Plan 2 The North Atlantic showing ports detailed in Part II ... 66
Plan 3 General direction of current flow in the North Atlantic during December. Based on information from *The Atlantic Pilot Atlas* ... 69
Plan 4 General direction of current flow in the North Atlantic during June. Based on information from *The Atlantic Pilot Atlas* ... 69
Plan 5 Atlantic coast of Europe to 60°N. Ports and passage distances ... 75
Plan 6 Prevailing winds and currents off the Atlantic coast of Europe during August. Based on information from *The Atlantic Pilot Atlas* ... 77
Plan 7 Cork (Cobh) Harbour ... 79
Plan 8 Crosshaven, Ireland ... 81
Plan 9 Falmouth, UK ... 83
Plan 10 Brest, France ... 87
Plan 11 La Coruña, Spain ... 90
Plan 12 Baiona (Bayona), Spain ... 93
Plan 13 Cascais, Portugal ... 96
Plan 14 Strait of Gibraltar and the Atlantic Coast of Morocco to Madeira and the Canary Islands. Ports and passage distances ... 97
Plan 15 Tidal charts for the Strait of Gibraltar. Tidal information by Dr Sloma of Gibraltar *Yacht Scene*, reproduced with permission from Imray ... 99
Plan 16 Prevailing winds and currents off the Atlantic coast of Morocco during October. Based on information from *The Atlantic Pilot Atlas* ... 100
Plan 17 Gibraltar ... 102
Plan 18 La Linea, Spain ... 105
Plan 19 Ceuta, Spain ... 107
Plan 20 Mohammedia, Morocco ... 109
Plan 21 Agadir, Morocco ... 112
Plan 22 Ports in the Madeiran archipelago ... 113
Plan 23 Porto Santo, Madeira ... 115
Plan 24 Marina Quinta do Lorde, Madeira ... 117
Plan 25 The Canary Islands ... 119
Plan 26 Puerto de la Luz, Las Palmas de Gran Canaria ... 123
Plan 27 Marino Atlantico, Santa Cruz de Tenerife ... 125
Plan 28 Ports and passage distances from Madeira to the Cape Verdes and West Africa ... 127
Plan 29 Prevailing winds and currents off the coast of West Africa, 10°N to 35°N, during November. Based on information from *The Atlantic Pilot Atlas* ... 128
Plan 30 Ports in the Cape Verdes ... 129
Plan 31 Porto Grande, Mindelo, São Vicente, Cape Verdes ... 131
Plan 32 Typical trade wind routes across the Atlantic Ocean ... 135
Plan 33 Winds and currents across the Atlantic during December. Based on information from *The Atlantic Pilot Atlas* ... 136
Plan 34 Caribbean island chain ... 140
Plan 35 Prevailing winds over the Caribbean island chain during January. Based on information from *The Atlantic Pilot Atlas* ... 145
Plan 36 Prevailing winds over the Caribbean island chain during May. Based on information from *The Atlantic Pilot Atlas* ... 145
Plan 37 Prevailing currents through the Caribbean island chain during March. Based on information from *The Atlantic Pilot Atlas* ... 145
Plan 38 Bridgetown, Barbados ... 150
Plan 39 Port St Charles, Barbados ... 150
Plan 40 Chaguaramas, Trinidad ... 154
Plan 41 Rodney Bay, St Lucia ... 158
Plan 42 English/Falmouth harbours, Antigua ... 162
Plan 43 The Virgin Islands ... 164
Plan 44 Road Town, Tortola, BVI ... 166
Plan 45 Virgin Gorda Yacht Harbour, Virgin Gorda, BVI ... 167
Plan 46 The Caribbean Sea showing common transit routes ... 168
Plan 47 Winds and currents in the Caribbean Sea during March. Based on information from *The Atlantic Pilot Atlas* ... 169
Plan 48 Colón, Panama ... 174
Plan 49 Ports between the Caribbean Islands and Florida ... 176
Plan 50 Prevailing winds and currents between the Caribbean Islands and Florida during May. Based on information from *The Atlantic Pilot Atlas* ... 177
Plan 51 North coast of the Dominican Republic with details of Luperon and Ocean World ... 181
Plan 52 Providenciales, Turks and Caicos ... 182
Plan 53 Georgetown, Great Exuma, Bahamas ... 184
Plan 54 Marsh Harbour, Great Abaco, Bahamas ... 187
Plan 55 Fort Lauderdale, Florida, USA ... 188
Plan 56 Ports along the Atlantic coast of the USA ... 191
Plan 57 Prevailing winds and currents off the Atlantic coast of the USA during July. Based on information from *The Atlantic Pilot Atlas* ... 191
Plan 58 Iceberg limits and the percentage chance of encountering fog off the North American coast during July. Based on information from *The Atlantic Pilot Atlas* ... 193
Plan 59 Entrance to West Palm Beach ... 198
Plan 60 Entrance to Fort Pierce ... 199
Plan 61 Entrance to St Mary's River ... 200
Plan 62 Entrance to Charleston ... 201
Plan 63 Entrance to Cape Fear River ... 201
Plan 64 Beaufort/Morehead City, North Carolina, USA ... 203
Plan 65 Approaches to Norfolk, Virginia, USA ... 206
Plan 66 Norfolk harbour ... 207
Plan 67 Annapolis, Maryland, USA ... 210
Plan 68 New York, New York, USA ... 214
Plan 69 New York to Cape Cod showing approaches to New York, Newport and the Cape Cod Canal ... 216
Plan 70 Newport, Rhode Island, USA ... 219
Plan 71 Portland, Maine, USA ... 222
Plan 72 Typical routes in the middle latitudes of the North Atlantic ... 224
Plan 73 Prevailing winds and currents in the North Atlantic during June. Based on information from *The Atlantic Pilot Atlas* ... 225
Plan 74 Bermuda ... 230
Plan 75 St Georges, Bermuda ... 232
Plan 76 Ports in the Azores ... 234
Plan 77 Prevailing winds and currents around the Azores during July. Based on information from *The Atlantic Pilot Atlas* ... 235
Plan 78 Lajes Harbour, Flores, Azores ... 237
Plan 79 Horta, Faial, Azores ... 240
Plan 80 Ponta Delgada, São Miguel, Azores ... 242
Plan 81 Ports and passage distances in the higher latitudes of the North Atlantic ... 245
Plan 82 Prevailing winds and currents across the North Atlantic in the higher latitudes during June. Maximum limits of ice and icebergs are also shown. Based on information from *The Atlantic Pilot Atlas* and *Arctic Pilot Vol II* ... 246
Plan 83 Halifax, Nova Scotia, Canada ... 251
Plan 84 St John's, Newfoundland, Canada ... 254
Plan 85 Stornoway, Isle of Lewis, Scotland, UK ... 258

Appendix plans
Appendix A
- *Imray charts for the North Atlantic, passages and island groups.* Reproduced with permission from Imray ... 260
- *Imray charts for the Atlantic coast of Europe, passages and some of the port charts.* Reproduced with permission from Imray ... 261
- *Imray charts for the Caribbean Sea, eastern area.* Reproduced with permission from Imray ... 262
- *Admiralty passage charts for the North Atlantic Ocean.* Reproduced with permission from UKHO ... 263

Introduction

Hundreds of cruising yachts sail across the Atlantic Ocean every year. Some of them make a single crossing on their way to or from peripheral cruising grounds such as the Mediterranean or the Caribbean. Others make a return crossing and complete a circuit. There are several different route options. Most cruising yachts crossing the Atlantic from northern Europe tend to head south to join the trade wind route, although a few hardy souls head westwards in the high latitudes. Those departing from the Mediterranean usually set their sights on Madeira or the Canaries, but the Moroccan coast is becoming more popular as an alternative.

The classic trade wind route runs from the Canaries to the Caribbean. For those with more time, the coast of West Africa can prove to be a memorable cruising ground before heading west. The Cape Verde Islands are a logical stop-off as they sit on an ocean crossroad within the trade wind belt and are a good departure point for passages westwards or southwest towards Brazil. Each year some yachts sail up from the South Atlantic to join the North Atlantic circuit. A few boats sail eastwards through Panama on their way towards Europe. Many more will leave the circle by way of Panama as they head for the Pacific. The classic route out from the eastern shores of the USA is via Bermuda and the Azores, however there are always some who are tempted northwards, despite tales of high winds, fog and ice.

There is a wealth of information now available to the would-be ocean passage maker, including books, websites, courses and seminars, some of which go into great depth on a specific topic. Reference to some of these is made in the appropriate sections of the text. This guide does not attempt to go into great detail on any specific aspect of cruising. Rather it is intended as an introduction and an overview, appropriate to the North Atlantic and its peripheral cruising grounds. It covers a wide range of related topics brought together with a depth of experience from all the contributors, both past and present. Hopefully it will confirm your hopes, ease your concerns and encourage you to consider making your own Atlantic crossing.

A note about websites
Most readers will be familiar with the internet and should find many of the website links useful. Some of the websites may not remain live for the lifetime of this edition. In most cases it should be possible to use a search engine to find the current address for a particular website.

Well proven Atlantic cruising yachts on the wall in Horta, Azores. Photo: David Ridout

I PREPARATIONS

I THINKING IT THROUGH

The dream of sailing across the Atlantic Ocean is shared by people from a diverse range of backgrounds and age groups. You may be a retired couple who have been planning it for most of your lives. Perhaps you are grabbing the chance of a year out from work or studies. You may be a youngster who has to do it on a tiny boat and a tiny budget. It could be your first ocean crossing, but some of you will be approaching the Atlantic having already experienced other ocean passages.

Whoever you are, your approach to it will be specific to you. Even if you plan to join a rally, your preparations and route plans should reflect your own ideas. There is seldom only one right way to prepare, but the more you have thought it through, the better organised you will be to cope with both the routine and the unexpected.

ASKING THE RIGHT QUESTIONS

If you are at an early phase of planning your Atlantic crossing, it may be useful to ask yourself the following questions:

What is your budget? If you are retired from a well-paid career your decisions will be very different to those of a 20-year-old who is doing it on a shoestring. Think through your budget for each phase:

- Buying the boat and equipment
- Ongoing running costs
- Your daily needs and extras like inland travel and emergency situations

On a low budget you will have fewer options, but not necessarily poorer ones!

What is the timescale? The necessity of a tight schedule will lead to solutions which differ from those who are happy to drift for as long as it takes.

Who will I go with? Unless you are planning to be a single-handed sailor you will need to consider all the many aspects of sharing a boat with other people. Whether you plan to sail as a couple, be fully-crewed, or if you are intending to take children, you should plan accordingly.

What route will I follow? Are you heading for the trade winds, with no intention of cruising higher latitudes? Or are you hoping to test yourself in colder waters?

Why do I want to do it? Your answer to this may well change over time. Nevertheless, if you know what you are trying to achieve, your planning will be simplified. For example, if your dream is to slow down and escape as far as possible from the life you have had on land, your choice of boat and equipment may differ markedly from someone who wants modern conveniences on board.

BEING SELF-SUFFICIENT

Sailors who are used to coastal cruising in home waters have a tendency to assume that there will always be help on hand if problems arise. Even in an era of satellite phones and EPIRBs, and when sailing on a rally, there can be times, mid-ocean, when the nearest practical help is many hours, if not days away. It does not matter whether your vessel is a

THINKING IT THROUGH

6.7m (22ft) plywood home-build or a state-of-the-art superyacht. What is most important is that the combined vessel and crew is a self-sufficient unit. The crew need a vessel that is properly seaworthy. They need to know how to maintain that seaworthiness, and how best to look after themselves.

In the preparation phase, a useful way of testing your level of self-sufficiency is to repeatedly ask the question 'What if…?'. For example, 'What if the steering cables part?' or 'What if the furling gear jams?' or 'What if there is a man overboard?' or 'What if the watermaker fails?' or 'What if one of us gets appendicitis?' The same 'What if?' question could and should be asked about all aspects of the boat, its equipment and its crew. Some of the questions will seem small and easy to answer, others will seem catastrophic and nightmarish. But if you have imagined those scenarios, and if you have thought through a response, two things will be true. Firstly you should have equipped yourself with whatever is necessary to solve the problem, and secondly you will be mentally prepared to get on and do whatever is needed. The attitude 'It worries me so I'm trying not to think about it.' will leave you unprepared to deal with even minor issues. Whereas 'I've thought about it and I know exactly what I would do.' leads to a good degree of self-sufficiency.

If you think there could be problems with something, don't ignore that instinct. One more headache before you go is nothing compared to the pain of problems whilst on passage. Whether you have owned your boat for years or just taken delivery of a brand new yacht, it is important that you really know the boat inside and out. Investigate all the systems, practise servicing all the mechanical parts. If you know how everything fits together you will be less daunted about trying to fix things when they go wrong. Living on board for a period before you set off can be a good way of ensuring that you really know your boat.

The flip side of preparing for every eventuality is that it may sometimes feel as if you are never going to finish the list of jobs and get away. Most people find it useful to set a date for departure. Then, even if you haven't completed your preparations, you can start with a short passage to make the first break from your land-based life. Try to keep a perspective about the things that are not essential to seaworthiness and survival. Don't delay your departure for the sake of niceties. Once you are cruising you will probably find that you have a lot more time to potter about and improve on the basics.

JOINING A RALLY

Joining a rally to cross the Atlantic is a popular choice for many cruisers. More than 200 boats each year take part in the Atlantic Rally for Cruisers (ARC) from the Canaries to the Caribbean. The Atlantic Rally to Europe (ARC Europe)

Living the dream – *Al Shaheen* enjoys a romp in the trade winds. Her equipment shows that she is a serious ocean cruiser with many sea miles under her keel. Photo: www.yachtshotsbvi.com

PREPARATIONS

The start of the 2008 Atlantic Rally for Cruisers (ARC). Photo: Graham Adam

is for boats heading from the Caribbean to Europe and is often joined in Bermuda by boats heading out from the USA. There are other transatlantic rallies which are smaller and take different routes; for example Les Iles du Soleil Rallye Transatlantique leaves from the Canaries and goes via the Cape Verdes to Brazil and into the Amazon. On the western side of the Atlantic there are several rallies such as the Cruising Rally Association Caribbean 1500. The European coast plays host to numerous rallies every year.

There are pros and cons to joining a rally. Whether or not it is right for you is really down to personal choice. A rally will provide you with a vast array of information and advice which can be an invaluable confidence boost. The ARC runs a whole series of pre-voyage seminars and training sessions, including an information-packed weekend. These are occasions when lasting friendships can be formed, giving mutual encouragement in the weeks and months pre-departure. The ARC does require you to meet certain requirements for length of vessel, types of equipment carried on board and levels of pre-rally training. These are sensible pre-requisites for anyone intending to undertake an extended cruise for the first time. But some of the requirements may be beyond those on a small boat or a tight budget. A popular reason for choosing to rally is that it forces you into setting a departure date and dictates the pace of your cruising. A downside of this is that you may then feel obliged to stick to that date and that pace, whatever the weather pattern and however your plans may have changed since leaving home waters. Rallies offer the reassurance of an extended cruising community with organisational back-up, the possibility of a certain amount of competition even outside the racing divisions, and the sociability of numerous parties and celebrations with like-minded people.

If you want to dictate your own pace and itinerary and don't think that a rally is for you, be assured that most non-rally yachts travelling similar paths also evolve into their own cruising communities. These smaller groups of yachts look out for each other, keeping in touch via radio. They frequently go to each other's rescue in various ways, and certainly get together to celebrate. It would be wrong to assume that if you don't join a rally you will remain isolated from other cruisers. It would be equally wrong to gain a false sense of security and think that joining a rally will automatically protect you from worst case scenarios. It is better to assume that, whether you are with a rally or not, once you are offshore, you are on your own. There are several incidents each year where rally yachts do help other yachts in mid-ocean, but such assistance could never be guaranteed and organisers of rallies are the first to recognise the need for proper preparation and thorough self-reliance.

Websites
If you want to find out more about joining a rally, the following websites may be useful:

www.worldcruising.com *The ARC and ARC Europe*
Within this site you can opt to download a PDF file of the Entry Pack, including the Safety Equipment Requirements. Whether or not you choose to join the rally, this gives a useful perspective on assessing how well your boat and equipment shape up for an Atlantic Crossing.
www.ilesdusoleil.eu *Canaries to Brazil*
www.carib1500.com *USA to the Caribbean*
www.yachtrallies.co.uk

2 PREPARING THE BOAT

In an era when the Atlantic Ocean is regularly crossed in rowing boats or even on wind-surfers, it would seem ridiculous to be too narrow-minded about what kind of sailing boat constitutes the right sort of ocean-going vessel. However, there are certain characteristics that are critically important for any vessel to be safe on an ocean voyage.

HULL, DECK AND THROUGH FITTINGS

There are pros and cons to all the various designs of boat and types of build materials. The vast majority of ocean cruising yachts are GRP monohulls, but there are also many cruisers who do not subscribe to this norm. What matters is that the boat is seaworthy. Fundamental to this is a sound hull. If you are uncertain about the state of the hull or deck it may pay to have a survey and/or strip away the paint layers and thoroughly investigate any corrosion, rot or chronic osmosis. Keep a sense of perspective. For example, many fibreglass boats cruise for years with some degree of osmosis. But knowing the real condition of your hull and deck allows you to remedy any areas of potential weakness. This will remove a great deal of nagging anxiety, and probably save you time and money in the long run.

Once you are confident about the hull, you need to think about all hull and deck fittings and openings. This is as true for a new boat as an old one. Imagine the boat upright in the water and consider all the skin fittings below the waterline. Then imagine the boat in a knock-down position and consider hatches, lockers, companionways, vents, stove pipes, toilets and so on. How watertight would you be? Then take that thought even further and imagine the extreme situation of being rolled over. Again, think about where water could get in. No-one, and especially not multihull sailors, will want to consider any scenario other than remaining upright. But although it is extremely unlikely that you will ever be rolled over or even knocked down, it is quite possible that you will experience waves breaking over the deck and filling the cockpit. It is far better to feel confident that you are a corked bottle bobbing about on the water than to be at all doubtful about your seaworthiness.

Skin fittings

Every hole in the hull below the waterline should be protected by a seacock. There are many different types of seacock and the type you use may depend, in part, on the material of your hull. Some seacocks are more corrosion resistant than others. A major benefit of the traditional,

A less common choice but well suited to the task, *Allegro*, a Heavenly Twins catamaran, has successfully crossed the Atlantic several times. Photo: Richard Woods

PREPARATIONS

lever-operated types is that it is immediately obvious whether they are open or shut by looking at (or feeling for) the lever position. Gate valves with turn handles, such as are used for domestic plumbing, are not suitable for use on ocean-going boats. They will disintegrate or seize in the marine environment and should be replaced at the first opportunity. Whatever type of seacock is fitted, they should regularly be stripped and examined, cleaned and greased, or renewed if suspect. Aim to check them each time you apply antifouling. Hose connections should be secured with two all-stainless steel clips. Reinforced plastic hoses should be renewed if they have hardened. Ideally, each skin fitting should have a conical softwood bung attached on a lanyard, ready for use if the skin fitting fails. Failing that, keep an appropriate range of bungs on board that are easily accessible.

Stern glands, propeller shafts and cutless bearings

Understand your stern gland! Traditional stuffing boxes or packing glands rely on an appropriate thickness of greased packing material wrapped around the propeller shaft. They are designed to allow a small but steady leak of water. Too little packing or lack of grease will cause significant leakage. But too much packing material can prevent the shaft from spinning freely and cause overheating and wear on the shaft. Once the shaft is worn it becomes impossible to pack or grease effectively and needs to be replaced. Always carry spare packing and the correct grease and remember to turn the greaser regularly (one turn every eight hours) when motoring. Packing material should be replaced every year because it is liable to harden over time.

The more modern designs of stern gland are drip free. There are two distinct varieties. The first incorporates a 'mechanical' seal which depends upon two perfectly smooth discs – usually of ceramic or carbon materials – pressing against each other to maintain a seal. One disc revolves with the shaft, while the other, connected to the hull, remains stationary. The second variety is a 'lip' seal. This is composed of a sleeve around the shaft log (stern tube) with one or more rubber seals embedded within it. Most of these types now have at least two seals with lubricating oil in between. These seals are usually maintenance-free over a long period of time, but eventually they may deteriorate and have to be replaced. This requires partial withdrawal of the propeller shaft in order to remove the shaft coupling. In the mean time, if failure has occurred, there may be a flood of incoming water. If the gap between the propeller shaft and the stern tube is too wide, the inflow may be greater than a bilge pump would cope with. Replace your seals if you have any doubts about their longevity.

Boat engines are usually on flexible mounts and the stern gland has to accommodate this movement. It is common to use a length of hose to attach the stuffing box to the stern tube. Failure of this hose would result in a rapid inflow of water. The hose should be examined for any signs of deterioration and should be replaced if necessary. It should be fixed in position with two all-stainless steel hose clamps at each end.

Because the stern gland is an integral part of the motorised drive system of the boat, it shouldn't be dealt with in isolation. There is little point in carefully renewing your stern gland whilst failing to check the condition of other parts of the system. Do not renew your stern gland without also checking the state of the engine mounts. Similarly, a worn cutless bearing will cause excessive shaft movement which will stress the stern gland seals. If you are removing the shaft to service one part of the system, check the condition of the other component parts.

Sail drives

Some yachts less than 16m (50ft) long are fitted with a sail drive. These are generally cheaper and more straightforward to install than more traditional propeller shaft systems. The most significant downside is that any damage to the main seal around the drive leg could allow a catastrophic ingress of water. Regular inspection of the main seal and oil seals should be routine and occasional replacement will be necessary. Drive legs protrude perpendicularly from the underside of the hull and may be vulnerable to impact damage and entanglement. Choice of a suitable propeller and rope cutter is relatively limited. It is often problematic to position the drive leg sufficiently close to the rudder which tends to result in reduced manoeuvrability under engine at slow speeds, ie the drive leg has to sit in a sealed well in the hull which makes it difficult to position it sufficiently close to the rudder for efficient steering (because of the reduced prop wash passing the rudder).

Marine toilets

Many boat toilets are below the waterline. They are susceptible to siphoning water into the toilet. This has been known to sink boats if left undiscovered. To prevent this, an anti-siphon loop should be fitted above the line of water at all normal angles of heel and as high as possible. These should be fitted on both inlet and discharge hoses.

Holding tanks

There are several cruising areas around the North Atlantic where it is illegal to discharge sewage. It is strongly advised that you have some form of holding tank on board. The holding tank is connected to the marine toilet via a switch valve which allows sewage to be pumped into the tank when required, or directly overboard when offshore. The tank can be pumped out via a deck fitting at pump-out stations found at marinas and yacht clubs in areas where restrictions apply. The simplest form of retro-fitted tank is a plastic jerry can

PREPARING THE BOAT

which can be disconnected for emptying. Officials may want to inspect your holding tank provision.

Above the waterline

Hatches, cockpit lockers, the companionway, deck fittings, windlass navel pipe, dorade vents and mast collar are all potential points of water ingress. Drip leaks through deteriorating decks or poorly sealed fittings may not appear to threaten the seaworthiness of your boat. In fact they can make the difference between a happy, effective crew and a miserable, over-tired one. All hatchways and lockers should be looked at with the thought of a knock-down or a large wave breaking across the deck. The amount of water that might enter the boat in such circumstances could be catastrophic, so check their basic strength, hinges and seals. Make sure that your decks can be as watertight as your hull.

In the event of the cockpit filling with water, the cockpit lockers should be well secured and sealed. The cockpit drains should be of a large enough diameter to allow rapid drainage. Make sure they do not get bunged up with debris. Water should not be able to run from a full cockpit into the boat through the companionway. If the companionway entrance is at a lower level than the cockpit seats (or coaming) it may be wise to seal in a lower washboard up to this level when on passage. It is important that you can seal the companionway from both the outside and the inside. Attach removable washboards to lanyards so they cannot be lost.

Bilge pumps

Inevitably, a little water will occasionally find its way below. With this in mind, at least two manual, high-capacity bilge pumps are essential. One should be operable from the cockpit, preferably within reach of the helmsman. It is important that you can use this pump without needing to keep a cockpit locker open. The second manual pump should be operable from inside the cabin. If an electric pump is fitted, it should be additional to, not instead of, these two pumps. Spare parts for all pumps should be carried.

No manual or electric bilge pump will be able to cope with the flow from even a minor below-water leak for very long. A fit man can pump about 90 litres (20 gallons) of water a minute, but only for a short period of time. A large yacht, or one with a weak crew, should consider fitting a large-capacity pump driven directly from the engine via a clutch; this is the only type of pump that has the slightest chance of coping for any length of time with the incoming water caused by significant underwater damage.

> **Further reading**
> *Boatowner's Mechanical and Electrical Manual: How to Maintain, Repair, and Improve Your Boat's Essential Systems* by Nigel Calder, Adlard Coles Nautical

THE RIG

Your rig is your power house. On a cruising boat, the spars and sails will be in almost constant use and they need to be up to the job. The majority of modern boats are bermudan sloops or cutters, but all the more traditional rigs, including junk rigs, have also proven their worth. Gaff rigs are enthusiastically recommended by many seasoned transatlantic cruisers. Modern materials have produced aero-rigs and the unstayed mast and wishbone rig adopted by the Freedom class, both of which have successfully crossed the Atlantic. It doesn't really matter what type of rig you have, as long as it is capable of working hard for you.

Mast and spars

Both keel-stepped and deck-stepped masts have their own advantages and drawbacks, and both have been well proven at sea. Both types require considerable reinforcement of the hull and deck to prevent distortion. This is usually achieved with a correctly positioned main bulkhead. A deck-stepped mast should also have a compression post to transfer its loading down to the keel. A keel-stepped mast may cause some leakage around the deck collar, but because it is supported at deck level, any break will probably occur high enough to furnish at least the beginnings of a jury-rig. A mast stepped on deck is dependent on the rigging for its support, and any failure there is likely to result in the loss of the whole rig.

Check your mast for any corrosion or wear. Aluminium spars are vulnerable to corrosion around steel fittings or at the heel, especially if stepped onto steel. There should always be a layer of insulating material between the dissimilar metals. It is possible for the aluminium to degrade unnoticed, until either the fitting pulls out under strain or the spar suddenly collapses. But there is usually some sign of corrosion, chalkiness or powder on the surface, which will prompt you to take remedial action.

Standing rigging

Before setting off on any long passage or extended cruise, it is really important to ensure that all standing rigging is in good order, as failure on an ocean passage may lead to disaster. Unless you have an unstayed rig, the shrouds and stays are what you depend on to keep the rig in one piece. Despite this, all too often, these vital parts of the boat are not given the attention they need. Faults in metal work are often invisible so, even if there are no apparent problems, unless you are certain of the history of your rig, you might want to consider replacing the standing rigging. The life of stainless steel wire is generally considered to be about ten years. Stainless steel wire is vulnerable to repeated bending stresses and it is essential that the load lies straight along the

PREPARATIONS

Checking the rig before starting an ocean passage is a sensible precaution. Photo: Graham Adam

axis of the wire and its fittings. All rigs move a little in relation to the hull, so toggles are designed to accommodate this movement and maintain the axial loading on the wires. Toggles should be fitted between the bottlescrew and chainplate of all shrouds and stays. Headsail stays are subject to extra bending forces, as a glance up the luff of a headsail will show. It is essential that these wires are fitted with toggles at the mast and at the deck.

Despite these measures there will be weak points, usually where the wire enters a terminal. Examine all your terminals, whether swaged or swageless, including those at the top of the mast. The fracture of a single strand of wire or distortion of the terminal indicates that something is seriously wrong, and the shroud or stay should be replaced as soon as possible. Because the condition of swaged joints is often hard to assess, swageless terminals (Norseman or Sta-lock) are preferable, although they are initially more expensive. These terminals can be fitted in a few minutes with no special tools, and they can be dismantled periodically to inspect the condition of the wire inside. They may also be reusable when the wire has reached the end of its life. Swageless terminals cannot be used with galvanised wire.

Remember that, either aloft or at deck level, the rigging is only as strong as its weakest point. The fittings to which the shrouds and stays are attached, top and bottom, are as important as the wires. It is preferable that shroud attachments to the mast are through-mast, conventional tangs rather than T bars. All the eyebolts and chainplates, including those for forestays and backstays, should regularly be examined. Any component that has been damaged or seems suspect should be replaced. Eyebolts eventually wear through. Chainplates are sometimes difficult to access, but it is important that you satisfy yourself that they are strong enough in themselves, and that their anchorage to the hull or deck, and the way in which the loads are spread, is adequate. Check your spreaders and think about upgrading your spreader fittings if necessary. The modern 'ball and socket' mast fitting, in which a hook-shaped terminal with a ball at its end is slotted into the spar, is unlikely to stand up to the continuous wear on an ocean passage-maker.

The old advice used to be to upsize the rigging if you are heading across an ocean. But with modern stainless rigging this is not necessarily the case. The rigging wire is an integral part of the whole rig which is designed to be in balance with the hull. By upsizing one or more of your rigging wires you might create destructive loads in another part of the boat. Many modern cruising yachts carry considerable weight and windage up the mast. In-mast furlers, mast steps and radar will all increase the loads and should be taken into consideration when assessing the rig's integrity. If in doubt seek expert advice.

In case of emergency, it is always wise to carry at least one spare length of rigging wire capable of replacing your longest, thickest shroud or stay and appropriate swageless terminals. You should also consider what action you might take if the worst happens and you lose the rig entirely. Do you have the means on board to cut the rig away? Standard bolt cutters, though frequently recommended for such situations, may be completely ineffectual on thicker gauges of wire. If in doubt, test a piece of your thickest gauge wire.

Running rigging

Most cruising boats are equipped with modern synthetic ropes. Although these are much stronger and more durable than traditional ropes, they are still susceptible to chafe. It is important to ensure that all turning blocks, sheaves and jammers are large enough for the ropes used, that they are in line with the direction of load, and that they are in good condition. Going aloft at sea is always unpleasant, and in rough conditions it is dangerous. Sufficient spare halyards will allow for some redundancy should a halyard be lost aloft or damaged. An oversize topping lift will double up as a halyard for the main or mizzen and a spinnaker halyard for the genoa. The fittings at the masthead must be appropriate for these secondary purposes because the spare halyard may be in emergency use for days on end.

The modern tendency is for running rigging to be led aft from the mast to the cockpit. This has the advantage of reducing the number of times that it is necessary to go forward, but even with the best hardware, friction will be increased and ropes will be subject to additional wear. The forward end of the cockpit is liable to become cluttered with lines, winches and jammers which can be confusing, particularly at night. One disadvantage of the 'lead everything aft' approach is that, in an emergency situation, the deck outside the cockpit, the positions of handholds, obstacles, clipping-on points and so forth, becomes unfamiliar territory. For a crew who routinely go forward, such things are second nature, so they are better placed to concentrate on the job in hand, whatever the situation may be. If you choose not to lead everything back to the cockpit, it may be worth considering fitting 'Granny bars' to support and protect you while working at the mast.

A word on noise: there is often a symphony of sound on board, something which can be pleasurable to be a part of. However, there is nothing worse than being subjected to the cacophony of intermittent twanging, tapping, and thrumming of unruly rigging, particularly if you are trying to sleep. It pays to have several short lengths of hook-ended shock cord or similar ties with which you can tame any unemployed halyards, reefing lines and so on. Use the ties in harbour or at anchor even when you are not on board, so as not to annoy the neighbours.

SAILS

Sun damage and chafe

The two main enemies of your sails during an extended Atlantic cruise will be sun damage and chafe. It is tempting not to bother with covering the mainsail or mizzen when they are not in use, but the damaging effects of the sun will quickly reduce their longevity. Many cruising yachts opt for a mainsail cover that is integral with a lazyjack system. The sail is thereby protected as soon as it is lowered. There is the added benefit of a more controlled sail when slab reefing although, if the positioning of the lazyjacks is not correct, they can sometimes foul up with the batten pockets. Roller-furling headsails must either have a cover or, more commonly, UV resistant strips on the leech and foot. Similar protection is needed on the clew of in-mast furled sails and the head of in-boom furled sails. Sails that have to stay on deck when in harbour should always be stored in UV resistant bags. All sails will last longer if they are triple stitched with UV-resistant thread.

Careful attention should be paid at all times to ways of avoiding chafe. The most likely place for this to occur is where a mainsail touches the shrouds when running downwind. This is one of the reasons that using two headsails is often favoured on long passages allowing the main to remain stowed. It is worthwhile positioning reinforcing patches on any potential chafe points. A fully-battened mainsail is very vulnerable to chafe where the battens press against the shrouds and at the luff; some extra protection will be needed here.

Most sailmakers will recommend a heavier cloth for cruising compared to racing. But unless those already on board are showing signs of wear and tear, there may be no need for new sails. If you choose not to replace existing sails, give them a very thorough inspection, get a sailmaker to put in new stitching or chafe patches where necessary and equip yourself with the means for on-board repair. Many cruisers end up with sail repairs on passage at some stage. After long periods of downwind sailing it is easy to become complacent about your sails. But as soon as you have to head up into the wind any weakness will be revealed, sometimes quite dramatically.

Sail plan

Some boats have crossed the Atlantic quite successfully with only a roller furling genoa and a roller furling mainsail. Traditionally rigged or racing yachts tend towards the other extreme and have hanked-on sails of every description. Most cruisers fall somewhere in the middle, minimising the need for constant sail changes but with a variety of sails to allow some flexibility of the sail plan.

A typical sail inventory for a Bermudan sloop might be:

- Mainsail
- Roller furling genoa
- Second headsail
- Storm jib
- Storm trisail
- Spinnaker and/or cruising chute or other lightweight sail

It is the second headsail which may require the most thought. Is it carried as a spare and therefore made to fit up the same foil as the genoa – either as a replacement or to form a double headsail rig – or should it be designed to hank onto a new, but temporary, snap-tensioned inner forestay as an entirely separate sail? Is the standing rigging designed to withstand the new loading? If the second headsail is a No 2 and designed for heavy weather, should a lightweight headsail be carried? And if so, should it be free flying, designed for the foil, or hanked? Decisions about the rig will largely depend on your existing boat and your wish to have the most efficient sail plan available to you to cope with all conditions. They will also depend upon your willingness to operate on the foredeck to make best use of that sail plan. Crew strength may dictate that the rig is kept very simple – and anyway, unnecessary complications should always be avoided – but, unless you are prepared to run the engine (with all the fuel and maintenance issues that implies) whatever you decide you must have confidence that your chosen rig is suitable for extensive, chafe-free, downwind sailing as well as the more varied conditions found in more northern waters.

PREPARATIONS

Reefing

Learn to love your reefing system! Whether at the mast or fed back to the cockpit, make sure that all your reefing systems are straightforward but effective. You will frequently need to reef at night, by definition in worsening conditions. Any system which causes you to delay making the decision to put in a reef could endanger the boat. Increasing numbers of cruisers use in-mast or in-boom furling systems for their mainsails. There are pros and cons to the various systems. Any in-mast system should be designed in such a way that it is impossible to jam, and for in-boom furlers you must have an effective method of reefing the sail should a jam occur. In this respect, in-boom furlers carry less risk, because you could revert to traditional slab reefs if necessary. All cruising mainsails should have three reefs. Traditionally a storm trysail would be set in place of a third reef, but for most cruisers a deep third reef is often simpler, quicker and therefore more useful.

Roller-furling and reefing headsails are now the norm rather than the exception, although many cutters retain a hanked-on staysail. If reputable furling gear is chosen and correctly fitted, the likelihood of problems is low. The gear will need to be well maintained and should anyway be dismantled periodically so that the condition of the forestay can be checked. If a jam does occur with the sail reefed it will be impossible to lower it. The best way to furl the sail in this situation is to motor in circles, passing the sheets around the sail. At least one reserve headsail (No 2 genoa or working jib size) should also be carried. This will need a spare stay, halyard and sheet leads. There are some systems on the market which rely on attaching the second genoa onto sheaves around the furled main genoa. Over time these will chafe and damage the main genoa. Regardless of what other headsails are aboard, you should carry a small, heavy storm jib, set on a wire luff, and fitted with shackles to pass around the stay at head and foot for extra security. If using roller furling, either a permanent or temporary inner forestay is essential for hoisting the storm jib. This forestay may need extra support, either from running backstays or additional lower shrouds swept well aft, and the deck fittings must be substantial.

Storm sails

If you are planning to head for the tropics and stay there you may never release the storm sails from their bags. However, most long-term cruisers do carry storm sails (at least a storm jib), because if you are caught out in bad weather you will be glad of them, and because they are a back-up in case of damage to your other sails. If you do carry storm sails it is very important that you understand how and where you will set them. You will only ever use them in the worst of conditions, so your system for setting them must be foolproof and able to withstand storm loads.

Downwind rig

The two most common downwind rigs on cruising boats are twin headsails or a mainsail and poled-out genoa. A true twin headsail rig, high cut and with twin poles stowed up and down the mast, was for many years the hallmark of the ocean cruiser. The rig evolved not so much for its efficiency as for its self-steering attributes. Before the advent of reliable vane gears or autopilots, twin headsail rig was the only way that most yachts could be persuaded to steer themselves before the wind. For this reason it remains the easiest rig on the helmsman, whether human, mechanical or electrical. Other advantages are that it is remarkably free from chafe; wear and tear on the mainsail is avoided and there is no danger of an accidental gybe. Drawbacks are that some yachts roll with no fore-and-aft canvas to steady them and, once the gear is rigged, manoeuvrability is considerably reduced. Setting a storm trysail and sheeting it hard amidships may ease the rolling. It will gybe repeatedly, but will come to no harm. The usual twin arrangement is for one sail to be the normal roller-furling genoa, and for the other to be a spare headsail hanked to a temporary stay. The advantage of this system is that the asymmetric rig will normally induce far less rolling than a true twin rig whilst still producing directional stability. It will also allow a large furling genoa to be reefed easily as necessary and the size of the inner sail to be chosen to suit conditions. It will be large and light until the trade winds kick in, when a smaller No 2 genoa will become more suitable.

Jammed furling gear can prove a real headache when you are mid-Atlantic. Photo: Richard Woods

PREPARING THE BOAT

An alternative is to have two identical or similar sails, each set in one of the twin grooves of the roller gear. These sails can be furled and unfurled together as the wind strength varies. Those who have used this arrangement are enthusiastic about it, but the loads on the furling gear will be larger than normal and it must be man enough for the job. Double headsails need at least one pole, and preferably two. With two poles on board you have some redundancy built into your systems should a pole or pole fittings fail. If only one pole is available, the main boom will serve as the other, supported by the topping lift and with a foreguy holding it as far forward as the shrouds will allow. The headsail sheet is run through a block at the boom end. Poles attached to a track forward of the mast also need to be controlled by a topping lift, together with a guy led to the quarter, and a foreguy led to the foredeck. This enables the sail to be reefed without the problem of the spinnaker pole leaping about uncontrollably. The foreguy will also prevent the pole being driven aft into the shrouds should the end dip into a sea. Ropes do chafe where they pass through the pole ends and you may need to remedy this – chandlers sell pairs of lightweight leather patches which can be sewn to sheets to save them from chafe.

The simplest downwind rig is mainsail and boomed-out genoa. The main is set to leeward, and the genoa poled out to windward, the pole being secured as described previously with topping lift, guy and foreguy. The advantage of this rig is that no special gear or sails are needed. More significantly, the yacht is much more manoeuvrable and can be brought onto the wind very quickly if required. The drawbacks are that there will be more wear and tear on the mainsail and it is vulnerable to chafe. This can be minimised by using a tightly set-up foreguy and, if necessary, a block and tackle between the centre of the boom and the lee rail to prevent the boom, and therefore the sail, from moving up and down against the lee rigging.

For the majority of ocean cruisers, a spinnaker would only ever be set under settled conditions and probably only during the day, but this usually depends on crew numbers. Many boats do carry a spinnaker and/or cruising chute with a snuffer for ease of handling. As with the other downwind sail arrangements, beware of chafe. It will be the sheets and guys that may suffer over time.

Further information
Heavy Weather Sailing by Peter Bruce, Adlard Coles Nautical
Yachting Monthly SAILPOWER: Trim and Techniques for Cruising Sailors by Peter Nielsen, Adlard Coles Nautical
www.stalok.com

This classic twinned-out arrangement reduces wear on the mainsail and lightens the load on the helm whilst trade-wind sailing.
Photo: Graham Adam

PREPARATIONS

GROUND TACKLE

Trustworthy ground tackle is your most fundamental insurance. Unlike many home waters where a cosy harbour may be within reach, on an extended cruise there will be many occasions when there is no alternative but to ride out bad weather at anchor, sometimes in indifferent holding or poor shelter, and possibly with rocks or coral heads astern. At these times, the safety of the yacht and crew will depend entirely on the ground tackle and the skill with which this is deployed. It is not possible to over-emphasise the importance of this equipment and the knowledge that must go with it.

It is not unheard of for a yacht to set out on an extended Atlantic cruise without either an anchor or a dinghy. Astonishing though this may seem, such yachts have only ever moored up alongside, either on a pontoon or against a harbour wall. But one of the greatest differences between cruising in home waters and cruising long distance will be the amount of time you spend swinging to your anchor. Even in port, once you are away from northern Europe and the major American yachting centres, it is normal to spend time at anchor. This may be because alongside berths are simply not available, but even when there is a marina, considerations of privacy, security, not to mention expenditure, often make the anchorage preferable. Other advantages in the tropics are that there will be less trouble from insects and other pests, and the cooling breeze tends to be more prevalent in an anchorage. And anyway, who would want to be moored up in an overcrowded harbour or marina when you could be anchored in a tranquil paradise?

Anchors

Many a cruising conversation amongst seasoned yachtsmen revolves around the subject of anchors and anchoring. There are several different types of anchor, and the pros and cons of each are frequently reviewed in the yachting press. It is likely that you already have at least one anchor on board. But every cruising yacht should carry at least three anchors, preferably of different types suitable for use on differing seabeds. For example, a traditional combination might be to have a CQR on the bow roller plus a Danforth and a Fisherman's anchor. Modern spade anchors such as the Rocna have a roll over bar which encourages the anchor to dig in, which can be a problem on hard sand for the CQR. Lightweight Fortress anchors are a very useful type to have on board. They can be broken down to stow easily, they are light enough to be moved around on deck or set from the dinghy, yet they have well proven holding power.

If you are buying a new anchor, it is wise to choose anchors that are one level heavier than those recommended for your tonnage. Anchor manufacturers and cruising reference books provide tables giving recommended weights for various types of anchor. When cruising yachts tended to be of relatively heavy displacement, it used to be recommended to carry a heavy anchor for use in extreme conditions. However, many cruisers would baulk at carrying such weight. Most would prefer to adopt mooring techniques for extreme conditions that use two or more smaller anchors to provide holding power greater than that provided by one big anchor. Backing the anchor or setting a forked moor are examples of such techniques (see page 13).

The combined weights of anchor and chain on yachts over about 9m (30ft) make a manual windlass an extremely welcome addition to the foredeck. Above around 11m (36ft), a power-operated windlass becomes increasingly attractive, particularly for a shorthanded crew. Although the current it draws is high, it is only used for brief periods, so overall power consumption is not excessive and, anyway, most cruisers opt to have the engine running during anchoring procedures. In crowded anchorages it seems prudent to have the engine running, even only as a back-up, in which case the power draw from the windlass is less of an issue. Although windlasses are a wonderful aid on board (and can also be used to winch a crewman up the mast for routine checking or repairs), it is a wise yachtsman who considers the possibility that the windlass may, at some stage, break down or seize. Is the crew physically able to pull up the chain and anchor by hand?

Depth is an important consideration here. Most fit adults could lift an anchor and 3–4m (10–12ft) of chain hanging down to the seabed. Fewer would be capable of lifting the combined weight in 10m or deeper without assistance. In such a situation it is possible to lead the chain to a mast or cockpit winch, but there is a possibility that you will damage the winch, particularly if the lead to the winch is not fair. Block and tackle systems may help – or a pair of chain hooks on rope which may be led to a winch and used in sequence to speedily recover the anchor. Whatever you rely on as a back-up, you should aim to keep your windlass in good condition. You will then be more confident about anchoring with a good amount of scope, re-anchoring if necessary, and sometimes anchoring deeper than you would otherwise be able to.

Self-stowing from the windlass will be improved if the chain falls straight down from the chain gypsy (wildcat) into a deep locker. The windlass, navel pipe and locker may have to be moved aft to get the necessary fall for reliable self-stowing.

Anchor cable or rode

It is important to remember that holding power is not simply a function of the anchor, but also the strength, weight and length of the anchor cable or rode. Most seasoned cruisers would agree that the main anchor cable should be made of chain. The chain should be of a size that is proportional to the size of boat and size of anchor. Make sure that the chain fits the windlass! Multihulls and light displacement yachts may prefer to use rope because it is

PREPARING THE BOAT

The forked moor
This is an excellent technique for situations when the wind direction is relatively constant and currents do not create repeated turning. It is possible to lay out the second anchor in deteriorating conditions. Holding power is increased, swinging area is reduced and yawing is dampened. Even if one anchor drags or one cable parts, the yacht should remain anchored, thereby allowing the crew the time to take further action if necessary.

1 Lay the main anchor.

2 Lay the second anchor either
a) under motor (You may have to lay out extra cable on the main anchor in order to reach the desired dropping point for the second anchor.)

Or

b) from the tender (This is usually reasonably straightforward although the weight of the paid out cable tends to make manoeuvering difficult.)

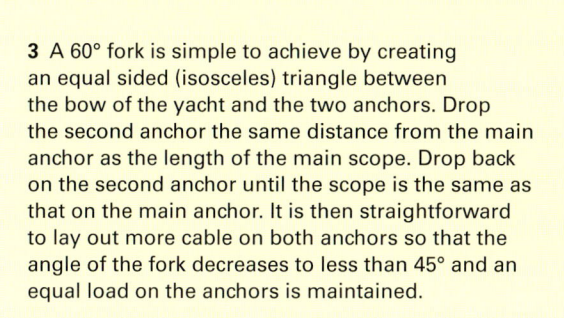

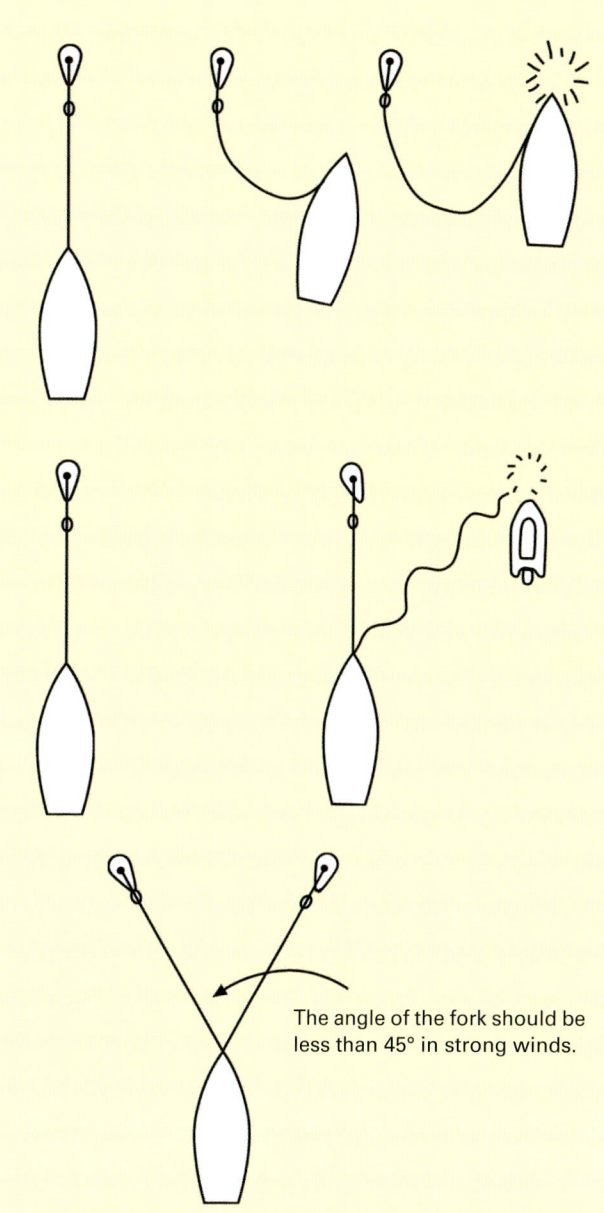

3 A 60° fork is simple to achieve by creating an equal sided (isosceles) triangle between the bow of the yacht and the two anchors. Drop the second anchor the same distance from the main anchor as the length of the main scope. Drop back on the second anchor until the scope is the same as that on the main anchor. It is then straightforward to lay out more cable on both anchors so that the angle of the fork decreases to less than 45° and an equal load on the anchors is maintained.

The angle of the fork should be less than 45° in strong winds.

Weighing anchor is usually possible without needing to use the tender. Shorten the scope on the second anchor and break it out, fall back onto the main scope and then weigh the main anchor as usual.

Backed anchors
This arrangement produces the greatest holding power from the anchors used but it is difficult to lay retrospectively once conditions have begun to deteriorate. Swinging and yawing are not reduced and the system is entirely reliant on the integrity of the main cable and all the component shackles.

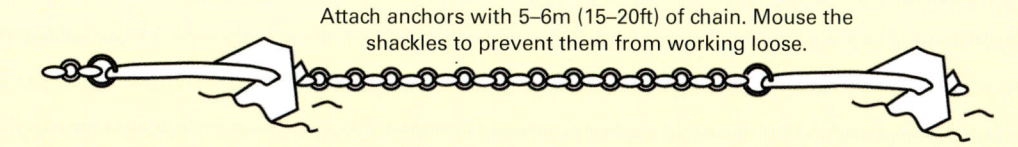

Attach anchors with 5–6m (15–20ft) of chain. Mouse the shackles to prevent them from working loose.

Weighing the anchors can be difficult because of the inceased weight, although this is not a problem if anchoring depths are less than the length of the attachment chain.

Fig 1 Techniques for increasing holding power: backed anchors and a forked moor. Adapted from *Anchoring and Mooring Techniques Illustrated* by Alain Gree.

PREPARATIONS

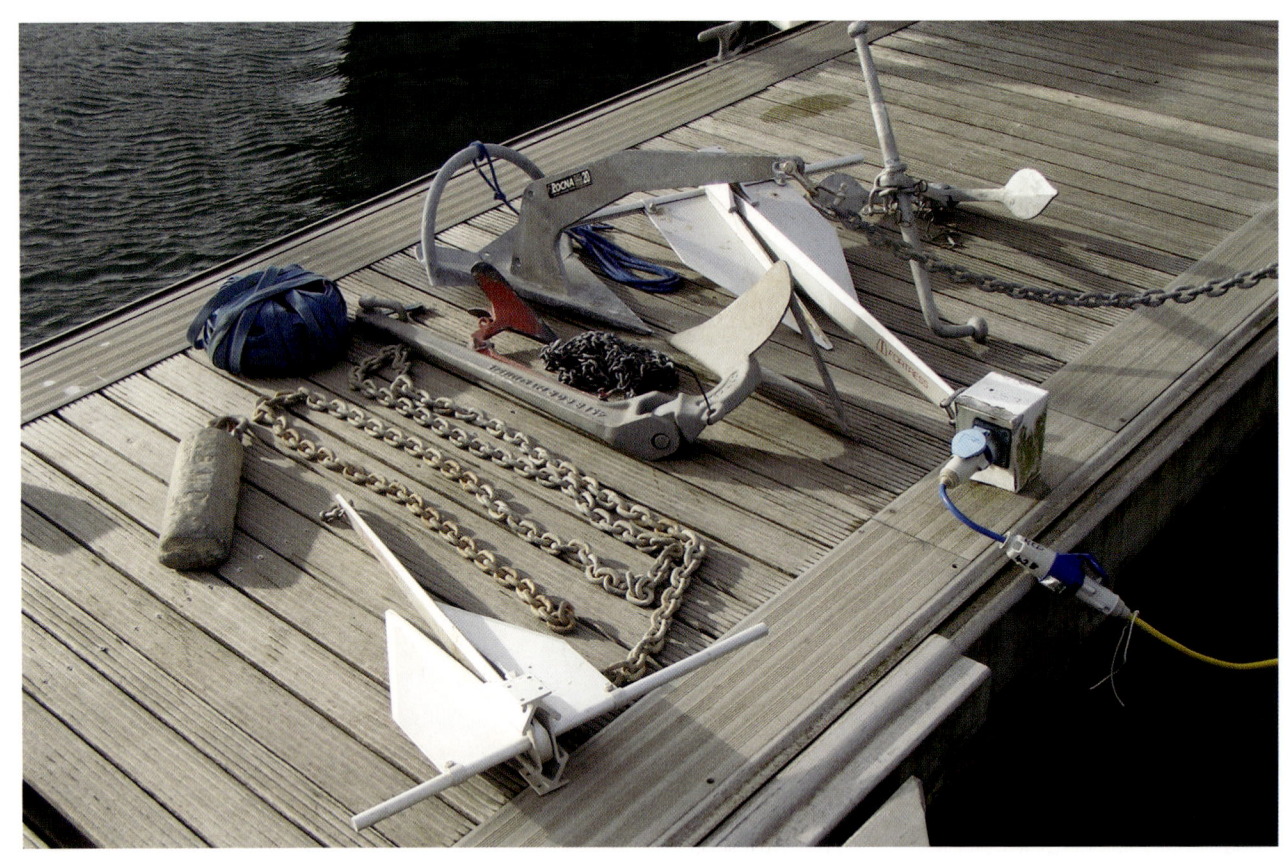

A collection of the ground tackle used on a 39ft steel cruising yacht. Photo: David Russell

much lighter. However, because rope is particularly liable to chafe on unseen rock or coral, at least the first 5–10m (15–30ft) of cable should still be chain. A cable made entirely of chain helps to ensure a horizontal pull on the anchor, which significantly increases the holding power. Rope cables do not hold such a favourable catenary. To compensate for this it is necessary either to use a longer scope or to use a 'chummy weight' to hold the cable more horizontally. A yacht lying to rope moves around its anchor considerably more than a yacht lying to chain, even without any extra scope. This can be a problem in a crowded anchorage where rope is also much more liable to be snagged by passing yachts or dinghies. However, rope does come into its own as a secondary cable. It is sometimes necessary to lay a second anchor from the dinghy. A lightweight anchor on a rope cable is much more manageable in this situation. Without the anchor attached, the rope doubles up as an excellent shore line when mooring to a steeply shelving, rocky shore.

Chain increases holding power to such an extent, both through its own weight dragging along the seabed and by encouraging the anchor to lie flat and dig in, that a scope of 3:1 is sufficient in mild conditions. As the wind increases, the scope should be increased. In a blow it is comforting to be able to lay a scope of 7:1. There are few anchorages along the normal Atlantic route with depths much in excess of 15m (50ft), and most are shallower than this so, for most yachts, 60m (200ft) of chain should be sufficient as a primary cable. A secondary cable of 15m (50ft) of chain plus 75m (250ft) of multi-plait nylon is ideal for the second anchor.

It is seldom a steady pull that breaks out an anchor. It is usually the snatching and jerking caused by gusts or swell that causes a problem. The best way of absorbing the jerking is to use a spring or snubber. Once the anchor has been set and all but the last few metres of scope paid out, attach one end of a 3–4m (10–13ft) length of nylon rope to the chain using a rolling hitch or chain hook. Secure the other end of the rope to a substantial strong point in the bow. Veer out some more chain until the nylon takes the strain, leaving the chain hanging in a bight beneath it. As well as smoothing the ride at anchor, routine use of a snubber reduces the noise transmitted up the chain and it also takes the strain off the windlass. However, always cleat off the chain as usual in case the nylon parts. It is important to have at least one, preferably two or three, good strongpoints in order to make fast your cable and snubber. A Samson post or substantial cleat bolted through a large backing plate under the deck is ideal for this job.

There are times when you may want to hold the yacht stern to the shore or to anchor fore and aft. With this in mind you need at least one deck strongpoint at the stern.

Further reading
Anchoring and Mooring Techniques Illustrated by Alain Gree, Adlard Coles Nautical (dated but still useful)
Yachting Monthly: Anchor Tests in December 2006 and November 2009. www.yachtingmonthly.com

PREPARING THE BOAT

FENDERING

As well as the usual fenders carried on board it is very useful to have a builder's plank with a hole at either end. This can then be suspended outside the fenders when alongside a rough wall or commercial harbour with widely spaced fendering. It also doubles up as a walkway when you are moored bow or stern-to.

Well protected with fenders and tyres on transit through the Panama canal. Photo: Mike Robinson

AUTOMATIC STEERING

Every ocean-going yacht should have some means of self-steering. For most long-term cruisers the self-steering is not just an extra helmsman but, in fact, the principal helmsman. It becomes such a relied upon member of the crew that it is frequently personalised with a nickname. Even with several crew on board, there are times when it just makes life easier. If you are single-handed or have just two or three crew on board, a well functioning self-steering device can make a real difference to your safety. Needing to hand steer constantly can quickly become exhausting. A yacht with a chronically exhausted crew is a yacht in danger.

Depending on the design of the boat, it is sometimes possible to set the sails in balance with the helm such that the boat will self-steer. However, most modern cruising yachts depend on either vane gears or autopilots. Both devices have their advantages and disadvantages, and many ocean cruising boats are fitted with both. This is the ideal situation, particularly for short-handed crew. Whatever method of self-steering is used, the boat must be properly balanced and the system must be arranged so that it can be disconnected instantly in an emergency.

Vane gears

The main advantage of a vane gear is that it is a purely mechanical device and requires no electrical power. It is a self-sufficient system, silently in tune with the wind and the sea. This alone is often enough to outweigh any disadvantages. Vane gears can seem a mysterious beast to the uninitiated, but they are actually quite straightforward and it is well worth getting to grips with them. They steer relative to the apparent wind, so when the wind direction changes, the yacht's course will change too. All types have a vertical wind vane arranged so that when the yacht is on course the vane is in line with the apparent wind. When the

A good wind vane on a well-balanced boat adds an extra crew-member who has unlimited stamina and no power requirement. Photo: Clive Ellis

yacht veers off course the vane is blown over or around on its axis which, in turn, causes the gear to steer the yacht back onto the correct heading.

There are three types of system. In the oldest type, a linkage connects the wind vane directly to the yacht's rudder (or to a trim tab on its trailing edge). It is the simplest gear, and the only one that the average owner is likely to be able to build himself: but as it generally lacks power it is suitable only for smaller yachts. It is now seldom seen.

The second type of gear, for example a hydrovane, is completely self-contained and uses an auxiliary rudder. The

15

PREPARATIONS

wind vane turns this rudder, or a trim tab attached to it, when the yacht is off course. The boat's main rudder is either left free to trail or, more commonly, set in a position that helps to balance the vane gear. This type of gear avoids complicated connections to the wheel or tiller, and has the considerable advantage of providing the yacht with an auxiliary rudder.

The third type of vane gear is the servo-pendulum, for example Monitor and Aries. In these systems, movement of the wind vane rotates a servo-oar, or blade, in the water. Once this blade has been rotated out of the fore-and-aft line, the changes in pressure from the water flowing past it cause it to swing up to one side or the other. This swinging movement (hence the name servo-pendulum) causes a gear wheel to rotate, which turns the yacht's rudder via a system of steering lines connected to the wheel or tiller. Servo-pendulum gears are powerful and, as the power comes from the flow of water past the servo blade, the faster the yacht is travelling the more powerful they become. However, the converse is also true, in light airs they may steer an erratic course, although this may often be alleviated by using a tall, light windvane.

The choice of gear comes down to personal preference, availability and cost, but you should also consider where the gear will be bolted to the boat and whether the extra loading should be compensated for. All vane gears work better on a well balanced boat. Over time you will be able to interpret the signals from the gear that indicate that it is working too hard. Depending on the conditions you may need to adjust the sails, give it a notch more weather helm, or put a reef in to maintain the balance. A good gear should be capable of steering a yacht however heavy the weather. But this does rely on the crew understanding how to get the best out of the system. This really is worth it, but it can take quite a long time, so some practice before you set off on your extended cruise is highly advisable.

It is wise to carry a range of spares for vane gear. The control lines work very hard and are liable to chafe through. Because the blades are an aerofoil section and are very strong but light, they are quite complicated to re-create yourself. Both vanes and blades, positioned proud of the stern, are particularly vulnerable in port. They should be removed when not in use. The gears are liable to corrode over time and you should service them periodically. If you are afloat, make sure you have a dinghy positioned underneath to catch all the components!

Autopilots

Electronically operated autopilots are increasingly reliable and popular. There are many skippers who are unwilling or unable to carry vane gear and who rely entirely on an autopilot for self-steering. Other yachts generally rely on vane gear, but also carry an autopilot for use when motoring or motorsailing or for very light airs when the vane gear becomes less reliable. Autopilots are generally seen to be affordable enough to enable you to carry a spare complete unit on board. The main disadvantage is the complete dependence on electric power. It is quite possible that the autopilot will be in use all day every day, and you should plan for the increased power consumption. If you have a wind vane and only use the autopilot in light airs, it is possible to rig a tillerpilot such that it manoeuvres the vane rather than the tiller or wheel itself. Because of the gearing ratios within the vane gear you then effectively reduce the workload on the tiller pilot and therefore minimise the power consumption. Converting a windvane system by swapping the windvane itself for a small tiller pilot is particularly useful for use under engine or when using a spinnaker – but, as this cuts out the natural give of the vane system, some gear wear may result.

An autopilot uses a compass sensor, an electronic control system and an electric power unit to steer the yacht. In smaller sizes, these three components may be combined into a single unit and models are available for either wheel or tiller steering. Larger units for wheel-steered yachts may either be mounted in the cockpit and turn the wheel via a belt and wheel drum, or may be mounted below decks and connected into the steering system there. Below-decks systems are more reliable and benefit from the power unit being out of the weather and less vulnerable to accidental damage, or to theft. The electronic control systems vary in sophistication, with the most advanced models incorporating circuits that automatically adjust the autopilot for weather helm, sea state and steering load; these are said to reduce the power the autopilot will use. Autopilots can be linked to other instruments including the GPS in quite a sophisticated fashion. However, constant use of linked functions will increase power consumption, and anyhow should be used with caution and not at the expense of basic sailing skills and good seamanship.

THE ENGINE, ELECTRICAL SYSTEM AND ELECTRONICS

It is now very rare to find a cruising yacht without an auxiliary engine. Manoeuvring under sail has become more difficult in congested anchorages and impossible in some harbours and most marinas. But it is the increasing dependence on electronics and electrical systems on board which has made a well-functioning engine and electrical system an essential requisite for many long-term cruisers. On many Atlantic cruises an engine is not needed so much for propulsion on passage as for battery charging and harbour work. Although, in an increasingly impatient world, crews do resort to using their engine on passage, either to try to find some wind, or to speed up their arrival at their destination. Either way, there are increased demands on yacht engines and electrical systems. Yet, despite this, it remains true that many yachtsmen lack knowledge about engine and electrical maintenance and are heavily reliant on shore services to keep their systems running efficiently. More extended cruises are delayed, curtailed or abandoned as a result of engine, electronic or electrical failure than for any other reason. The irony of this, on a sailing boat, is not lost on many seasoned sailors who go to some lengths to ensure that there are always non-electrical back-ups for all the essential systems, including the possibility of hand-cranking the engine.

Further reading
Marine Diesel Engines: Maintenance, Troubleshooting, and Repair by Nigel Calder, Adlard Coles Nautical

Good engine access encourages routine maintenance. Photo: Lilian Duckworth

The engine

Engine problems are usually caused by lack of maintenance or poor installation. Poor access to the engine can be a real disincentive to maintenance, particularly at sea, so it is worth improving your engine access if at all possible. The engine should be given a thorough service before any extended passage-making. If you lack confidence, consider attending an engine maintenance course. If you depend on the services of a mechanic, at least try to be on board while he is working, watch what he does and ask questions about any areas of concern or confusion. Engine mounts should be examined, as should all flexible hoses, belts and impeller. If in doubt about their condition, renew them. If the engine is past the first flush of youth it may be wise to have the alternator and starter motor overhauled and to renew the thermostat. It is also worth checking the accuracy of the thermostat. More than one skipper has spent weeks or months tearing hair out over an apparently overheating engine, only to eventually discover that the temperature gauge was reading high. Injectors and fuel pumps will benefit from being serviced before departure. But there is little point in renewing the fuel system if the fuel tanks are thick with sludge. If it seems likely that they may be dirty, fuel tanks should be opened up and cleaned. The exhaust system should be thoroughly checked and any suspect components renewed as corrosion in this system is particularly common. Ideally, there should be some method of closing off the exhaust overboard discharge. Water flooding back through the exhaust system in heavy weather has destroyed countless engines. Fresh-water and salt-water cooling systems need de-scaling periodically. A fresh-water cooling system should contain the correct proportion of antifreeze. Icing is unlikely to be a problem, but antifreeze is also an effective anti-corrosive. It is difficult to hand-crank anything other than the smallest engines, so most cruisers should carry a spare starter.

Having set off with an engine in good condition it is relatively easy to maintain. Follow the manufacturer's service schedule. Modern, lightweight diesel engines are hard on their lubricating oil and filters which should be changed at the recommended intervals. If the engine is regularly run on light load – to power a fridge or to charge the battery for example – then the oil and filter should be changed more frequently. Fuel filters should also be changed regularly, and it is good practice to install double fuel filters in parallel so that a clean one is always available for use. Working on the engine is much easier if it, and its compartment, are kept clean. It is then much easier to detect oil leaks.

Corrosion

Any water-cooled engine is liable to be affected by galvanic or electrolytic action. A salt-water-cooled installation should have sacrificial zincs somewhere in the water jacket, and these will need regular inspection and replacement. Even when fresh-water cooling is used, the heat exchanger is exposed to the corrosive action of hot salt water and an anode may be needed for its protection. Galvanic corrosion is rapid in tropical waters and must be guarded against. Most boats will need at least one external hull anode correctly bonded to the metal fittings. This is a complex subject and, unless you are an expert, you should ask a surveyor who specialises in this field to check your system during your preparations. Anodes should be in good condition before departure, and at least one spare carried.

Electrical systems and electronics

The borderline between electrics and electronics has become increasingly blurred. Many items that would in the past have been thought of as part of the electrical system now contain quite complex electronics – for example, alternators, regulators and battery chargers. The yacht's electrical and electronic systems should therefore be considered together, and if a lot of electronics are to be fitted then the basic electrical installation may need modification. The key to a good electrical system is balance. Whatever power is

PREPARATIONS

consumed must be replaced by recharging. Unlike a shoreside existence, where unlimited electricity is available on demand, once you are away from the land, life onboard can become a constant struggle if the balance is ignored. When you are planning the electronic and electrical equipment onboard, it is worth considering to what extent you want to be held hostage by the power demands of a hungry system. It may be that you place a high priority on all the modern technology and take for granted the consequent frequency of hours spent recharging. On the other hand, if you want to enjoy a real sense of freedom in your cruising, you might want to prune your onboard electrical and electronic expectations. Passage-making on a small yacht is, after all, a lifestyle decision and perhaps part of this is a realisation that some modern luxuries carry a heavy price in terms of their power consumption. A little sacrifice in luxury could actually enhance your enjoyment of unique cruising experiences. An engine or generator running at sundown in an otherwise perfect, peaceful anchorage is enough to spoil the moment, both for those on board and also those anchored near by.

System overhaul Even on relatively modestly equipped yachts, the demands placed on electrical systems have increased dramatically in recent years. Unfortunately, the systems themselves have often not developed at the same pace. Deficiencies in the system may not reveal themselves during a home-waters cruise. Such cruises are likely to involve regular use of the engine, and therefore the alternator. And at least the occasional night may be spent connected to shore power, when the battery can get a good charge. But the ocean voyager must be independent of the shore for long periods of time, and electrical demands must be met entirely from onboard resources. It is worth giving your electrical system a thorough review, both of its existing condition, but also of its overall capacity. Open the electrical panel (isolate it first) and check all connections are tight and corrosion free. Many fires have started from loose electrical connections. Think of your most important equipment (navigation lights, radio, autopilot etc), and trace through the whole installation looking for any signs of trouble and checking connections. The voltage drop between batteries and instrument is exacerbated by thin or corroded wiring, poor connections and surrounding dust and dirt. So make sure that you maintain the system in good condition with periodic checks. Damp, salt-laden air or, worse still, an actual drenching, is not a good environment for electronics. Even marine products are not necessarily adequately waterproofed. It is worth taking the trouble to ensure that all electronic equipment on board is kept as dry as possible. If you have any doubts about your electrical system or the condition of any on-board electronics, seek professional advice.

Usage It is relatively simple to estimate your total daily usage in terms of amp hours. After a few days of occasional monitoring, these estimates can be honed. Figures are quoted in all instruction books and can be adjusted according to how many hours a day an item will be used. Fridges are slightly more complex as there is a cycle time to consider. A well insulated fridge should run approximately 50 per cent of the time, freezers slightly more. Lights can be a major consumer. At sea, a tri-colour will typically run for 12 hours near the tropics, and compass lights and instrument lights for a similar time if left on. If your yacht is riddled with halogen down lighters, you may want to remove every other bulb or replace them with LED bulbs. LED bulbs can also be used for navigation lights and are particularly suited for a tri-colour that is used only when sailing.

Capacity Once you have estimated your energy consumption you need to consider how you will replace that energy. Because of the characteristics of batteries, every amp hour taken out must be replaced by more than that – usually about one and a quarter amp-hours. The battery bank is the fulcrum in this balancing act. Batteries are a subject in their own right and advice should be sought for the best options available with in budget and space constraints. The banks should be checked before departure and replaced if necessary. As a rule of thumb, a battery bank should never be discharged more than 50 per cent. So if you require 100 amp hours a day you will need an absolute minimum of 200 amp-hour bank, even if you recharge every day. And this does not take into account the need to put back more amp-hours than you use. In fact it is better if the domestic battery capacity in amp-hours is not less than three times your estimated usage. Electronic equipment may need a comparatively stable supply voltage to run reliably, which can prove difficult to provide. A yacht's battery voltage might vary from 14.4 volts when being charged by a smart alternator, down to 11.5 volts when a heavy load is being taken from it by, for example, a fridge or autopilot. The bigger the battery, the less the variation in voltage under a given load. So when fitting electronic items, a larger battery bank may be needed – not only to provide the power, but also to steady the voltage.

Batteries can only be recharged quickly to about 80 per cent of full charge after which a float charge is required to reach full capacity. Most specialist marine regulators and battery chargers have 3 or 4 stage charge cycles to achieve full charge. Slower charging devices can achieve 100 per cent as they charge at lower amperage over a long period. The options for recharging are via the main engine alternator, via a generator (diesel or petrol), or via wind, water or solar generators. Alternatives to the main engine are covered in the next section. The rated continuous alternator output in amps from the engine should be around a third of the battery capacity in amp-hours. A larger alternator will do no harm, though to gain full benefit a 'smart regulator' should be fitted. These are general guidelines for a system to

PREPARING THE BOAT

be maintained with less than two hours of engine or generator running each day. A system that falls significantly outside these parameters will need longer and/or more frequent periods of charging.

Dedicated start battery Unless it can be started by hand, the engine should have its own dedicated start battery, kept fully charged. The electrical system should be designed so that this battery cannot inadvertently be used to power the domestic system, while at the same time provision should be made for the domestic batteries to be used to start the engine should its own battery fail. This is usually achieved either by manual switches or blocking diodes. A battery state indicator is also useful, and should be installed in such a way that it can indicate the state of each battery individually.

AC power

Many yachts now have some form of AC circuit fitted. AC voltages are potentially life-threatening and an inadequately fitted circuit plugged into poorly earthed shore power has been shown to be lethal to anyone in the water nearby. It is extremely important that any AC circuitry is fitted and maintained by someone with sufficient expertise and understanding. An isolation transformer or galvanic isolator should be fitted to the shore supply. The circuits should be protected with the appropriate circuit breakers and residual current devices (RCDs, RCBOs, GFCIs).

AC supplies will come from shore power, an inverter, or a generator. It is important to ensure that only one supply source is powering the system at any one time, so a selector switch is needed if more than one supply source is fitted.

Shore power

The voltages and frequencies used around the Atlantic vary from 50–60Hz and from 110–240 volts. Some types of equipment, particularly those with an in-built timer (for example a microwave), are frequency sensitive and will be damaged if they are connected to the incorrect frequency. A large yacht may fit frequency converters and an isolation transformer to cope with the variations. Smaller yachts are unlikely to have the space or resources to do this. Some battery chargers are now dual voltage and are not frequency sensitive. So it is possible to plug the battery charger into shore power and then run an inverter (set to the correct frequency and voltage) from the boat's batteries. An alternative is a small plug in transformer, but these only change the voltage, not the frequency. It is usually possible to obtain 220 to 110V transformers, but going the other way may be more difficult. Shore power connections are anyhow likely to vary, so a variety of adaptors may be needed or leads will need to be made up locally. It is a good idea to carry a socket for your shore lead which can then be made up for local connections to the shore.

Inverters

Never forget that any AC power coming through an inverter is still drawing from the on-board batteries. High load items such as kettles and hair driers will create a significant drain on the batteries. You can run a laptop from a 12V cigar socket at the chart table using a laptop car power supply (which acts as a DC/DC converter to take the 12V up to a variety of voltages suitable for many laptops). This is more efficient than going from 12V to 240V then down via a transformer back to the laptop voltage. The saving is several amps per hour.

ALTERNATIVE POWER GENERATION

Many yachts rely solely on their main engine for the generation of electricity. However, additional demands on the electrical system have led to an increasing use of alternative energy sources. There are advantages and disadvantages to each source, which should be weighed against where and when the extra power will be needed. For example, wind generators are hardly productive at all on long downwind passages, but come into their own in a trade wind anchorage. So, consider whether you need extra power to drive your autopilot on passage, in which case a wind generator may let you down, or whether you want it to power the fridge for cooling beers in a Caribbean anchorage, in which case you'll think it's great. Whatever system you choose, consider the noise and fumes that may be produced and the consequent annoyance to other yachtsmen.

Wind generators

There are several wind-generators on the market specifically designed for the yachtsman. They vary greatly from small trickle chargers to large machines capable of producing up to 250 watts in a reasonable breeze. In most types an alternator is driven by a propeller with three to six blades, and the unit is mounted aft on a pillar or on the mizzen mast above head height and clear of all rigging. Some have the blade tips protected by a guard, but even with this they can inflict lethal injuries. There is at least one type that can also be used with a water impeller which revolves on a bracket under the transom, and this is not as vulnerable to inquisitive or hungry fish as an impeller towed astern. To a greater or lesser extent, all wind generators make a noise. This can be detrimental to the crew as well as to any neighbours and should be taken into account before committing to purchase.

PREPARATIONS

A perpetual balance of power – the wind generator is tied off and the solar panels are partially shaded, but the wind vane remains hard at work. Photo: Andy O'Grady

Noise levels may be influenced by the type of mounting as well as hull resonance. Some combinations can produce a wearing, if not downright terrifying, din even at relatively low wind speeds. Conversely, it is possible to mount a generator such that it is a low level, background sound even in moderate winds. The increasing or decreasing pitch of the wind generator can act as a useful indicator of changes in wind speed. Different types of wind generator will provide a trickle charge or a quite realistic alternative supply of power. None of them produces a significant output without at least 10 knots of relative wind.

Water-powered generators

Towed water-powered generators are capable of producing more power than wind generators, but they have some disadvantages. They will only produce a charge when underway at reasonable speed and they do create some drag. They can be quite a handful to get back on board. It may be necessary to slow or stop the boat to do so. A towed impeller is an attraction to predatory fish, which can become expensive. It may be similarly disastrous to start the engine with the generator in tow, particularly if engaging reverse.

Solar panels

Solar panel technology has improved markedly in recent years and modern panels are considerably more efficient than older ones. Theoretical output is significantly reduced if any part of a panel is in shadow. Ideally the panel should be on a pivoting mount such that it can be positioned at right angles to the sun and adjusted at intervals throughout the day or according to how the boat is lying. Many cruising yachts do not achieve this and output is correspondingly compromised. Wiring should be maintained in good condition. Even with optimal mounting and under tropical skies, solar panels will produce no power at all during the hours of darkness, but on long downwind passages they are a useful contributor to the onboard power bank.

Auxiliary generators

Fitted or portable auxiliary generators are increasingly popular on board as they provide the only sure means of keeping the batteries charged without frequent recourse to the main engine. If your yacht has any significant AC loads, a generator will probably be fitted from new. Diesel generators have the advantage of using the same fuel as the main engine, but small diesel generators tend not to be reliable. Portable petrol generators are reliable and relatively cheap, but require you to carry significant amounts of petrol on board – much more than just a jerrycan for the outboard. The downsides to any auxiliary generator are the noise, the heat and the air pollution, commonly for two hours each day. Even if these factors do not concern you, they may be a repeated annoyance to your neighbours in harbour or in an otherwise idyllic anchorage.

DINGHIES AND OUTBOARD ENGINES

A good dinghy is an essential piece of equipment for a long-distance cruising yacht. Cruising dinghies lead a hard life. They carry heavy loads of people and stores, sometimes even containers of fuel and they are repeatedly dragged up on beaches or left to fend for themselves at the dockside. They sit out in the full sun for hour on hour, day on day. They need to be seaworthy enough to cope with headwinds and chop across an open anchorage and yet they need to be stowable on passage. A dinghy, either tied alongside or pulled up on the beach, seems to be a natural playground for young children and filled with tropical rain also doubles as a fantastic bath tub. Hard dinghies and RIBs are excellent work horses, but finding stowage space for them can be an issue. Inflatables are easier to stow, but always involve some compromise in performance. Choice of dinghy will therefore ultimately depend on deck space, affordability and personal preference. Hypalon inflatables withstand the rigours of cruising life better than PVC, but a UV-resistant canvas cover will prolong the life of both. Whatever the weight, it can be useful to have wheels for beaching.

Most cruisers power their dinghy with an outboard motor, although there are still a few who prefer to row or sail. Outboard motors may fail or get flooded in surf so all dinghies must be manageable under oars or paddle. The choice of outboard will depend on the type and size of dinghy, but most cruising dinghies benefit from having more

PREPARING THE BOAT

horsepower than they would normally need to potter about in home waters. Increased horsepower means increased weight. For security reasons most cruisers bring their dinghies and outboards onto the deck overnight in port. If your dinghy or your outboard is too heavy to lift, you will need to create a system for hauling them up on deck. It is sensible to use wire or chain bicycle locks to secure your outboard to the dinghy and the dinghy to the boat or the shore.

In addition to the practical problem of handling the dinghy/engine on board – often with a sea running – consider the need to be able to handle the dinghy quickly on and off a beach through modest surf without capsizing or flooding. Unless you have a strong crew, avoid heavy boats with big engines or boats with small tubes and few grab handles. Also consider how easy it is to climb aboard from your dinghy. Ladders are not always helpful once the dinghy is bashing into them in the chop or swell. A good alternative is a fender step – a fender strung at both ends and tied to lie horizontally at an appropriate height or a similar commercial version.

Electric outboards are an increasingly common sight. However, they may not give you the range you need without a heavy and voluminous battery bank. The technology is improving, but for a cruising work-horse it is perhaps not quite there yet.

Carry a photo such as this to show lift operators your hull shape – it will help them to position the slings correctly. Photo: Jane Russell

MAINTENANCE AND SPARES

All around the Atlantic circuit there are facilities for yacht repair and maintenance, including several haul-out facilities. To help the lift operators in far flung places, it is a good idea to carry photographs which show sling positions, hull shape, length of keel, and positions of underwater fittings. In tropical waters it is easy to inspect and scrub below the waterline with snorkel and facemask.

Spares and repairs

Try to standardise types and sizes of equipment throughout the boat wherever possible so that spares can be interchangeable and the number of spares you need to carry is reduced. Equipment that can do more than one job is always a bonus. Depending on the reasons for renewal, you can sometimes keep old, replaced equipment to use as an emergency spare. If you are properly familiar with your vessel you probably know what things might be needed. If you rely on a boatyard for all your maintenance you might need to ask them to compile a spares list for you. The engine maker's recommended list of spares and tools will help. Store the tools and spares securely (some are very heavy and potentially dangerous) and protect them from corrosion. Factor in the different gauges used on either side of the Atlantic. See Appendix E for conversions.

PREPARATIONS

SUGGESTIONS FOR MANUALS AND SPARES TO TAKE WITH YOU

Engine
Boatowner's Mechanical and Electrical Manual by Nigel Calder, Adlard Coles Nautical
Marine Diesel Engines: Maintenance, Troubleshooting, and Repair by Nigel Calder, Adlard Coles Nautical
Workshop user manuals
Circuit diagrams
Pump valves and gaskets
A complete spare bilge pump
Engine/generator fuel and oil filters
Moulded engine hoses
A complete spare alternator
A complete spare starter motor
Stern gland packing and grease
Cutless bearing
Selection of relevant bearings

Steering and deck gear
Winch handles
Winch internals
Steering cable
Emergency tiller

Sails and rigging
Sewing machine (manual or manual/electrical)
Sewing machine spares
Sail cloth and adhesive sail repair tape
Double sided seam tape
Thread and twine of various thicknesses

Palm, needles, beeswax
The Complete Canvasworker's Guide by Jim Grant, International Marine Publishing
A length of wire suitable to replace the longest shroud or stay
Spare lengths of sheet and halyard of each diameter used
1m (3ft) lengths of wire
Bulldog grips (wire rope clamps)
Selection of rigging screws and swageless terminals
Mast slides
Rope clamps

Paints, glues and other spares
Specialist paint
Underwater epoxy
A range of glues
Specialist batteries
Selection of bulbs for all lights and instruments, including nav lights
Wind vane paddle, vanes and control lines
Cooker parts, particularly burners and jets
Toilet seals
Anodes
Log impeller
A siphon pump
VHF aerial
WD 40
Grease and oils

TOOL BOXES

Mechanical tools
Allen keys (hex wrenches) of a range of sizes and different gauges
Spanners of a range of sizes and different gauges
Adjustable spanners
Propeller puller
Screwdrivers of both types and all sizes
Monkey wrench
Bolt cutters
Hacksaw and blades
Blow torch and gas canisters
Rivet gun and rivets
Mole grips
Pliers
Workman's knee pads
A range of common woodworking tools
Sandpaper
Inspection mirror on a stick
6mm/7mm socket on a flexible stem to access nuts on jubilee clips

Electrical tools
Soldering iron
Solder

Fuses
Multi-meter
12V rechargeable Dust Buster

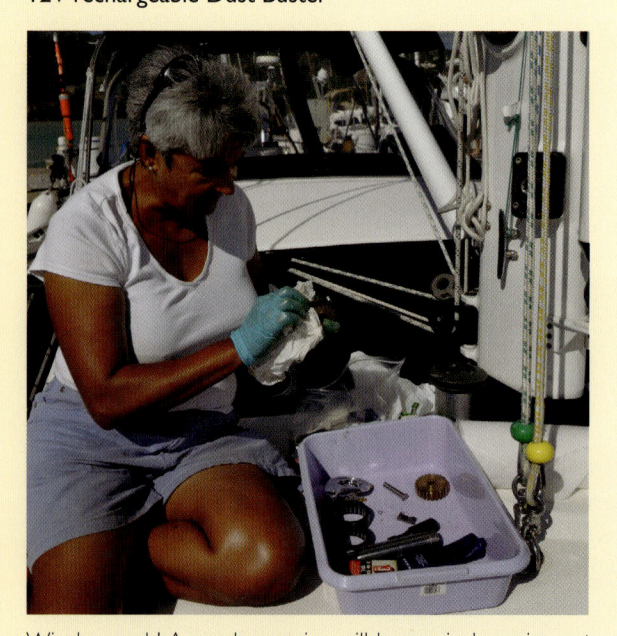

Winch wench! A regular service will keep winch equipment running smoothly. Photo: Mike Robinson

3 CREATING A HOME-FROM-HOME

This chapter covers all the practical aspects of living aboard when you are cruising for any length of time.

AWNINGS AND SCREENS

In benign conditions, the cockpit of your boat is quite likely to be the place on board that you spend the majority of your waking hours and probably some of your sleeping ones as well. It is worth thinking about ways to make the space more comfortable.

Sun protection

Even in the higher latitudes of an Atlantic circuit, both yacht and crew are very susceptible to the damaging effects of UV radiation. Because of the amount of time spent outside, receiving UV light from above but also reflected from the water, yachtsmen are at a significantly increased risk of long-term skin damage, including various forms of skin cancer. This risk is not restricted to the tropics. All yachts cruising around the Atlantic circuit should have some form of sun protection over the cockpit, for use both on passage and while in harbour.

Harbour awnings

For anything more than a relatively short cruise, a proper cockpit awning makes a huge difference to living conditions on board. In the tropics, the awning shields the crew from the sun, but in all climates it protects them from rain or even snow and converts the cockpit into a worthwhile porch where wet gear can be shed before going into the cabin. Traditional harbour awnings cover the whole deck at least from mast to backstay. Apart from protecting wooden decks as well as the crew, large awnings may have a dramatic cooling effect for life below decks. Aboard a modern, well-insulated yacht such a large awning may not be necessary and could become a concern in even moderate wind strengths. The simplest awnings are the best, often a single piece of fabric supported over or under the boom and tied off to guardrails, backstay or sprayhood. If it is too complicated and time consuming you will be less inclined to bother erecting it. If the awning is too high you may need additional side-screens. If it is too low it inhibits movement around the deck or into a dinghy or onto the pontoon. Bamboo or similar battens may be needed to support the width or length of material. Similarly, a halyard attachment

When in harbour in the tropics, you will want to create as much shade as possible over the cockpit. Photo: John Aldridge

in the middle may be needed to help to support it. Whatever the design, it is essential that it can be dropped and cleared from the deck quickly.

An important secondary use for an awning is as a rainwater collecting device. An awning will collect a surprisingly large amount of water in a tropical downpour. Plastic pipes can be attached at the natural drainage point (not necessarily central) using plastic through-fittings. Ideally these should be long enough to reach the tank filler.

Awnings should be made from a light-coloured, fairly heavyweight synthetic material such as the acrylic used for many sprayhoods. Nylon is degraded by sunlight and lets UV light through. It also tends to flap and rattle in any breeze.

Sailing awnings (biminis)

Many long-term cruising yachts never remove their sun awnings whilst on passage, even if the original intention was to do so. It can sometimes be quite problematic to find a workable sailing awning, but it is worth persevering. A bimini top is a popular type of permanent awning over the helmsman's position, but alternative designs of fabric sea awning can be just as effective. In order to be usable under way, it must not interfere with the working of the sails, and it should not obstruct the all-round view from the cockpit. Nor must any struts or strops prevent the crew from moving rapidly from cockpit to deck. Ideally it will not obstruct the view of the masthead from the helm however, while automatic steering is engaged, it is usually easy enough for the crew to keep an eye on the sails.

PREPARATIONS

Different boats have varying solutions to the sea awning issue. Some even utilise oversized umbrellas. What is important is that it protects the areas of the cockpit where crew will be for any period of time, plus it is strong enough to withstand normal sailing conditions, but is easily removable in bad weather.

> **Further reading**
> *The Complete Canvasworker's Guide* by Jim Grant, International Marine Publishing

Mosquito screens

All around the Atlantic circuit, mosquito netting may occasionally be needed as a protection from the nuisance of biting flies. In certain areas it is significantly more important as the primary protection against malaria, which is carried by mosquitoes and which is potentially lethal. If you intend to visit West Africa or Central or South America you should seek advice about the malaria risk in those areas and prepare the boat accordingly. Nets can be fitted onto lightweight frames which slot into the washboard area, or across hatchways. Alternatively you can attach netting with Velcro or use a roll-out net blind. These methods tend to restrict air flow through the cabin. A better method may be to hang a large mosquito net above the cockpit such that it protects the cockpit and the companionway, allowing you to leave the companionway open to air flow. Whichever method you use, make sure that the edges of the net do not allow any gaps, and that the mesh size is small enough to be effective. Anti-mosquito coils are widely available in the tropics. In malarial zones these can be used as well as, but not instead of, nets.

Where biting insects are merely a nuisance, coils can be an effective defence, but will not last through the night. There tends to be a peak of biting activity at dawn and at dusk, but the risks may remain at any time of day or night. Anchoring further out from the shore tends to decrease the likelihood of being bitten, but this is not a secure enough defence against insect-borne diseases such as malaria and yellow fever. A standard or battery powered insect swat is useful for the odd mosquito or fly that makes it past the defences.

> **Websites**
> www.who.int/malaria/docs/Tech-ConsultNetting Materials.pdf
> www.who.int/topics/malaria/en/
> www.who.int/topics/yellow_fever/en/

A good sailing awning is seldom put away. Photo: Mike Robinson

CREATING A HOME-FROM-HOME

BELOW DECKS

The cabin of your cruising yacht should be your sanctuary. When you are down below you should be safe, dry and comfortable. The cabin is your home in every respect. It is your kitchen, bathroom, and bedroom. But it is also your study, perhaps your classroom, your workshop and your sail loft. Whatever the layout of your boat, you should think about how to use the various spaces in ways that are best suited to you and your crew. On a long-term cruise you will need to use the space very differently compared to weekend or holiday sailing. Most cruisers use the spaces below in at least two quite different modes. They usually have an 'on-passage' mode and a 'non-passage' mode. There might also be a 'guests-aboard' mode. It is worth thinking through the various scenarios. This will be helpful when it comes to planning your stowage, and it may mean that you realise that some changes to your layout are needed. If you haven't already experienced them on board, imagine yourself in every situation and assess whether the space will work.

Berths

Human beings who are deprived of sleep cease to function effectively much earlier than human beings who are deprived of food. In order to sleep whilst on passage you need to have access to a good seaberth. A good seaberth is one in which it is possible to sleep safely in any weather and on any angle of heel. Ideally, to reduce the motion, it should be as close to the centre of the boat as possible and should be parallel to the fore-and-aft line. It should also be located so that normal watchkeeping and ship's activities do not disturb the sleeper too much. Berths in the forward cabin, which may be ideal when in harbour, can be untenable at sea. Ideally there should be one seaberth for every crew member. At the very least there should be one for every off-watch crew member. In this situation, crew members 'hot bunk'. In other words, the retiring watch climb into the warm bunks just vacated by those going up on watch. Wherever the berths, it is absolutely essential that the sleeper cannot be thrown out however extreme the conditions. High leecloths are more forgiving than bunkboards, but either should be fitted. They and their attachment points must be strong and well secured, not simply reliant on the weight of the sleeper to hold them in place. When in harbour it is much better if the living space of the saloon is not needed for berths other than for occasional guests. A separate sleeping cabin makes life in port much easier. Having to make up bunks each evening and stow them each morning feels acceptable for a few weeks, but is a real nuisance in the long term.

Ventilation and air-conditioning

When you are in the cabin, particularly if you are trying to sleep, there is nothing more unpleasant than feeling stifled and airless. Make sure that the cabin can be ventilated safely, even on passage. Traditional dorade-type ventilators have two holes in the top of the box, one over the watertrap and the other immediately over the deck inlet. In port, the vent can be put directly over the inlet with a cover on the other opening. The reverse position is used at sea. There should also be an emergency cover for the deck inlet in case the box is smashed. Modern versions often only have one hole because an adjustable mushroom cap over the deck inlet allows the vent to be sealed. It is often possible to have at least some hatches or ports open or on vent while on passage, but you should always assess the risks according to conditions. Having an opening hatch in the heads

Sleeping like a baby – high lee cloths and extra cushions create a safe sea cot for crew of any age. Photo: Jane Russell

PREPARATIONS

Dorade-type ventilators (left) improve conditions below.
Photo: Graham Adam

compartment is a real bonus, as is having one above the galley. If you are in a position to choose or change your hatches you could opt for ones which open in both directions. Alternatively you might want to have some forward-opening and some aft-opening. This way you will maximise your chances of directing some air flow through the cabin. The simplest method of forced ventilation when in harbour is by means of windscoops: lightweight sailcloth triangles, shaped rather like miniature spinnakers, set above each hatch to direct the breeze below. Like awnings, they are better when made of canvas rather than nylon which tends to flap noisily in the breeze.

In harbour, opening both port and starboard hull ports will promote a cross breeze which will rapidly reduce the temperature below decks. This can be further enhanced at anchor by adding temporary wind scoops in the form of cut plastic bottles. However, you should consider the security of the yacht before opening hull ports and ensure that pre-departure drills include checking that none have been left open.

When it is very still and hot, electric fans make life more pleasant, particularly in the galley. Power consumption may be high, so check before purchase. Cheaper fans tend to be noisy, demand power and are often short-lived. It is worth investing in ones that are quiet at full and low speed, use little power and have a long life. Small solar-powered ventilators are available, but they are not powerful enough to cool the main interior significantly. They do make a difference in the heads or for a boat left closed up and unattended.

Larger yachts (over 12m/40ft) might be fitted with air conditioning, either at build or retrospectively. In order to provide enough power, these units are all AC and, if you are not plugged in to shore power, an appropriate diesel generator is the only sensible way to power them (see comments on auxiliary generators in Chapter 2). Small self-contained units are relatively simple to fit. They require power, a cooling water inlet and an outlet seacock. Larger, more complex systems with remote compressors require specialist installation. Any of the main suppliers will provide advice on the size of unit required for a particular boat. All air conditioning systems are most efficient if windows and hatches are closed. It is personal choice as to whether your desire to be cool warrants being cocooned down below. Many would prefer the shade of an awning with all their senses still in tune with the environment around them.

Heating systems

In the northern latitudes, some sort of heating system is beneficial if not essential. There are two main types of onboard heating systems. Traditional systems rely on a stove-style heater with the burner situated in the cabin to be heated. A calorifier can be integrated into the system to produce hot water. More common to modern yachts is a system whereby the burner unit is fitted remotely from the cabins and the heat is transmitted to the cabin or cabins by blown hot air or by a hot water circuit. This type of system is more powerful and has the ability to heat even a large yacht. However, it is more complex to install and requires some form of electrical power as well as fuel. Both types require a flue (exhaust) and enough air to allow efficient burning without creating deadly carbon monoxide. Most remote burners use diesel as fuel. Traditional stoves will burn either diesel, paraffin (kerosene) or solid fuel (wood or charcoal). Any type of heater can get very hot and is a potential burn risk.

Insulation

Whether you are in the tropics or frozen into the ice, comfort below is greatly improved by proper insulation. In a steel or aluminum boat the whole of the area under the deck, coachroof and topsides should, if accessible, be covered with one of the proprietary forms of expanded polyurethane foam, the thicker the better. Many glassfibre boats will have a foam or balsa core in the deck and possibly the topsides. If they do not, or if the amount is not considered adequate, extra insulation can be added. This should not be done in a wooden boat where it might promote rot, but timber provides relatively good insulation anyway.

The galley

The galley is the heart and soul of a cruising yacht. Nothing impacts so immediately on the spirits of the crew as the production of appropriate and timely meals and drinks. The happiest crews are those with a well-equipped, well-stocked galley that remains functional and safe in all sea states.

The stove must be gimbaled to swing freely to at least 35° in either direction and should have a surrounding rail and pot-clamps to hold pots in position over the burners. A protective 'crash bar' in front of the stove protects the cook and decreases the likelihood of gas taps being turned on or off by accident. Linear galleys can leave the cook dangerously unbalanced and should at least have a stout strap to hold the cook in place or to lean against. It is preferable that other crew members are able to enter and exit the cabin without the cook needing to move aside. The very best sea galley is a cosy U or L shape with fiddled work surfaces, where it is comfortable to prepare food, cook and wash up whilst braced against the galley sides, outside of which the rest of the crew can come and go unhindered, and from where a quick escape is possible should a boiling pot fall towards you. It is possible to enclose a galley in this way on even quite a small yacht.

Good stowage is critical to a well-functioning galley. All the day-to-day items should be within easy reach, but securely stowed. Tea caddies, mugs, knives and salt cellars can all become lethal missiles on an unexpected wave. Non-slip maps or cloths to stop things sliding around in lockers and on work surfaces are remarkably effective in all but the most extreme conditions. A deep sink is essential and it should drain on either tack. As well as its normal use for washing up, the sink will often be the best place to stow things temporarily during cooking operations. It can also be fitted with a chopping board lid if workspace is restricted. There should be a salt-water supply at the sink to encourage salt-water usage whenever possible. It is also a good idea to have a foot pump for the cold fresh-water supply to the galley. It is much easier to monitor your water usage and minimise waste of water and gas if, for example, you know that you need four squirts for two cups of tea. But beware the probability that for weeks after coming ashore you will find yourself standing at sinks, pumping your foot up and down, holding your hands foreward beseechingly and only belatedly realising why no water is coming out of the taps!

Cooking fuel

Paraffin (kerosene)
Paraffin (kerosene) stoves used to be the favourite of cruisers, but this fuel is increasingly hard to obtain. Supplies of spares for paraffin stoves have also dwindled worldwide. Some boats still prefer to use paraffin, sometimes to simplify fuel storage where a paraffin heater is also used. If you decide to follow this route, keep at least three months supply of fuel on board and be careful to filter any fuel that you buy. Beware of language differences and misunderstandings about which type of fuel you are buying. It has been known for yachtsmen to unwittingly buy petrol instead of paraffin. This can have explosively disastrous consequences.

Propane or butane
Most cruisers rely on bottles of propane or butane gas for their cooking fuel. Although propane and butane are widely available, they are marketed in different parts of the world in a variety of bottles at different pressures and needing different regulators.

Propane is stored at a higher pressure than butane so propane cylinders usually (not always) incorporate a pressure release valve. Depending on where you are around the Atlantic, your bottles may be filled with either propane or butane and in some places by a mixture of the two. Propane should always be used at higher latitudes because butane does not vaporise below 0°C. It is perfectly safe to put butane into a propane cylinder, whereas it is very dangerous to put propane into a butane bottle. With this in mind, most cruising yachts carry propane cylinders which they re-fill when necessary. Most gas appliances will run off either fuel, provided that it is supplied through the correct regulator. With two or three crewmembers it is a good idea to carry two or three 6kg or 3.9kg cylinders, rather than fewer bigger ones, even if you have the space. That way the bottles remain small enough and light enough to carry ashore easily and you are better able to monitor your gas consumption. The process of re-filling is often protracted, particularly in Europe where exchange of butane cylinders is common practice. But the trip to the fuelling plant can sometimes be a memorable experience in itself and such trips are part of the tapestry of the cruising lifestyle.

The simplest and most flexible system for European yachts is to be equipped with propane bottles and regulators and to have the capability to attach any nation's authorised system into the yacht's system without compromising any of the built-in safety systems – particularly below decks. Containers for gas bottles must drain overboard and not into the cockpit, lockers or below decks. Camping Gaz bottles will be redundant once you have left Europe. Calor propane bottles can be refilled using the standard US fittings (but see note below). An American yacht will find her propane system quite adequate until she reaches Europe. There it may be possible to get gas cylinders refilled, provided that there is the documentation to prove that they are suitable for the purpose and in test date, but it may be a time-consuming process. If planning to remain in a single European country for a length of time, it may be preferable to lease local propane cylinders, and to fit the necessary adaptors to connect them to the yacht's propane regulator. If the intention is to visit several European countries over an extended period, you may be advised to convert to a butane system using Camping Gaz cylinders. But be aware that this may be a costly alternative and if you plan to visit the Scandinavian countries, only propane may be available.

Note
Although American and Calor propane connectors appear identical, they are not absolutely so. An American propane connector can be attached to the female fitting on a Calor bottle and a gas-tight seal can be made. However, it is physically impossible to get a UK Calor connector into an American female bottle fitting.

PREPARATIONS

Safe systems

All on-board fuels, including gas, are potentially dangerous and it is vital that all crew members observe basic safety procedures. Turn gas off at the bottle as soon as it is no longer required. If this means going out into the cockpit and opening a locker, a shut-off valve for routine use should be fitted where the piping enters the cabin. Electrically operated shut-off valves at the bottles can be operated by a galley switch. Any device must be far enough from the stove to be accessible in the event of a galley fire. Newer gas stoves and other gas appliances are likely to be fitted with some form of flame failure device. However, this will not prevent leaks from defective piping. As with your other onboard systems, you are only as safe as the weakest point. Stove and gas system spares should be carried. If burners rust out or a regulator fails, replacements may be difficult to find. It is worth carrying a simple alternative method of heating food such as a miniature camping stove with its own fuel supply. On an ocean passage, a diet of uncooked food palls quickly.

All yachts should ensure that their bottles are new or in very good condition before departure, and that they will remain within their test date throughout the cruise. Bottles that are dented or have become rusty are unlikely to be acceptable for refill, so it is worth looking after them. But be cautious about painting bottles in order to protect them. Some refill plants will automatically reject them if they have been painted. Varnishing would be more acceptable.

Bottles should be marked with their tare weight and should never be overfilled. In tropical or semi-tropical regions cylinders should only be filled to 70 per cent of their capacity to allow for expansion of the LPG with increase in temperature. Overfilling could lead to burst bottles.

A great deal of useful information on gas systems is contained on the calor gas website, including a section on marine use.

Website
www.calormarineshop.co.uk/marine_safety/marine_safety_and_you.htm

BBQs

Many cruising boats now carry some form of marine barbecue. These are usually a lidded, ventilated stainless steel bowl which clamps to a stanchion or similar support. The simplest versions use solid fuel – either wood or charcoal, but marine gas barbecues are also available. Either sort is very useful on board, particularly for cooking fish, even more so in the tropics where cooking on deck is considerably more pleasant than cooking in the cabin. The main downside to the solid fuel varieties is the time delay between lighting them and reaching cooking temperature, but they are also considerably messier. Gas barbecues are instant, easier and cleaner to use, but are subject to the same safety concerns as any other on-board gas appliances.

Whatever the latitude, most crews will find themselves at various 'beach barbecues' along the way. These are usually gatherings around an open fire. It is very useful to have a spare oven tray or similar metal grill which can be taken ashore and propped over the fire. Some tongs are also helpful, and kitchen foil is great for wrapping around food to cook in the base of the fire.

Fridges and freezers

If your home cruising ground is in relatively high latitudes you may not think of an onboard fridge as a major priority. However, beer and meat aside, once you are in tropical or sub-tropical regions even fruit and vegetables will have an extended life if you are able to refrigerate them. You may still have edible fresh tomatoes after three weeks at sea, which is unlikely to be true at ambient temperatures. Perhaps more important to many cruisers, when you land that prize-winning tuna or dorado you will be able to enjoy it for several days. So, although not absolutely essential, some method of keeping food and drink cool in the tropics should be on your wish list. The basic choice is either an insulated icebox or a refrigeration system.

Refrigeration systems fall broadly into two categories, those that are directly driven from the yacht's engine (or auxiliary generator), and those that run from the ship's electrical system. Directly powered systems enable cooling of larger volumes and to lower temperatures, but the larger the volume or the lower the temperature, the more power required. Even a relatively small-volume freezer will require the engine or generator to be run at least once every single day, which may be antisocial and can render the crew hostage to their vessel. Regularly running the main engine on such a comparatively light load in harbour does it no good.

Power usage increases considerably in the tropics but is reduced in proportion to better (thicker) insulation. Ideally, if space allows, any onboard fridge should have a minimum of 10cm (4in) of closed cell polyurethane foam. 15cm (6in) of foam would be even better and should be considered a minimum for any part of the fridge that is against an engine compartment bulkhead or being used as a freezer. The insulation should incorporate a vapour barrier, and a reflective layer to reduce radiated heat transmission. Air-cooled fridges are hopelessly inefficient in hot climates where it is better to use a keel cooled compressor. However, on larger systems where several keel coolers would be required, a water cooled system should be considered. Make sure that the lid fits tightly with proper (neoprene) seals. A drain with a swan-neck to prevent cold air escaping is also a good idea. All fridges contain a cocktail of metal compounds, so ensure that sacrificial zincs are fitted in the cooling circuit.

CREATING A HOME-FROM-HOME

Boat fridges have tended to be top opening in order to minimise the escape of cold air. However there is an argument for the ease, and therefore speed, of access of front opening boxes, which potentially reduces the time that the door is opened.

Stowage

Life on board is always improved by proper stowage. There is an enormous amount of stuff squirreled away into every last corner of most cruising boats. But quantity of storage is not necessarily as important as quality of storage. For example, although beneath the sole boards may seem to offer gaping caverns of space crying out to be filled, be cautious about what you actually store there. Anything that will rot or spoil or corrode on contact with water should either be sealed into watertight containers or stored elsewhere. Production boats tend to lack locker space but have more berths than are required. It is usually possible to convert a bunk into storage space. Think about the possibility of being slammed by a big wave and make sure that lockers are not going to fly open and release their stores. Lockers should be lined so that any water trickling around the inside of the hull cannot rot the locker itself or spoil the contents. For similar reasons, make sure that locker shelves are not fitted right up flush with the hull. It is better to divide locker space up into several smaller areas. That way it is much easier to know where everything is stored and to keep everything to hand.

Most live-aboard cruisers develop ingenious storage systems that work for them. This might be using fold-away plastic crates, or stringing up net or cloth storage hammocks. Keep priority equipment such as flares, medical kit, and emergency grab bags readily to hand and close to the companionway. Think carefully about which items can go into deeper, longer-term storage. Always provide a locker or similar stowage for each crew member. Clothes stored in hanging lockers may need to be protected from chafe. If personal storage space is limited, make that clear to new crew members before they come aboard.

Every bit of storage space is useful. But be selective about what to store in any areas below the cabin soles – tissue boxes would be a very optimistic choice on some boats. Photo: Mike Robinson

Clothing

An Atlantic cruise calls for a variety of clothing. In the higher latitudes, oilskins are likely to be in daily use at sea and they need to be of good enough quality to withstand such constant wear. It is worth looking after them properly. In the tropics they may be forgotten for a while, although a tropical downpour on nightwatch might have you reaching for them again. When you arrive in a new country, a reasonably clean and tidy crew makes a better impression on customs or immigration officials than a dirty and dishevelled one. It is worth having at least one decent set of clothes on board for this purpose if nothing else. Be aware of local customs. It is possible to cause offence by failing to conform to local standards of dress. Shoes are considered a part of normal dress in many areas. Most voyaging sailors spend a great deal of time exploring ashore on foot, so have appropriate footwear.

A good sunhat is essential, particularly for youngsters. Photo: Rhianon Darwall

The effects of sun damage to skin are often not revealed for ten or more years. But the damage is cumulative, and it seems common sense that all crewmembers, and most importantly young crew, should use sun-screen and wear a wide brimmed hat (or a peak cap with a neck flap) and sunglasses as a routine. In the tropics, lightweight long-sleeved shirts and lightweight trousers do a great job of protecting you, and there are now some excellent UV resistant swim wear products that protect back and shoulders, particularly when you are snorkeling. At the very least, a T-shirt will help to protect your shoulders and back when you are in the water.

PREPARATIONS

Laundry

Some yachts do have washing machines installed on board. But it is more usual for crew to hand-wash laundry, either onboard or ashore, or to have clothes and bed linen laundered for them ashore. If you are hand-washing on board and want to avoid permanently salty clothes and bedding, the volume of fresh water required for rinsing will probably be the main issue. If water is restricted, several rinses of a few items in small volumes of fresh water are more effective than one or two rinses of a whole load at a time. A couple of buckets or trugs are useful for this. Drying the clean laundry is not necessarily straightforward on board, even in harbour. If it is a windy anchorage the salt spray will be absorbed into the material, particularly if it is draped over guard rails, quickly undoing any painstaking rinsing. Plastic laundry driers with multiple pegs attached are great for smaller items and can be clipped up in the lee of the spray hood or similarly protected position. Washing lines strung between stays and shrouds are a common practice, although this is frowned upon or even prohibited in some harbours and marinas. Consider the biodegradability of your washing products, especially if you are washing on board.

Waste disposal

If you are heading off from northern Europe or North America it is easy enough to take waste disposal for granted. But you need to think through the consequences of how you will dispose of waste from the boat. Onboard provision must be made for rubbish disposal, and most of us are now

Sewing your yacht's name onto clothing may help you to keep track of it all at the laundry. Photo: Mike Robinson

familiar with the concept of separating our rubbish. Within the galley area there should be a container for biodegradable rubbish that can be disposed of at sea. This can contain paper and cardboard packaging (ripped up or shredded) as well as food waste. Somewhere convenient, ideally a deck locker, there should be a bag or container for plastics and other non-degradable items. It is a good idea to rinse any food or drink containers with sea water before storage. Metal cans and glass can be disposed of by filling them with sea water and sinking them overboard, but it is against international regulations to do this within 12 miles of the shore. In some special areas such as the 'Wider Caribbean Region' and the Mediterranean it is an offence to dump any form of waste overboard. All vessels cruising within US waters are required to adhere to US regulations appertaining to discharge overboard of oil and garbage. US vessels are

Pirates of the Caribbean: a laundry service with a certain style. Photo: Graham Adam

CREATING A HOME-FROM-HOME

required (and foreign vessels are recommended) to post in a prominent position on board two placards summarising these regulations. These placards, each measuring about 9in x 6in (22cm x 15cm) are obtainable from yacht chandlers in the UK or by mail order from the USA. The US Coast Guard always look for these on boarding and can fine the owner for non-compliance.

The International Convention for the Prevention of Pollution from Ships (MARPOL) gives the following guidance for all vessels.

GARBAGE DISPOSAL		
	All vessels outside special areas	All vessels inside special areas
Plastic – including synthetic ropes, fishing nets and plastic bags	Disposal prohibited	Disposal prohibited
Floating dunnage, lining and packing materials	> 25 miles off shore	Disposal prohibited
Paper, rags, glass, metal, bottles, crockery and similar refuse	> 12 miles	Disposal prohibited
Paper, rags, glass, etc, comminuted or ground	> 3 miles	Disposal prohibited
Food waste: cooked, not comminuted or ground	> 12 miles	> 12 miles
Food waste: comminuted or ground*	> 12 miles	> 12 miles
Fresh fish remains	> 3 miles	> 12 miles
Ash (inert) comminuted (slurry)	> 12 miles	Disposal prohibited
Ash (inert)	> 12 miles	Disposal prohibited

*Comminuted or ground garbage must be able to pass through a screen with mesh size no larger than 25mm (1in)

Time taken for objects to dissolve at sea	
Paper bus ticket	2–4 weeks
Cotton cloth	1–5 months
Rope	3–14 months
Woollen cloth	1 year
Painted wood	13 years
Tin can	100 years
Aluminium can	200–500 years
Plastic bottle	450 years

Source: Hellenic Marine Environment Protection Association (HELMEPA)

Note
Most 'disposable' nappies are not bio-degradable! There are many excellent washable varieties now available which would completely remove the horror of storing soiled nappies on board for any length of time or, worse still, dumping them at sea or ashore in a community that has no way of dealing with them. Sanitary or feminine hygiene products are another necessary problem for female crew to deal with on board. It is possible to source washable or totally bio-degradable varieties. Moon Cups (not the 'disposable' varieties) are a 'monthly' option worth considering as they completely eliminate disposal of sanitary towels or tampons.

PREPARATIONS

Not what you would expect to see on an idyllic tropical island – but, sadly, many a Caribbean windward shore is littered with rubbish from the sea. Photo: Richard Woods

You may, anyhow, disapprove of putting any waste overboard even on passage. However, it is worth considering the problems that island communities may have with waste disposal. On some islands it is impossible to landfill. Such islands, unless they have the population to warrant an incinerator, are often scarred by massive dumping areas which then have to be burned off at intervals. Avoid taking sackfuls of non-degradable waste ashore to isolated communities. It may be a relief to get rid of it, but it would be much better if you kept it on board until you reach a port or harbour where there is the possibility of an infrastructure to deal with it. Keep this in mind when you are provisioning at major centres. Try to remove as much plastic packaging as possible when you stow, and take it ashore before departure.

Websites
www.marinewastedisposal.com/regulations.htm

www.imo.org/environment/mainframe.asp?topic_id=297

www.greenboatstuff.com/feminineitems.html

www.keeper.com (Moon cups)

FOOD AND WATER

Provisioning

Many aspects of life on board, except for occasional maintenance periods and dealings with officialdom, can be very self-contained within the community of yachts. But the need for food creates every opportunity for going ashore and becoming immersed in local markets and local culture.

Provisioning in many and varied places is one of the golden threads of going cruising. The experience should be shared by all the crew, partly because it's interesting and partly because more hands make lighter bags. Unless your departure from your home port is your point of departure across the Atlantic, it is entirely unnecessary to weigh the boat down with mountains of home provisions. Local people all around the Atlantic do eat food! Most of the major centres around the Atlantic circuit have well-stocked modern supermarkets as well as local markets of fresh produce. In West Africa and on some smaller islands the supermarket facilities may not be quite so good, but local produce is generally available. Particularly in North America, it may be necessary to organise transport to a large supermarket to stock up with all the basics. Crews on neighbouring yachts often share a hire car if buses or taxis are not available. Take strong bags with you to minimise the need for flimsy plastic bags. Some yachts use telescopic trolleys to help with the loads.

Any tins to be kept in the bilge should have the contents marked in indelible pen and their labels removed. This is to prevent the possibility of soggy labels clogging bilge pump strainers, but it also removes the potential for confusion with numerous unmarked cans.

Before leaving home, lay in a stock of 'national' foods – those items that are likely to be expensive or simply unavailable elsewhere. Instant coffee, English tea bags, bread mixes, concentrated fruit 'squash' and yeast extract (Marmite) fall into this category, as do favourite branded products. However, avoid overstocking staples that can be found almost everywhere such as bread, flour, sugar, pasta, rice, canned fish, canned fruit and vegetables and fresh eggs. A couple of weeks' supply of all of these should be ample.

Mid-passage treats

If you are provisioning for a longer passage it is a good idea to sit down with all the crew and make a list. There will be individual likes and dislikes to take into account, but also make sure that any allergies are known about. Work out how many meals you need to cater for and then build in a safety margin in case of delays. Your choice of provisions will largely depend on how much storage space is available on board. For example dried pulses, rice, oats, quorn, popping corn and dried milk all score highly on a ratio of nutrients gained to storage space required. Cartons of milk and cans of beans would not score so well, and are heavier too. There are some really very palatable powdered milk varieties available in bulk once you get into the hotter areas where fresh milk is unavailable. Aim for variety, keep a stock of biscuits and crackers, and always have a stash of little culinary treats like a tin of cream or a jar of char-grilled artichokes – whatever you fancy! It is good for morale to have mini-celebrations to mark sections of the passage, so stock up accordingly. On a long passage it is 'fresh crunch' which tends to run out first. Bean sprouts and sprouting seeds, such as mustard and cress or alfalfa, are an excellent way of keeping that need fulfilled. But preserved vegetables such as pickled dill cucumbers can also help to satisfy that

CREATING A HOME-FROM-HOME

craving. Bottles or jars of stronger flavours to liven up an otherwise drab meal are always worth keeping in stock. These are things like jams and chutneys, curry paste, lime pickle, mustard or hot chilli sauce.

There has been a great advance in recent years in the quality and variety of dried or dehydrated foods and crews in long distance ocean races use them almost exclusively. This may not be your first choice, but they are a good standby.

Shelf-life

The length of time that fresh stores will keep depends both on their quality and the care with which they are stored. They will deteriorate rapidly in warm ambient temperatures if they have been chilled prior to purchase. It is worth sourcing fruit and vegetables from a local market where produce has not been refrigerated in storage. Sound potatoes, carrots, beetroot, white cabbage and onions will last for a month-long voyage even in tropical latitudes, provided they are picked over regularly and any suspect ones removed. Green tomatoes will ripen gradually in a warm atmosphere, and do not need daylight, but should be protected from bruising. Aubergine, courgette, cucumber and capsicums will last for a couple of weeks un-chilled, but longer if there is fridge space available. It is always worth trying local tropical fruits and vegetables and experimenting with storage, but don't depend on their keeping qualities.

Nearly all citrus fruit will keep for weeks if not months but, again, check that they haven't been pre-chilled. Lemons keep well if wrapped in foil. It is also worth having some bottles of lemon juice and lime juice on board. Bunches of bananas are notorious for being green and inedible for several days, but then ripening all at once. One ripe banana will cause the other bananas (and other nearby fruits such as tomatoes) to ripen, so you can delay the domino effect to some extent by separating the fruit off into smaller 'hands' and storing them in different places. Fresh eggs will last a long time without treatment, but not so long if they have been chilled at any time. There are various methods of

Preparing meals before a passage. Photo: Mike Robinson

preserving eggs that have been chilled. Keep them dry and free from condensation. Coating with Vaseline (petroleum jelly) certainly works, and eggs treated in this way will last for at least six weeks. A less messy alternative is to wrap individual eggs with cling-film. All eggs should be turned twice a week to prevent their shells from drying out and the yolks from settling – it's this that makes them turn bad.

Meat and cheese

Many cruising yachts now have the refrigerator capacity to cope with fresh meat on board. Vacuum-packed meat lasts longer, providing that the process has been done properly. Some boats may find it easier to carry their own small vacuum packer rather than rely on the need to keep a refrigerator properly cooled. On smaller boats or ones without a fridge it may not be worth trying to have fresh meat on board other than for an immediate treat. If you catch fish on passage you probably won't miss having meat anyway – fresh tuna steak is pretty red meat. Some salamis and chorizos will keep un-chilled for a long time, but only if they have been appropriately cured. You need to source them from a market where they are clearly unrefrigerated. These varieties are drier and saltier than the chilled ones, but don't melt when temperatures increase. Cheese is a similar conundrum. Waxed cheeses keep quite well without refrigeration. It is sometimes possible to find tinned cheese, though it tends to be very processed and not to everyone's taste. It is possible to keep yoghurt cultures going on board and even to create your own cream cheese, but this can take practice.

You can buy portable vacuum packers; see below.

Storing citrus fruit in a hammock. Soft fruits would crush against the net if packed in too tightly. Photo: Graham Adam

Further reference
www.juiceland.co.uk (Vacuum packers)

Voyaging on a Small Income by Annie Hill, Thomas Reed Publications. This book is full of useful provisioning tips for boats constrained by both budget and space

PREPARATIONS

Food pests

Various forms of pest will find their way on board through contact with the shore, particularly when provisioning. Anchoring off gives good protection except for stowaways brought aboard in the food itself or in container boxes. These include weevils and cockroaches. Cardboard cartons and bunches of fruit and vegetables often harbour cockroach eggs. It is worth sorting through any fresh stores and cardboard containers before taking stores down below. In particular, discard cardboard egg boxes and store the eggs in ventilated plastic containers. Vigorously dunk large hands of bananas in the sea to rid them of unwelcome guests.

To avoid general insect infestation, any dry produce should be stored in small-volume, airtight, plastic storage containers. It is likely that some of your dry produce will at some stage be infested with weevils. But by dividing your stores into smaller, separate volumes you minimise the chance of everything becoming infested at the same time. The weevils themselves are not really a problem and in small numbers can be sifted out. However, larger infestations result in the produce becoming tainted and unpalatable.

Water

Most production boats will not have sufficient built-in water-carrying capacity for an ocean voyage. About 2.5 litres (just over 1/2 Imperial gallon or nearly 3/4 US gallon) per person per day is really the minimum amount that should be carried. Allowance should always be made for a longer than anticipated passage time. It is prudent to check the actual capacity of each of your tanks. If you decide to increase your capacity with flexible water tanks, be aware that they are susceptible to chafing. Position and protect them accordingly. The calculation for water needed for the Canaries to Barbados voyage with a crew of three in a slow boat might be:

> 2.5 litres x 3 people x 24 days = 180 litres
> 50 per cent reserve = 90 litres
> Total required = 270 litres (about 62 Imperial gallons or 75 US gallons)

It should be stressed that this is the absolute minimum water supply consistent with safety, even if you have a water maker. Even if you have a good water-catching system, you should not assume that you will catch water on passage.

Emergency water

At least 45 litres (10 Imperial gallons) should be carried in plastic 'grab' containers, and kept reasonably accessible in case of emergency. Fresh water is lighter than salt water so, depending on the weight of the containers themselves, they should float. But it is a good idea not to completely fill them, leaving some air trapped to help flotation. It is easy to test whether yours float. These containers will also be needed for filling up where it is not possible to fill the tanks via a shore hose. The small 5 or 10 litre (1 or 2 Imperial gallon) cans are easiest to handle in and out of dinghies and are also easiest to stow on board. It is possible to buy collapsible water carriers. These are probably useful as a back up, but may not be hard-wearing enough for constant use.

Monitoring consumption

The main water supply should be split between at least two separate tanks. The water distribution system should be valved so that an individual tank can be selected for use. The tanks should be used in turn every few days through the passage. This helps you to monitor consumption (essential when on passage); it can help to balance the boat, and also reduces the risks of contamination or leakage of a whole tank. Water should draw out through the top of each tank via a standpipe into the bottom. This reduces the chances of the tanks leaking into the bilge. Tank gauges may be unreliable, and a better method of keeping track of consumption at sea is to use a small-volume service container. Water should only be drawn from this container. Keep a record of each time it is refilled.

There are other useful ways of monitoring water consumption. If you disconnect the electric water pump and rely on a hand or foot pump for fresh water when on passage you will minimise waste. It is also useful to keep a fresh-water rinse bottle: take an empty 1 litre plastic drink bottle and punch or drill a series of holes in its lid. Use this as a hand held fresh-water shower after a salt-water wash. Some boats are only fitted with electric water pumps and, worse still, have sealed in tanks that are inaccessible for hand bailing or pumping. This is a potentially lethal situation on a long passage as you are entirely dependent on a functioning electrical system to gain access to fresh water.

Watermakers

Reverse osmosis watermakers, which produce fresh water from sea water, are increasingly popular on cruising yachts. The most productive ones are driven directly from the engine or a generator or are AC powered. DC units are very power hungry, so if you are retro-fitting one you should consider upgrading the whole electrical system. Manually-operated models are also available, but these are only suitable for use in survival situations. As long as it continues to work, a watermaker can transform life whilst on passage. But watermakers should never be completely relied upon, and there ought always to be sufficient water maintained in tanks or grab containers to make it to the nearest port. A watermaker may eliminate the need to fill up from the shore. This would allow more extended cruising of unpopulated areas and also allows for more generous use of water for laundry and cleaning. However, some watermakers cannot be used in harbours or anchorages. Here the water is more liable to be contaminated with oily substances which can

CREATING A HOME-FROM-HOME

damage the membranes of the machine. Despite these drawbacks many long distance cruisers would not choose to cruise without one.

Rain catchers

More traditionally-minded cruisers feel just as strongly about their rain water harvesting systems. Around most of the Atlantic circle rainfall is normally abundant enough to at least provide an occasional top up of the fresh water supply. With a good system in place it can be possible to keep your tanks filled with rain water for long periods of time without any reliance on shore supplies. It is sometimes the case that the rain is contaminated with, for example, desert dust. But rain water is most likely to be purer than other sources. In any case it is a good idea to install an in-line carbon water filter in the fresh water tap feed. The designs of water harvesting systems tend to be individual to different boats. The most common systems tend to combine water catching with a sun awning. Some excellent systems rely on collecting rain water off the decks, but in this case you need to allow for a longer period of surface cleaning before you start collecting.

Plastic contamination

When you fill up from the shore, be aware that some types of plastic hose soften in the sun and leach unpleasant tasting compounds into the water held within them. Without being too wasteful, it may be necessary to run some water out from the length of the hose before filling your tanks. A quick taste test before you fill up will save you from contaminating your tanks with chemically tainted water. A similar problem can occur with new flexible water tanks. These should be thoroughly rinsed and then taste tested before being relied upon.

Alcohol on board

The old system of Bonded stores of alcohol is no longer common practice. Most sailors prefer to experiment with the local wines and spirits as the cruise progresses. France, Spain, Portugal, Madeira and The Canaries are good areas to stock up on wine, port, sherry, madeira and brandy. Rum is a staple in the Caribbean, and most of the islands produce their own. The French islands (Martinique, Guadeloupe, St Barts and St Martin) are also good places to stock up with wine or brandy. The United States produces some lovely wines, and spirits (liquor) are reasonably priced by European standards. Imported alcohol is more expensive, particularly Scotch whisky. You can stock up on Portuguese and local wines in the Azores. Beer, either in bottles or in cans, is available almost everywhere. Beware of aluminium beer cans, which can be very thin-skinned and vulnerable to damage if they are not well stowed.

Some countries have regulations about consumption of alcohol on board. In the UK, the Department for Transport has issued a consultation paper regarding draft regulations for alcohol limits for non-professional mariners and inland boaters. The consultation document proposes that alcohol limits should not apply to vessels with an overall length of less than 7m (23ft) and a 'maximum design speed' not exceeding 7 knots. It is not yet clear whether (or how) this legislation will be enforced, but cruisers in UK waters should be aware that alcohol limits similar to those for drink-driving may become legally enforceable.

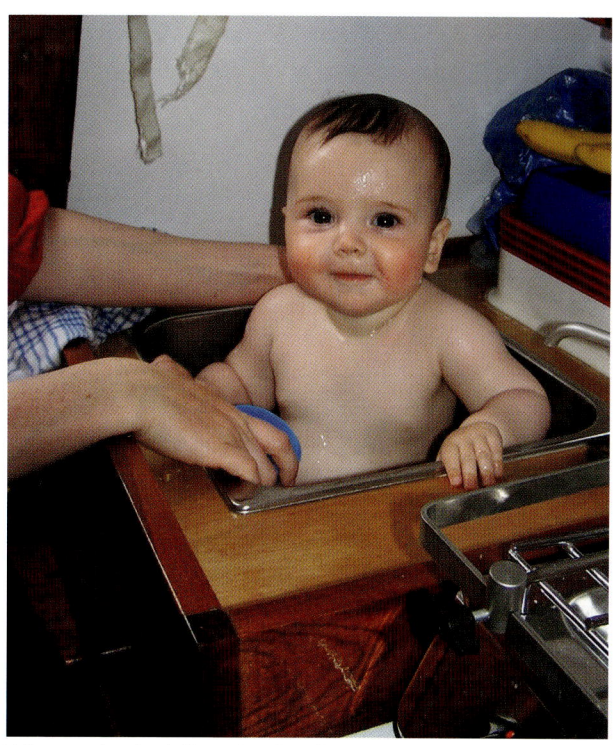

Who needs a bath if a sink will do? Monitor fresh water consumption and avoid waste. Photo: Dan Darwall

Website
www.rya.org.uk/alcohollimits

Fishing

Size of tackle

Although it is impossible to guarantee that you will be a successful passage fisherman, it is nevertheless very common for cruising yachts to supplement their stores with unforgettably fresh and delicious tuna, dorado, kingfish (mackerel) and sometimes even swordfish. A common learning curve for novice ocean fishermen might go as follows. You walk into your local fishing shop and ask for some line and lures appropriate for trolling at sea. They provide you with a very pretty array of lures and some lengths of line. After an astonishingly short amount of cruising time you realise that every single lure has gone. You visit another fishing shop and upsize. You do catch a fish, but when you try to gaff it the gaff straightens out under the weight and the fish gets away. On down the track you make friends with a

PREPARATIONS

seasoned Aussie crew and you have a 'Crocodile Dundee' moment over your fishing tackle. Opening your fishing box you say 'This is my fishing tackle.' There is an answering guffaw, followed by 'You call that fishing tackle? Nah Mate! This is fishing tackle!' A tackle box is opened to reveal an enormous gaff, huge lures, line as thick as your finger and, most importantly of all, substantial wire leaders.

It's not actually the case that bigger is better when it comes to lures, except that a bigger lure will tend to attract a bigger fish. But unless you have a large number of crew on board you probably don't want to catch a monster. What does make a difference to success is the wire leader. Even quite small tuna and dorado will easily bite through fishing line.

Tricks of the trade

It's not advisable to leave your line out overnight. Partly because you can end up catching some rather scary species which live deep during the day but come closer to the surface at night, and partly because sorting lines and landing fish is not really conducive to the off-watch crew getting any sleep.

Some yachts opt for a rod and line which tends to be the preference of anyone with game fishing experience. However it is often just as successful to tow a line from the stern. The line should be cleated off at the deck but it is common practice to run a few turns anti-clockwise around a winch before making up the inboard end. Any pull on the hook then causes the winch to spin, alerting the crew immediately. It is also sensible to leave a loop of slack in the line at the inboard end and take up the strain with a short length of shock chord. This means that when the fish strikes the sudden load is slightly dissipated and the line is less likely to snap.

Various types of lure are commonly used. The polished spoon can work well, as can a hook camouflaged among strips of coloured polythene or ragged rope end. Several varieties of 'plastic squid' are commercially available; these are relatively cheap yet effective. It makes sense to have more than one type of lure on board.

Landing a fish

Once you have a fish on the line you need to get it safely on board, which is sometimes easier said than done. You are likely to need a strong gaff, probably laced firmly onto an extension handle to give you enough reach. Once a large fish has been landed and is thrashing around, a little neat spirit poured into the gills is said to kill it immediately. However, it is sometimes quite difficult to execute this manoeuvre skilfully and you can end up with prolonged and even wilder thrashing. Ideally keep some alcohol in an old spray bottle and spray it into the gills before the fish is brought on deck.

Anaesthetisation should be instant so any drama and mess on board is avoided. The alternative method is a hard blow on the head with a winch handle. This process is likely to be more bloody and it is not a job for the faint-hearted. Wear gloves when you are handling the line. The wire leader will act as a bacon slice if your hands are not protected. It is a good idea to keep a pair of gloves on deck for this purpose. It is also a good idea to have a sharp knife to hand on deck.

Trolling at dawn. Leaving the line out overnight is inadvisable. Photo: Mike Robinson

A perfect catch on passage – just the right size of dorado (also known as dolphin fish or mahi mahi). Photo: Mike Robinson

Ocean fresh and straight to the pan – you'll never taste better fish. Photo: Mike Robinson

This will help with the gutting and filleting, but it is also there should you need to cut the line away in a hurry. Never leave this knife on deck when you are moored up or at anchor. There has been at least one occasion when unwanted boarders have used just such a deck knife as a weapon against the crew.

Spear guns

As well as line fishing, many yachtsmen use various forms of spear gun to catch reef fish and crayfish when snorkeling. Many cruising areas are nature reserves where fishing is either restricted or banned. Spear fishing is forbidden in the Tobago Cays, parts of Antigua, the Virgin Islands and Bermuda among other places, although local people may be allowed to fish by traditional methods, usually traps or pots. In the Bahamas a fishing permit is needed, and fishing of any sort is prohibited in the Exuma National Park. Check local cruising guides for details before you go spear fishing. Spear fishing with scuba gear is usually considered unethical.

Ciguatera poisoning

Eating fish caught on ocean passage is generally safe. However, owing to the prevalence of ciguatera poisoning in parts of the West Indies, fishing should not take place there without seeking local advice. Ciguatera is caused by a toxin derived from dinoflagellates found on coral and seaweed, eaten by fish, and passed along the food chain from small to bigger fish and thence to man. It accumulates over time, so a bigger fish is a greater potential danger. A rule of thumb in coastal waters is not to eat any fish that is longer than your forearm. Ciguatera causes nausea, vomiting, abdominal pain and diarrhoea and in extreme cases can lead to paralysis and death. The only cure is to make the sufferer vomit to empty the stomach. If you have any doubts about fish caught, be extremely cautious about what you eat. Barracuda tend to prey on reef fish and have a reputation for carrying ciguatera.

Flying fish

In the tropics you are likely to have the occasional flying fish landing on deck during the night. Displaying a light will tend to attract them. It is tempting to put the small ones back overboard, but many are so stunned that they do not appear to recover in the water. If you collect them through the night there is a chance that you will have enough for a meal, but it is by no means certain.

Inflatable dinghies are the first choice of most long-term cruisers. They are relatively easy to climb into from the water when scuba diving or snorkelling. Photo: Richard Woods

4 THE CREW

CREW DYNAMICS

Most Atlantic crossings take place as part of a longer cruise. The majority of extended cruising is done by couples, sometimes with children. Guests join from time to time. These are normally friends or relatives who seldom stay for more than a few weeks. But many couples choose to have extra crew on board for the longer ocean passages. By far the best situation is to be joined by an old friend who has sailed with you before. But, out of necessity, your crew may be complete strangers or only loose acquaintances, and this aspect of an Atlantic voyage needs careful thought. With a happy ship of people who know how to live afloat and who enjoy one another's company, long voyages can be a wonderful experience. Whereas friction or arguments among a dysfunctional crew will be a source of lasting regret.

Whenever possible you should try to keep arrangements flexible until you know that you will definitely be where you plan to be. It is very common for advance arrangements to be made to rendezvous at a particular port on a particular date, only for headwinds to blow or an unplanned cruising ground to beckon or engines to fail. The result is always a self-imposed nightmare of racing against time to be somewhere that you didn't really need to be except for the fact that someone is waiting for you. Anyone who has ever been cruising will appreciate that sometimes you don't end up where or when you think you will. Anyone who has not been cruising may not understand this at all. Travel arrangements should be flexible enough to cater for a change in timings or a change to the rendezvous point. The crew should realise that they may need to find accommodation and look after themselves for as long as it takes, or perhaps get on an inter-island ferry or connecting flight. Do not underestimate the potential stress on crew and vessel in trying to keep to a rigid rendezvous.

Recruitment and timings

Before approaching anybody to be passage crew, it is best to have the cruise planned in broad outline. To avoid misunderstandings, certain points should be agreed at the outset, at least verbally. The issues most likely to cause upset to either party tend to revolve around money. For example:

- Who pays any travelling expenses to or from the points of embarkation and disembarkation?
- What financial contribution, if any, is expected?
- What liability does the owner accept in the event of accident or injury, or for the costs of any changes to, or cancellation of, the arrangements? Even the best of friendships will be strained by an unexpected demand for a considerable sum of money, or a complete change of itinerary after flights have been booked.

Amateur yachtsmen who are cruising for pleasure need to find the right balance so that both owners and temporary crew feel that they have given in some way, but also each gained in some way. Typically, the crew may pay their own air fares but be glad of the ocean experience. In turn, the owners may not expect any contribution towards on-board provisioning because they appreciate having the extra crew onboard. The arrangements will be different depending on each situation, but you should agree them together before making any commitments.

In most countries, a yacht's skipper is liable for the costs of repatriating any crew member who leaves the vessel, for whatever reason. Usually this occurs by pre-arrangement and the crew holds the requisite airline ticket, or transfers to another yacht. With relatively unknown crew, however, particularly those who have been picked up off the dock, it is a sensible precaution to insist on a deposit to cover the cost of a flight from the furthest point of the cruise to their country of origin. All prospective crew need valid passports, with visas where necessary, and it is important that these should not expire during the duration of the cruise.

Who you choose as crew is a personal decision. Temperament, character, and a willingness to learn are really more important than any sailing experience. However, if there will only be the two of you on board, you need to feel confident that you can trust the boat to the crew at least while you are asleep, but also in the event of you suffering illness or injury. Taking on casual crew who are thumbing a lift from the quayside is not recommended. If it must be done as a last resort, take precautions. Screen quayside applicants carefully by taking up references from previous skippers. Examine passports and visas, and insist on the flight deposit already mentioned. Ensure that the crew joins the yacht several days before departure and helps with the provisioning, stowage and preparations, both to get some idea of what they are really like and to find out if they will pull their weight. Do not be naïve about the possibility that an unknown crew member may be carrying drugs. If these are discovered by the authorities, the consequences would be serious. Ignorance is not a good enough defence.

THE CREW

> **Websites**
> www.noonsite.com
> www.crewseekers.net

ONBOARD ROUTINE

Every yacht has her own routine. Whenever you have new crew on board you should explain to them, early on, whatever is necessary to help them to fit in with that routine. On land you would never normally brief visitors about how to behave during their stay, and when old friends come on board it can sometimes feel awkward to give any sort of skipper's briefing. But most crew will be reassured by knowing where the boundaries lie. Your approach can be more or less formal depending on your relationship to the crew. Some aspects of life on board are quite arbitrary arrangements which should be flexible depending on the differing dynamics of changing crew. Some aspects are down to the needs for privacy and house-keeping and should be gently monitored so that you can step in more firmly if the need arises. Other aspects are crucial to safety and these should be laid down very clearly and repeated as often as necessary.

Division of responsibilities

On most cruising yachts the permanent crew are a couple, married or otherwise. The dynamic of this core relationship will differ from yacht to yacht and will have a knock-on effect on the relationships with any temporary crew members. On some yachts the couple are very much equal partners in every aspect of life on board. More commonly, at least to start with, one person is the more experienced sailor and tends to take on the role of skipper. In these situations, the tasks associated with running the boat tend to occupy the skipper while the partner tends to have the, perhaps more familiar, house-keeping responsibilities. It is understandable that this might be the situation at the start of a cruise, but it is not at all ideal. It is a matter of self-preservation that with only two people on board, both should understand how to sail the boat and operate all the essential systems. Otherwise, what would happen if the skipper is ill or injured? Confidence comes with practice.

The experienced partner should encourage the inexperienced partner to practise sailing skills whenever possible. Practise helming and setting up the automatic steering. Learn about setting the sails. Practise using the navigational equipment. It is likely that the stronger, more experienced partner usually goes forward to put in reefs. Nevertheless, it is important for the other partner to practise

Keeping everyone involved makes a happy ship. Assess individuals' strengths and weaknesses and assign jobs accordingly. Photo: Jane Russell

39

PREPARATIONS

this occasionally too. Both should feel completely confident about starting up the engine and manouevring under power, particularly to anchor. If only one of you was on board and the anchor dragged, would you know what to do?

However many crew are on board, it is a good idea to keep everyone involved. When you apportion responsibilities, work to individual strengths and don't ignore weaknesses. How often have you seen a burly bloke remain clamped to the helm during anchoring procedures whilst his petite partner struggles with the hardwear on the foredeck? Take advantage of existing skills, but also allow for the crew to learn new skills. That might mean ocean navigation, or changing a fuel filter, or it might mean producing a meal for six people without losing any of it into the bilges. The core crew (the couple or the skipper) should always retain overall responsibility for the running of the yacht, but morale will be best if everyone feels as if they are contributing to life on board.

Seasick crew
At the start of every passage some of the crew are likely to suffer from seasickness. This might be demonstrated by all-out vomiting, but is equally likely to be revealed as sleepiness or considerable bad temper. Novice crew may not realise what is happening to them or may feel embarrassed to acknowledge their discomfort. Make very clear to all the crew that seasickness is extremely common and encourage sufferers to rest or accept a treatment as necessary. Non-sufferers should draw on their wells of patience and kindness until everyone is restored to normal. Onboard routines and responsibilities may need to be restructured to take account of those who are incapacitated. See also page 43.

Keeping watch

A happy voyage depends to a great extent on establishing a sustainable daily routine which allows everyone on board sufficient time to relax and sleep whilst ensuring the safe passage of the yacht. This applies as much to singlehanders, who must work out for themselves whatever compromise between sleep and watchkeeping they feel they can live with. The watch system takes into account sail changes and navigation, cooking and ongoing maintenance, but its main focus is having someone on deck at frequent intervals, if not continuously, to keep an all around watch on the horizon for any other vessels or likely hazards. AIS is increasingly popular as an aid to watch keeping (see Chapter 5), but it has its limitations and should never be used as a replacement to visual watch keeping.

Some yacht crews choose to ignore the International Regulations for Preventing Collisions at Sea and do not keep a regular watch on an ocean crossing. Sometimes such crews will leave an alarmed radar on a timed cycle. But it is not unusual to hear that, in order to save power, passage yachts have turned off their navigation lights and VHF radio. It may be true that, in certain sections of the Atlantic, a yacht can go for many days and never see a commercial vessel. However, depending on your route and timings, it is increasingly likely that a yacht with no watch keeper could, quite literally, bump into another passage yacht.

A near-miss
A scenario has actually occurred where a young singlehander in a small plywood boat, invisible to intermittent radar in the swell, was almost run down by a larger, crewed yacht with no-one on watch. The singlehander was keeping a regular watch but had not seen the approaching yacht because they were not showing any navigation lights. By the time he saw them he was only just able to disengage his wind vane in time and collision was avoided by a matter of a few feet. Even then he was unable to rouse the other crew because they were asleep down below and, he later discovered, never maintained a VHF watch on passage.

The danger is not just that many yachts make an Atlantic crossing at the same time, it is also probable that several of them will have departed from the same port and be heading to a similar GPS waypoint. Even if a collision is never imminent, any yacht on passage is reliant on its nearest neighbours if things should go wrong. It is a sickening thought that a yacht in peril, perhaps your own, could be putting out a call on the VHF, yet fellow yachtsmen could be passing by just over the horizon, their VHF switched off, oblivious to lives in danger. The power drain of a VHF radio and navigation lights is tiny compared to the drain caused by many other onboard electrics that are taken for granted. When crew avoid maintaining the best possible watch, fail to show navigation lights or fail to monitor the VHF it is at best thoughtless, probably illegal, and at worst potentially life-threatening.

The rhythm of the watches
The rhythm of the watches will depend on the number of crew on board, the prevailing conditions and also the needs of various crew members. Some crew will be up with the dawn whatever their watch, and others will be able to sleep at any time of night or day. Few people will be able to hand-steer for more than two hours even in good conditions, which is why an automatic steering system is so crucial on yachts with only one or two crew. With automatic steering engaged it is quite possible to maintain a watch for three or even four hours in good conditions. In rough weather at night, a two-hour watch is enough for most mortals. Some watch systems run formally through the night and more flexibly through the day, allowing for meal times and companionship. Others

THE CREW

are more rigidly set throughout. With larger crew numbers, and anyway with inexperienced or young crew, it may be preferable to double up the watch keeping so that there are always two or more crew on watch at the same time. Sometimes the crew prefer to have overlapping watches, but that depends on the relationships between the crew members. If you find it hard to sleep without darkness and quiet, investing in an eye mask and some earplugs may help your chances of catching up on sleep.

The most important factor is that the system should be on a 24-hour cycle. If it is anything other than this, the off-watch times for each crew member will shift on a daily basis. At first this will not be a problem, but after a few days the crew effectively become permanently jetlagged. To maximise the possibility of restorative sleep, the crew should be off watch at the same time each day. The body then gets into a rhythm of waking and sleeping. For example, with a crew of three on board and a three-hour watch system with no gaps, a 27-hour cycle is produced. Over a week or more the crew will become permanently sleep deprived. If instead they have 18 hours of watch keeping and 6 hours of flexible, communal time, the crew will be off watch at the same time each day and will be better rested, stronger and happier.

Ship's time

It is best to alter the ship's clocks periodically during the course of an Atlantic crossing. The time change is one hour for every 15° of longitude, the clocks being put back when heading west, and forward when heading east. Make the change whenever it is convenient and according to prevailing conditions. You can split the difference between the watches or, depending on your watch system, just ignore ship's time and continue with the watch changes. In this way a 0300 to 0600 watch would become a 0200 to 0500 watch and then a 0100 to 0400 watch and so on. The time is changing but the body's rhythm of sleep and waking remains constant. With only two people on board this can be quite an enjoyable way of experiencing different segments of the night and the day. But you should do what suits the crew best. Always record UTC as well as ship's time in the log to avoid any confusion.

Communications with home

Communications are discussed further in Chapter 5. The telephone system around the north Atlantic is now excellent and it is possible to make direct-dialled calls practically everywhere or to use mobiles when near to land. Mobile phone coverage has expanded enormously in the past few years. Using a mobile phone with a locally purchased SIM card may be cheaper and more convenient than using the local telephone system. The use of e-mail has now become usual almost everywhere, with WiFi access quite common in many anchorages and marinas. There are various systems for sending e-mails on board which are discussed further in Chapter 5. Satellite phones are now carried on board many yachts and may be a pre-requisite for rally membership. Many voyagers continue to rely on the international mail services to keep in touch and to send or receive packages and parcels. Mail may be sent poste restante (general delivery) to post offices in most towns, to be collected on arrival – but

---

ON BOARD ENTERTAINMENT

Paperback books (crews tend to swap them as they go along)
Dictionary
Atlas
Reference books such as the Pocket Guide series:
- *Stars and Planets*
- *Whales, Dolphins and Porpoises*
- *Rocks and Fossils*
- *Birds* (especially sea birds and migratory species)
- *Botanical*
- *Coral Reefs*

Travel guides
Cookery books (crews often swap favourite recipes)
CD-ROMS and DVDs
Playing cards
Board games (mini travel versions)
Paper, notebooks, pens and pencils
Painting set
Musical instruments
MP3 players/iPods

Have a range of onboard entertainment to occupy all the crew.
Photo: Jane Russell

PREPARATIONS

the time that it will be retained varies from country to country. Some marinas, yacht clubs and harbour offices will hold mail for visiting yachts. Local pilot books should give details.

Mailing addresses for the ports in Part II are given in the text. Mark the envelope with 'Please hold for arrival'. Wording should be kept clear and simple, without titles or honorifics. The sender's address should be clearly marked on the envelope, although uncollected letters will not necessarily be returned.

Children on board

Issues revolving around having children on board for long periods of time will differ according to the ages of the children involved. With very young children, the main concern will be their safety on board. Certain areas of the boat will be more dangerous for them than for an adult, but any parent will be used to thinking through similar concerns ashore. For example, a steep, deep companionway is a potentially damaging tumble zone, mainsheet cars can be finger slicers, a gimbaled stove is a scalding danger and table corners may be at eye level. But a berth can be converted into a fabulous cot and play pen with good use of lee cloths or netting. Similarly, a car seat can be strapped to the saloon table or cockpit seats to provide a safe high chair or viewing platform.

Slightly older children will need to be given clear boundaries to keep them safe. Involving them in planning and provisioning as well as sailing will help to keep them interested and occupied. A good idea for older children is to give them some responsibility and freedom in the form of a seaworthy dinghy or canoe. Good harnesses and harness lines are critical for keeping them safe on deck.

Probably the biggest concern for parents of children of school age is that they will miss having a peer group. The reality is often that, particularly with pre-teens, they are happy to make new friendships on board or ashore, with other children of every nationality, wherever they happen to be. A more constant peer group might be achieved by cruising in company with another family or by joining a rally with other families involved. But it may also be achieved through regular connections with friends, either on boats or ashore, via the internet. 'Skyping' is an excellent way for them to keep in touch.

Computers and the internet have also revolutionised the possibilities of home schooling, although you cannot yet assume that you will be able to access the internet from anywhere and everywhere (see Chapter 5). If you are planning to take the children out of school for a relatively short period of time, perhaps a few months, it may be possible to arrange course work directly with the children's schools, using occasional e-mail communication between the children and their teachers and classmates. Alternatively you may decide that the learning acquired while you are cruising will far outweigh any concerns about continuing with a particular curriculum. Indeed, even if you are planning a longer period of cruising with children you should investigate the various options available for home schooling, including the option of 'unschooling'. In the USA, guidelines vary from state to state. France has its own system for home or distance learning which works towards the International Baccalaureat. In the UK, the requirement is that every child receives an 'efficient full-time education suitable to his age, ability and aptitude ... either by regular attendance at school or otherwise'. Other home nations may vary in their schooling requirements.

Avoid mutiny by giving him his own command.
Photo: Rhianon Darwall

> **Further reference**
>
> For more information and advice about cruising with children and schooling on board go to:
>
> www.yachtmollymawk.com/2007/09/sea-school/
>
> www.primaryhomeeducation.co.uk (UK based) Primary School level
>
> www.oxfordhomeschooling.co.uk (UK based) Key Stage 3, GCSE and beyond
>
> www.home-schooling-uk.com
>
> www.homeschoolcentral.com (US site with links to UK courses)
>
> www.calvertschool.org/calvert-school (US based but used by many nationalities)
>
> www.weshome.com (Worldwide Education Service, UK qualifications)
>
> www.globalstudentnetwork.com
>
> For more detailed information, advice and wisdom about the various aspects of cruising with children of all ages read:
>
> *Kids In The Cockpit* by Jill Schinas, Adlard Coles Nautical. A pilot book for safe and happy sailing with children.
>
> *A Family Outing in the Atlantic* by Jill Schinas, Imperator Publishing

KEEPING HEALTHY

This section is intended to inform rather than to terrify. Cruising is a remarkably healthy way of life and, though incidents grab the headlines, serious illness or injury is rare. It is worth remembering that during the typical Atlantic cruise, a yacht will only be out of reach of help for a very small proportion of the time. However, the risks are there, and everybody on board should be aware of potential problems and have some knowledge of first aid. Medical and dental check-ups before departure are an obvious precaution. A chronic condition is not necessarily a barrier to crossing the Atlantic, but you and the rest of the crew should be informed and prepared for possible crises. Such conditions would include any food allergies or similar anaphylactic shock susceptibilities. Take advice from your doctor about the appropriate medication or drugs, including antibiotics for treatment of appendicitis. Drugs should be accompanied by a doctor's certificate to show to customs officials. Most medical practices have travel health clinics or offer travel advice, and you should ensure that you are given all the appropriate vaccinations for your cruising areas.

Websites
There is a comprehensive and helpful medical section at www.noonsite.com/General/Medical

Other useful websites include
www.fitfortravel.nhs.uk

www.who.int/en/

Seasickness

By far the most common cruising ailment, which affects most people at some time or other, is seasickness. Seasickness is caused by mixed messages being sent to the brain. The messages from your eyes are telling the brain that you are stable within your environment (because you are moving with the boat), but the messages from your balance centres are saying that you are all over the place. The resultant confused message causes nausea. This is why staring at the horizon can help, but it gets tiring over long periods. Some people are more susceptible than others and everyone recovers at different rates. Only a tiny minority never acclimatise.

Seasickness is exacerbated by many things including fear, tiredness and hunger. It can also be made worse by anything which the body treats as a toxin or finds harder to process. Removing caffeine, alcohol and meat from the menu before setting sail has been known to help sufferers. Conversely, if you insist on having steak and chips with lashings of beer or wine during a late night 'send-off', you only have yourself to blame! Of the various remedies on the market, Stugeron (cinnazarine) is very effective, particularly if you take the first dose several hours before departure.

Ocean cruising is a generally healthy lifestyle which periodically tests your fitness! Photo: Tim Wright www.photoaction.com

However, once you have begun to vomit it may not be possible to keep a pill down for long enough for it to be effective. With this in mind some people choose suppositories. However, sufferers of seasickness can experience diarrhoea simultaneously with the vomiting, which would not favour suppository use. For many cruisers, a hyoscine (scopolamine) patch, worn behind the ear, is the veritable wonder drug. The patches slowly release chemicals through the skin over a period of a few days and their effectiveness is not diminished by actual sickness or diarrhoea. If you feel that you are experiencing side effects it is worth trying a half patch at a time. Anti-sickness wrist bands, which act on pressure points inside the wrists, can be helpful. Ginger helps to settle stomachs and gingernut biscuits have a loyal fan club.

It is worth mentioning that seasickness can affect the efficacy of any drug regime. It may also reduce protectiveness of oral contraceptives. It may be necessary to take extra precautions unless you want to add to your crew numbers.

Diarrhoea

This is an ailment common to most travellers at some stage. There are several possible reasons including sunstroke and seasickness as well as various illnesses and forms of food

PREPARATIONS

poisoning. It is possible to make up your own simple re-hydration fluid as follows:

- One level teaspoon of salt
- Eight level teaspoons of sugar
- One litre of clean drinking or cooled boiled water

Dangers from the sun

Ultraviolet (UV) light is a small component of sunlight consisting of UVA, UVB and UVC. UVC light is completely absorbed by ozone in the atmosphere and the remaining radiation that reaches us consists of approximately 5 per cent UVB and 95 per cent UVA. UVB is mainly responsible for sunburn, skin ageing and, in time, various forms of cancer. The highest levels of UV light occur when the sun is at its highest point in the sky during the middle of the day. UV is not absorbed by clouds, so it is possible to experience the damaging effects of the sun even on cool cloudy days. White surfaces such as rippling water and rough seas reflect more UVB radiation than calm, open water. The immediate effects of sun damage are sunburn, which can be soothed with creams, and sunstroke, which is really caused by dehydration. Mild sunstroke can be cured by drinking plenty of water and taking mild pain killers. Severe sunstroke can result in vomiting and diarrhoea and may need to be treated with re-hydration fluid. Prevention is better than cure! Babies and children, fair-skinned people, people with certain medical conditions or on certain treatment regimes are most vulnerable to the effects of the sun and should take all precautions necessary. Wearing wide brimmed hats and long loose clothing, using UV resistant swim-wear, and regularly applying high factor sunscreens are all important. Sailors can suffer from temporary sun blindness which can be prevented by wearing dark glasses.

Website
Further information can be found on Cancer Research UK's SunSmart website:
cancerresearchuk.org/sunsmart

Insect bites

Around most of the Atlantic circuit, insects are a nuisance rather than a danger and tend to be a problem only when ashore or moored close to the shore. Insects are attracted by carbon dioxide, heat, smells and movement. Different species of biting insects are active at different times of day or night. Sand flies tend to bite at night, but will bite during the day if they are disturbed. In some areas (particularly South America) they transmit a nasty disease called leishmaniasis. Tsetse flies are found in sub-Saharan Africa. They bite during the day and are attracted to dark, contrasting colours, particularly blue. Vessels exploring The Gambia should take note of this as the bites are very unpleasant. Ticks usually live in long grassy areas and attach themselves to the clothing of a human when they brush past. They crawl up the clothing until they find an area of exposed skin where they can attach. They may carry disease, and any tick bites should be recorded in case subsequent symptoms develop.

The best way of avoiding bites is by timing your trips ashore, using nets aboard and wearing long, loose-fitting clothing (tucked into your boots in tick areas). DEET repellents are very effective and can be used on adults with caution and according to instructions. Alternative products such as Autan or Mosi-guard can also be protective. Insecticide coils burnt in well-ventilated areas are a useful deterrent. There is no scientific evidence that sonic buzzers are at all protective. Nor has it been proven that taking vitamin B tablets, marmite or garlic reduces bites. If you do get bitten, and react badly to the bites, anti-histamine tablets may provide some relief. If you remove a tick be careful to pull out the mouthparts without crushing the body. You'll need tweezers or a tick removal tool (available from veterinary supply stores if not from your medical centre).

Yellow fever

Yellow fever is a viral disease found in tropical regions of Africa and the Americas including Senegal, The Gambia, the Cape Verde Islands, Trinidad and Tobago, Venezuela and Panama. It is transmitted via the bite of some types of mosquito. Infection causes a wide spectrum of disease including jaundice – the yellow that gives its name. Yellow Fever vaccination is strongly recommended for anyone who might decide to travel to any risk zones. A vaccination certificate lasts for 10 years and is a condition of entry for several countries, particularly any country that you enter subsequent to visiting a risk zone. It is a good idea to be vaccinated before leaving home. However, the vaccination is available in other countries including travel clinics in Spain and The Canaries.

Malaria

Malaria is caused by tiny parasites in the blood which are transmitted via the bite of some types of mosquito. Take advice about malaria risks before leaving home. If you plan to visit a potential malarial zone you should have a supply of anti-malarial (prophylactic) pills on board. The most threatening form of malaria is cerebral (falciparum) malaria. In the worst cases this can take only a couple of days to progress from onset of fever to irreversible coma. The advised types of pill will vary according to the type of malaria prevalent in different geographical areas. Some pills need to be taken for a period of time before exposure to any risk, so be careful to follow the recommended regime.

Doxycycline is sometimes recommended – this drug can make you more susceptible to sun damage and may also decrease the efficacy of oral contraceptives. If you have been travelling in a malaria area and develop a fever seek medical attention very promptly. If relevant and possible, it may be advisable to carry at least one treatment course of drugs in case of developing symptoms while on passage. Some forms of malaria can develop up to one year after exposure.

Dengue fever

Dengue is widespread in the Caribbean Islands, northern and eastern parts of Central and South America, and sporadically in Africa. There was a major outbreak in the Cape Verdes in 2009. Outbreaks are common and often occur after the rainy season when mosquitoes breed more actively. It causes a feverish illness with headache and muscle pains like a bad, prolonged, attack of influenza. There may also be a rash. The cause is a virus spread by a type of mosquito which predominantly bites during the day. Avoid mosquito bites and seek medical attention for feverish illness if you have been in an area where dengue is present.

Contraception

This is not a topic that is commonly discussed in the pages of nautical publications. But there are plenty of women of child-bearing age who go cruising, and it is a subject worthy of some forethought. Seek advice about contraception before leaving home. Contraceptives may not necessarily be readily available to you in some countries. The efficacy of oral contraceptives may be reduced by bouts of seasickness, traveller's diarrhoea, and also some forms of antibiotic. Changing time zones or altering watch-keeping cycles may interfere with the narrow time bands required for daily use of some varieties of oral contraceptive. Injected contraceptives may be an alternative. Diaphragms/caps are susceptible to perishing in tropical conditions and the applied spermicide may also lose its efficacy if allowed to become too warm. Weight change, which is not uncommon for women on an extended passage or cruise, may result in losing a good fit for the diaphragm. Coil positioning requires relatively frequent check-ups which may not be available. Reliable condoms may be difficult to find in some countries and they are also susceptible to perishing over time with warm storage.

Websites
The International Planned Parenthood Federation (IPPF) and the Family Planning Association of Britain can provide extra information.
www.fpa.org.uk
www.ippf.org

THE MEDICAL CABINET

Inform your doctor of your travel plans before you leave home, take advice about which drugs to take with you, and ensure that you have sufficient supplies of any medication that you use routinely. Check whether any of the drugs require signed documentation in the countries you plan to visit. If children are on board ensure that the medical cabinet caters for their needs.

Some traveller's medical kits are very well equipped, but they may need supplementing to include:

Waterproof adhesive dressings in various sizes
Burn dressings
A range of plasters and microporous tape
A range of bandages including finger bandages
Cotton wool and sterile gauze
Equipment for stitching a wound
Scissors, tweezers, safety pins
Sterile needles and syringes (5ml syringes are most useful)
Skin disinfectant eg iodine tincture or equivalent
Local anaesthetic wipes
Eye bath
Thermometer
Basic dental kit including emergency fillings and tooth repair (clove oil or just sucking on a clove is good for mild tooth pain relief)
Seasickness remedies (see p 43)
Strong pain killers
Sedatives
Antibiotics (range of types – always continue the course for the recommended length of time)
Antifungal cream (and pessaries for women)
Antimalaria pills if required (check which areas are risk zones)
Rehydration packs
Antihistamine pills and creams or sprays
Contraceptives (see above – these can be difficult to source in some countries)

Useful books to have on board:
Where there is no doctor by Carol Thuman, Hesperian Foundation
Ship Captain's Medical Guide. Maritime and Coastguard Agency (UK), HMSO
An up-to-date medical formulary – ask your doctor

WEBSITE
www.noonsite.com/General/Medical

5 NAVIGATION AND COMMUNICATION

Ocean navigation and communication systems have been revolutionised in recent years and, increasingly, there is a cross-over of use between the systems. The Global Positioning System (GPS) is now familiar to most people as a navigational tool and it is very rare to find an ocean-going vessel that does not carry one. Linked to DSC it becomes a vital component of safety communications. Satellite telephones, more advanced HF radios and the internet mean that phone calls, e-mails and downloads at anchor or even mid-ocean are increasingly commonplace. These advanced communication systems allow access to pilotage, tidal and weather data to aid navigation. Electronic charts have become more widely available and are extremely popular because of the ability to link onboard systems and overlay information.

The benefits of such modern electronics are clear, but it remains extremely unwise to be entirely reliant upon them. Batteries may die, electrical or electronic circuits may succumb to the marine environment and fail. Several yachts are struck by lightning every year, and it is not uncommon to lose all your electrics and electronics in such a strike. So there remains a need for old-fashioned, seamanlike commonsense when it comes to navigation. Enjoy all the latest technology as much as you want to or can afford, but always carry sufficient back-up systems to enable you to make safe landfall if your main electronics fail.

SHIP'S LOG

Maintenance of a ship's log is an internationally recognised legal requirement. Even if you keep an electronic log, it is still a good idea to record the daily position and other basic information in a hand-written copy. This should be a bound notebook, to protect you from any accusations of inserting or removing pages in creation of 'a story'. Customs and immigration officials may ask to see the log for reasons such as timings of entry into port or a record of ports previously visited. The log is also a place for recording other observations such as whale sightings, and could be used to record parameters such as sea temperature (see Chapter 8).

NAVIGATIONAL EQUIPMENT

It is assumed that anyone planning to set off across the Atlantic has a reasonable level of navigational knowledge and experience. If you lack confidence, there are a multitude of courses available at all levels, both theoretical and practical, and it never hurts to refresh your understanding.

What will you need?
- A good-quality steering compass (corrected for deviation before leaving home waters)
- A hand-bearing compass
- Aneroid barometer
- Thermometer (Air and water temperatures can be useful, for example at the edges of the Gulf Stream.)
- Relevant charts
- Tidal information (electronic and/or paper tables)
- GPS (connected to 12V system or battery powered hand-held, plus a hand-held back up)
- Sextant plus all supporting tables and texts if desired (see discussion below)
- Log plus spare impeller or spare towing log (or piece of degradable paper thrown overboard at the bow and timed to the stern!)
- Echosounder (plus spare or lead line)
- Masthead wind instruments (can be damaged by visiting birds) are helpful for optimising rig and course steered but should be interpreted sensibly – some crew are liable to become overly anxious when masthead windspeed figures rise, but such figures do not necessarily give a balanced picture of the prevailing conditions)
- A good pair of polaroid sunglasses and a shroud ladder or mast steps (to help with eyeball navigation in coral waters – see page 49)
- Binoculars

Chart accuracy

Very few cruising sailors keep their charts and pilot books corrected up-to-date. Once you are away from home waters it becomes difficult to access the information regularly. New editions of charts use WGS 84 which is the same as the GPS system. If a different datum is used, a correction may be given. Worldwide, even apparently modern charts, both paper and electronic, are quite often based on ancient surveys. These surveys were remarkably accurate, but there were sometimes errors, more usually in longitude than in latitude, and these can be as much as half a mile. In other words, the GPS position of a feature or even a whole island may not be the same as its charted position (paper or electronic). With this in mind it is prudent to be cautious when making a new landfall at night or in poor visibility.

NAVIGATION AND COMMUNICATION

This catamaran relied too heavily on the GPS on approach to Tortuga. Photo: Richard Woods

Until you have visual evidence that supports the charted information it is wise to assume that some differences are possible. Also never assume that buoyage will be exactly as charted or described. For example, on the coast of West Africa it is common for buoys to remain as charted but to be unlit. Elsewhere, local buoyage may change overnight.

Gnomonic charts and Great Circle sailing

The shortest distance between two points on a globe is a Great Circle. A rhumb line, the straight line on a Mercator chart, goes by a longer route. In practical terms, the difference is negligible except in high latitudes. For routes between the northern part of the United States and northern Europe, the saving of distance made by keeping to a Great Circle route is likely to be considerable. GPS receivers usually display course to the destination waypoint as a Great Circle bearing, although on many the rhumb line option can be selected.

GPS, chartplotter or sextant

There are now very few cruising yachts which rely entirely on traditional means of navigation. For most cruisers the GPS, often in the form of a chartplotter, is the primary navigational tool. Some choose also to carry a sextant, either simply as a back up, or to learn, or practise the ancient art. The downside of this is that you also need to carry all the relevant tables which add up to several reference volumes. If you have never or only rarely used a sextant it is questionable that you would then use it to any good effect in an emergency situation. Nevertheless, just knowing how to establish ship's latitude would greatly assist in emergency navigation if all electronics were destroyed by lightning. Increasing numbers of cruisers carry one or two GPS or chart plotters and have a hand-held GPS for emergency situations. If a thunder storm approaches you can put the hand-held GPS into your oven to protect it (see lightning section in Chapter 7). Then even after complete electrical failure you should still be able to switch the GPS on once or twice a day to get a position reading. A hand-held GPS can also be useful for surveying a new anchorage from the dinghy.

GPSs are available in a range of complexities. How you use your GPS will determine what functions you feel you need. If you are a gadget person you probably spend many happy hours pre-programming your machine and monitor the readouts continuously. Other cruisers may prefer to keep things simple and monitor only distance and bearing to a single waypoint, or even just record a current position at regular intervals. In mid-ocean this is really all you need. Your log and compass complete the picture. However in coastal situations, and particularly in tides or currents, the SOG (speed over the ground) and COG (course over the ground), seen in relation to a bearing to a waypoint, can be an extremely useful and immediate tool for assessing the strength and direction of water flow. This can help to prevent you from being set down onto danger, particularly at night or in poor visibility.

Waypoints should always be used with caution. Always check waypoints on a chart before programming them in but, above all, check that you, your charts and your GPS(s) are all working to the same datum. Even then remember that, particularly at night or in poor visibility, if you have created or confirmed a waypoint from a chart, there may nevertheless be a significant difference between the charted and actual positions. Don't be lured into blindly following the course laid out on the screen. Use your common sense and make the best use of your GPS as only one of the navigational tools that you have at your disposal and confirm its information by visual or radar observation.

PREPARATIONS

Those were the days! But take the opportunity on passage to learn to use the sextant – you may be glad of the knowledge one day. Photo: Lou Newman

Echosounder

Even an ocean-going yacht spends most of its time within soundings, often in unfamiliar waters, and a reliable echosounder is a top priority. A lead line can be tricky to use, particularly for shorthanded crew, so it is worth carrying a spare echosounder. Its transducer can be fitted before departure and the set itself stowed away in a protective environment.

Radar

Radar has obvious uses as an aid to collision avoidance in poor visibility or at night and it also helps with spotting approaching squalls and thunderstorms. It is a useful tool when making landfall if used in conjuction with other information and instruments. In the north Atlantic, radar is a real bonus for boats planning to cruise in Maine and Nova Scotia or on the north European coast, particularly in the western approaches to the English Channel, where fog is common. It is an essential tool if you are considering the northern or 'Viking' routes. However, sailors should be aware that, under the Collision Regulations, vessels fitted with radar are obliged to use it, and use it properly, when visibility is poor. Failure to do so, resulting in an accident, might result in an insurance claim being rejected. Radar is not a substitute for maintaining a visual watch.

AIS

The Automatic Identification System (AIS) is a short range, electronic, vessel tracking system. Class A systems are now required to be fitted to commercial vessels. They integrate AIS transceivers with other components to allow shore stations or other vessels to track nearby ships. Information transmitted on AIS includes the vessel's unique identification number, position, course and speed. There are a variety of ways in which the information can be displayed.

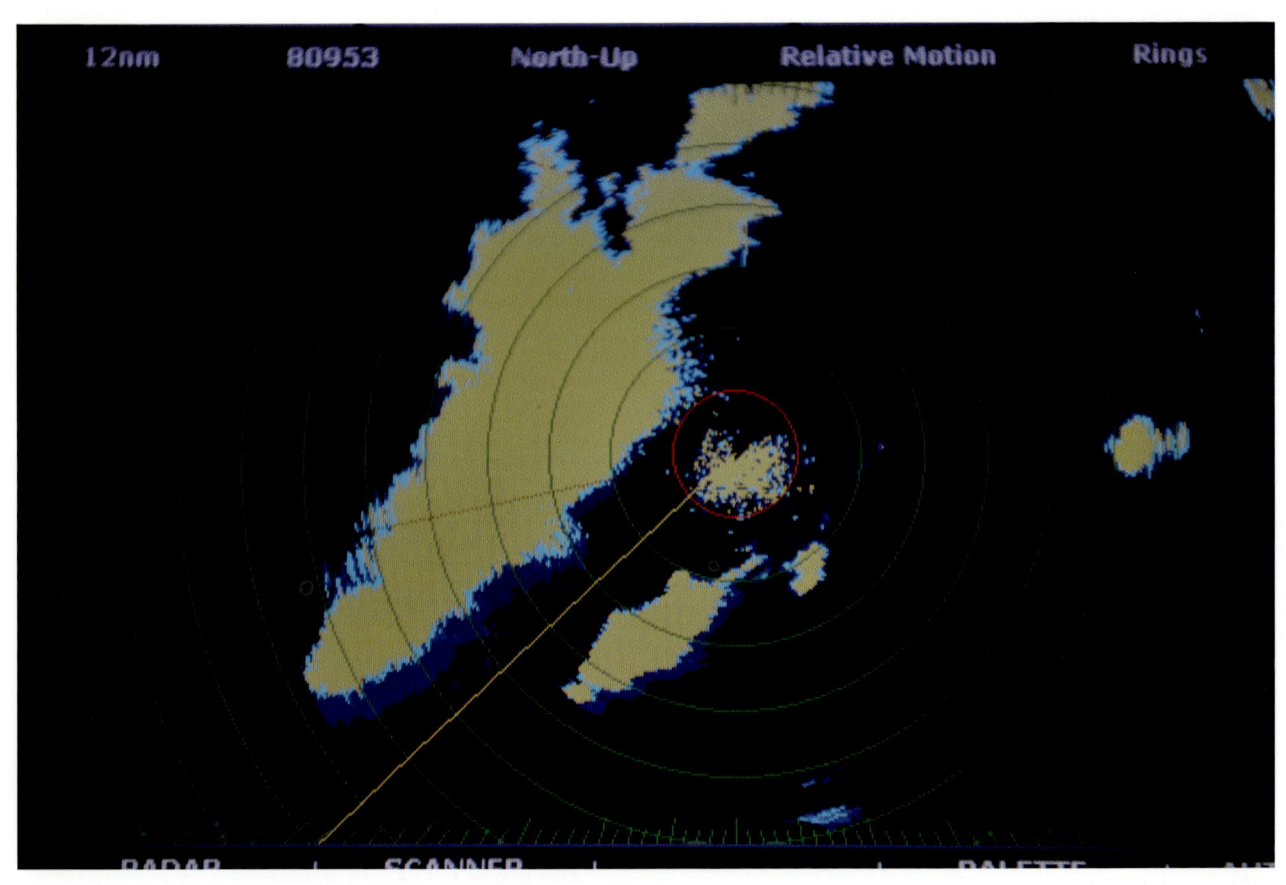

Radar can be useful for tracking squalls. Photo: Mike Robinson

Class B AIS systems are becoming increasingly popular watch keeping components on pleasure vessels such as cruising yachts. AIS signals are transmitted via VHF and the most simple 'receive only' AIS sets use the yacht's normal VHF aerial to receive Class A and B signals. These sets use relatively little power. Transceivers can share the yacht's VHF aerial but must also be connected to a dedicated GPS aerial. Transceivers are more power hungry than 'receive only' sets and they have to be registered in a similar way to VHF and EPIRBs. If you have a Class B transceiver on board, do not assume that other vessels will 'see' you. Ships and shore stations may choose to switch off any Class B signals if their screens become cluttered.

Eyeball navigation

Eyeball navigation is the name commonly given to judging depths by eye around shallow coral-strewn waters. For the first timer, the technique can seem daunting, but some of the most magical anchorages are accessed this way so it is worth getting to grips with. The trick is to get one of the crew as high as possible above the deck so they are looking down into the water for a good distance all around the boat. Polaroid sunglasses help to reduce the glare and improve colour differentiation for this look-out crew member. In areas where you know there will be shoals and coral it is important to make your approach with the sun high in the sky and, preferably, behind you. Once the angle of the sun is relatively low, and particularly if it is ahead of you, the sunlight reflecting off the water becomes a barrier to seeing down through the surface.

Shallow water over clear sand looks turquoise. Pale turquoise becomes darker as the depth increases and becomes a much darker blue in a deep channel. Coral heads generally appear as a browny-green colour. Confusion can sometimes arise where a sandy bottom has patches of sea grass. From a distance these can look a similar colour to coral, but on closer approach, the difference is more obvious.

Local cruising guides for coral waters usually have helpful advice about navigation techniques and passage timings.

Integrated systems

Many boats are now fitted with fully-integrated, linked systems. A major drawback of this would be if the failure of a single component affected the function of the whole system. For example, should an electronic wind direction indicator fail on passage it is unlikely to be more than an inconvenience. But if that failure led to the loss of other instrumentation, the situation might be more serious. If you do have an integrated system it is a good idea to keep

It is sensible to maintain a paper log. Plotting a daily position whilst crossing the Atlantic is usually a morale-boosting ritual.
Photo: Mike Robinson

PREPARATIONS

separate a basic log, GPS and autopilot that are independent of other instruments and can be used as back up.

Laptops

Laptop computers and printers are now commonplace aboard voyaging yachts. Appropriate software enables them to fulfil a variety of useful roles including navigation, weather monitoring, communication and record keeping. They have also helped to revolutionise the distance learning possibilities for cruising families as well as onboard entertainment. Marinised computer units are now available, but most onboard computers are vulnerable to the effects of life afloat. Secure, dry stowage should be a priority. Carry plenty of memory sticks or similar storage devices and always back up anything of importance. You can run a laptop from a 12V cigar socket at the chart table using a laptop car power supply (which acts as a DC/DC converter to take the 12V up to a variety of voltages suitable for many laptops). This is more efficient than going from 12V to 240V then down via a transformer back to the laptop voltage. The saving is several amps per hour.

COMMUNICATION

In recent years, communication at sea has benefitted from an ever-increasing, ever-accelerating tidal wave of technological advances. For the uninitiated, this whole topic can appear to be a mind boggling jumble of acronyms, frequencies and other technical jargon. The aim of this section is to try to introduce and explain various components, without getting too caught up with technical details. Anyone who wishes to immerse themselves more fully will find the various links helpful.

It is important that both yacht and crew carry all the relevant certificates and licenses appropriate to the communication systems on board. Links to courses are given in each section.

A thorough overview of the subject, including some product reviews, is given in *Ship and Boat International* Nov/Dec 2008 – Sea changes in maritime communication by George Marsh.

Website
www.rina.org.uk/sbi

VHF

VHF (Very High Frequency) radio is the most common form of onboard communication. It is generally operable to a range of up to 50 miles, depending on various factors. It is really limited to line of sight. It is now universally recommended that a yacht will carry a main VHF with DSC capability. An operating certificate is required. All VHF emergency traffic is conducted on channel 70 DSC off Europe and North America.

Cruising yachts routinely use their VHF to contact each other on passage or in port and also to alert commercial vessels to their position. Communications with harbour authorities are also often dependent on VHF. A waterproofed, handheld VHF set is very useful for crew going ashore in the dinghy, and is an extremely valuable component of an emergency grab bag. Floating, submersible units are now available.

VHF channels are preset and operators do not themselves tune to the frequencies. Internationally, VHF channels are duplex, with transmission and reception on different frequencies on the same channel. In the United States, some channels are simplex, with both transmission and reception taking place on the same international ship transmitting frequency. Modern VHF sets now all have a facility for selecting either the international or US set of frequencies. US frequencies allow reception of the continuous, dedicated US VHF weather transmissions.

UK VHF training courses are run by the RYA.

Website
www.ryatraining.org/leisure/specialist/Pages/SRC.aspx

DSC

Digital Selective Calling (DSC) is one of the most important parts of GMDSS. DSC is a digital dialling system which can carry information such as a vessel's identity, and the nature of the call. If there is GPS input to the radio, a position will also be transmitted. In a distress situation, all necessary information can be sent automatically at the touch of a single button. The entire message is transmitted in one quick burst, thus reducing the demand time on the calling channel. The digital calling information is transmitted on specially designated channels. VHF Channel 70 is dedicated for DSC use and must not be used for anything else.

GMDSS

The Global Maritime Distress and Safety System (GMDSS) is a fully automated system which forms a part of the Safety Of Life At Sea (SOLAS) Convention. All ocean-going cargo and passenger ships of 300 tonnes gross or more, engaged on international voyages are required to be GMDSS-equipped. SOLAS is an international treaty responsible for ensuring the safety of merchant ships but is also relevant and applicable to cruising yachts. GMDSS incorporates various communications technologies including **NAVTEX, DSC, INMARSAT** and **EPIRB** (see following sections). GMDSS is designed to optimise rapid and accurate communications via a shore-based Rescue Co-ordination Centre (RCC) in the event of a vessel in distress, such that a co-ordinated Search and Rescue (SAR) operation can be implemented with the minimum delay. The system alerts vessels to any safety or distress information and allows for subsequent communications. It also provides for the promulgation of Maritime Safety Information (MSI) such as navigational and meteorological warnings and forecasts and other urgent safety information. GMDSS weather information is produced by meteorologists who have interpreted the raw data. It is useful in addition to alternative sources such as GRIB files (see following section) which are generated exclusively via computer models. Under GMDSS, all vessels are allocated a Maritime Mobile Service Identity (MMSI), which is a unique nine digit code. While GMDSS now provides a safety net that may increase the chances of survival in a marine disaster, it should always be treated as a last resort (see Chapter 7).

> **Websites**
> www.icselectronics.net/GMDSS.php
> www.weather.mailasail.com/Franks-Weather/Gmdss-Weather-Forecasts

NAVTEX

NAVTEX (Navigational Telex) is part of GMDSS and is an international system for the broadcast and automatic reception of maritime safety information. NAVTEX provides continuous weather and navigation warnings and frequent weather forecasts by means of narrow-band telegraphy through automatic printouts from a dedicated receiver. It is included as an element of GMDSS. NAVTEX transmissions are sent via a single frequency from local stations situated worldwide. The power of each transmission is regulated so as to avoid the possibility of interference between transmitters. NAVTEX is broadcast in English, and often in the local language too. The receivers are relatively cheap and easy to install; they can have either a direct readout screen or produce the same information on a paper roll. NAVTEX is the most economical means – in terms of cost and power requirements – of receiving continual weather information. The only disadvantage is the limitation of range to about 300 miles from the stations. The European and West African coasts are covered in Regions I and II. The western area of the North Atlantic is Region IV.

> **Website**
> A comprehensive updated list of NAVTEX stations is found at www.icselectronics.net/NAVTEX.php.

Marine SSB and amateur (ham) radio

Single Side Band (SSB) radio, operating in the Medium Frequency/High Frequency (MF/HF) bands, remains a mainstay on board many cruising yachts and is generally referred to as SSB or HF radio. SSB radios are available as two separate types – either marine SSB or amateur (ham) radio. Marine SSB radios must be 'Type Approved' – they use simplex or duplex frequencies within specified marine bands. Ham radios operate throughout the amateur bands but are restricted from use on marine frequencies. It is common practice amongst cruising yachts to 'open up' an amateur radio to marine frequencies, but there are licence implications (see modifications website below). Although they are not yet necessarily 'Type Approved', it is now also possible to program the latest marine SSBs into amateur bands, but only with proof of an amateur licence. To fully access all the potential communication links, rather than simply being a passive listener, you need to fit a transceiver (transmits and receives) rather than just a receiver. Only qualified, licensed amateurs (hams) may transmit on the amateur bands, but anyone may listen. You will be able to find amateur radio courses available locally if you would like to qualify. There is no longer a requirement to use Morse Code.

Installation
HF radios, whether marine or amateur, require proper installation. They are not just a single component but also consist of interconnected components – antenna (aerial), tuner, and modem. They are power hungry when transmitting, and are particularly sensitive to a reduction in input voltage, so heavy supply cables are essential. An insulated shroud or backstay creates the aerial, but providing a good earth for the set and aerial tuning unit is equally important. In a steel yacht, the hull itself will provide an excellent earth, but wooden or glassfibre yachts need an external ground plate below the waterline.

Computer links
It is now common practice to link a laptop computer to an HF radio to send and receive e-mails and to receive GRIB files and other information without online charges, although file size is restricted due to limited data speed. AirMail is a radio mail software program (equivalent to Outlook) for sending and receiving messages via a modem (modulator/demodulator) over HF radio, either via the ham radio system or participating marine and commercial services. Sailmail is a subscriber SSB e-mail system that uses Airmail. The frequencies used are mostly within the marine bands. Winlink is a free communication system, produced by and for licensed radio amateurs, which also uses Airmail.

Safety networks
HF operators can use the Sailmail and Winlink systems to send distress messages, but it is also possible to buy an HF

PREPARATIONS

Communications are changing worldwide. In this San Blas village in the western Caribbean, villagers now have mobile phones. Photo: Richard Woods

radio with DSC – operation of such a set requires a GMDSS Long Range Certificate.

HF radio also gives access to weather voice broadcasts, stations such as the BBC World Service and the French 'Meteo', international time signals, and multi-party conversation with other HF operators.

> **Websites**
> www.sailmail.com – Marine SSB e-mail
> www.winlink.org – Amateur Radio (ham) e-mail
> www.siriuscyber.net – Airmail
> www.mods.dk – Set modifications
> www.icomuk.co.uk or www.icomamerica.com – ICOM training courses
> www.pactor.info – Modems

Satellite telephones

Satellite communications are increasingly affordable and available for use on board. They allow you to phone, e-mail and access the internet even in mid-ocean. The latest generation of satellites has opened the door to continuous broadband while at sea. The original Inmarsat systems (International Mobile Satellite Organisation) are still the choice of many ocean sailors and are integrated within GMDSS. Iridium is an increasingly popular alternative which provides the option of a handheld unit which you could take with you into a liferaft. The MailASail website gives a good description of the various satphones available and a comparison table of their characteristics. Make sure that you understand the usage tariffs and take these into account when costing the different systems.

> **Websites**
> www.mailasail.com
> Satphones and e-mail compression software
> www.sailmail.com
> E-mail via Sailmail (Inmarsat and Iridium)
> www.oceancruisingclub.org/content/view/1381/85#ocean
> A wealth of information about various ways of accessing weather information can be found on the Ocean Cruising Club's website
> www.weather.mailasail.com/Franks-Weather/Home
> Frank Singleton's weather site for yachtsmen is extremely informative and useful

Long range communications – SSB versus satphone

Transatlantic yachts are now commonly fitted either with an SSB radio, a satphone or both. Either system allows voice calls, e-mails and downloads from the internet such as GRIB files. There are pros and cons to each system depending on how much they are used. With the reduced cost of satellite phones, SSB may appear to be an expensive alternative, but probably not if you take into account usage costs over a period of time. The flip side of this is that SSBs cost more in amp-hours. SSBs are 'plumbed in' to the boat and consist of several separate components, whereas some types of satphone are single units which could be taken into a liferaft. You need the appropriate training and licences for an SSB, which is not always the case with a satphone. If you want to be able to participate in daily radio nets with other yachts you will need an SSB – a satphone will only allow one-to-one calling. But file downloads are more restricted with an SSB. The various technologies are progressing at such a fast rate that any detailed discussion quickly becomes out of date. If you are considering the advantages and disadvantages of various onboard long range communications it is worth investigating the current options. Whichever system you choose, it is recommended that you use compression software.

> **WEBSITE**
> www.mailasail.com – Ed Wildgoose at MailASail is an excellent source of help and information
> www.freewebs.com/seawrite/lusradiopage.htm
> For good advice about HF radios go to Rod Heikell's website
> www.yachtcom.info
> www.saildocs.com
> www.sailcom.co.uk

6 PROTOCOL, PAPERWORK AND PROCEDURES

FORMALITIES

Customs and Immigration regulations, and the formality with which they are applied, vary from country to country. In some areas, a yacht entering a remote harbour or anchorage may be treated with suspicion. To allay these fears, always contact the authorities on arrival, even if only the local police.

There is a universal ban on the import of hard drugs, and many countries look carefully at prescribed medicines which should be accompanied by a letter from the prescribing doctor. Import of fresh meat is forbidden in some countries, as are growing plants and some fresh vegetables. Many countries place restrictions on the import of alcohol and tobacco. All firearms, including flare guns, must be declared and failure to do so will incur very heavy penalties, particularly in the United Kingdom. In the United Kingdom and Irish Republic there are very strict regulations regarding bringing live animals of any kind into the country. If you have pets on board it is essential that you contact the authorities at your intended port of arrival well in advance. The anti-rabies laws are taken very seriously indeed. Animals must be micro-chipped, and you must carry all the relevant documentation to show that the appropriate vaccinations have been given to your animal.

CITES

Be aware of the Convention on International Trade of Endangered Species of Wild Flora and Fauna (CITES). Seemingly innocent collections of empty shells or pieces of already broken coral from remote beaches may get you into trouble and make you liable for a fine. If you buy shells, for example turtle shell from a licensed turtle farm, ensure that you have the appropriate certification. Cruisers have been caught out in the past when they have flown home with collected treasures such as Queen Conch shells, only to find them confiscated and a heavy fine imposed. The same may be true on arrival at any port of entry.

Website
www.cites.org – Click on CITES species.

Clearing in on the Customs' dock at Jolly Harbour, Antigua. In many ports of call it is more usual to go ashore by dinghy to clear in or out. Photo Graham Adam

PREPARATIONS

DOCUMENTATION

Requirements for documentation vary from country to country. In most cases original documents will be needed, although it is useful to have several sets of photocopies on board. Keep a further set safe ashore in case the originals are lost. Not all the documents listed here will be examined in every country, but items 1–6 will be regularly required.

1. Valid passports for everyone on board, with visas as necessary. If the crew are multi-national it must be remembered that some may need visas for a particular country, while others will not. Neither passports nor, if possible, visas should expire during the course of the cruise. Visa requirements for yacht crew are sometimes different to visa requirements for other forms of visit. You should make it clear that you will be on a yacht when you make your visa applications.

2. RYA or International Certificate of Competence, at least for the skipper.

3. Crew list. Normally everyone aboard should be listed as crew rather than passengers, as some countries levy high fees for charter yachts or other passenger-carrying vessels.

4. Certificate of Registry, or Small Ships Registry Certificate. American yachts should have national, as opposed to state, documentation. For British yachts, both full and Small Ships Registry need to be renewed periodically; if possible, ensure that this will not happen during the cruise.

5. Value Added Tax (VAT). All private yachts owned or used by EU residents must be VAT paid if they are used in EU territorial waters. Non EU residents may own and use a private yacht VAT free on a temporary import basis for up to 18 months. Pleasure yachts built before 1985, and in EU waters on 31st December 1992 are treated as VAT paid – you will need to have evidence that the yacht was in EU waters on this date. Documentary evidence should be carried at all times as you may be asked by customs officials within the EU to provide evidence of your vessel's VAT status. Documentary evidence might include: original invoice or receipt; evidence that VAT was paid at importation; and/or invoices for materials used in the construction of a 'Home-Built' vessel.

6. Clearance papers from the previous port of call. In certain countries, notably Spain and the Canaries, these can be difficult to obtain. A dated receipt from your departure port may be a useful alternative.

7. Stores list, which should differentiate between opened and unopened items. In practice, very few countries are interested in stores other than alcohol, although fresh fruit and vegetables should always be mentioned, as these may have to be destroyed to prevent the spread of pests.

8. Cruising permit if applicable (issued to visiting yachts in the USA, Canada and some Caribbean islands)

9. VHF and other radio licences and operator's certificates as applicable.

10. Insurance papers – a few marinas will not allow boats without at least third party insurance to berth. It helps if a certificate in the language of the countries visited can be obtained.

11. Bill of Sale – to prove legal ownership of vessel.

12. Yellow Fever Vaccination Certificate. This is valid for ten years from vaccination. It is unlikely that you will be asked to produce it in Yellow Fever areas such as West Africa and, occasionally, the Cape Verdes. However, the countries you wish to visit thereafter may require proof that you are not carrying the disease.

13. Bills of Health or Pratiques acquired en route. Few countries now demand a Bill of Health, but a sudden epidemic could alter the rules overnight.

14. Charter documents, if applicable.

15. Ensign Warrant for British yachts, if applicable.

16. Firearms Certificate, if applicable (see section on firearms in Chapter 7)

PROTOCOL, PAPERWORK AND PROCEDURES

Ship's stamp

A stamp with boat name, port of registry and call sign used to be a necessary piece of onboard equipment. Few port officials now ask for papers to be stamped, although in Morocco and West African ports, a ships stamp may ease the path through officialdom. A more useful item is a boat's 'business card' with boat name, home port, registration number and radio call sign, plus the skipper's or owner's mailing address and e-mail address. Small adhesive address stickers are a basic alternative. These are also useful for entries in the visitors' books which are carried by many cruising yachts.

ENTRY PROCEDURES

If you are entering a new country you will need to check in at a Port of Entry. Some suggested Ports of Entry are indicated in Part II. Familiarise yourself with the entry procedures before arrival. As procedures do vary, the easiest way to do this is to talk to other yachts which have already arrived. Hoist the national ensign if it has not been worn at sea, and have both the Q flag and a courtesy ensign ready to hoist on entering territorial waters. Not surprisingly, yachts flying an incorrect, tattered or upside-down courtesy ensign will be disapproved of. Establish whether it is necessary to report to the authorities by radio before entering the harbour. In most places the skipper (with or without the First Mate) should go ashore to report as soon as the yacht is secured, but occasionally all the crew are required to remain on board until the officials visit. In the USA all the crew now have to be fingerprinted, which is usually done ashore. If you are unsure about procedures, another yacht in the anchorage may be able to advise. In some places you will be charged extra for checking in outside office hours. However, a delay in going ashore to check in may make you liable for a fine. Harbour launches sometimes monitor any anchorages close to the check-in port on a regular basis, so you should not assume that your entry has gone unnoticed while you wait for office hours.

Any new country that you arrive in will be well aware that you are visiting for pleasure, and you are likely to be welcomed with courtesy if not outright warmth. Checking in can be time consuming, but if you have all your necessary paperwork to hand and remain pleasant and patient with all the officials you may find that things go more easily. Collect all the documents needed and make out a crew list with full names, dates and places of birth, and passport numbers. It is useful to have photocopies of a blank or partially complete crew list form which you can fill in with updated details. Alternatively you can generate a crew list on the computer and print out copies as required. Different countries demand different information, and many insist that the details should be written on their own printed forms.

Apart from the documents, in many places procedures will take less time if you take your own pen, a supply of carbon paper, some blank paper for making notes and a phrase book if applicable. Having some cash in the local currency is helpful, but US dollars are usually acceptable and occasionally preferred. Some ports of entry have cash machines within the harbour compound.

Boarding by officials

There are several Ports of Entry where officials may choose to visit you on board. In some countries the officials may carry firearms. There are also occasions when you might be boarded at sea whilst on passage, particularly on approach to a landfall. This can be quite a frightening experience,

Being boarded at sea by the Coast Guard can be an alarming experience. Put out lots of fenders and manoeuvre as directed. Photo: Richard Woods

PREPARATIONS

particularly at night. If you are at all unsure of the identity of an approaching vessel, call them up on the VHF and ask them to identify themselves. If they do not respond and it is dark, a strong flashlight shone downwards towards their hull – not in their eyes – should reveal any Coast Guard or similar livery. If the approaching vessel shines a light on you, make it clear that you would like to talk to them on the VHF. Try to ascertain whether they require you to heave-to or stop your engine, or whether they wish you to proceed slowly on a fixed course. Put out lots of fenders. Their behaviour may seem disproportionate and heavy-handed but, if they are involved in an effort to restrict trafficking of any sort, their modus operandi will tend to assume that you may be carrying weapons on board. They may wish to search the whole vessel and they will probably separate crew members for individual questioning. Try to stay calm, and be helpful with any documentation they may want to see. Depending on the prevailing weather conditions they may require you to put into a nearby port.

Courtesy flags

The appropriate courtesy flags for each country are shown beside the chapter headings in Part II. Some people choose to buy a set of courtesy flags, others take appropriate materials to make their own. Some of the flags have complicated designs which make sewing them quite a challenge. An alternative is to take sufficient white cloth – off-cuts of sail cloth are good – and a range of acrylic paints and paint brushes. You can then accurately reproduce the flag.

Further reference
Reeds Maritime Flag Handbook, Miranda Delmar-Morgan, Adlard Coles Nautical

MONEY

Cash machines (ATMs) are found worldwide, and it is usually a very straightforward process to access local currency on arrival in a new country. Just be sure that you do not forget your PIN numbers and ensure that your cards will remain in date for the duration of the cruise. Managing your funds will be up to you, but using a credit card to obtain cash is often considerably more expensive than using a debit card. Different cards are linked to different networks, for example MasterCard or Visa. Although both systems are widely available, it is sensible to carry cards of both types. Don't keep all your cards together in one place, so that any loss or theft will not be completely disastrous. Obtaining replacement cards abroad can be a complicated process. If losing your card in a machine worries you, most banks will allow you to use cards to obtain cash over the counter as long as you have a passport for identification.

It is useful to carry a small reserve of cash on board. Small denomination euros and US dollars are the most useful. Some yachts carry a larger concealed reserve of cash in case of emergency. If deciding to do this, the cash should be split into reasonable-sized amounts and hidden separately. Never tell anyone where this cash is hidden, or even that it is aboard.

DUTY-FREE IMPORTS

Many countries allow yacht equipment or spares for a visiting foreign yacht to be imported duty free. It is always wise to enquire about current regulations concerning paperwork, labelling and notification before such equipment is dispatched. Parcels should be clearly labelled 'FOR VESSEL IN TRANSIT' (unless other wording is specified locally). Personal imports are nearly always subject to duty.

INSURANCE

Marine

Third-party insurance is relatively inexpensive and is recommended as a minimum on an Atlantic cruise. The risk of a third-party claim against you is not worth taking. Some

Flying courtesy and Q flags as you approach a Port of Entry will get you off to a good start with the officials. Photo: Mike Robinson

PROTOCOL, PAPERWORK AND PROCEDURES

harbours and marinas will not allow entry to uninsured vessels. It is sometimes difficult for yachts sailed by two or even three people to get comprehensive insurance, and the benefits of having such cover may have to be balanced against the undesirability of being forced to carry extra crew. Companies are much more likely to provide cover if they have confidence in you. This may come from a shared insurance history, for example if your boat has been insured with a company for several years already, or from current evidence that you and the boat are well prepared. Willingness to accept a high excess (deductible) will demonstrate that trivial claims are not being contemplated. Apart from the more obvious hurricane issues, insurance cover in other areas such as Biscay may come with strings attached, regarding timing or crew numbers, so plan well ahead. It will always be difficult to obtain insurance cover for the Caribbean during the hurricane season, but you should consider carefully the reasons for this before deciding to keep a boat there during that period.

Insurance-approved storage for use during the hurricane season at Marina del Rey, Puerto Rico. Photo: Marina del Rey

Medical

A standard medical insurance policy may not protect you while cruising, and you should make amendments if necessary. Europeans should obtain a European Health Insurance Card, which entitles them to free, or reduced-cost, emergency treatment in EU countries. The French islands are part of the EU. Private medical fees are high in the West Indies and the United States compared with Europe, though many West Indian islands have free health schemes based on the UK National Health model, and in some islands reciprocal arrangements for free treatment have been established with the United Kingdom and with some other EU countries. Medical attention in the United States is very much more likely to be prompt if evidence of US-valid medical insurance is produced at the outset.

TRAFFIC SEPARATION SCHEMES

In many areas where shipping is heavy – particularly around headlands, where a number of major routes converge, and in constricted waters – IMCO Traffic Separation Schemes (TSS) have been set up. Typically they consist of two lanes down which vessels pass port-to-port, a central separation zone, and usually an inshore traffic zone. The rules governing separation schemes are detailed in the International Regulations for Preventing Collisions at Sea, but as far as yachts are concerned the most important points are as follows:

1. As far as possible, avoid crossing traffic lanes, but if obliged to do so, cross on a heading as nearly as practicable at right angles to the general direction of traffic flow. (It should be noted that it is the heading rather than the ground track that is to be at right angles to the traffic flow.)

2. Use inshore traffic zones whenever possible.

3. Do not impede the safe passage of a power-driven vessel following a traffic lane.

Traffic Separation Schemes are often monitored by Coast Guards or other official bodies, usually by radar, and sailors have been prosecuted for ignoring the regulations. The Traffic Separation Schemes that yachts might encounter going across the Atlantic are: off Lands End, off Ouessant, off the north-west corner of Spain, off Cape St Vincent, in the Gibraltar Straits, around Cuba, and the many along the east coast of the United States and Canada.

Scuba diving
Many cruising yachts carry scuba gear on board and larger yachts may carry the necessary generators and compressors for filling tanks. In most of the popular diving areas it is possible to have tanks refilled ashore. Many cruisers take the opportunity to learn to scuba dive somewhere on their route. Depending on where you are, it may be necessary to gain permission to scuba dive. You may need some form of licence or be required to dive with a local operator. Check out the local regulations before you dive.

57

7 DEALING WITH RISK

When fear and anxiety stick their claws into your guts it is worth reminding yourself that, by crossing an ocean aboard a seaworthy yacht, you probably face less inherent risk than you do every time you get behind the wheel of a car. This is partly a function of speed. Most potential catastrophes develop relatively slowly on a cruising yacht, giving you time to react.

On a passage in the open ocean there is no risk of grounding. Relative to coastal sailing you are unlikely to collide with another vessel, whatever the visibility. Gales, or worse, are generally less hazardous in deep water because of longer wavelengths and, by definition, more sea room. However, in the event that something serious does go wrong, assistance is unlikely to be available immediately. So, you need to feel confident that you can deal with any possible eventuality. This confidence will come through experience, but it also comes from imagining the worse before it happens and planning what your response should be. On a moonless night with a gale blowing you will do nothing but terrify yourself if you start to dwell on nightmare scenarios. But before you set sail it is a very worthwhile exercise to think through all the things that could go wrong and then take relevant precautions and equip yourself with the means to deal with the situation. If you are a couple, it is helpful to go through this thought process together. Everyone reacts differently to a crisis, and the unknown is often the most frightening. Facing up to the risks that might be there, making them known, helps to dispel that fear.

Falling overboard

Don't! Prevention is infinitely preferable to cure. Non-slip surfacing on the decks, decent guard rails, a strong pushpit and pulpit, and plenty of strong handholds, clipping on points and properly thought-out jackstays are essential. More important is the practice of actually using these features. This is one area where onboard rules should be established: when harnesses and safety lines are worn and what to clip onto. A harness must be allocated and fitted to each crew member before departure. Never clip onto the shrouds, in case of knockdown. Harnesses should have crotch straps and safety lines should be about 2m (7ft) long, with a clip at each end, and preferably one in the middle also. This allows you to clip to the next point before unclipping from the first. In higher latitudes it is more comfortable to have harnesses built into oilskins, but in the tropics you will need separate harnesses. In heavy weather the dangers are obvious and no-one will need reminding to clip on. But on a balmy tropical day it is easy to become complacent. There can be few worse horrors than coming up on deck, after being asleep down below, to discover that the deck and cockpit are empty and your partner or friend is nowhere to be seen. It has happened. A common reason for people falling overboard from leisure craft is because they go to the guard rail to relieve themselves. If you are solo, or alone on deck, either clip on or use a bucket in the cockpit.

Every cruising yacht should carry life jackets appropriate for the numbers and sizes of people on board at any time and fitted to each individual before departure. There are pros and cons to auto-inflating or pull-chord varieties, depending on the age and ability of the wearer. If the life jacket is for a child it is worthwhile testing the jacket on the child before heading offshore. Make sure that you carry spare auto-inflate gas cylinders. Regulations in some countries require life jackets to be carried in the dinghy when going ashore.

In the event that someone does go overboard the whole crew needs to know the drill for recovery. When you plan

It is essential to prevent any crewmember from falling overboard. This crew is safely clipped on in his harnessed life jacket complete with crotch strap. Photo: Dan Darwall

the drill, take into account the boat's handling characteristics as well as the capabilities of the crew and think about the different scenarios on various points of sail. You also need to consider how you will get the person back up on deck. Assume that the heaviest crew member will be the one in the water and then work out how you would retrieve them – possibly while they are unconscious. You may need to use a halyard and winch or windlass. Rope ladders tend to swing in under the hull and can be very awkward to use even in a non-emergency. Solid ladders are more difficult to stow and are often too short – ideally the lowest step should be far enough below the waterline that the user does not need to be a contortionist to get a foot onto it. A fender step can make all the difference to being able to get on and off a boat with high topsides easily, even from a dinghy.

Two fluorescent lifebuoys, both equipped with automatic lights and one attached to a danbuoy, should be within reach of the helmsman and ready for throwing overboard. The combination should also have a small drogue attached to slow down any drift once in the water. The danbuoy pole will need a brightly-coloured flag on top with a counterweight to keep it upright. The whole assembly must be carefully stowed so that danbuoy, lifebuoy, light, drogue and connecting line can be deployed instantly without fouling. Danbuoy, lifebuoys, harnesses and lifejackets all benefit from having reflective tape stuck on them for location in the dark. Some materials do not hold their reflective quality indefinitely, so make sure that those in use at the start of the voyage are in good order and replace as necessary.

There are now several Man OverBoard (MOB) and Personal Locator Beacon (PLB) products on the market available through most good chandlers.

Gales, hurricanes and line squalls

By keeping to the recommended seasons, yachts undertaking a standard Atlantic circuit should manage to avoid any really unpleasant weather. However, every cruising yacht should be prepared for heavy weather. Further north you are more likely to have to cope with a few inescapable gales. Hurricanes are discussed in Part II.

A trough in mid-Atlantic causes unstable weather patterns. Resulting line squalls are a reasonably common occurrence on an Atlantic trade wind crossing. It is usually possible to track squalls on radar or to follow them with a hand-bearing compass, enabling you to adjust your course to cut across the squall track. If you run with the squall you will be in it for longer, but may then lose the wind completely once it has passed, leaving you wallowing. Squall clouds are high up and their track will not be the same as the surface wind direction. If there is rain under the squall cloud there is also likely to be an increase of wind strength for ten minutes or so as the squall passes. Dark, heavy clouds with no rain may cause a brief increase in wind followed by lighter winds beneath the cloud.

An approaching line squall. Photo: Mike Robinson

PREPARATIONS

As long as you have seen it coming, the arrival of a squall can be exhilarating. Photo: Mike Robinson

Lightning

Many yachts are struck by lightning every year, and the effects can be catastrophic. A lightning strike or near strike is something which you should be prepared for. If you see a nearby boat get struck, make sure that the crew are safe and that the integrity of the hull is also checked. You are more at risk in certain areas of the Atlantic, including the east coast of the United States and Central America. The worst time of year is between June and September. It is important that your boat is protected as much as possible. Methods of protection differ depending on the materials of hull and rig. As the equipment of modern cruising yachts becomes more complicated, the consequences of a strike are more likely to be totally disabling.

> **Further reference**
> Nigel Calder covers the subject of lightning in some depth in *Boatowner's Mechanical and Electrical Manual*, Adlard Coles Nautical
>
> www.marinelightning.com is a very informative site

Emergency steering

If you have wheel steering you need to have some sort of emergency steering arrangement should the linkage to the wheel fail. Also, carry spare steering cable. With tiller steering, the point of attachment of a tiller to the rudder may be a weak link and may need strengthening. A hydrovane provides auxiliary steering, so if you have one fitted this is a bonus.

Using an oven as a Faraday cage may help to protect electronic equipment during lightning storms. Photo: Richard Woods

DEALING WITH RISK

Collisions

The best guard against collision is to maintain a proper, continuous watch (see Onboard Routine, Keeping Watch in Chapter 4). Radar is an aid, but should not be treated as a substitute for watch keeping. A radar reflector, as high as possible on the mast, will improve your radar visibility to other vessels, but you should never assume that you have been seen. Some yachts and all commercial ships are now fitted with an Automatic Identification System (AIS). This can help with watch keeping. It is automatic and uses low power. If you are unsure of the intentions of another vessel on the open ocean, it never hurts to call them on the VHF, clearly stating your current position as well as your position relative to them and your direction of travel. Your call may alert them to your existence even if they don't respond. It is sometimes the case that you will not have been seen or heard. Be prepared to take avoiding action even if you should be the stand-on vessel, but if you do have to alter course, make your course change very obvious.

According to many reports, the chances of colliding with a semi-submerged object such as a shipping container are on the increase. If you are lucky you might notice an area of water with an altered wave pattern and have time to take avoiding action. At night you probably wouldn't see anything, although yachts have reported seeing strangely geometrical patches of phosphorescence. It is worth considering some sort of collision bulkhead, but otherwise there's not really any way of safe-guarding against this kind of collision. If you do see a container, note the position and try to relay the information to warn other vessels.

Oil rigs are not something that you are likely to bump into unless you are keeping no watch at all. But they are an alarming spectacle if you come across one under tow at night. Rigs on the move are attended by several tugs, whose long towlines are largely submerged and therefore invisible. Night or day, fixed or moving, oil rigs should be given a very wide berth. International regulations require all vessels to keep 500m (0.25 miles) away from rigs, but at least a mile would be preferable.

There have been a number of accounts of yachts having close encounters with whales. It is relatively rare for any direct contact to take place, but collisions with whales do sometimes occur. Sperm whales snooze at the surface and can be quite oblivious to an approaching yacht. If there are whales in the vicinity and you suspect they may not be aware of your presence, starting the engine, running the echo-sounder or playing some music may help to alert them. From some reports it seems possible that menstruating crew members may encourage the approach of various predatory species, including sharks, orca and dolphins, but their approach is most likely to be curious rather than threatening. If you think that any discharge from the heads is attracting undue interest it might be advisable to resort to 'bucket and chuck it' which will break any association with the boat.

Any sightings of whales, dolphins or other marine species are valuable information for the scientific community. See Chapter 8 for ways in which you can contribute and further information sources.

Fire

Serious fires on cruising yachts are very uncommon, but the consequences of a major fire on an ocean passage might be disastrous. A fire blanket within easy reach of the galley is a sensible precaution. You should also ensure that your cooking fuel system is well maintained and has appropriate safeguards. Several in-date fire-extinguishers should be positioned around the boat, including one for discharging into the engine compartment. Opening up the engine space admits oxygen and causes the fire to flare or even explode. So if you don't have an automatic extinguisher in the engine compartment itself, you should have a hole in the wall of the compartment so that you can discharge a cylinder into the engine space without needing to open it.

The chances of an electrical fire are greatest on boats where additional loads have been added to the system without the wiring being upgraded. Some batteries generate explosive gases when being charged and must have adequate ventilation.

There are various types of extinguisher, but dry powder extinguishers are the best choice. Although they make a lot of mess, so does a fire. They should be shaken regularly to prevent the contents of the extinguisher from settling. CO_2 is very effective in confined spaces because it denies the fire oxygen, but is dangerous to the operator for the same reason. Water should not be used on electrical, fat or fuel-based fires.

Liferaft and grab bags

If your liferaft will over-run its service period within a year of leaving home waters it is worth having it serviced before you go. When you book the service, ask to watch the raft being inflated so that you can see how it works and what equipment it contains. Most service centres are happy for customers to do this. It is sometimes possible to add extra equipment into the liferaft at service, but it may be better to create your own waterproof and floatable 'grab bags' which can be inspected routinely and refreshed with in-date products. Always keep the bags within emergency grab range of the cockpit and make sure they have a lanyard so that they can be tied to you or your rescue craft. Bear in mind that any grab bag must be positioned in such a way that every member of the crew is aware of it and so that it can be grabbed quickly and easily. If you have to evacuate without warning, it might be to the liferaft, your dinghy, another craft or into the sea.

PREPARATIONS

Depending on what is already contained in your liferaft, the grab bags might contain the following:

Grab bag contents
- Handheld (travellers') watermaker/solar still
- EPIRB
- Handheld VHF
- Handheld GPS
- Satellite telephone
- Medical kit including routine medication
- Seasickness patches and pills
- Foil survival blankets
- A selection of warm clothing
- Flares
- Fishing gear
- Sunscreen
- Sunglasses
- Heliograph or mirror
- Wind-up torch
- Wind-up or solar-powered radio
- Emergency food
- Water (leave some air in the containers to ensure that they float)
- Athlete's isotonic drink powder
- Notepad and pencils
- Playing cards
- Ship's papers and passports

You should assemble and check the contents of your grab bag(s) before each offshore passage. Make sure that the bags are watertight and will float.

Website
An interesting discussion about what to take in a grab bag in a real life emergency is at:
www.sailingcatamarans.com/grab%20bag.htm

Flares

Until modern equivalents such as lasers become the norm it makes sense to carry a good selection of flares. In an emergency situation it is said that the first draws attention, the second confirms it wasn't an illusion, and the third provides the opportunity to take a bearing. An ocean cruising yacht should carry at least a dozen rocket flares, together with orange smoke markers, handheld red flares, and handheld white anti-collision flares. A supply of white parachute rockets will greatly help the search for a man overboard at night. They should never, however, be used to warn of an impending collision situation at night, despite any advice given to the contrary. They will simply serve to surprise and distract the bridge crew of the approaching ship, who are unlikely to realise that they were launched from a yacht close ahead.

EPIRBs

As discussed in Chapter 5, the Global Maritime Distress and Safety System (GMDSS) is now in place worldwide. It is a fully automated system relying on dedicated terrestrial and satellite radio to link shore and ships for alerting and any subsequent communications. An incident will be triggered by an emergency DSC transmission or an activated EPIRB.

Emergency Position Indicating Radio Beacons (EPIRBs) are self-contained devices that can be activated in an emergency to alert the rescue authorities. EPIRBs are an integral part of GMDSS, and any activation of an EPIRB will be reacted to almost immediately anywhere in the world. EPIRBs with an in-built GPS will transmit their current position. EPIRBs should be secured with a hydrostatic switch so that they will release underwater if the yacht sinks before manual release. The identity and details of all vessels carrying an EPIRB must be registered with the national authority (for example, HM Coastguard, Falmouth, for UK vessels). In the event of accidental activation you should not switch the EPIRB off, but make every effort to contact the nearest Maritime Rescue Co-ordination Centre to inform them of the situation.

Whether or not you choose to have an EPIRB is a personal decision. Some yachtsmen and women consider that the risks taken at sea should fall on their own shoulders, and they baulk at the idea of triggering a costly international rescue effort when they have chosen to take those risks. However, it is certainly true that the chances of rescue from a disaster at sea have been greatly increased with the development of these systems. Nevertheless, it would be erroneous to assume that help will always be promptly at hand wherever you might be. It is much wiser to be self-reliant and to think of an EPIRB as a very last resort.

CAUTION
EPIRBs now operate on 406MHz. Signals from older EPIRBs which operate on 121.5 or 243MHz are no longer recognised or received.

SARTs

Radar-SARTs (Search and Rescue Transponders) or AIS-SARTs (Search and Rescue Transmitters) are portable locator devices intended for deployment in liferafts to facilitate the homing-in of search and rescue teams. They are part of the GMDSS and can greatly reduce the searching time in bad weather, fog or at night.

Security and firearms

The risks to cruisers of violent crime and piracy are a common concern amongst would-be cruisers and stay-at-homes. There are occasional horror stories which are truly appalling for all involved and there are periodic 'hotspots' which are worth avoiding. The island of Margarita and the adjacent coast of Venezuela are one example. However, the chance of being the victim of such crimes on the water is considerably less than ashore in cities such as London or New York. Mostly, wherever you go, the local people will be friendly, welcoming to strangers, hospitable, kind and just as horrified by atrocities as anyone else.

It is wise to be cautious – lock the companionway when you leave the boat, pull dinghies and boarding ladders out of the water overnight, secure dinghies and outboards when ashore. If you feel vulnerable on board at night, a metal grill which fits over the companionway may act as a deterrent while still allowing a flow of air. When you do go ashore, don't take all of your money or all your credit cards, but leave some behind, hidden away. In general, by displaying obvious wealth you will make yourself more vulnerable. A small backpack to carry camera, video and other luxuries is more discreet than wandering around with various gadgets hanging off your shoulders.

Marina security, Guatemalan-style, Rio Dulce. Photo: Richard Woods

The subject of whether or not you should carry a firearm onboard is sometimes hotly debated. The relevant page on www.noonsite.com is a good indication of the strength of feeling. In most countries firearms will be impounded on arrival and not returned until departure. A Verey or flare pistol needs a firearms certificate in the United Kingdom and Europe before it can be carried on board. It may not be accepted at all as safety equipment in other countries. Some yachts choose to hide firearms on board, but if you are caught, having failed to declare at ports of call, you are liable to severe penalties. Coast Guard and naval patrol vessels do occasionally 'stop and search' vessels on passage.

For most cruisers, the real questions should be 'Would you be prepared to use it in anger?', 'Are you experienced and practised enough to use it confidently and effectively?' and 'Is it kept safely stowed, yet easy enough to access and activate in a surprise situation?' If the answer to any of those questions is negative, it is more likely that you will endanger yourself rather than protect yourself by having a gun on board. Serious piracy situations involving yachts are relatively rare, and a gun on board is only likely to make such incidents worse.

Pests

In some areas, including the Caribbean, rats may make their way onboard, and once they are established they are very difficult to get rid of. They can do a phenomenal amount of damage in a short time, chewing through food containers, wiring and plastic hoses, including those attached to open seacocks. Rats can swim, and will run up anchor cable, so it is not only shore-side yachts which are at risk. Commercially available rope 'rat guards' are not an effective protection. If you do get a rat on board, the best way of dealing with it is via a baited trap or by baiting into an appropriately confined space and then bludgeoning or shooting it with a spear gun.

Cockroaches can be very unpleasant if they are allowed to gain a firm hold. They are adept at finding places to nest. If a yacht does become infested, the only really effective solution is fumigation of the yacht. A period of time in colder climates will also see them off. See also Food and Water (Provisioning) in Chapter 3 and Keeping Healthy (Insect bites) in Chapter 4.

Other risks

Anywhere that you travel there will be certain risks ashore or in the water. There may be poisonous plants or venomous fish or other potential dangers – few areas of the world are devoid of such things. Any such risks tend to be highlighted in the various cruising and travel guides.

8 CONTRIBUTION TO SCIENCE

The worldwide community of cruising yachts has great potential as a source of observations and recorded data for marine biologists and oceanographers. The world's oceans remain 'the great unknown' compared to our knowledge of land and sky. It is easy to assume that everything you see has been seen before and understood. But when you cross an ocean in a small sailing vessel you are really still a human pioneer in this habitat. It is highly likely that you will observe dolphins and whales on several occasions while on passage. Likewise you will probably snorkel or dive on many different reef systems. There may be other things which strike a chord with you – sightings of sea birds, a strange fish caught, unusual patches of bio-luminescence. Recording your observations and passing them on to the relevant scientists may help to advance our understanding. The problem, for most of us, is in knowing what to note down. But if in doubt, record it. The following links may help to guide you.

Further reference
For a useful aid to identification see *Whales, Dolphins and Porpoises* by Mark Carwardine, Dorling and Kindersley Publishing.

ORCA is an organisation which collects and processes data about whales, dolphins and other marine species. It has been running since 1966 and is very dependent on the observations of volunteers. Before you leave your home waters, download the ORCA survey forms from: www.orcaweb.org.uk/surveyforms.htm Click on Excel versions for recording sightings directly onto the computer, or print off the PDF versions for hand-written recordings. You can volunteer as an observer by emailing ORCA at volunteer@orcaweb.org.uk

Every encounter with dolphins is an uplifting, joyful experience. Your logged observations may help our understanding of these extraordinary creatures. Photo: Mike Robinson

CONTRIBUTION TO SCIENCE

The Whale and Dolphin Conservation Society www.wdcs.org.uk are also developing observation links on their website. For details of the 'Marine Code of Conduct' for vessels observing cetaceans go to: www.seawatchfoundation.org.uk and click on 'Observing'.

Reef Check is another organisation which depends on volunteers to help to monitor reefs, including those in the Caribbean. Visit www.reefcheck.org/ecoaction /ecomonitoring_program.php Click on Data Sheets. For more information about species to look out for click on Indicators or use the Reef Check EcoMonitoring Instruction Manual, which is available in book form or online. Contact rcinfo@reefcheck.org to find out more about contributing information. Reef Check teams record four temperature readings for each reef site they survey: air, water surface, 3m depth, and 10m depth. These fields can be found on their site description sheet.

OceansWatch undertakes marine conservation projects and offers humanitarian aid to coastal communities in developing countries. It aims to strengthen global links between yachtsmen, divers and marine researchers, teachers and conservationists: www.oceanswatch.org/main/page/info-yachtsmen

Observations of coral reefs are fundamental to our understanding of how the oceans are changing over time.
Photo: Mike Robinson

Many turtles are endangered, and recorded observations could help to ensure their survival.
Photo: Mike Robinson

65

II
PASSAGES AND LANDFALLS

Overview of
THE NORTH ATLANTIC

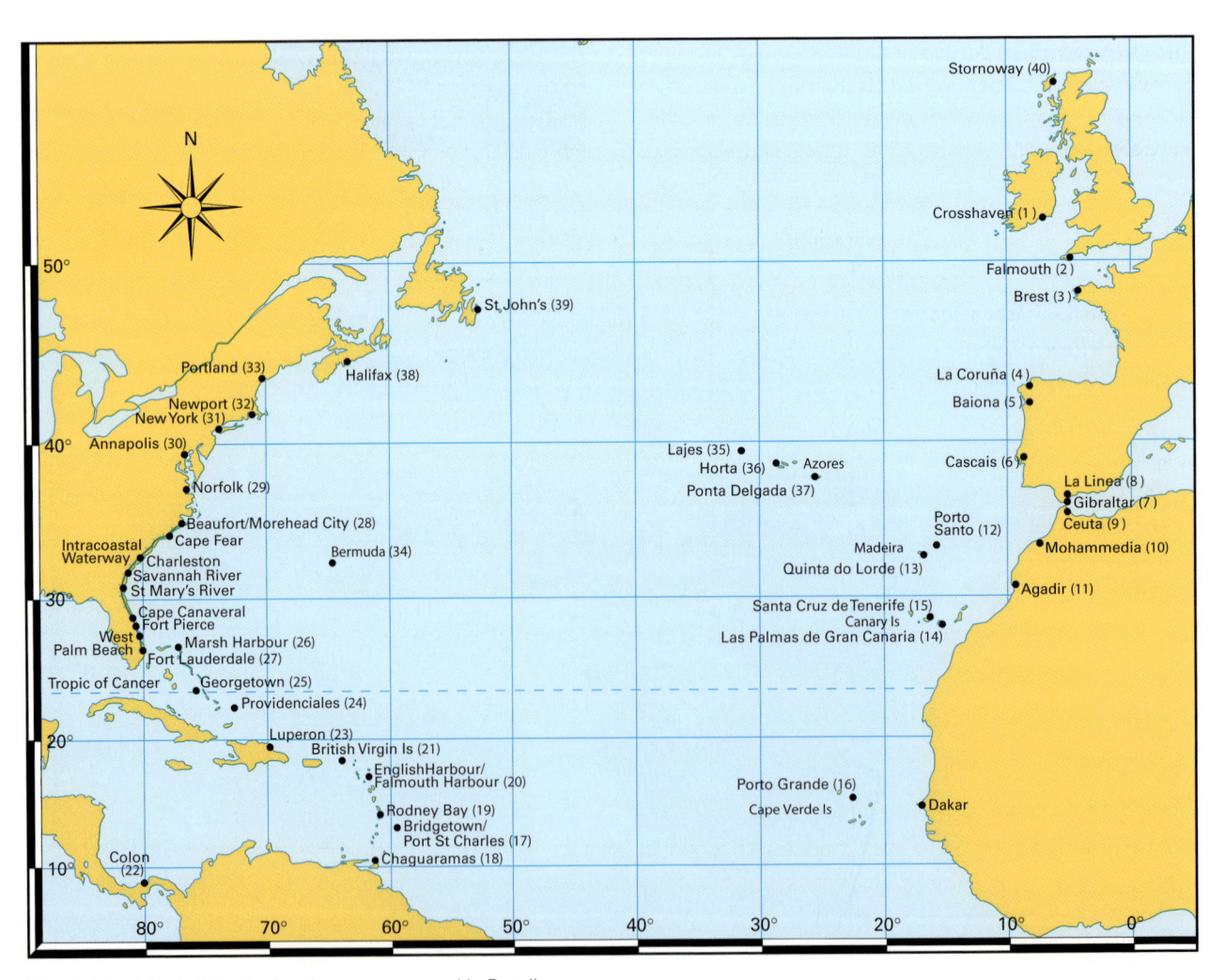

Plan 2 The North Atlantic showing ports covered in Part II

OVERVIEW OF THE NORTH ATLANTIC

ROUTE TIMING

The timing of passages around the North Atlantic is dependent on the prevailing weather patterns through the seasons. In tropical areas the optimum timings will be when the trade winds are properly established, but avoiding the hurricane season. In higher latitudes, frequencies of gales and the extent of ice fields should be taken into account. At the eastern and western margins, seasonal continental weather patterns become significant.

Winds

Winds and weather in the North Atlantic revolve around a central high pressure, the Azores High. This is characterised by a band of variables which usually encompasses the Azores and Bermuda and is surrounded by outer rings of relatively low pressures.

At the western margin, the land mass of North America and the confluence of the warm Gulf Stream with the cold Labrador Current results in unstable conditions. These give rise to a succession of depressions, or lows, which form over the western North Atlantic and are then propelled east or north-east towards Northern Europe. Each of these depressions creates its own wind system anti-clockwise around its centre. The northerly latitudes of the 40s and 50s lie at the bottom edge of these anti-clockwise lows and at the top edge of the clockwise Azores high. This results in a corridor of prevailing westerlies. Gales, caused by steep pressure gradients within the lows, are frequent in this area, but are generally less common and less severe in the summer. In the high latitudes of the 60s it is sometimes possible to pick up easterly winds over the tops of the low pressure systems as they go through.

At the eastern margin during the summer months, the Azores High dominates which, together with low pressure over Spain, causes north easterly winds to become established down the Spanish, Portuguese and North African coasts. The Azores High is generally weaker during the winter months when the band of variables extends to the southern European and North African coastline.

South of the variable band lies the trade wind belt where the winds are predominantly easterly or north-easterly. The trade winds are usually established winds of around 15 to 20 knots, but may be weaker or stronger than this. Because the Azores High fluctuates in its position and its intensity year on year, the trade winds establish at slightly different times and with varying strengths at any particular latitude. The trades have usually not fully established before December or January although, earlier than this, it may be possible to find more reliable winds by heading further south.

	MAY	JUN	JUL	AUG	SEP	OCT	NOV	DEC	JAN	FEB	MAR	APR
The British & European Coasts	■	■	■	■	■							
Southwards in the Eastern Atlantic	■	■	■	■	■	■						
The Madeiran, Canary & Cape Verde archipelagos	■	■	■	■	■	■	■	■	■	■	■	■
The Trade Wind crossing							■	■	■	■	■	■
The South Atlantic (Cape Town to Caribbean)								■	■	■	■	■
The Caribbean	■						■	■	■	■	■	■
The Bahamas & Florida	■							■	■	■	■	■
North from the Caribbean	■	■									■	■
East coast of North America	■	■	■	■	■							
Transatlantic in the middle & northern latitudes	■	■	■	■								
Viking Route		■	■	■								

Fig 2 Timing your passages. Green shading indicates the best times for each region.

PASSAGES AND LANDFALLS

The Azores High is sometimes disrupted by a cold front which causes a mid-Atlantic trough, resulting in a band of light variables. Further west in the trade wind belt, it is common to experience squalls or even, depending on the season, a tropical wave. Squalls can be intense, with a short but sharp burst of gale force winds. Tropical waves are most common during the hurricane season, indeed they are the progenitor of most hurricanes. Tropical waves are caused by weather systems which form over Africa and then track westwards across the top of the Inter Tropical Convergence Zone (ITCZ). They sometimes carry clear skies, but their passage is more usually characterised by strong south-easterly winds, rain and thunderstorms. See Appendix B.

Currents

There is a close but complex relationship between prevailing winds and surface currents (see plans 3 and 4 opposite). Thus the north-east trade wind gives rises to the North Equatorial Current, flowing east to west across the Atlantic between about 10° and 25°N. This creates a head of water in the Gulf of Mexico and the Caribbean Sea which becomes the Gulf Stream. This emerges through the Strait of Florida and flows in a north-easterly direction until it meets the Labrador Current flowing south around Newfoundland and Nova Scotia. From 50°W westwards, the interface between the Gulf Stream and the Labrador Current is known as the Cold Wall and is normally very noticeable because of the change in water temperature and in colour – the cold Labrador Current is light green, whereas the warm Gulf Stream is a deep blue. Where it meets the Gulf Stream, the Labrador Current divides. One part forces a passage down between the Gulf Stream and the American coast, and the other turns eastward and combines with the Gulf Stream to form the North Atlantic Current. The North Atlantic Current, urged on by the prevailing westerly winds, eventually meets the obstruction of the continent of Europe. Again it divides, one stream going north of Scotland, and the other being deflected south-east and then south to form the Azores Current, the Portuguese Current and finally the Canaries Current. This in turn feeds the embryonic North Equatorial Current to complete the giant circle.

South of latitude 10°N there is a region of equatorial countercurrent which weakens close to South America. Along the north-eastern shoulder of the South American coastline the southern and northern Equatorial Currents combine into a strong north-westerly flow.

In addition there are local features, such as the currents flowing into the English Channel, the Bay of Biscay and the Mediterranean. There are also vertical currents which are turned downwards from the surface when surface current meets a land mass. So, for example, some of the water arriving at the Caribbean flows down to the ocean floor and back towards Africa. When it meets the African continental shelf it is forced back up to the surface, bringing with it a richness of nutrients which feed an abundance of ocean life in this area.

When a current flows along a continental coastline its course tends to be orderly, but in mid-ocean, or on encountering islands in its path, its track may split or become very ragged at the edges. In some places there are well-documented changes of course due to land masses, and there are areas in which eddies or countercurrents occur predictably. Knowledge of these can be important because parallel courses only a few miles apart may be in waters moving in opposite directions. When this happens the choice of the right track can make a significant difference to the day's run. In areas where currents run strongly, even moderate contrary winds can create steep and confused seas. Stronger winds, certainly a hurricane, could make the sea state disastrous.

> **Further reference**
> *World Cruising Routes* by Jimmy Cornell is aimed specifically at cruising yachts and discusses regional weather and currents for each ocean and cruising area, together with tactics to be adopted should a tropical storm be met at sea.
> www.noonsite.com

Hurricanes

Tropical revolving storms, known as hurricanes in the North Atlantic, are triggered near the equator during the summer months, often as a development from a tropical wave. They form over warm water (27°C or above). They intensify while moving north-west towards the western margin of the North Atlantic between Grenada and Cape Hatteras. They tend to recurve to the north or even north-east, but sometimes continue westwards towards Central America or into the Gulf of Mexico.

An old saying about hurricanes goes:

> June too soon,
> July stand by,
> August come she must,
> September remember,
> October all over.

Hurricanes are among the most destructive forces of nature. Sustained winds can reach 135 knots, with gusts far in excess of that. Huge waves are generated which, depending on the relative track of the storm, may become violently confused. When a hurricane reaches land, the surge associated with it may temporarily raise the sea level by as much as 3–4m (10–13ft). Even large commercial ships encountering such storms are often damaged and sometimes lost.

OVERVIEW OF THE NORTH ATLANTIC

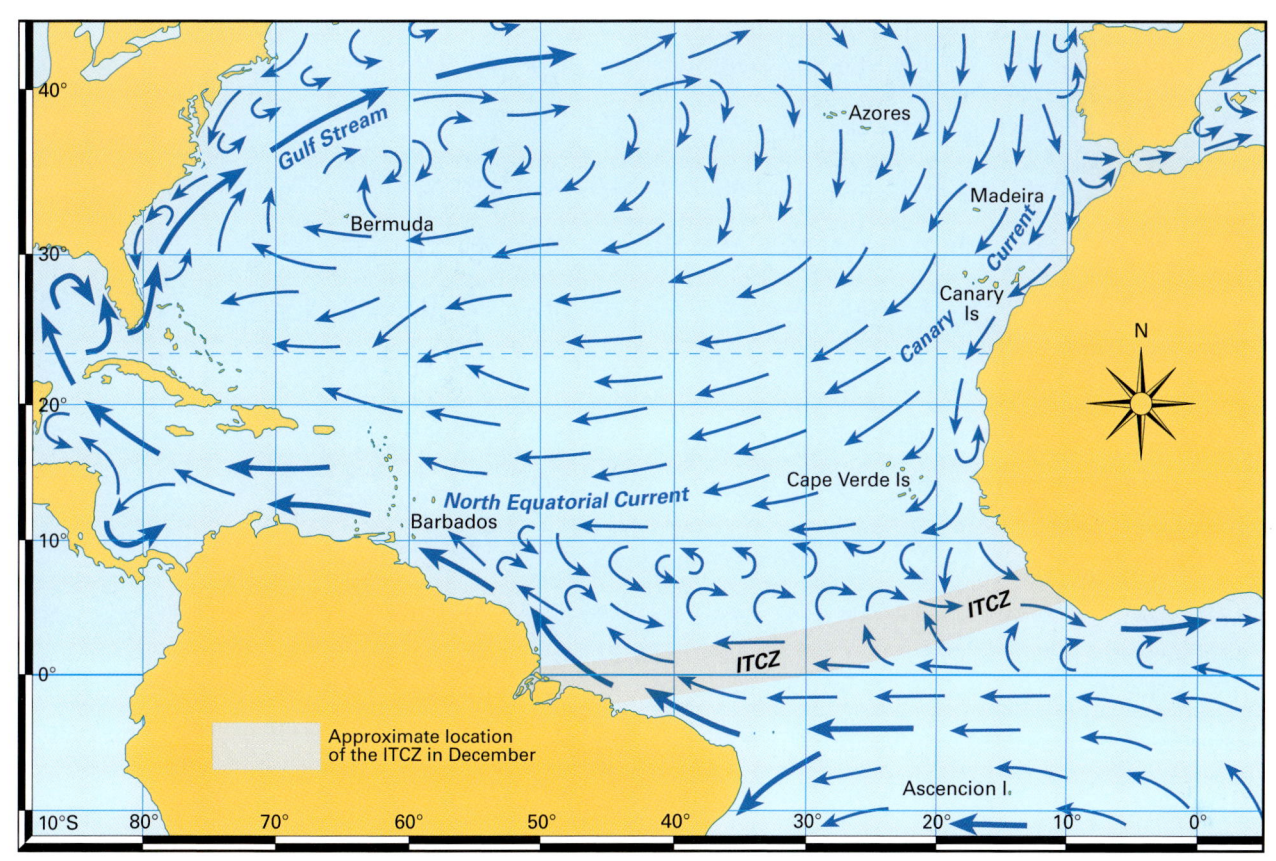

Plan 3 General direction of current flow in the North Atlantic – December

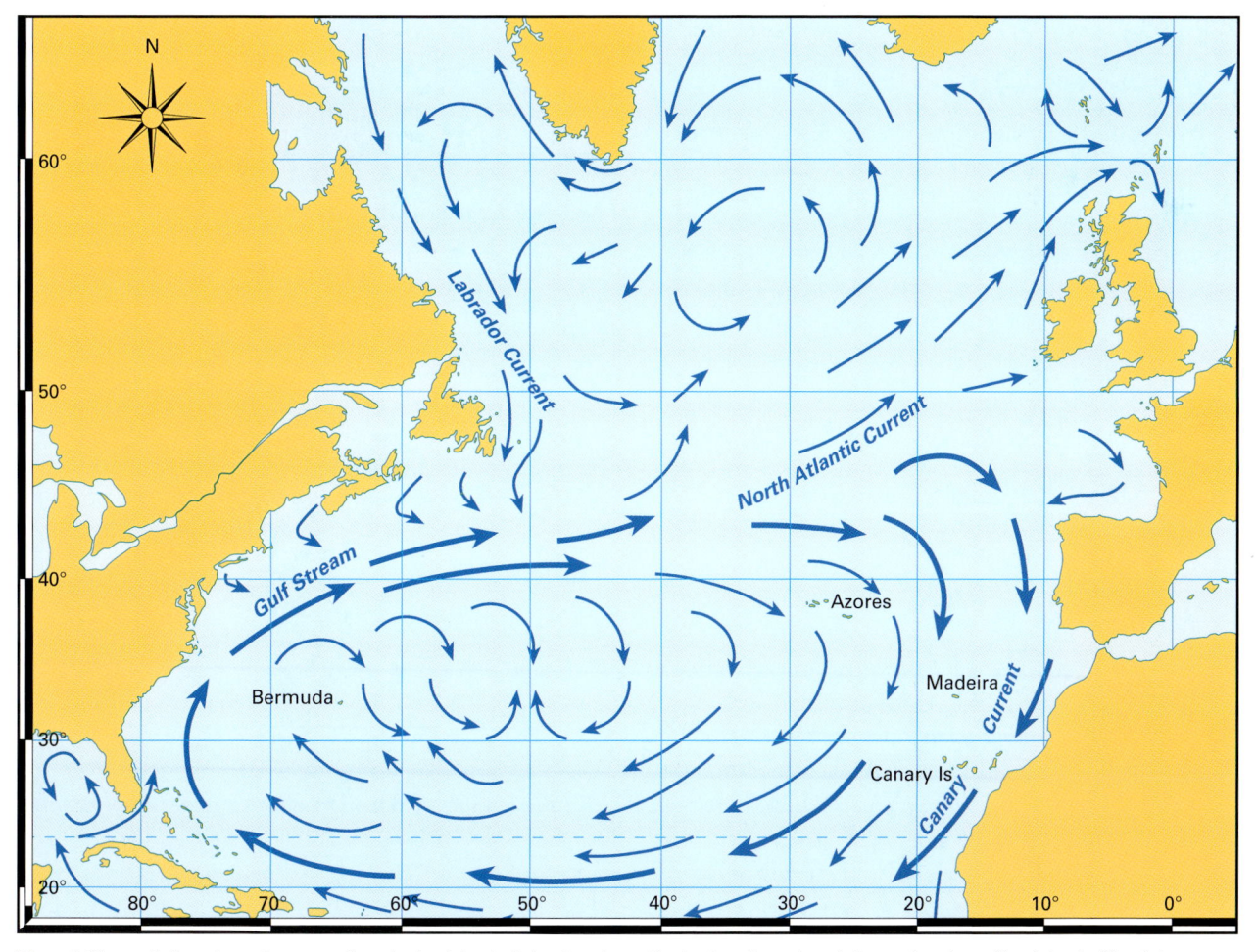

Plan 4 General direction of current flow in the North Atlantic – June. Both plans based on information from *The Atlantic Pilot Atlas*

69

PASSAGES AND LANDFALLS

Yachts piled up on the beach in the lagoon at St Maarten following Hurricane Luis. Photo: Malcolm Page

One of the main considerations in timing passages around the North Atlantic should be the avoidance of the hurricane area during the hurricane season. In general, the following advice will minimise the chances of experiencing a hurricane:

1. If bound for the Caribbean, do not leave the Canaries or Cape Verdes before the middle of November.

2. If remaining in the Caribbean for the summer, be south of Grenada by the beginning of June.

3. If sailing directly to Europe, leave the Caribbean by mid-May; if going via Bermuda, leave earlier to allow for time spent there. Whether bound for Europe or for the north-eastern United States, leave Bermuda by early June.

4. If transiting the Bahamas and the US Intracoastal Waterway northwards, be north of Cape Hatteras by the beginning of June.

5. Monitor the forecasts regularly when on passage between late May and November.

The National Hurricane Centre is a part of the National Oceanic and Atmospheric Administration (NOAA). NOAA is a US federal agency which focuses on the condition of the oceans and the atmosphere and produces excellent weather reports and forecasts, including hurricane forecasting and tracking.

For more information about hurricanes and storm shelters see Appendix B.

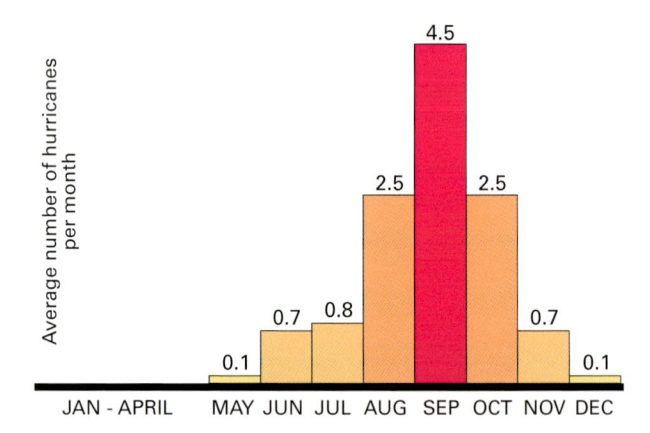

Fig 3 Average number of hurricanes per month in the Caribbean

Websites

www.nhc.noaa.gov/pastprofile.shtml#ori for zones of origin and tracks of hurricanes for different months

Other useful sites which report on hurricanes are:
www.stormcarib.com
www.crownweather.com

Fog

Fog is common on the coast of Maine and in the region of the Grand Banks. It is most prevalent in spring and summer, and can be expected to occur about ten days in each month. All of the coastal areas on the eastern side of the north Atlantic, from Norway southwards, are subject to fog. European sailors who tend to associate fog with light winds or calms should be aware that this is often not the case in the western Atlantic, where fog may be accompanied by steady winds of 25 knots or more.

OVERVIEW OF THE NORTH ATLANTIC

Fog is a common hazard in higher latitudes on both sides of the North Atlantic. In some regions it may be accompanied by strong winds. Photo: Richard Woods

Ice

North Atlantic icebergs form by 'calving' from Greenland's glaciers, and are then carried south by wind and currents. They are almost totally confined to an area north of 40°N and west of 40°W, though stray bergs have very occasionally been found south or east of this and there is some evidence that global warming is changing this pattern. Icebergs are most widespread between March and July. The International Ice Patrol locates the position of bergs and gives radio reports. Ice reports are also given on Navtex. Further information about ice is given in Chapters 16 and 18.

Website
www.uscg-iip.org/General/mission.shtml
(US Coastguard, International Ice Patrol)

An iceberg off the entrance to St Johns, Newfoundland in June. Photo: Paul Heiney

WEATHER FORECAST TRANSMISSIONS

In a printed guide like this it is quite difficult to provide information which will stay in date for all the various weather forecast transmissions. Frequencies and transmission times do change, and the latest technologies are enabling an ever-increasing amount of continuously available information to be transmitted around the world. Nevertheless, the following information should at least put you on the right track to accessing all the weather information you need. Once you are actually on the cruising circuit you will find that fellow cruisers will swap information about what is available and useful. The important thing is to ensure that you have the means to receive such information (see Chapter 5).

Further information
A wealth of information about accessing weather information can be found on the RCC Pilotage Foundation and Ocean Cruising Club websites:

www.rccpf.org.uk/technic/weather_%20websites.pdf

www.oceancruisingclub.org/content/view/1381/85#ocean

Also Frank Singleton's weather site for yachtsmen is extremely informative and useful:

www.weather.mailasail.com/Franks-Weather/Home

The French Weather service, Meteo France is a mainstay of information, particularly on the trade wind route:

www.meteo.fr/meteonet_en/index.htm

For a dictionary of French terms and the Meteo areas see Appendices C and D.

71

PASSAGES AND LANDFALLS

WEATHER NETS
Mostly Upper Side Band, USB (J3E)

Herb
Herb Hilgenberg, Southbound II (call sign VAX498). 12359kHz at 2000UTC. This gives a detailed forecast to each boat that checks in; those who are only listening in will gain useful information and may well find that a forecast is given for a boat close to their position. To check in, call via e-mail giving your planned route. A donation is usually not asked for but greatly appreciated.
E-mail: hehilgen@aol.com

Trudi's Transatlantic Maritime Net
Trudi in Barbados (call sign 8P6QM), broadcasts at 1300UT on 21400kHz USB (J3E). Yachts throughout the Atlantic check in, giving positions and actual weather conditions. If it is available, a translation of the Radio France weather forecast is broadcast at around 1330UT. This net is most useful for those crossing west on the trade wind route. It may not operate for certain periods during the hurricane season.

Caribbean Weather Service
Chris Parker in Florida www.caribbeanwx.com (who has taken over from David Jones) broadcasts (USB (J3E)) daily except Sunday on 8137kHz at 1100UTC (0700 local), 4045kHz at 1130UTC, 8104kHz at 1230UTC, 12350kHz at 1330UTC and 16525kHz at 1345UTC. This gives comprehensive weather for the South West North Atlantic (south-westNA) area including the Caribbean region. Subscribers may talk to Chris and obtain a personalised forecast for any area within the Caribbean and the east coast of the USA as well as passages between the two. Chris also formulates two daily e-mails which are sent to subscribers, one covering the Caribbean and the other covering the Bahamas.
E-mail: chris@mwxc.com

Eric's Net
The Antilles Emergency and Weather Net (Ham) on Lower Side Band (LSB) on 3855kHz every day at 1030UT and 2230UT has all sorts of weather information from the Caribbean islands and has a wide audience in the Eastern Caribbean.

Caribbean South-west Net
8107kHz at 1330UTC. Weather and information Caribbean coast of Panama and Colombia.

Caribbean Maritime Mobile Net
Run by Lou, call sign KV4JC, on 7241kHz at 1100UTC. At 1115 UTC weather forecast from St. John (USVI).

European Maritime Mobile Net
14297kHz at 1900UTC. HAM net.

UK Maritime Mobile Net
14303kHz at 0800 and 1800UTC. HAM net.

Atlantic, Bahamas, Bermuda, Caribbean, Mexico, & Panama Nets
For a comprehensive list of frequencies and times go to www.docksideradio.com/east_coast.htm

CRUISERS' NETS

OCC Caribbean Net
This is on every day during the Winter months, November to May at 1130UTC (0730 local) on 4027kHz (J3E). This net is now open to members of the OCC (Ocean Cruising Club), RCC (Royal Cruising Club) and CCA (Cruising Club of America).

Coconut Telegraph Net
Operates every day within the Caribbean Sea at 1200UTC (0800 local) on 4060kHz (USB (J3E).

Cruiseheimer's Net
Operates mainly on US East coast at 0930 EST on 6227kHz.

'Doo Dah Net' (associated with the Cruiseheimer's Net) Run by Dick Giddings from North Carolina (Call sign Saint Jude) at 1700 EST on 8152kHz in the summer and 6227kHz in the winter. Covers mainly US east coast and Bahamas.

East Coast Net
This is an on-line net at www.cruisersnet.net. It has a wealth of information covering the whole of the east coast of the USA and Bahamas.

INMARSAT, SafetyNET and NAVTEX

Navareas UK – I, France – II and USA – IV

The Admiralty Lists of Radio Signals contain complete details of all weather and safety broadcasts. They also contain details of the NAVTEX broadcasts together with all the harbour and marina frequencies, telephone numbers, websites and e-mail addresses on both sides of the Atlantic.

UK Hydrographic Office: *Admiralty Digital List of Lights* and *Admiralty Digital Radio Signals* are available as programs www.ukho.gov.uk/ProductsandServices/Digital Publications/Pages/Home.aspx which can be updated online at updates: www.ukho.gov.uk/adll

Marine Service Charts (MSC) list frequencies, schedules and locations of stations disseminating NOAA's National Weather Service products. They also contain additional weather information of interest to the mariner. Charts are available via the Internet. For more information visit www.nws.noaa.gov/om/marine/pub.htm

Once a day an Extended Outlook, published at 2200, is broadcast via each of the UK NAVTEX stations on 518 kHz. The extended outlook signposts expected hazards for the Cullercoats, Niton and Portpatrick areas during a three-day outlook period beyond the period of the 24-hour forecast. The Niton area covers SW approaches to the UK, Portpatrick covers NW approaches. www.bbc.co.uk/weather/coast/shipping/outlook.shtml

UK High Seas forecasts, Met Area 1, are broadcast by the GMDSS Inmarsat EGC SafetyNET service twice a day at 0930 and 2130 UTC. The bulletin is in three parts: storm warnings, general synopsis and forecasts for the sea areas. Storm warnings are broadcast at other times when necessary. At 0800 and 2000 UTC the text of the High Seas forecasts, Met Area 1 is updated on the website: www.bbc.co.uk/weather/coast/shipping/highseas.shtml

Canadian NAVTEX forecasts are in English on 518 kHz and in French on the secondary 490 kHz frequency. Text forecasts and further information can be found on the Environment Canada website: www.weatheroffice.gc.ca/marine/index_e.html

GRIB

GRIB files (GRidded Information in Binary) is the format used by international meteorological institutes to transfer large data sets and is the foundation of modern weather forecasts. GRIB files are now available as free downloads from the internet. This enables yachts to view weather data for anywhere in the world whenever they want to, and wherever they are. GRIB files can be accessed ashore or on a limited bandwidth connection on board, either by HF radio or satellite telephone. It is possible to choose and save your settings for future use, which can speed up access to relevant data. GRIB files can be downloaded via compression software – which reduces file sizes and minimises the time to download. GRIB files have now largely superceded Weatherfax technology.

> **Websites**
> There is a great deal of information about GRIB for sailors at:
> www.weather.mailasail.com/Franks-Weather/Grib
> The GRIB US site is at www.grib.us/

Voice forecasts

BBC marine forecasts 0048, 0520, 1201 and 1754 (local time) daily on Radio 4 LW on 1515m (198 kHz). Also some VHF transmissions. Forecasts give a summary of gale warnings in force, a general synopsis and area forecasts for specified sea areas around the UK (see Appendix D). The radio bulletins at 0048 and 0536 also include the coastal weather reports. Weather information is updated 4 times a day. A text version is posted on www.bbc.co.uk/weather/coast/shipping/. There is also a listening link on the website.

Detailed Inshore Waters forecasts for 19 areas around the coast of the UK are broadcast on Radio 4 LW on 1515m (198 kHz) at approximately 0526 (local time). The forecasts generally cover up to 12 miles offshore and consist of a 24-hour forecast followed by an outlook for the following 24 hours. The forecast for Shetland covers up to 60 miles offshore and consists of a 12-hour forecast followed by an outlook for the following 12 hours. Local radio and Coastguard stations also broadcast on VHF. A text version is posted on www.bbc.co.uk/weather/coast/inshore/.

See Appendix D for BBC and Meteo forecast areas.

Radio France Internationale 'Le Meteo' 1130UTC daily on the following AM (A3E) frequencies: 6175kHz in Europe, 15300, 15515, and 17570 and 21645kHz for the Atlantic.

This forecast is the only voice forecast which covers the whole of the trade wind crossing. It is read clearly in French. Even if your French is not very good, you will soon pick up all the necessary vocabulary to understand the forecast. See Appendix C for a translation of terms. Write it down as it sounds and work it out afterwards. You may find that someone on another yacht will give a translation on a daily net.

For more information about forecast transmissions go to: www.marine.meteofrancecom/ Click on 'Bulletins Large' or 'Bulletins Grande Large'.

US Coast Guard Portsmouth, Virginia (call sign NMN) Western Atlantic north of 3°N and west of 35°W together with the Gulf of Mexico and the Caribbean Sea; American High Seas forecast: any hurricane warnings will be transmitted before the forecast. In addition, some broadcasts include a Gulf Stream analysis. This forecast is read by a computer-generated voice synthesiser, which takes some getting used to.

USCG broadcasts offshore forecasts and marine warnings on 2670 kHz following an initial call on 2182 kHz. The 'Iron Mike' High Seas HF Voice Broadcast is on 6501 kHz (USB) at 0203 UTC and 1645 UTC.

PASSAGES AND LANDFALLS

VHF forecasts Most coastal areas around the Atlantic have local maritime weather forecasts on VHF. Forecasts are usually announced on Channel 16.

On US VHF frequencies, continuous marine weather forecasts are available on one of 10 VHF weather channels and cover all of the USA, Puerto Rico, The Virgin Islands and some of the Bahamas. Depending on your itinerary it may make sense to purchase a US handheld VHF.

US Maritime Safety Information Broadcasts are given on Channel 22A and announced on Channel 16. Further information about US Coast Guard broadcasts can be found at www.navcen.uscg.gov/marcomms/vhf.htm Continuous forecasts for Canadian waters are given on Channels 21B AND 83B. Text forecasts and further information can be found on the Environment Canada website: www.weatheroffice.gc.ca/marine/index_e.html

PORT INFORMATION

There is, of course, a degree of personal choice involved in the selection of ports for each region. However, emphasis has been placed on their suitability for making safe landfall. With the exception of ports in Chapter 15 (Dominican Republic, Turks and Caicos and Bahamas), the majority of the primary ports in each section may be approached and entered even in bad conditions and at night and most are official Ports of Entry. The extensive lists of shore facilities from previous editions have no longer been included. It is safe to assume that, unless otherwise indicated, all the ports included have a selection of reasonable facilities for yachts and are appropriate places to prepare for departure or recover on arrival. Many cruising yachts prefer to anchor wherever possible and in this respect the listed ports are not always ideal. No attempt has been made to cover all viable harbours and anchorages for which local cruising guides should be consulted. Further guidelines on the use of this book are as follows:

- The area and harbour plans in this book should not be used for navigation: they are intended only to illustrate the text. In many areas developments are taking place that could render information out-of-date at any time. Current charts, pilot books and yachtsmen's guides should be consulted before attempting to enter any harbour for the first time.

- Further information about ports of call worldwide can be found at www.rccpf.org.uk and at www.noonsite.com (Click on 'Countries' and then on the relevant country which will come up in a list under cruising areas. Then select from the list of ports.)
- The relevant courtesy flags are shown for each port. These are not always the same as the national flag.
- The co-ordinates given for each port, rounded to the nearest half degree, are not intended to be used as waypoints. They merely indicate location.
- Bearings, where given, are in true from seaward.
- Local time (LT), in relation to the Universal Time Constant (UTC), is quoted for each port. In many places, including Great Britain, clocks are advanced during the summer months. The dates when this operates are decided by the government of each country and may vary from year to year. The times quoted are therefore subject to the appropriate adjustment for local 'summer' time if applicable.
- Wind and current diagrams are based on information in the *Atlantic Pilot Atlas*, James Clarke, Adlard Coles Nautical.

Tides

Tidal heights quoted are Mean Level above Datum, as listed in the British Admiralty Tide Tables NP 202. All heights are given in metres.

Websites
Admiralty Total Tide program:

www.ukho.gov.uk/ProductsandServices/DigitalPublications/Pages/Home.aspx

Tidal information on line from the UK Hydrographic Office:

www.easytide.ukho.gov.uk/EASYTIDE/EasyTide/SelectPort.aspx

www.tide-forecast.com

www.wxtide32.com

www.bbc.co.uk/weather/coast/tides

www./tidesandcurrents.noaa.gov/ (Click on Tidal Current Tables and follow the links)

Buoyage

The IALA A system (red to port, green to starboard when entering a harbour or heading upstream) is standard in European waters, including the Azores, Madeira and the Canaries. The IALA B system (green to port, red to starboard when entering a harbour or heading upstream) is used throughout American waters, as well as Bermuda and the Caribbean.

CAUTION
Maintenance of navigation aids is poor in some areas, and even major lights may sometimes be out of service for long periods. Where a change is notified, it may also take several months for it to appear in *Notices to Mariners* or on newly bought charts. If approaching in darkness and in any doubt at all about entry, it is always prudent to stand off until daylight. Do not assume that a total absence of lights is indicative of an absence of buoys – in some instances the buoys remain in position but are not maintained. They are a considerable hazard if approaching in darkness.

9 The Atlantic Coast of Europe

1	Crosshaven, Cork, Ireland	78
2	Falmouth, United Kingdom	82
3	Brest, France	86
4	La Coruña, Spain	89
5	Baiona (Bayona), Spain	92
6	Cascais, Lisbon, Portugal	95

The Atlantic coast of Europe encompasses a rich diversity of landscapes, climates and cultures. As well as some stunning scenery, a journey down this coast can provide a glut of historic and religious sites, a revelation in beer and wine sampling, certainly a mouth-watering gastronomic progression. But through the diversity along the way there is also a strong connecting thread of music, language, maritime tradition and, some might say, rebelliousness which runs between the peoples of the coast, from the Scots, Irish and Welsh, down through the Cornish, the Breton and south at least to the Basques and Galicians, perhaps beyond. Throughout the cruising season there are many festivals and events which are worth taking into account when you are at the planning stage. You may happen across them serendipitously, but it would be a shame to miss them for want of a day or two. Where possible, annual festivals are mentioned in the port details.

Gateway to northern Europe

The English Channel is also the main gateway to and from the coasts and many of the capitals of northern Europe. The Baltic Sea, the Scandinavian fjords or the Dutch and German coastal waterways are diverse and popular cruising grounds in the summer season, giving access to several great cities as well as to a range of more natural wonders. From the North Sea coast, sailing up the River Thames into the heart of London is a truly memorable experience. It is also possible to voyage up the Seine from Le Havre all the way into Paris, although this does require you to take your mast down. But from there, with a maximum draught of 1.9m (6ft), you can follow a network of interlinked canals and rivers all the way down through France and into the Mediterranean.

Websites
www.michaelbriant.com/french_canals.htm
www.vnf.fr/

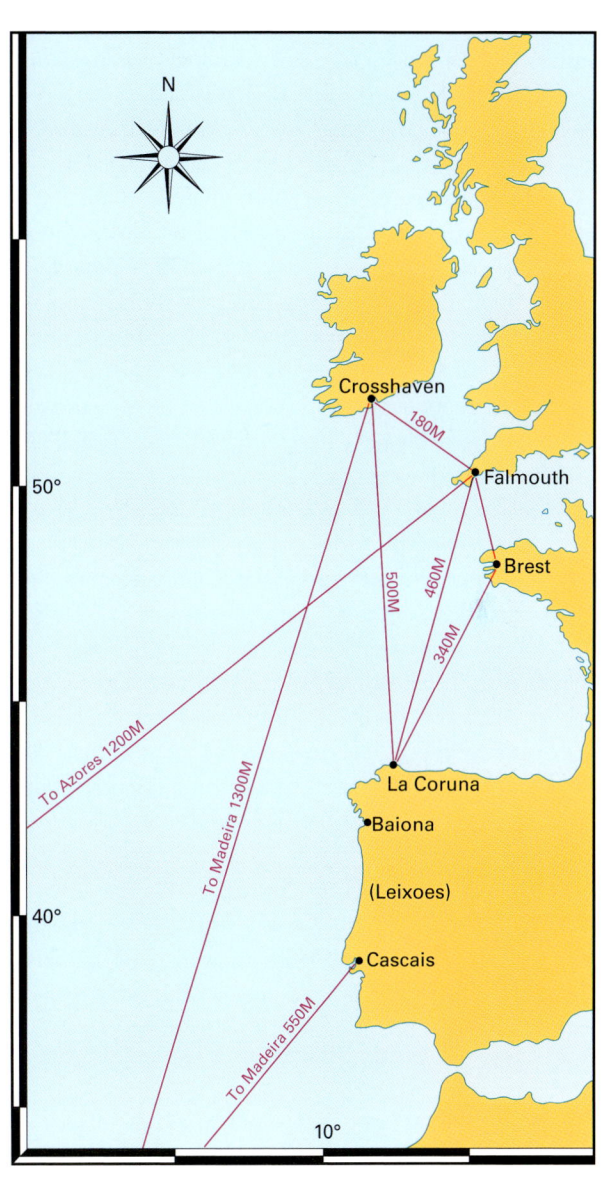

Plan 5 The Atlantic Coast of Europe to 60°N. Ports and passage distances

REGIONAL WEATHER AND PASSAGE TIMINGS

The Atlantic coast of Europe reaches from 36°N at Gibraltar to the Arctic Circle and beyond. The cruising season runs from May until early October. The window of opportunity for favourable weather is shorter than this as you head towards the north of the region, but extends later into the year as you progress south.

From northern Spain (La Coruña) northwards, the weather pattern is unstable because it depends on the

PASSAGES AND LANDFALLS

relative movements of areas of high and low pressure. Winds blow predominantly from south-west through to north-west, although winds from other directions are common. Conditions can change very quickly and weather forecasts should be monitored regularly.

The Bay of Biscay has a reputation for particularly unpleasant sea conditions, largely due to the effects of the continental shelf. The rapid change in depth from the North Atlantic to the relatively shallow Bay of Biscay causes the sea state to be rougher than you might otherwise expect. Vessels heading south from home ports in the UK, the Republic of Ireland or northern France encounter the Bay of Biscay within hours of leaving home. The crew are often anxious, seasick, tired from crossing busy shipping lanes, and have not had any time to settle into a rhythm. If you add this to the pot of unstable weather and rough seas, not to mention the unfathomable behaviour of some of the large Biscay fishing fleets, it is unsurprising that Biscay can prove too much of a challenge to inexperienced crew. If you are at all unsure about how well you and your crew will stand up to a Biscay crossing, it is well worth having extra, experienced crew on board for this passage. Alternatively, if you leave early enough in the season and want to take more time over your passage south, it is perfectly feasible to coast hop down the Biscay coast of France and along the north coast of Spain, where there are many unspoilt ports amidst stunning scenery. The coast of Brittany and the 'rias' in the north-west corner of Spain are cruising areas in their own right. Whichever route you take, you should plan to be south of Biscay by the end of August, after which the incidence of gales increases.

If you leave the English Channel late in the year you will run the gauntlet of the autumn weather. The incidence of gales in Biscay increases from an average of one day a month in August to nine in November. Timing of departure will rely on detailed long-range forecasts. Consider sailing from England to southwest Ireland to await suitable conditions, or head west of your direct track as you cross the Channel approaches. This puts you well to the west of the continental shelf and increases your sea room in the Bay of Biscay if you are caught in a gale.

Once you have passed Cape Finisterre you should start to experience more favourable conditions, when even the more doubtful crew members will be able to relax and enjoy the passage-making. A large area of low pressure usually forms over the Iberian Peninsula in early summer, dominating weather patterns until late autumn. The western edge of this depression coincides with the eastern margin of the Azores High, giving rise to the Portuguese trades. These are northerly winds that blow down the coast of Spain and Portugal in a band some 100 miles wide. These winds are most reliable from July through to September or October, and may be accelerated by the sea breeze along the coast to strong or even gale force winds for a short time in the afternoon. If the Portuguese Trades have not settled in, this coast can become fog bound for days at a time. However, south of Baiona, ports are spaced at intervals of 50 miles or less down the Portuguese coast and it is possible to hop down the coast in short passages.

Leixões, with its well-protected entrance, is a good port of refuge that can be entered in almost any weather. There is a small marina in the northern corner of what is otherwise a purely functional fishing and commercial port. Inevitably, it can sometimes be rather dirty, but a stopover here is worthwhile because of its proximity to the ancient city of Porto on the Douro river with its famous bridge, port wines and sailing wine barges. The marina monitors Channel 09.
Contact: Marina Porto Atlantico, Molhe Norte de Leixoes 4450-718 Leca da Palmeira. Portugal
Tel: 964 895   Fax: 966 636
E-mail: info@marinaportoatlantico.net
Website: www. marinaportoatlantico. net/english.html

Falmouth to Madeira

Although the direct course from the English Channel to Madeira passes close to the Spanish coast, it is worth making enough westing to remain a safe distance off shore. The greatest concentrations of commercial traffic are found near the coast which is an area known for its poor visibility. By staying 50–100 miles offshore, you should escape both these problems while still receiving the full benefits of the northerly Portuguese Trades and Portuguese Current.

To Madeira via the Azores

Depending on your onward plans, any period between late May and early August is the best time for the passage from Falmouth to the Azores. Keep as near the rhumb line as conditions permit. The current sets south-east and prevailing winds are likely to be between south-west and north-west. The Azores High may extend a considerable distance to the north-east of the islands, in which case you may need plenty of fuel.

Onwards to Madeira a pleasant passage can be anticipated, with winds between north-west and north-east backed by a favourable current. There is generally good visibility and relatively little shipping. Though there may be a temptation to linger in the Azores, it would be wise to leave before the middle of September.

NORTH ATLANTIC CURRENT

The relatively warm water of the North Atlantic Current (previously the Gulf Stream) divides into two as it approaches the British Isles. One part runs up the west coast of Scotland towards Scandinavia and the other is deflected south-east and then south past Spain and Portugal. Smaller branches enter the English Channel and the Irish Sea. This

THE ATLANTIC COAST OF EUROPE

warm water provides a moderating influence on temperatures in the coastal fringes of western Europe, which tend to be much less extreme than those inland.

TIDES

Both tidal range and strength of stream vary a great deal along the Atlantic coast of Europe. Spring tidal ranges of 12m (39ft) occur in the Bristol Channel, around the Channel Islands and the adjacent French coast. Around Gibraltar the spring tidal range is only 1.1m (3.4ft). The greater tidal ranges naturally give rise to strong tidal streams. These are generally much more significant than any underlying current. On the coast of the British Isles and France, tidal streams regularly reach speeds of 3–4 knots. In the famous 'Alderney Race' between the Channel Islands and the Normandy peninsula the flood can exceed 9 knots. Tidal streams can be especially strong off headlands and between islands, with heavy overfalls. If these are marked on the chart you should avoid the area during the periods of strongest flow. If winds blow contrary to the tidal stream, conditions may become dangerous.

SHIPPING LANES

The English Channel has one of the world's highest concentrations of shipping traffic. Maintain a good lookout and proceed with caution if visibility is poor. Yachts are required to cross the charted shipping lanes as quickly as possible and on a course as close to perpendicular (90°) to the lanes as they are able. Stay outside the lanes except when crossing them. Most of the traffic is concentrated on two main routes, one on the northern side between the Scilly Isles and the Dover Strait, and the other on the southern side, between Ushant and the Dover Strait. Each of these corridors has an east-bound and a west-bound lane. There are also ferries sailing between England and France, and many coastal trading vessels, fishing boats and yachts are continually on the move.

Other charted shipping lanes exist off Cape Finisterre and the Portuguese coast and in the Straits of Gibraltar. The whole Atlantic coast of Spain and Portugal tends to be busy with shipping and with fishing vessels.

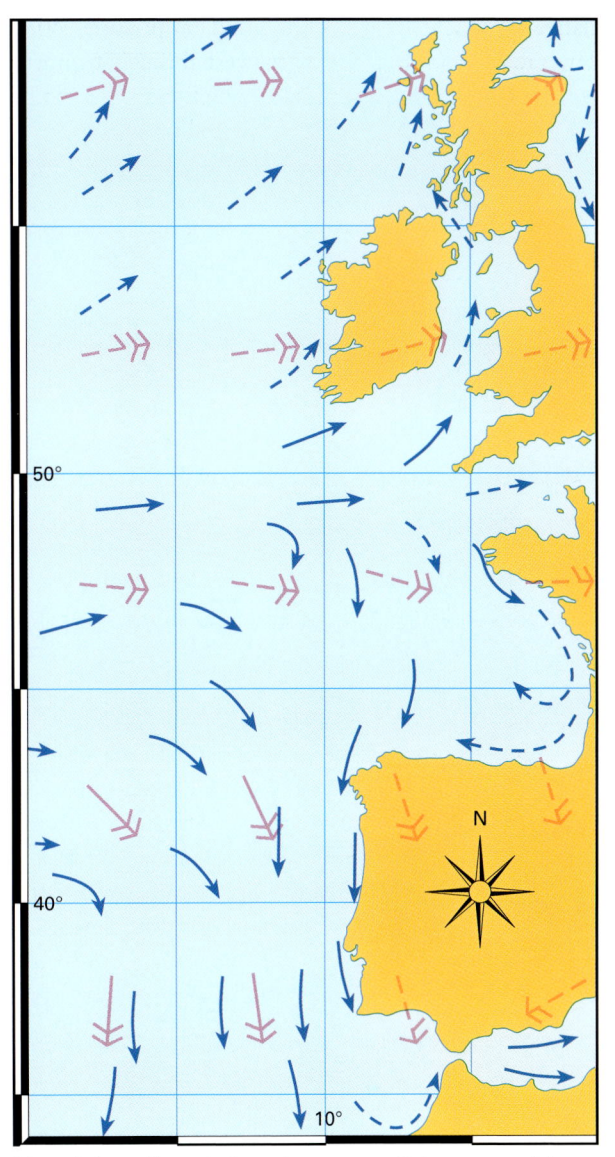

Plan 6 Prevailing winds and currents off the coast of Europe during August. Based on information from *The Atlantic Pilot Atlas*

Website
For details of the major pilot books available for this area, together with passage planning guides see www.rccpf.org.uk

PASSAGES AND LANDFALLS

Crosshaven
Cork, Ireland

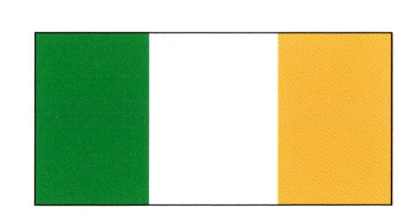

Location:	51°48´.5N 8°17´.5W
Springs:	4.1m Range: 3.7m
Neaps:	3.2m Range: 1.9m
Time zone:	UT
Currency:	Euro
Tel/fax:	Country code: 353 Area code: (0) 21
Language:	English (Irish Gaelic)
Emergencies:	Tel: 112 or 999

The oldest yacht club in the world

The south-west of Ireland is a green and pleasant land with a stunningly beautiful coastline and many lovely harbours and anchorages. Cork Harbour is a large natural harbour and a busy commercial port which can be entered safely in all conditions.

Crosshaven, on the Owenboy River, is on the west side within the entrance and is the centre for yachting in the estuary. It offers good shelter in all weathers and is the home of the Royal Cork Yacht Club which is the oldest yacht club in the world, founded in 1720. The RCYC has a fine

Crosshaven looking east down the Owenboy River. The Royal Cork Yacht Club and marina can be seen on the right. Roche's Point lighthouse is in the background (top right). Photo: Kevin Dwyer

THE ATLANTIC COAST OF EUROPE

clubhouse overlooking the river, a thriving social and sailing programme and an established reputation for hospitality to visiting sailors. You may well be tempted to try some of the creamy-headed Irish Stout brewed at the local Beamish and Murphys breweries.

It is said that Sir Francis Drake once evaded a superior Spanish force by taking his fleet of ships up the Owenboy River to Drake's Pool. More common now are fleets of racing yachts and dinghies. Cork Week is a world class regatta held in mid-July every two years and is an exuberant week of competitive sailing and parties. There is plenty to interest visitors in and around Cork, including a visit to Blarney Castle. You may want to try to kiss the Stone of Eloquence, otherwise known as the Blarney Stone, but not if you suffer from vertigo.

Websites
www.corktourist.com/
www.discoverireland.ie/southwest

CROSSHAVEN CORK — IRELAND

Plan 7 Cork (Cobh) Harbour

PASSAGES AND LANDFALLS

Approach

Landfall on the south-west or southern Irish coast is pretty straightforward. If coming from the Atlantic then Fastnet Rock, Mizzen Head and further north the Skelligs and Blasket Islands are conspicuous and well lit. In bad weather Dingle Bay, Bantry Bay (Bare Haven) or Crookhaven, Schull or Baltimore in Roaring Water Bay offer good shelter. Further east you have Castle Haven and Glandore also available before you reach the Old Head of Kinsale which is a distinctive headland that has a powerful light and is very easily identifiable [Fl (2) 10s 72m 25M]. Kinsale itself has a safe harbour with two marinas and is popular with visiting sailors.

Approaching Cork Harbour from any direction you have no hazards that are of consequence to boats drawing less than 3.5m (12ft) and all the possible hazards for craft deeper than this are well buoyed and lit. Roches Point (on the east side of the harbour entrance) had a sectored red and white light that covers both Daunt and Pollock Rocks. Cork Buoy safe water mark (a red and white pillar) is situated 5M south of Roches Point and 0.8M south-east of Daunt Rock Buoy and is a good initial waypoint. From there the 24m (80ft) Hammerhead Water Tower, south of Crosshaven to the west of the entrance is very conspicuous. If approaching from the UK, the red and white power station chimney north-east of Corkbeg to the east of the entrance is very useful. An approach waypoint of 51°46´.60N, 08°15´.40W puts you on the leading line/lights of 354°.

Dangers

All dangers are well marked and lit. Rock ledges extend up to 180m (600ft) offshore on either side of the entrance channels. Tidal streams can run strongly in the entrance, reaching two knots at springs, though the strength of the ebb can be somewhat lessened by keeping to the west side of the channel.

Entrance

The entrance is wide (0.8M) with two shipping channels that are fully buoyed, each with leading marks and lights. Boats drawing less than 5m (16ft) need not worry about draught anywhere other than off Ram's Head where it is advisable to keep at least 200m (656ft) to the east. The entrance narrows to 0.5M between the Forts. Once past the Forts, alter course to the north-west to pick up the buoyed channel into Crosshaven. This channel is fully buoyed with a minimum depth of at least 3m (10ft) LWS.

Radio

Cork Coastguard Radio broadcasts weather forecasts, and monitors VHF Channel 16 and working Channel 26. It should not be confused with Cork Harbour Radio which

An Irish coastal guard ship enters Baltimore harbour to the west of Cork. Photo: Robin Pharaoh

monitors commercial shipping on working Channels 12 and 14, and Channel 16. The Royal Cork Yacht Club and Crosshaven Boatyard both monitor Channels 16 and M(37) during working hours.

Formalities

There are no entry requirements for vessels arriving from within the EU. Yachts owned by EU residents should at all times carry proof of VAT paid status. In the case of a non-EU registered vessel, or if arriving from a non-EU country or with non-EU nationals aboard, hoist the Q flag on closing the land.

Customs and Immigration may be contacted by telephone (Tel: 4324444/6027700, or Freephone 1 800 295295), through any of the marina offices, or via the police station (Tel: 4831222) situated across the road from the Royal Cork Yacht Club.

Berthing and facilities

There are three marinas at Crosshaven on the south side of the river. Other facilities are available elsewhere within Cork Harbour.

The Crosshaven Boatyard has 20 visitors' berths; 40m (130ft) maximum, 4m (13ft) draught. A 40-ton boat hoist and storage on the hard are available.
Website: www.crosshavenboatyard.com
Contact: Tel: 4831161 Fax: 4831603
E-mail: cby@eircom.net

Salve Marina will accommodate visitors up to 30m (100ft) and 3.5m (12ft) draught. Fuel is available alongside.
Website: www.sailingireland.com/salve1.htm
Contact: Tel: 4831145 Fax: 4831747
E-mail: salvemarine@eircom.net

THE ATLANTIC COAST OF EUROPE

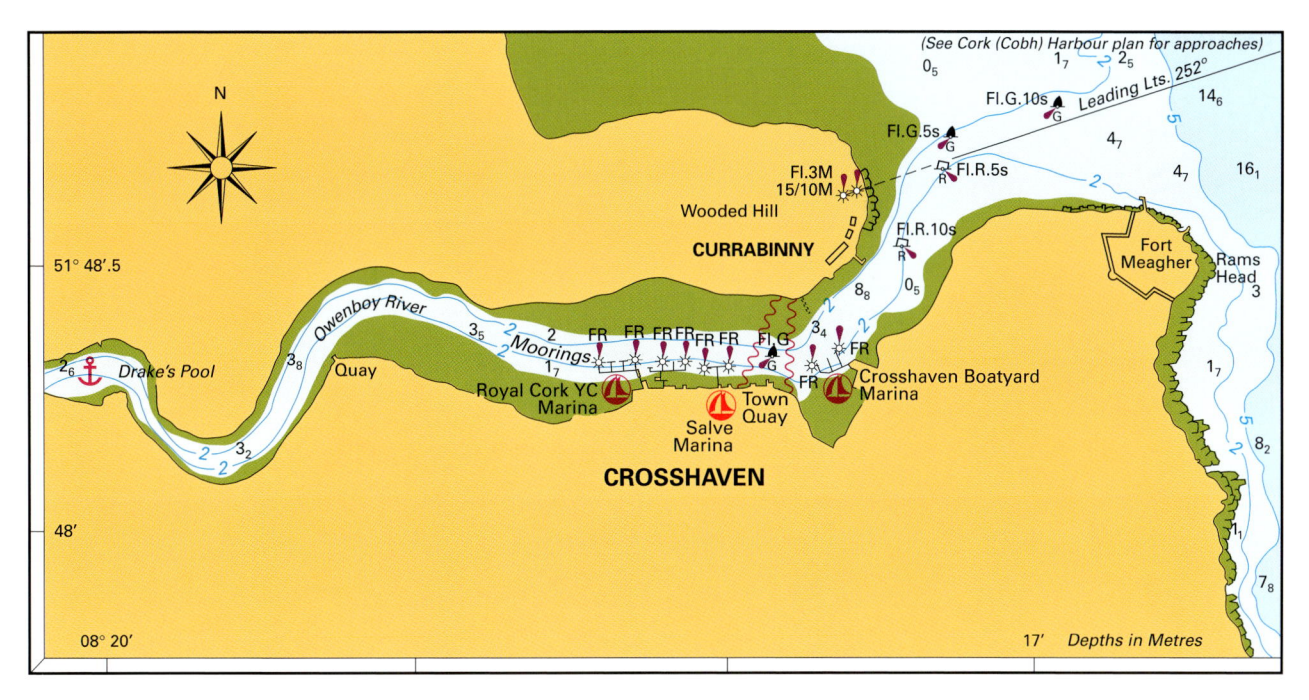

Plan 8 Crosshaven, Ireland

The Royal Cork Yacht Club will accommodate up to 20m (66ft) and 3m (10ft) draught. The least depth in the Owenboy channel up to the Royal Cork Yacht Club is 3m (8ft), but there are deeper parts beyond, up to Drake's Pool.
Website: www.royalcork.com
Contact: Tel: 4831023 Fax: 4831586
E-mail: office@royalcork.com

Castlepoint Boatyard has a 15-ton hoist and storage.
Contact: Tel: 4832154.

Anchorage and moorings

There is no good anchorage in the lower river, which is crowded and has cables and numerous old chains fouling the bottom, but a mooring may be available through the Royal Cork Yacht Club or Salve Marine Ltd. Drakes Pool, 1.5M up the river, offers anchorage in mud in 2m (7ft) in delightful surroundings, but has no facilities. Use of a tripping line is recommended.

Transport connections

A regular bus service operates to Cork City, from where there are trains and buses to Shannon or Dublin Airports for transatlantic flights. Cork Airport, with regular daily flights to the UK and the Continent is about 16km (10 miles) away. There are daily ferry connections to the UK and services to Brittany from Rosslare three times a week. A weekly ferry service to Brittany (Roscoff) from Cork operates on Saturdays from April to October. The Cork to Swansea (South Wales UK) Car Ferry is due to resume in 2010. A taxi service based in Crosshaven can be contacted on Tel: 4831122.

Medical services (telephone numbers)

Doctor in Crosshaven:	4831716
Crosshaven Health Centre	83 1839
Cork University Hospital	454 6400
Emergency	999 or 112.

CROSSHAVEN CORK IRELAND

PASSAGES AND LANDFALLS

2

Falmouth
United Kingdom

Location:	50°09′N 5°03′W
Springs:	5.4m Range: 4.6m
Neaps:	4.3m Range: 2.2m
Time zone:	UT (Winter), UT +1 (Summer)
Currency:	£ pounds sterling
Tel/fax:	Country code: 44 Area code: (0) 1326
Language:	English
Emergencies:	Tel: 999 or 112 (includes Coastguard)

The land of St Piran

Falmouth is the most westerly of the large English Channel ports and is one of the finest natural harbours in the world, with several miles of sheltered deep water branching off into inlets and creeks which just cry out to be explored. The entrance is well marked and safe under all conditions. Falmouth has excellent and extensive facilities for yachts and is well used to looking after transatlantic sailors, whether they be preparing for departure or making landfall.

The Royal Cornwall Yacht Club always welcomes visiting yachtsmen, and in August each year hosts a Classics regatta and Falmouth Week. The local gaff-rigged Falmouth Working Boats race in Carrick Road on two or three afternoons each week in summer. The racing is a wonderful spectacle but is also taken very seriously, so be careful not to get in the way. You might also see some gig racing – another very competitive Cornish sport. Many of the local boats may be flying the distinctive Cornish flag – the black and white crossed flag of St Piran. The National Maritime Museum overlooks the harbour and has plenty to interest visiting sailors of all ages. Pendennis Castle, built in the 1540s, and facing its sister fort across

Visitors' Yacht Haven with National Maritime Museum beyond. Photo: National Maritime Museum/Visit Cornwall

THE ATLANTIC COAST OF EUROPE

Plan 9 Falmouth, UK

the water at St Mawes, is a good view point and is well worth a visit. But don't be surprised by the Noonday Gun which is fired from the castle every day during July and August. The area around Falmouth and the cathedral city of Truro is rich in musical events and is famous for a number of wonderful gardens which are a delight to wander around. Cornwall is developing a reputation for internationally renowned restaurants, but you may also be tempted by the more humble delights of a Cornish pasty and a cream tea.

Websites
www.royalcornwallyachtclub.org/Visitors/index.html
www.falmouthport.co.uk
www.discoverfalmouth.co.uk/

Approach and entrance

Heading for Falmouth from points west, the Bishop Rock lighthouse, which marks the south-western extremity of the Scilly Isles, is a likely first landfall. There can be strong tidal streams off the Bishop Rock and overfalls on the Pol Bank, three miles to the south-west. There may also be strong streams off Lizard Point and heavy overfalls extending to the south for three miles or more. Give these points a wide berth, and in strong south-westerlies make no attempt to close the coast until well round the Lizard. Once round the Lizard [Fl 3s 70m 25M] the only danger is the group of rocks known as the Manacles, clearly marked by an east cardinal buoy to seaward. An easterly wind combined with a flood tide can produce a race between Black Head and the Manacles on the direct course to Falmouth. In these conditions, after rounding the Lizard, head towards the Lowland Buoy at about 50°N 5°W which will put you east of the race on your approach. The entrance is passable under all conditions – even with a southerly gale and ebb tide a yacht can enter in safety, if not comfort. The main channel lies between St Anthony Head and the east cardinal buoy which marks the Black Rock Beacon.

Dangers

The Black Rock Beacon is unlit. In daylight a yacht can safely pass either side of Black Rock with an offing of 100m

(330ft), but at night you should use the main channel. There are sometimes shipping movements, often tug assisted, within the harbour and dock area. Some commercial fishing takes place and lobster pot marker buoys may be encountered anywhere in the coastal area, either singly or in attached strings, sometimes well offshore. They are often poorly marked and are a hazard to a yacht under power, particularly at night.

Radio

Falmouth Harbour radio: Channel 12 and 16
Falmouth Pilot radio: Channel 09 and 16
Harbour launch *Killigrew*: Channel 12
Visitors Yacht Haven: Channel 12
Falmouth Premier Marina: Channel 80
Port Pendennis Marina: Channel 80
Falmouth Docks: Channel 11

Formalities

Entry requirements are waived in the case of an EU registered yacht arriving direct from another EU country (including the Azores). In the case of a non-EU registered vessel, or if arriving from a non-EU country or with non-EU nationals aboard, hoist the Q flag at sea and telephone Customs on 0345 231110 immediately on arrival.

Berthing and facilities

There are three marinas in Falmouth itself. There are further berthing, mooring and anchoring possibilities within the Fal estuary and the nearby Helford River.

The Yacht Haven Falmouth Harbour Commissioners run the Yacht Haven which provides pontoons berths, shower and laundry facilities for up to 100 visitors. The Yacht Haven is suitable for use by vessels up to 16m (52ft) length and 2.5m (8ft) draught (larger vessels may be accepted on application). A dredged approach channel is marked by orange triangular leading marks. The pontoons are very conveniently situated close to shops, pubs, restaurants, cafes and the National Maritime Museum. WiFi is available.
Website: www.falmouthport.co.uk/leisure/html/yachthaven.php
Contacts: The Visitors Yacht Haven (Tel: 310991) or Falmouth Harbour Commissioners, 44 Arwenack Street, Falmouth, TR11 3JQ
Tel: 312285 Fax: 211352,
E-mail: admin@falmouthport.co.uk

Falmouth Marina is situated about 0.7M up the Penryn River. The approach and marina have a minimum depth of 2.0m (7ft) and can accept yachts up to 25m (83ft) by arrangement. The river is buoyed, and a narrow dredged channel into the marina is marked with beacons. Secure to the clearly marked reception pontoon until directed to a berth by marina staff. Falmouth Marina accepts some live-aboards and is a pleasant marina in which to winter. There is a supermarket close by.
Website: www.premiermarinas.com/pages/falmouth_marina
Contact: Falmouth Marina, North Parade, Falmouth, Cornwall, TR11 2TD.
Tel: 316620 Fax: 313939
E-mail: falmouth@premiermarinas.com

Port Pendennis Marina is a marina village development with space for a few visiting yachts. It lies in the southern part of the harbour between the docks and the town and is convenient to the town shops and other facilities. The marina basin, containing about 60 berths, is enclosed within a single tidal barrier with access for about half the tide. The outer section has a 3m (10ft) draught limit, and can accommodate boats up to 50m (165ft) or more, and keeps space for visitors.
Contact: Port Pendennis, Challenger Quay, Falmouth, Cornwall, TR11 3YL
Tel: 211211 Fax: 311116
E-mail: marina@portpendennis.com

Hoist and hard standing are available at Falmouth Marina and Port Pendennis. Fuel is available at all the marinas listed.

Anchorage and moorings

Visitors to the UK should be aware that in popular anchoring areas, particularly on the south coast, there is often a charge made to lie to your own anchor. In some harbours a charge will apply anywhere within the harbour limits, even if you are well off the beaten track. These charges may well exceed the charges for a marina pontoon berth in other countries.

In Falmouth, an anchorage area, suitable for use by small craft in most conditions, is situated near to the Yacht Haven between Custom House Quay and Falmouth Docks. Holding is generally good in firm mud, though there are a few soft patches, and protection is adequate. In northerly winds more shelter may also be found east of the moorings that run between Flushing and Trefusis Point. All vessels that anchor must have a working engine as there may be a requirement to vacate the area, sometimes at short notice, to facilitate commercial shipping movements to and from Falmouth Docks. Skippers of vessels using the anchorage should contact the harbour patrol craft or the Harbour Office or consult the notice board at the top of the Yacht Haven access bridge for information on shipping movements. Skippers should avoid leaving their vessels unattended for prolonged periods at the anchorage.

There are 19 deep water moorings for visiting yachts by the main channel in the northern part of the harbour,

THE ATLANTIC COAST OF EUROPE

Looking SW from St Mawes Castle over the main approach channel. Black Rock Beacon can be seen to the right of the castle and St Anthony Head light is to the left. Photo: Bob Berry/Visit Cornwall

including four moorings appropriate for yachts up to 24m (80ft). The moorings are managed by the Falmouth Harbour Commissioners and are marked with green pick-up buoys. These moorings cannot be pre-booked and there is a maximum stay of three weeks during the high season (1 June–30 September), beyond which the tariff rate is doubled. If you have paid for a mooring you are entitled to use the shower and laundry facilities at the Yacht Haven. The moorings officer can be contacted at the Falmouth Harbour Office.
Contact: Tel: 312285 during working hours.
E-mail: mo@falmouthport.co.uk
Website: www.falmouthport.co.uk/leisure/index.php

Take dinghies into the Yacht Haven or the Royal Cornwall Yacht Club (Tel: 312126, Fax: 211614) The RCYC does not have any moorings available for visitors, but has a dinghy landing, showers, a bar and an excellent restaurant (Tel: 311105).

Transport connections

There is bus and rail access to the nearby cathedral city of Truro and onward for nationwide connections. Daily flights to London depart from Newquay airport about 48km (30 miles) away.

Medical services (telephone numbers)

Falmouth Health Centre	01326 210090
Royal Cornwall Hospital Treliske	01872 250000
Emergency	999

FALMOUTH
UNITED KINGDOM
2

85

PASSAGES AND LANDFALLS

3

Brest
France

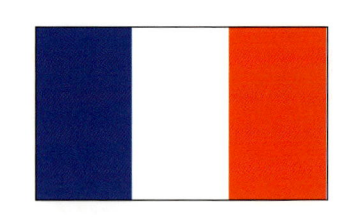

Location:	48°23′N 4°29′W
Springs:	7.5m Range: 5.9m
Neaps:	5.9m Range: 2.8m
Time zone:	UT+1
Currency:	Euro
Tel/fax:	Country code: 33 Area code: (0) 2
Language:	French
Emergencies:	Tel: 112

Maritime festival

Brest is a large city with a proud maritime history. It remains one of France's primary naval bases, no doubt partly due to its protected and easily defensible position inside the relatively narrow Goulet de Brest some 10 miles from the open sea. The surrounding coast is also the home of many renowned single-handed yachtsmen and women, and the city plays host to Le Figaro single-handed yacht race. Every four years (2012, 2016…) Brest hosts a spectacular maritime festival. This summer festival is a gathering of over 3000 craft from all over the world and celebrates a shared international heritage of sailing vessels, folk music and maritime art. The newly developed Marina du Chateau is conveniently located right in the heart of Brest allowing easy access to transport links and a whole range of facilities for visiting yachts.

Website:
www.brest2008.fr/fr/historique/

The Rade de Brest and the surrounding coast of Brittany is an interesting and varied cruising ground. There are many lovely harbours and anchorages, including Camaret-sur-Mer which is just eight miles by sea from Brest itself.

Brittany is a region of France with strong local traditions, linked with Cornwall through a shared Celtic influence. The Breton and Cornish languages have considerable similarities, and the folk music and dance demonstrate threads of common history. You are sure to notice the distinctive Breton flag which shares with the Cornish its black and white colouring. The Brittany region is famous for its abundant and delicious shellfish, which are served at almost every restaurant as *fruits de mer*, and for its many more gastronomic delights.

Approach

The Brittany coast of France is particularly dangerous to approach in bad weather because of the many off-lying rocks and strong tidal streams. There is also heavy shipping in the Traffic Separation Scheme lanes off Ushant. The many dangers are well marked but it is essential to have an accurate position before closing this coast. The direct approach is to head eastwards through the wide passage between Ile d'Ouessant (Ushant) and Ile de Sein. Heading east or north-east into the Goulet de Brest, off Pointe de St Matthieu at the southern end of the Chenal du Four or from the Chenal de Toulinguet, align the light towers of Pointe du Petit Minou [Fl (2) WR 6s] and Pointe du Portzic [Oc (2) WR 12s] on 068° to leave the well-marked Plateau des Fillettes shoal to starboard. In daylight this shoal can be left to port, but good clearance must be allowed around the Pointe des Espagnols where a wreck on a rock close to the north-east is marked by a white beacon.

If approaching from the north, yachts may use the shorter route through the Chenal du Four between Ile d'Ouessant and the mainland. The approach from the south cuts through the Raz de Sein between the Ile de Sein and the mainland. The northerly and southerly approaches are tidally dependent as the tidal streams run very hard round this corner of France. In particular the Raz de Sein can be very dangerous in strong wind-against-tide situations and should only be used at slack water in those conditions.

Radio

French coastal stations do not answer an initial call on VHF Channel 16 unless it is a Mayday call. The commercial port working channel is Channel 12, with Channel 74 used in the military port. The marinas may be contacted on Channel 09 or by telephone between 0800–2200 (reduced hours on public holidays and out of season).

Entrance

On approaching Pointe du Portzic, the city and port complex will be seen some two miles beyond. For the Marina du Château, use the main harbour entrance which

THE ATLANTIC COAST OF EUROPE

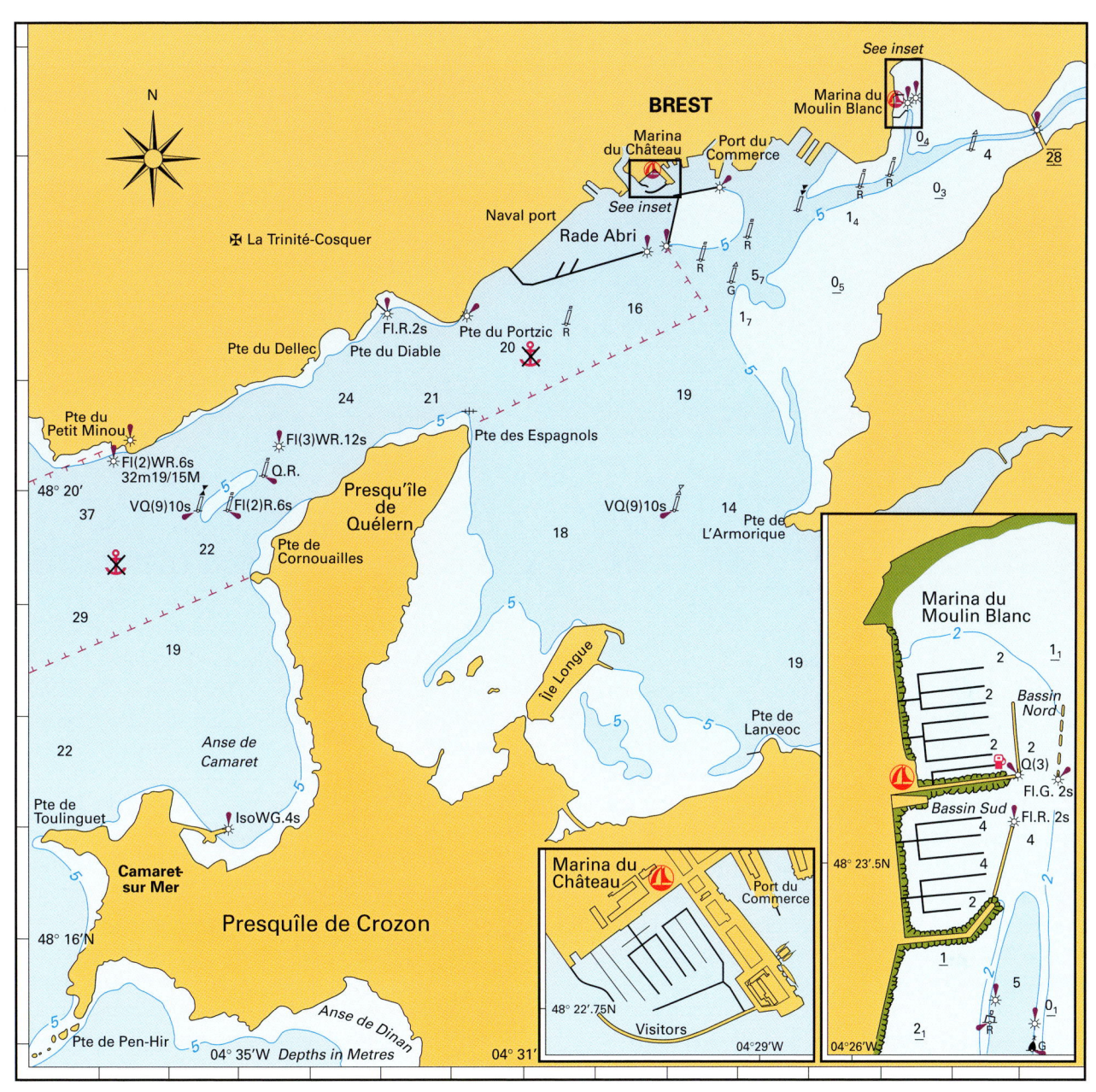

Plan 10 Brest, France

is used by all naval and most commercial ships. The Marina du Château can then be seen on the starboard bow with its entrance facing northwest. It is advisable to go beyond the entrance before turning in so that you have a clear view of vessels manoeuvring inside the entrance.

The Marina du Moulin Blanc is three miles further up the Goulet de Brest, on the eastern edge of reclaimed land near the mouth of the Elorn River, one mile below the two bridges. The marina is approached via a narrow dredged channel with a minimum of 2m (7ft), and the buoyage should be observed.

Formalities

It is not necessary for a yacht registered in the EU to report to Customs if arriving from another EU country, but failure to do so implies a formal declaration that the vessel complies with all the detailed Customs and health regulations. Non-EU-registered yachts, those arriving from a non-EU country or those with non-EU nationals aboard should report arrival without delay. All yachts must carry some form of registration and insurance, and it is important that these documents are originals and in-date. Officials may visit yachts, sometimes boarding at sea. In addition to checking registration documents and passports, they may check such things as liferaft service dates and expiry dates on flares.

Berthing and facilities

Marina du Chateau is a new 700 berth marina with 125 pontoon berths for visiting yachts of any size. It is situated close to the heart of Brest which has a wide range of shops

87

PASSAGES AND LANDFALLS

Marina du Château looking SE with the main harbour breakwater beyond. Photo: SOPAB

and restaurants. The railway station is also close by. The marina has an arrangement with one of the supermarkets for free delivery of large orders of stores. There is water and electricity on the pontoons, toilets and showers. Fuel is available 24 hours a day by credit card at a self-service pump where there is also a pump-out facility. In 2009, further marine facilities were planned but not yet complete. If major repairs are needed it may be advisable to proceed to the Moulin Blanc Marina which is under the same management and where there is a 40-tonne boat lift.
Contact: Tel: 98 331 250 E-mail: marina.lechateau@sopab.fr
Website: www.brestclubnautiquemarine.fr

The Marina du Moulin Blanc is a large marina complex with more than 1,460 berths, of which 120 are reserved in the northern basin for visiting yachts of up to 30m (100ft). The marina has all facilities including a 40 tonne hoist and hard standing. Fuel is available from a fueling berth. The marina is a half-hour bus ride from the centre of Brest but has an arrangement with a supermarket for the free delivery of stores.
Website: www.portmoulinblanc.com/uk/enter.html
Contact: Port de Plaisance du Moulin Blanc, 29200 Brest, France.
Tel: +33 298 022 002 Fax: +33 298 416 791
E-mail: marina.lemoulinblanc@sopab.fr

Anchorage and moorings

There are many sheltered anchorages within the Rade de Brest, but not adjacent to the port of Brest itself where anchoring is generally either forbidden, or the water too shallow.

Transport connections

Frequent buses into the city from Moulin Blanc. Trains from Brest leave for Morlaix, Rennes and Paris. Brest airport has national and international flights.

Medical services

There are a number of medical facilities. Ask for advice at the marinas.

Moulin Blanc Marina looking SW. Photo: SOPAB

THE ATLANTIC COAST OF EUROPE

4
La Coruña
Spain

Location:	43°21′.5N 8°23′W
Springs:	4.2m Range: 3.9m
Neaps:	2.8m Range: 1.2m
Time zone:	UT+1
Currency:	Euro
Tel/fax:	Country code: 34 Area code: 981 or 881
Language:	Spanish (also Galician dialect)
Emergencies:	Tel: 112

The world's oldest working lighthouse

La Coruña is a major city in the green and mountainous region of Galicia in the north-west of Spain. It is a busy fishing and commercial port, and facilities are good for visiting yachts. The British were not always so welcome and the heroine of the city is Maria Pita who helped to defend it against an attack by Sir Francis Drake in 1589. The roots of the city itself go back to Roman times and its most famous and ancient landmark is the 2nd century Tower of Hercules, the world's oldest working lighthouse. The water front is overlooked by many multi-storey buildings with glassed in balconies which have given rise to the name the 'crystal city'. Although these newer parts of the city are largely commercial, the older quarters are very picturesque and well worth exploring. Like Ireland, Cornwall and Brittany, Galicia has a strong regional identity rooted in Celtic traditions. August is a month of fiestas in La Coruña when you will be sure to see the *gaita* (a kind of bagpipe) being played.

Website
www.turismocoruna.com

Approach and entrance

Yachts on passage southwards across the Bay of Biscay may first sight Pta Estaca de Bares [Fl (2) 7.5s 99m 25M] nearly 40 miles to the north-east of La Coruña or Islas Sisargas [Fl (3) 15s 108m 23M] just over 20 miles to the west. Cabo

Marina Coruña looking south-east along the Dique de Abrigo. Photo: David Ridout

PASSAGES AND LANDFALLS

Plan 11 La Coruña, Spain

Prior [Fl (1+2) 15s 105m 22M] is about 10 miles north of La Coruña. Overlooking the entrance to La Coruña itself is Torre de Hércules (Tower of Hercules) [Fl (4) 20s 104m 23M] which is conspicuous, day or night. The entrance is straightforward by day or night. Dique de Abrigo is visible from some distance and lit at its eastern end. The tall, white twin towers near its root house the port authorities.

Dangers

There are various banks and shoals in the approaches which, although not of depths to trouble yachts, can cause the seas to break severely in bad weather. In these conditions the best approach is from the west on a bearing of no more than 145° on the Torre de Hércules, until the prominent Punta Mera leading line on 109°, which leads inside the off lying banks, can be picked up. The Punta Fieitera leading line on 182° will then lead in close to the south-east end of Dique de Abrigo. Two floating breakwaters some 200m (660ft) long lie across the water between the Dique de Abrigo and Castillo de San Anton. These are positioned such that they protect the south-east side of the Marina Coruña. They are low in the water and may be difficult to see, particularly at night.

Radio

La Coruña port control operates on VHF Channel 12. The marinas monitor Channel 09.

THE ATLANTIC COAST OF EUROPE

Darsena Marina showing the entrance. Photo: David Ridout

Formalities

In theory it is not necessary for a yacht registered in the EU to report to Customs if arriving from another EU country unless there are non-EU nationals aboard. However, it can do no harm to check in, and non-EU-registered yachts should report arrival without delay. Enquire at the marina or yacht club as to current procedure.

Berthing and facilities

Marina Coruña (43° 22´N 008° 23´W) is a new marina at the root of the Dique de Abrigo breakwater, just on the south side of the conspicuous harbour control twin towers. Entrance is very easily accessible by day or night. Two wave breakers protect the marina from the south-east. The marina provides a wide range of facilities including WiFi access. There is a restaurant in the port control towers which gives fantastic panoramic views.
Website: www.marinacoruna.es/e_index.htm
Contact: Marina Coruña, Paseo Alcalde Francisco Vazquez, s/n. 15001. La Coruña.
Tel: 881 920 482 Fax: 981 228 181
E-mail: marinacoruna@marinacoruna.es

Marina Seca (43° 20´.94N 008° 23´.05W) is a sister facility to Marina Coruña, located next door. Marina Seca has extensive boatyard facilities including a 50-tonne travel hoist and dry storage under cover.
Website: www.marinaseca.com/e_index.htm
Contact: Darsena Deportiva Faro de Oza s/n.15006, La Coruña.
Tel: 881 916 351 Fax: 881 913 649,
E-mail: marinaseca@marinaseca.com

Darsena Deportiva de La Coruña is situated in the Darsena de la Marina (43°22´.2N 008°23´.6W) which is the old fishing harbour in the heart of the city. There are 40 visitors' berths and a range of facilities.
Website: www.darsenacoruna.com/
Contact: Tel: 981 914142 Fax: 981 914144
E-mail: info@darsenacoruna.com

Fuel is available alongside at Marina Coruña. Haul-out may be possible at any of the listed marinas. Harbourmaster contact: Tel: 226001, Fax: 205862

Anchorage and moorings

The area for anchoring has now been considerably reduced by the expansion of Marina Coruña. It is possible to anchor further out, in about 12m (40ft) over mud. However, there is little shelter from winds from the south-east sector, holding is patchy, and a trip line is advisable. Various other anchorages exist in the Ría de la Coruña, but none are convenient to the city. There are few moorings.

Transport connections

Local buses, trains to Madrid and elsewhere. Airport with national flights and flights to UK. The main regional airport at Santiago de Compostela, about 60km (38 miles) away, handles many international flights. Ferries to the UK from Santander.

Medical services (telephone numbers)

Hospital	981 277905
Doctor	981 287477
Ambulance	061

LA CORUÑA
SPAIN
4

PASSAGES AND LANDFALLS

5
Baiona (Bayona)
Spain

Location:	42°07′N 8°51′W	
Springs:	3.5m	Range: 3.0m
Neaps:	2.7m	Range: 1.3m
Time zone:	UT+1	
Currency:	Euro	
Tel/fax:	Country code: 34 Area code: 986	
Language:	Spanish	
Emergencies:	Tel: 112	

In the wake of the *Pinta*

Baiona was Columbus's first Iberian landfall where he proclaimed his discovery of the new world on his return from the Caribbean in 1493 aboard the *Pinta*. The harbour remains a popular landfall for cruising sailors and can be entered in all weathers by day and night. Shelter is good. Baiona is picturesquely overlooked by a walled fortress which is now a Parador hotel. The views from the walls look down over the harbour and town and northwards to the Islas Cies. Many mediaeval buildings remain in the town, including the well preserved cathedral. As in La Coruña, August is a fiesta month in Baiona, particularly around the weekend nearest to 15/16 August. Try some of the local speciality seafood dishes or buy the ingredients at the busy fish market. The Monte Real Yacht Club is an old established yacht club which hosts local, national and international competitive sailing events. The busy, ship building, port city of Vigo is only a few miles up the Ria Vigo and is likely to provide any facilities that cannot be found in Baiona. The Islas Cies lie within the Galician Atlantic Islands National Park and are a lovely place to anchor and explore for a few days while you are in Baiona.

Approaching Baiona from the north. The Islas Cies are distinguishable from the mainland beyond them. Photo: Graham Adam

THE ATLANTIC COAST OF EUROPE

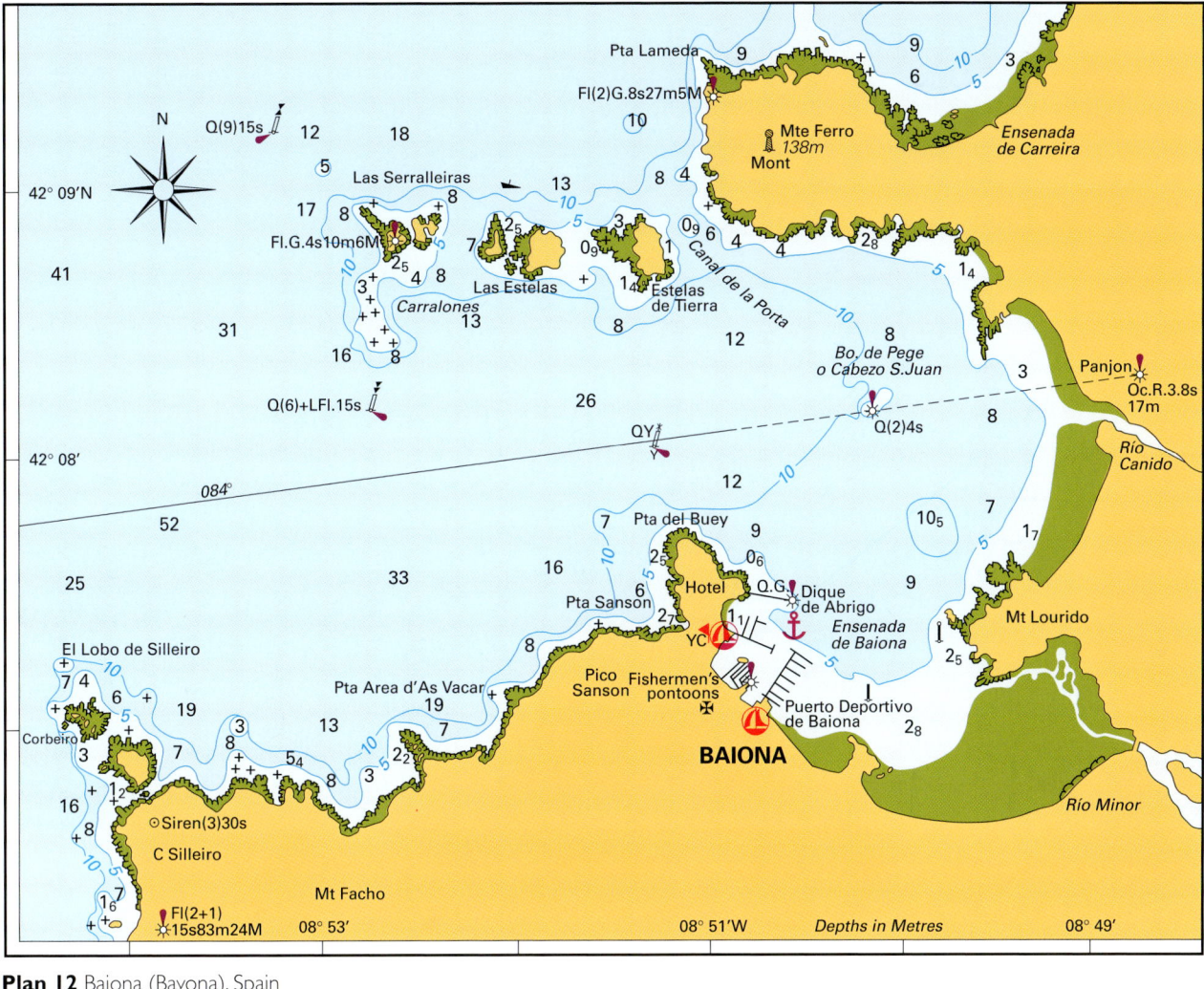

Plan 12 Baiona (Bayona), Spain

Website
www.baiona.org

Approach and entrance

Approach may either be made from the north, passing inside the Islas Cies and with Cabo de Home and Punta Robaleira [Fl (2) WR 7.5s 25m 11/9M] to port, or from the west, to the south of the Islas Cies and leaving the Islote Boerio (or Agoeiro) [Fl (2) R 8s 21m 6M] to port and Cabo Silleiro [Fl (2+1) 15s 83m 24M] to starboard.

The main entrance to the harbour leaves Las Serralleiras [Fl G 4s 9m 6M] well to port. Two cardinal buoys mark the western extremity of Las Serralleiras and Islas las Estelas. The leading lights then bear 084°, with the front one, Cabezo de San Juan, being on a shoal almost in the centre of the bay. In daylight, both Pta del Buey and the breakwater head can be left relatively close to starboard.

Dangers

If coming from south of west, note that off lying rocks extend some distance northwards of the Cabo Silleiro headland which itself lies nearly one mile north of the Cabo Silleiro light. The Canal de Porta inside the Estelas islands shoals to 0.9m (3ft).

Radio

The Harbourmaster and marinas monitor VHF Channel 06.

Formalities

In theory it is not necessary for a yacht registered in the EU to report to Customs if arriving from another EU country and crewed only by EU nationals. However, it can do no harm to check in, and non-EU-registered yachts should report arrival without delay. Enquire at the marina or yacht club as to current procedure.

Berthing and facilities

Puerto Deportivo de Baiona is a new marina which welcomes visiting yachts and offers pontoon berthing and all facilities including a 45-tonne hoist and fuel dock. PDB is situated south of the breakwater and to the south-east of the fishermen's mole.

PASSAGES AND LANDFALLS

BAIONA (BAYONA)
SPAIN

Looking south over Baiona. Photo: www.patrickroach.com

Website: www.puertobaiona.com
Contact: Puerto Deportivo de Baiona, Avenida Monterreal s/n 36300, Baiona.
Tel: 38 51 07   Fax: 35 64 89
E-mail: puertobaiona@puertobaiona.com

Monte Real Club de Yates de Baiona occupies an imposing building overlooking the harbour. The yacht club administers its own marina pontoons, moorings and facilities and may have visitors' berths available. There is a restaurant in the yacht club which welcomes visiting yachtsmen. There are draught restrictions in some parts of the yacht club marina. Repair facilities include a 17-tonne travel lift which may be tidally dependant. Fuel is available alongside.
Website: www.mrcyb.es/
Contact: Avda. Arquitecto Jesús Valverde, s/n, Reciento del Parador Nacional, 36300 Baiona
Tel: 385 000   Fax: 355 061   E-mail: mrcyb@mrcyb.com

Anchorage and moorings

There is an area of yacht anchorage to the south and southwest of the mole, outside the mooring buoys. It has excellent holding but is subject to swell in some conditions. The fairway leading to the fishermen's mole south of the yacht club pontoons should be left clear. The moorings are administered by the yacht club, so you should consult the MRCYB berthing master rather than the marina. The yacht club does not like dinghies from anchored yachts being left tied to its pontoons, but there is generally space to leave a dinghy on the pontoons at the fishermen's mole.

It is a short sail to the Islas Cies where there are some delightful anchorages. Islas Cies is a protected area and you need prior permission to land.

Transport connections

There are good train and bus connections from Vigo and national and international flights from Vigo Santiago de Compostela (about an hour away), or Porto.

Medical services (telephone numbers)

| Health Centre | 356 113/356 206 |
| Hospital Vigo | 816 000 |

6
Cascais
Lisbon, Portugal

Location:	38°42′N 9°25′W
Springs:	3.8m Range: 3.3m
Neaps:	3.0m Range: 1.5m
Time zone:	UT
Currency:	Euro
Tel/fax:	Country code: 351 Area code: 21
Language:	Portuguese
Emergencies:	Tel: 112

Home of 'The Navigators'

Cascais lies on the northern shore at the entrance of the River Tagus which runs up to Lisbon and beyond. There are very good train links between Cascais and Lisbon which are about 10 miles apart. Lisbon is the vibrant and modern capital of Portugal with a history of seafaring and exploration. Vasco de Gama set off from this region on his voyages of exploration. The maritime museum, just inland from the Tôrre de Belém, is particularly fascinating. Cascais itself has good shops, and restaurants where you can try the local *bacalhau* dishes made from dried and salted codfish. Throughout the region you will see buildings clad with beautifully crafted white and blue tiles (*azulejos*). Some tile compositions cover vast wall areas and tell elaborate stories.

An interesting day trip away from the coast is to the town of Sintra which is a World Heritage Site because of its 19th century Romantic architecture. The marina is a busy yachting centre and hosts a number of international sailing events.

Websites
www.visitlisboa.com/
www.visiteestoril.com/

Approach and entrance

If making landfall from north or west, the high cliffs of Cabo da Roca [Fl (4) 18s 164m 26M] are likely to be the first identifiable feature. Five miles further south is the lower headland of Cabo Raso [Fl (3) 15s 22m 20M]. The Bay of Cascais is approximately nine miles south-east of Cabo da Roca. The marina is just east of Santa Marta point. There are three cardinal buoys marking the breakwater. Leave these to port. Keep well clear of the end of the breakwater which extends further under water, leaving to port a small unlit red buoy. The reception quay is on the starboard side as you enter the marina beside the green and white striped entrance marker.

Radio

Cascais Marina is on Channel 09.

Cascais Marina in the approaches to Lisbon, looking NW. The anchorage is to the right of the marina. Photo Anne Hammick.

PASSAGES AND LANDFALLS

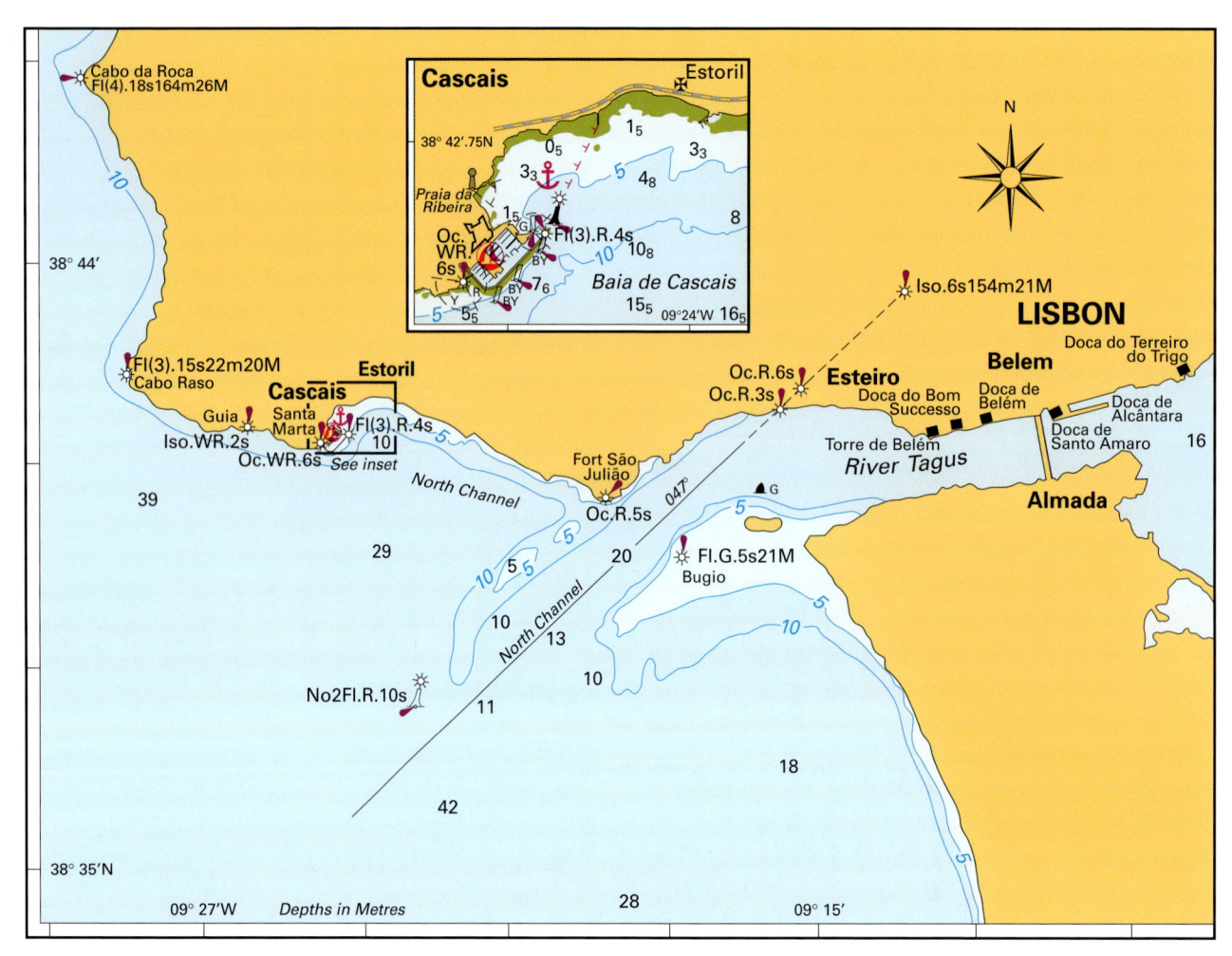

Plan 13 Cascais, Portugal

Formalities

All non-EU yachts should report their arrival to the relevant authorities. Report to the marina office with the usual papers and passports on arrival and fill in a standard form.

Berthing and facilities

Marina de Cascais has 650 berths, maximum draught 6m (20ft), with over 100 retained for transient visitors. There is berthing for larger yachts on a protected pontoon outside the marina. The marina has a full range of facilities, including a 70-tonne travel lift, fuel, water, electricity and a small supermarket on site.
Website: www.marina-cascais.com/eng/index_eng.html
Contact: Marina de Cascais, Casa de S. Bernardo, 2750-800 Cascais.
Tel: 4 824 800 Fax: 4 824 899
E-mail: info@marina-cascais.com

Other berthing facilities are available at Oeiras, halfway between Cascais and Lisbon, and in Lisbon itself.

Anchorage and moorings

The anchorage in Cascais Bay is good in sand and mud, but quite a large area is occupied by small-boat moorings. It is generally protected from the north but, in the summer, strong northerly winds can come down off the mountains. The anchorage is open to the south, although southerly winds are rare during the summer months.

Transport connections

There are frequent and swift train communications from Cascais to Lisbon every 30 minutes via Estoril and Belém. An efficient metro, frequent buses and trams run throughout the city, including connections to the international airport in the north-east part of the city, which is less than one hour away from Cascais.

Medical services

The British Hospital	Tel: 721 3400
	Fax: 721 3450
Website: www.bcclisbon.org/members?id=16	

10 Strait of Gibraltar and the Atlantic Coast of Morocco to Madeira and The Canaries

Harbours in the Strait of Gibraltar	101
7 Gibraltar	101
8 La Linea, Spain	104
9 Ceuta (Spanish enclave on the Moroccan coast)	106
Harbours on the Atlantic coast of Morocco	**108**
10 Mohammedia	109
11 Agadir	111
Harbours in Madeira	**113**
12 Porto Santo	115
13 Quinta do Lorde	117
Harbours in the Canaries	**119**
14 Las Palmas de Gran Canaria	122
15 Santa Cruz de Tenerife	125

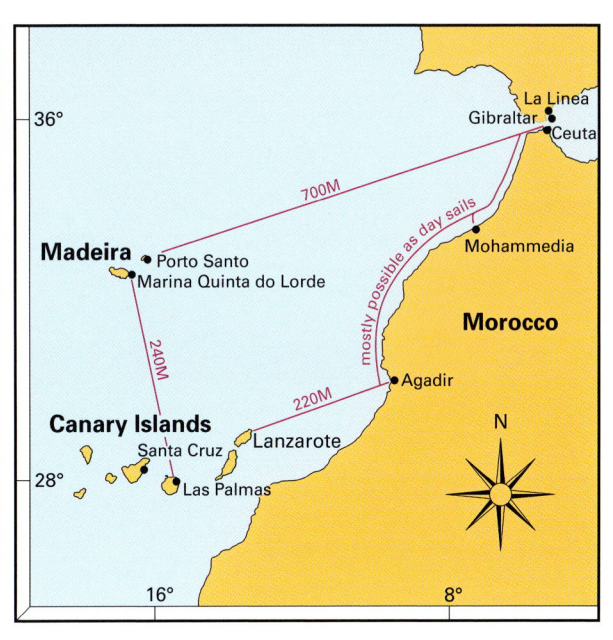

Plan 14 Strait of Gibraltar and the Atlantic coast of Morocco to Madeira and the Canary Island with port and passage distances

The Strait of Gibraltar is at a crossroad of sea routes – to or from Europe to the north, Africa to the south, the Mediterranean and through to the Black Sea or Red Sea to the east, and the Atlantic to the west. Many yachts head through the strait eastwards into the Mediterranean after crossing the Atlantic from the Caribbean or North America. Sailing in the opposite direction will be yachts which are leaving the Mediterranean and heading up the coast to northern Europe, down the African coast or out into the Atlantic. Departing from Portugal, south-west Spain or Gibraltar you can choose to head out to Madeira and continue southwards from island to island, or you can choose to explore the coast of Morocco before heading out to the Canaries.

GATEWAY TO THE MEDITERRANEAN

The Strait of Gibraltar is a major gateway into and out of the Mediterranean. Gibraltar has been the traditional port of call for the majority of yachts on this route, although this is now changing as alternative ports on the Spanish and Moroccan coasts develop and expand. Heading eastwards, from Cape St Vincent at the south-west tip of Portugal, there are a number of good harbours and anchorages. These allow you to coast-hop through the strait and use the wind and tides to your advantage. Lagos on the southern Portuguese coast has a very popular and secure marina in which to leave a boat for a period of time or to over-winter. Full coverage of this coastline will be found in Imray/RCC Pilotage Foundation *Atlantic Spain and Portugal*.

East of Gibraltar your route will depend on future passage plans.

Sailing northwards

A more northerly route will lead you to the Balearics. From here you can head further north to Sardinia and Corsica and up to the coast of France, or you can head further east to Sicily and Italy. Heading on through the Straits of Messina will take you towards the Greek Ionian islands or up into the Adriatic and the increasingly popular Croatian coast.

Continuing on through the Corinth Canal, or around the Peloponnese, opens up the cruising areas of the Greek Aegean. The eastern edge of the Aegean is bordered by Turkey. Here you can cruise north to the Dardanelles, Istanbul and into the Black Sea. Or you can cruise along the Turkish coast and islands to the south and east, perhaps heading on to Cyprus, Syria, Lebanon and Israel, or to Egypt and passages southwards into the Red Sea.

All of these areas are subject to seasonal weather changes. The topography of the Mediterranean creates localised winds in various regions which are given specific names – the *mistral, sirocco, vendavales, levante, gregale* and *meltemi*. Some of these winds can be unpredictable in their strength and suddenness of onset. The more general weather

PASSAGES AND LANDFALLS

Looking SSE down onto Lagos, Portugal; the marina is in the foreground, the fishing harbour and boatyard are beyond. Photo: Anne Hammick

patterns in the western Mediterranean differ from those in the east. To the west of Italy, summer winds tend to be light, with occasional periods of stronger winds. Force 9 winds have been recorded in recent summers. The winter brings frequent gales as Atlantic depressions move across the area. In the eastern Mediterranean fresh northerly winds establish during the summer, sometimes reaching gale force. During the winter, the winds are generally lighter but intense depressions with winds from any direction can develop very quickly. In the relatively confined and shallow waters of the Mediterranean, such depressions can produce seas of Biblical proportions within a very short period of time.

A more southerly route from Gibraltar runs along the African coastline where the easterly setting current may help your progress. Morocco and Tunisia are well used to visiting yachts and there are a number of good ports including several purpose built marinas. It is possible to cruise this coast even during the winter months as the weather is generally milder and more stable than further north in the Mediterranean. In the central Mediterranean, Pantellaria,

Further information
For details of the major pilot books available for this area, together with passage planning guides see www.rccpf.org.uk

RCCPF *Mediterranean Spain: Costas del Sol and Blanca* by John Marchment. See www.rccpf.org.uk if heading further east.

RCCPF *North Africa* by Graham Hutt

Red Sea Pilot by Elaine Morgan and Stephen Davies and *Indian Ocean Cruising Guide* by Rod Heikell

All published by Imray, Laurie, Norie & Wilson

The Pelagie Islands and Malta provide convenient and enjoyable stepping stones back up to Sicily and beyond. The Algerian and Libyan coasts are beautiful cruising grounds with many areas of great historical interest. Depending on the future political situation, these waters have the potential to become favourites, even for the less adventurous.

The varied delights of the Eastern Mediterranean seem to take a hold on many a cruising yacht. But for those with the urge to move on, Port Said is the Egyptian port at the northern entrance to the Suez Canal. A transit through the canal opens up the incredibly coral-rich cruising ground of the Red Sea and, beyond that, the Indian Ocean.

REGIONAL WEATHER

Prevailing winds in the eastern Atlantic have a northerly component, although Madeira, the Canaries, the Moroccan coast and Gibraltar are all occasionally influenced by the southern edge of winter depressions which bring south-westerly gales and rain. The passage of these depressions brings a substantial swell through the whole area. The swell is pervasive and may render anchorages untenable, even when they are protected from the direct force of the wind.

In the Strait of Gibraltar winds tend to blow east or west through the Strait. The general summer pattern is light overnight, rising to force 3 or force 4 in the afternoon and then dropping off again as the sun goes down. Winter winds also tend to be east or west except during a passing depression when they will be south-west. Very occasionally in winter winds will remain north-east for a long period during settled high pressure. There is a constant flow of surface current from the Atlantic into the Mediterranean, due to the high rate of evaporation in the confined area of

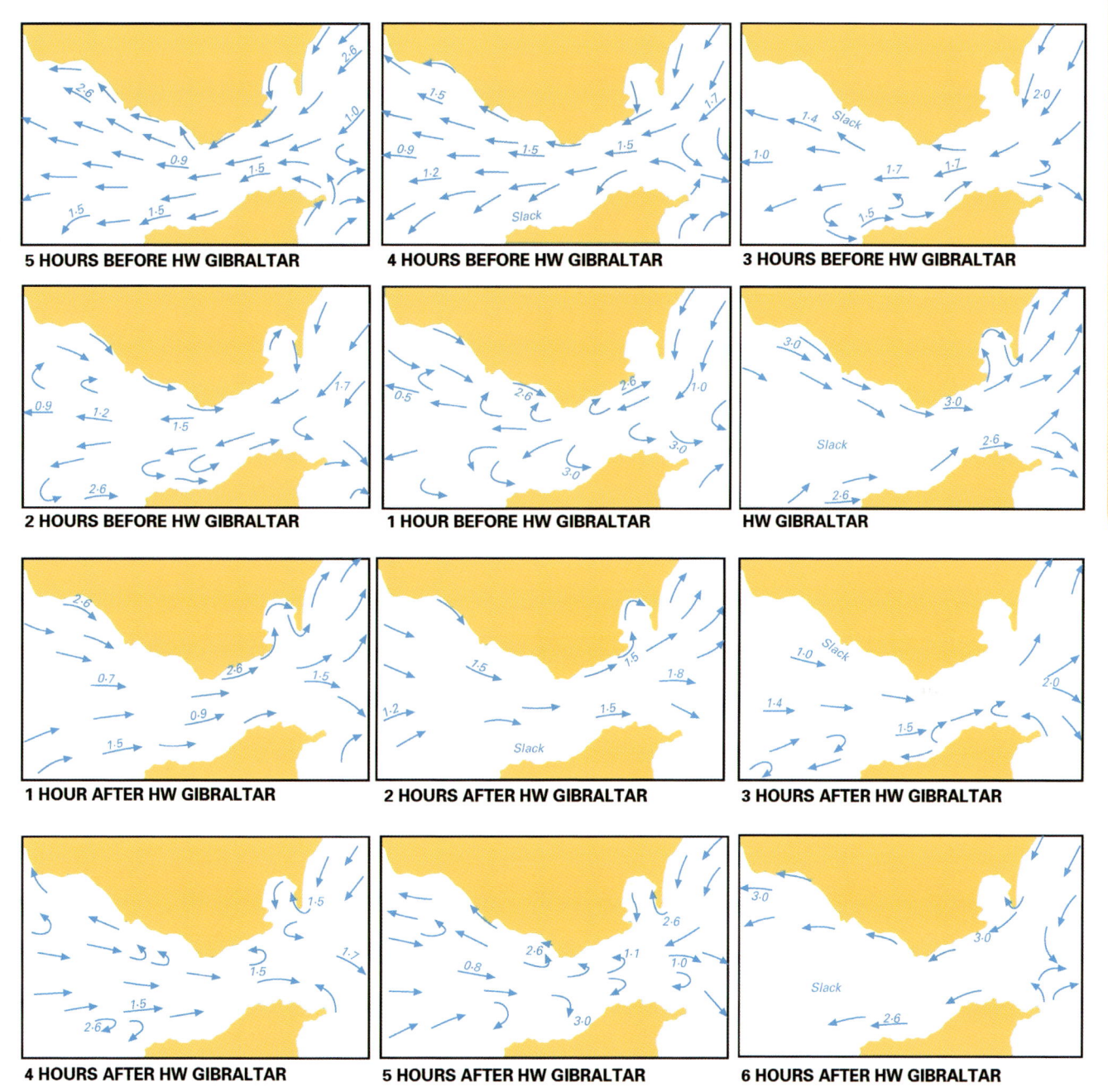

STRAIT OF GIBRALTAR AND THE ATLANTIC COAST OF MOROCCO

5 HOURS BEFORE HW GIBRALTAR

4 HOURS BEFORE HW GIBRALTAR

3 HOURS BEFORE HW GIBRALTAR

2 HOURS BEFORE HW GIBRALTAR

1 HOUR BEFORE HW GIBRALTAR

HW GIBRALTAR

1 HOUR AFTER HW GIBRALTAR

2 HOURS AFTER HW GIBRALTAR

3 HOURS AFTER HW GIBRALTAR

4 HOURS AFTER HW GIBRALTAR

5 HOURS AFTER HW GIBRALTAR

6 HOURS AFTER HW GIBRALTAR

Plan 15 Tidal charts for the Strait of Gibraltar. Tidal information by Dr Sloma of Gibraltar *Yacht Scene*, reproduced with permission from Imray

the Mediterranean Sea. The speed of this current is either diminished or accelerated by the tide and the wind. At springs, the currents in the Strait of Gibraltar can reach up to 6 knots. In moderate weather there is no difficulty in beating into Gibraltar, but against the *levante* (the local name for a strong easterly wind) it may be impossible for a small yacht to make much progress because of the steep seas kicked up by wind against current. Conversely, a strong westerly or south-westerly wind, which reinforces the current, can make it difficult for a yacht to get out from Gibraltar and into the Atlantic. In these conditions even a very slight easing of the wind strength makes an immediate and remarkable difference, and good progress may be made by hugging the Spanish or Morrocan coasts to escape the worst of the current. Fog is an occasional nuisance in the Strait and is associated with the *levante*.

The Moroccan coast tends to have stable weather from June to October, with light winds predominantly from the south-west. There will be occasional swings to the north-west or north-east. South of Essauira, the winds are mostly north-west, strengthening to 20 knots during the day and then dying off overnight. During the winter, fast-moving depressions move up from the Canaries causing periods of squalls or more prolonged gales. The weather patterns are relatively predictable and long-range forecasts are usually accurate. A long ocean swell, from the south-west or north-west, averages up to 2m (6ft) in summer and up to 5m (16ft) in winter. With the larger swells, even in light winds, the steadily shelving sea floor causes huge rollers to build and break near the shore. In stronger winds it pays to stay several miles offshore where the swell is markedly lower. The Atlantic coast of Morocco has a south-going current averaging 0.5 knots.

PASSAGES AND LANDFALLS

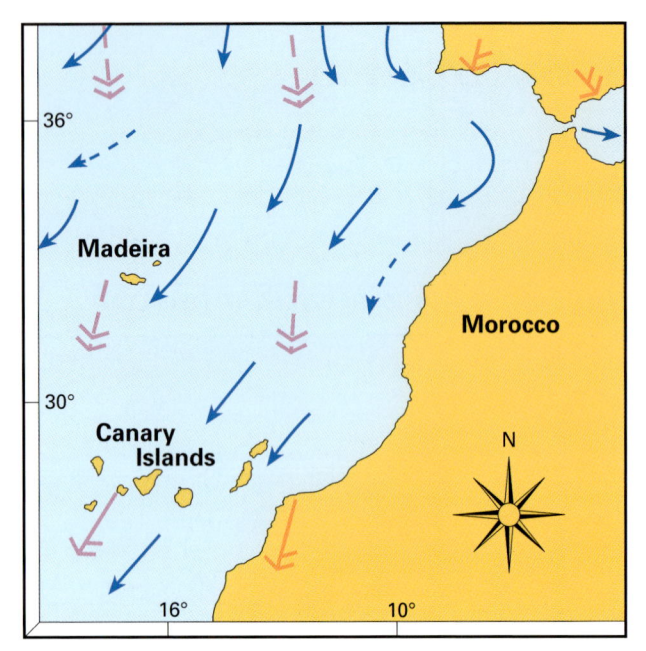

Plan 16 Prevailing winds and currents of the Atlantic coast of Morocco during October. Based on information from *The Atlantic Pilot Atlas*.

Within the Canary Islands, sudden and gusty increases in wind occur, typically around the south-west and south-east coasts of the higher islands. These 'acceleration zones' can be quite distinct and may produce an increase from less than 5 knots to 25 knots or more within a few hundred metres. A stronger than expected current or tidal flow can occur where it is accelerated as it is squeezed between islands. Madeira and the Canary Islands lie in the path of the south-westerly setting Canary Current.

Tidal range from the western Strait of Gibraltar to the Canaries and down the coast of Morocco is up to 3m (10ft), with similar timings to Gibraltar (a standard port).

PASSAGES TO AND BETWEEN THE ATLANTIC ISLANDS

Portugal or Gibraltar to Madeira

The passage from the Portuguese or southern Spanish coast towards Madeira is usually a pleasant one, often carrying north-easterly winds for the whole passage.

Madeira to the Canaries

This passage may be made at any time of the year, but the chances of increased wind and decreased visibility will be greater in the winter months. The south-going current is relatively constant. If intending to cruise the Canary Islands it makes good sense to head for Graciosa or Lanzarote. The direct passage to Santa Cruz de Las Palmas lies close to the

Cresting (RCC) moored in Sarsala, Turkey, in the eastern Mediterranean. Photo: Sally O'Riordan

Salvage Islands (Ilhas Selvagens). These pose a danger, particularly at night, as they are not well lit.

Morocco to the Canaries

Agadir is a common departure port for yachts heading the 220 miles to Lanzarote, though you are likely to be on a close reach with the prevailing wind.

Shipping lanes

A high concentration of traffic occurs in the Strait of Gibraltar. This fans out as soon as the narrowest part is passed, with the merchant shipping dividing into three main streams. One goes westward to Cape St Vincent, one coastwise to the south, and one in the general direction of Madeira and the Canaries. There will, in addition, be large numbers of fishing craft. A hundred miles from the coast, most of the traffic will be left behind, and little more will then be seen until the main north/south Atlantic shipping lane is crossed, west of the longitude of Cape St Vincent. The whole Atlantic coast of Spain, Portugal and Morocco tends to be busy with shipping and with fishing vessels.

STRAIT OF GIBRALTAR AND THE ATLANTIC COAST OF MOROCCO

Harbours in the Strait of Gibraltar

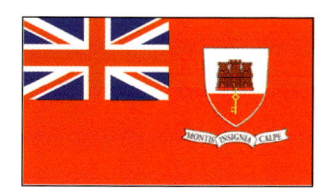

7 Gibraltar

Location:	36°8´.5N 5°22´W
Springs:	1.0m Range: 0.9m
Neaps:	0.7m Range: 0.4m
Time zone:	UT+1 (Winter) +2 (Summer)
Currency:	Gibraltar pound and pounds sterling
Tel/fax:	Country code: 350 Area code: none
Language:	English. Spanish is also widely spoken.
Emergencies:	Tel: 199

Crossroads

Gibraltar is a self-governing British colony, perched on the southern coast of Spain and overlooking the Strait of Gibraltar at its narrowest point. It is positioned at a crossroads of seas and of continents – between the Atlantic and the Mediterranean and also between Europe and Africa. The resulting population is a thorough mixture of cultures and language.

The Rock of Gibraltar, one of the Pillars of Hercules, is a spectacular peak which rears up out of the low-lying land around it, pointing towards its twin pillar near Ceuta in North Africa, which lies less than 20 miles away across the Strait. As well as being the gateway to or from the

The Rock of Gibraltar seen from Marina Bay. Photo: Lilian Duckworth

GIBRALTAR 7

PASSAGES AND LANDFALLS

Mediterranean for seafarers, it is also an important waypoint for migratory birds, including several species of birds of prey and thousands of white storks. Local residents include the Barbary partridge which is not found anywhere else on the European Mainland, as well as the famous Barbary apes. Gibraltar is a busy commercial harbour. Its marine facilities have undergone several changes in recent years and it is worth contacting the relevant operators before arrival if planning an extended stay or haul-out. It is advisable to pre-book a marina berth as it may be difficult to anchor.

> **Website**
> www.gibraltarport.com/yachting.cfm
> www.gibraltar.gov.gi

Approach

The Rock of Gibraltar is quite unmistakable from both west and east. After dark, the Aeromarine light flashes the letters GB in Morse from high on the rock itself [R 10s 405m 30M]. The sectored Europa Point light [Iso west 10s 49m 19M, Oc R 10s 15m and FR 44m 15M] is at the southern tip. The airport, which is on the low ground to the north of the Rock, is also well lit. Gibraltar Bay has deep water everywhere except for the offshore reefs on its western side, from Pta Carnero to just south of Algeciras. Depths in the area north of the airstrip shelve gradually.

Entrance

If making for one of the northern marinas, head north-east into Gibraltar Bay past the long breakwaters of the naval and commercial port. The airport runway will be seen ahead. Ocean Village sits in the eastern corner to the south of the runway. If heading for Queensway Quay Marina, pass between the south mole and the detached mole (both lit), from which the marina entrance (also lit) will be seen about 650m (0.5 miles) ahead. This entrance can be confusing if approached for the first time after dark, as two long floating pontoons produce a very distinct 'S' bend (an attempt to keep swell out).

Radio

Port control operates on VHF Channels 06, 12, 13, 14 and 16; Channel 12 is the Gibraltar Bay working channel. The marinas operate on Channel 71. The Queen's Harbour Master controls the military port on Channel 08.

Formalities

Report to one of the marina offices on arrival where all

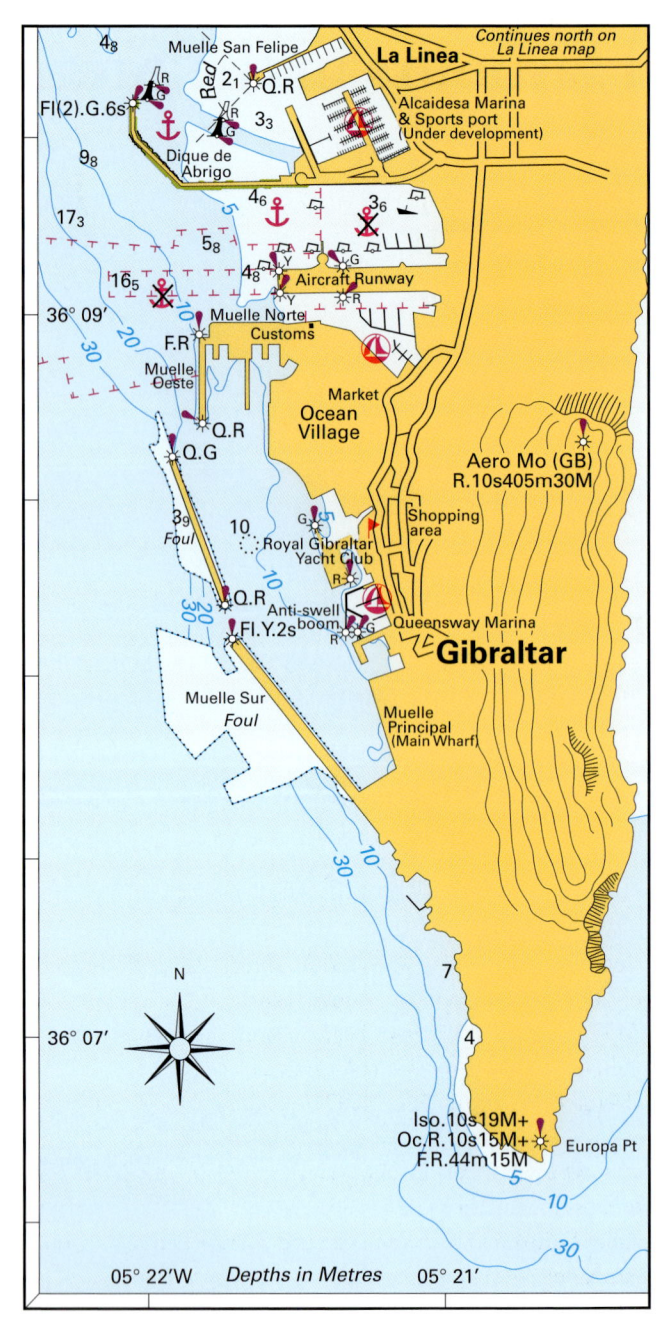

Plan 17 Gibraltar

formalities will be dealt with. The Gibraltar Port Yacht Reporting Berth closed down at the end of 2005 and responsibility for clearance of all yachts now rests with the individual yacht marinas.

Berthing and facilities

Ocean Village Marina (36° 8´.9N, 5° 21´.4W) incorporates the area once occupied by Marina Bay and Sheppard's Marinas. It has a wide range of facilities and caters for the largest super yachts.
Website: www.oceanvillage.gi/marina.html
Contact: Tel: 20073300 (24 hours)
E-mail: pieroffice@marinabay.gi

STRAIT OF GIBRALTAR AND THE ATLANTIC COAST OF MOROCCO

Leaving Gibraltar at sunrise. Photo: Richard Woods

Queensway Quay Marina (36° 8´.1N, 5° 21´.3W) is convenient for the shops in the town centre. It has a minimum depth of 3.5m (11.5ft) and can accommodate yachts up to 80m (262ft) in length. It has a range of facilities.
Contact: Tel: 44700 Fax: 44699 E-mail: qqmarina@gibnet.gi

Sheppard's Marine has a long history in Gibraltar. On going to press it is on temporary premises, providing haul out and repair facilities for six vessels up to 30 tonnes. A larger, more permanent facility is planned.
Website: www.sheppard.gi
Contact: Tel: 20075148/20077183 Fax: 20042535
E-mail: admin@sheppard.gi
or for repair workshop Tel: 20076895 Fax: 20071780
E-mail: yachtrep@gibraltar.gi

Anchorage and moorings

The possibilities of anchoring are restricted by the various marina developments as well as the prohibited zone around the airport runway. However it may still be possible to anchor north of the runway and south of the La Linea breakwater for short periods, but vessels should not be left there as they may be required to move at short notice. This anchorage is not well protected from winter storms.

Transport connections

Good bus services, including to La Linea which has ongoing connections to Spanish bus and train services and ferries to Ceuta and Tangier. There are several daily flights to the United Kingdom and Morocco. There are no flights to or from Spain.

Medical services (telephone numbers)

St Bernards Hospital	73941
Health Clinic, Casement Square	78337/77603
(Reciprocal arrangements with the British NHS)	

GIBRALTAR 7

PASSAGES AND LANDFALLS

8
La Linea
Spain

Location:	36°9′.5N 5°22′W
Springs:	1.0m Range: 0.9m
Neaps:	0.7m Range: 0.4m
Time zone:	UT+1 (Winter) +2 (Summer)
Currency:	Euro
Tel/fax:	Country code: 34 Area code: 956
Language:	Spanish
Emergencies:	Tel: 112

Moorish architecture, flamenco and fiestas

La Linea de la Concepción is an old Spanish port town just to the north of Gibraltar. It lies within the region of Andalucía which is famous for flamenco, fiestas and bullfighting. There is an old bullring in La Linea itself which has an interesting museum even if you don't feel inclined to witness a bullfight. Andalucía has several World Heritage sites which are all examples of the strong Moorish influence in its history, including the Alhambra in Granada, the Great Mosque of Cordoba and the Giralda Tower, Seville. These really are exceptional places and shouldn't be missed. There are good transport links from La Linea throughout the region.

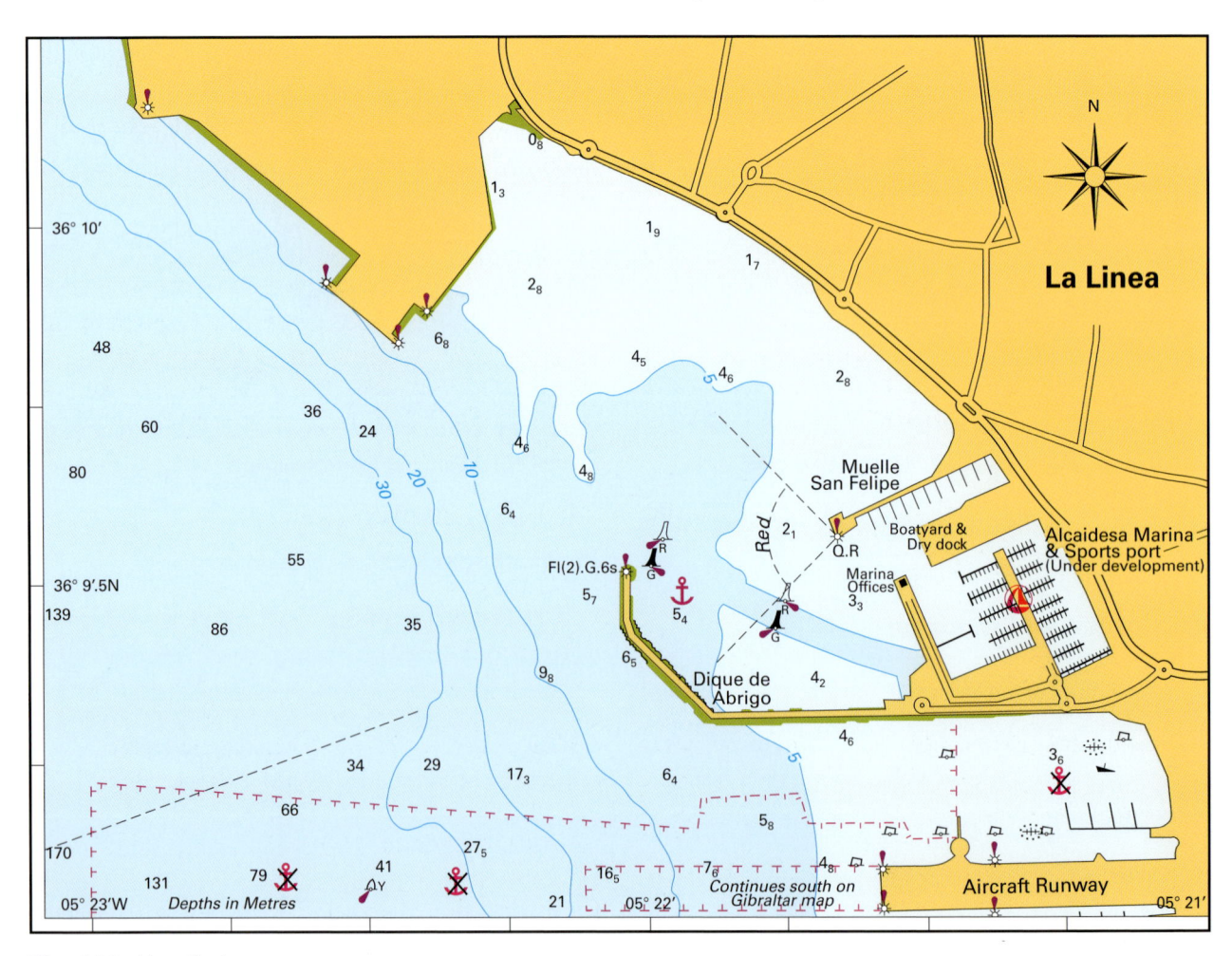

Plan 18 La Linea, Spain

Looking northwards from Gibraltar towards La Linea. The new marina development is seen top right. Photo: Lilian Duckworth

La Linea has an outdoor market every Wednesday. Local produce is abundant and delicious, including a number of fortified wines and sweet pastries. There is a pleasant quarter around the old harbour with several restaurants and bars.

Website
www.andalucia.com/province/cadiz/la-linea/home.htm

Approach and entrance

The approach to La Linea is the same as for Gibraltar. Continue north past the end of the airport runway and up the outside of the western breakwater. Turn to the east around the end of the breakwater and find a space to anchor inside the breakwater or head south-east to the marina entrance. The commercial harbour is further to the north.

Radio

VHF Channels 9 and 16.

Formalities

In theory it is not necessary for a yacht registered in the EU to report to Customs if arriving from another EU country and crewed only by EU nationals. Non-EU registered yachts should report arrival without delay. Enquire at the marina about current procedure.

Hazards

Until the marina works are completed, dredgers may be manoeuvring within the marina and anchorage, although this has not been reported to be a problem to visiting yachts.

Berthing and facilities

Marina Alcaidesa is a new Spanish marina in La Linea, due to open in March 2010. The marina will have 800 berths for yachts up to 50m (165ft) and a full range of facilities including a travel lift and hard standing, work shops and chandlery. Fuel will be available alongside a refuelling berth.
Website: www.puertodeportivoalcaidesa.es
Contact: Alcaidesa Puerto Deportivo, Avenida Príncipe de Asturias, s/n. La Linea 11315, Cádiz, Spain.
Tel: 791 040 Fax: 791 041

Anchorage

The anchorage behind the breakwater is well protected, even during westerlies when the rest of the bay becomes very choppy. Dinghy landing is available for a daily charge at the La Linea Yacht Club. It is not yet known whether there will be a dinghy dock within the marina.

Transport connections

There are good bus services, including connections to national Spanish bus and train services and ferries to Ceuta and Tangier. Jerez and Malaga airports are each one hour away. There are bus services to Gibraltar. It is possible to drive to Gibraltar but the queues can sometimes be prohibitive. An alternative is to walk across the border which entails crossing the airport runway. Don't forget your passport.

Medical services

Good local medical services including a local hospital. Services are also available in Gibraltar.

PASSAGES AND LANDFALLS

9
Ceuta
Spain

Location:	35°54′N 05°18′.5W
Springs:	1.0m Range: 0.8m
Neaps:	0.8m Range: 0.4m
Time zone:	UT+1 (Winter) +2 (Summer)
Currency:	Euro
Tel/fax:	Country code: 350 Area code: none
Language:	Spanish
Emergencies:	Tel: 112

Ancient fortifications

Ceuta is a Spanish enclave, 13 miles due south of Gibraltar's Europa Point and 27 miles east of Tangier on the Moroccan coast. The peak of Monte Hacho is thought to be a candidate as the second Pillar of Hercules, though it is modest in comparison. The view across the Strait to Gibraltar from here is worth the climb, as are the picturesque views over the old town. The strategic position of the city on the south side of the Strait has caused it to have a history of military occupation and fortification and the old walls make an interesting walk. The fort on Monte

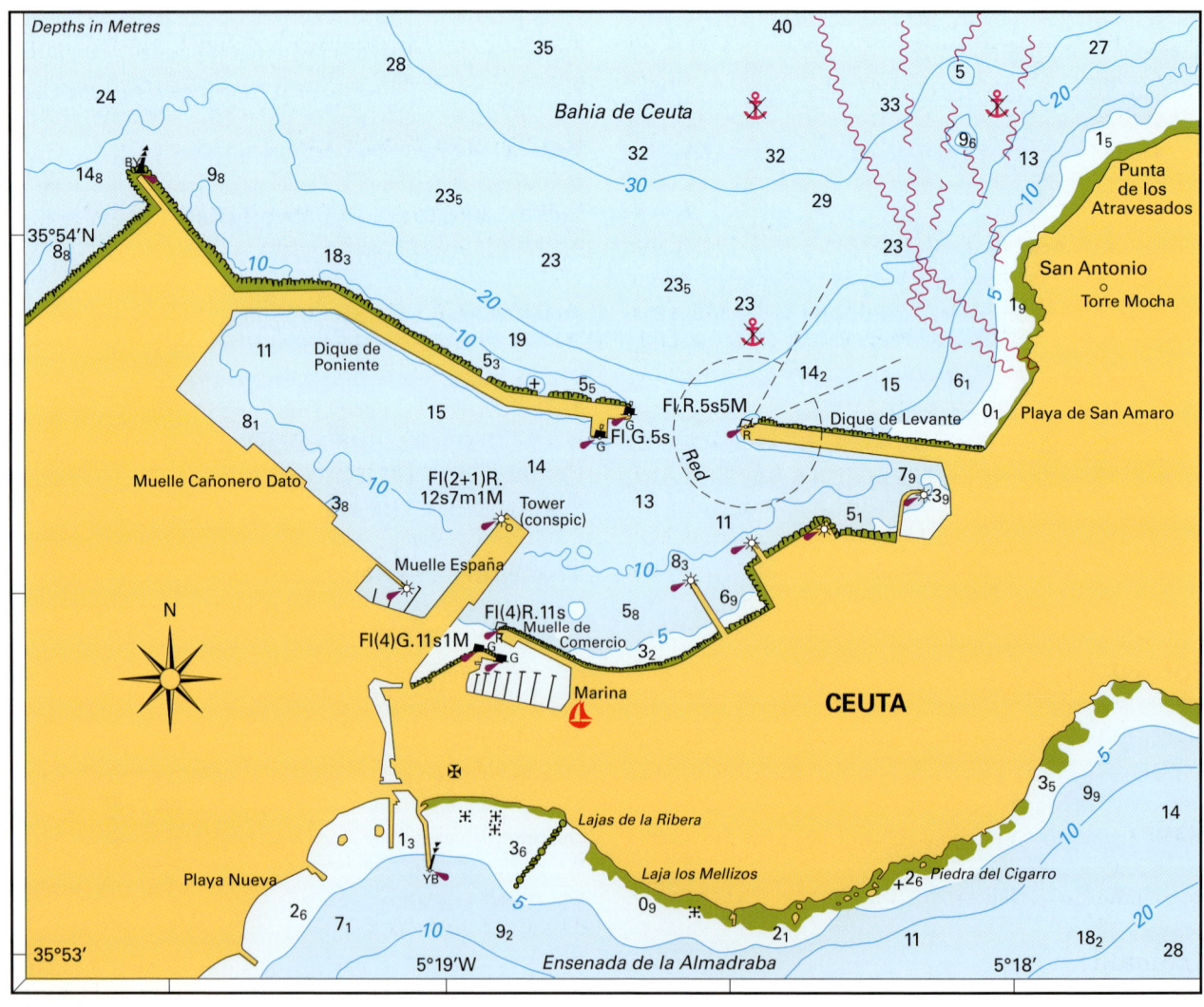

Plan 19 Ceuta, Spain

Entering Ceuta harbour looking towards the marina entrance. Hercules Marina is seen here distant far left, beneath the tower crane. Ceuta's unmistakable glass tower is on the right. Photo: Graham Hutt

Hacho is still a Spanish Army base. There is an excellent new marina, and the developing facilities for visiting yachts now rival Gibraltar.

Approach

The hills on the west side of Ceuta are high [850m (2788ft)] and very steep. To the east is a conspicuous lighthouse on the south face of Punta Almina [Fl (2) 10s 148m 22M]. Ceuta town itself is low-lying though the harbour is easily seen. There are rocks to the east of the entrance, north of Monte Hacho. The final approach has to be made from the north quadrant, so care must be taken with the set and tide in the Strait, especially in strong westerly winds. Ferries and hydrofoils from Algeciras will be seen entering and leaving the harbour throughout the day and until around midnight.

Once through the outer moles [Fl G 5s and Fl R 5s], continue south-westwards towards a large futuristic glass tower situated on the outer end of the harbour's central mole [mole end Fl (2+1) R 12s] which you leave to starboard. An ancient limestone observation tower will then be seen on the marina mole [Fl (4) R 11s]. Leave this to port to enter the marina.

Radio

Port Authority VHF Channels 16, 9, 12, 13, 14, 15 (24hrs).

Formalities

Formalities are usually observed in a friendly and relatively brief fashion – all paperwork is completed in the marina office when checking in.

Berthing and facilities

Hercules Marina has good facilities including an 8-tonne hoist and a refuelling station. Minimum depths within the marina are 2.5m (7ft).
Contact: Hercules Marina Office
Tel: 908 513738/908 502274 E-mail: mahersa@mahersa.com
Port Authority Tel: 956 502274

Marina Smir is only 10 miles to the east of Ceuta along the Moroccan coast. The marina monitors VHF Channel 09.
Website: www.portmarinasmir.com
Contact: Tel: +212 (0) 5 399772 50/51
E-mail: portmarinasmir@menara.ma

Anchoring and mooring

Anchoring is usually prohibited anywhere in the harbour.

Transport connections

The Moroccan border is 3km (2M) by bus or taxi; then a bus or taxi takes you to Tetouan. Daily ferries to Algeciras.

Medical services

Ask for advice about local medical services at Hercules Marina office.

PASSAGES AND LANDFALLS

Harbours on the Atlantic coast of Morocco

MINT TEA AND MEDINAS

The Atlantic coast of Morocco has become very popular and many yachts now call in along the route down to the Canaries. There are a number of new marinas and facilities for yachts at regular intervals down the coast. It is possible to mostly day-hop down to Agadir and to access the fascinating interior from the various ports on the way. There is now a superb new marina in Rabat on the Sale side of the river. It is very secure and well protected once you are inside, although the entrance may not be possible in strong winds. The channel has been dredged to 6m (20ft) and marked with buoys from the Atlantic inlet all the way to Bouregreg Marina. Casablanca has a new marina and is a good port of refuge in bad weather. Another excellent port of refuge in the event of a gale is Jorf Las Far. This is a huge phosphate harbour to the south of Casablanca, but yachts have been welcomed there, especially in bad weather. Tangier has been an important harbour for at least 2500 years since Carthaginian times – an ideal trading post at the gateway to the Straits. It might also seem an obvious point at which to start a cruise down the Atlantic coast of Morocco. However, visiting yachts have to take their chances amongst the fishing boats jostling for space in the harbour and facilities are limited.

This region has retained its strong and ancient cultural identity despite considerable modernisation of tourist facilities. Morocco is predominantly Muslim and the five daily calls to prayer become part of the rhythm of the day. Ramadan, the annual period of fasting, is a time when the usual opening hours and activities are curtailed during the day, but the evenings are periods of celebration and feasting. Moroccan dishes include *cous-cous* and *tajine*, and the drinking of mint tea is universal at all times of day or night. The whole coast is famous for its fishing which can involve vast nets laid out a considerable distance from the shore – a potential hazard when you are sailing down the coast.

A typical Moroccon souk. Photo: Graham Hutt

Further reference
An excellent pilotage guide to the area is *RCCPF North Africa* by Graham Hutt, Imray, Laurie, Norie & Wilson.
www.morocco.com

STRAIT OF GIBRALTAR AND THE ATLANTIC COAST OF MOROCCO

10
Mohammedia
Morocco

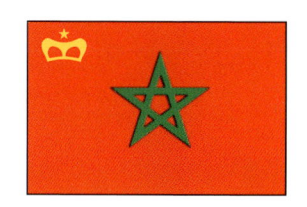

Location:	33°43′N 07°22′W
MHWS:	3.5m
MHWN:	2.7 m
Time zone:	UT
Currency:	Dirham (Dh)
Tel/fax: Language:	Country code: 00212 Arabic and French. Some English is spoken in commercial ports.

Built on liquid gold

Mohammedia is a busy commercial port with a friendly, welcoming yacht club and small marina. The port has been active since the 14th century but had gone into decline until the 1960s when prosperity returned with the development of a new oil refinery. The elegant town, pleasantly planted with trees and shrubs, has become a weekend and holiday resort for visitors from Casablanca or further afield. There has been a long association with horse breeding, training, racing and trading as evidenced by the prominent racecourse. Every July there is a popular festival of cultural and sporting events and exhibitions. Mohammedia Week is held during the first two weeks of August every year.

Website
www.morocco.com/grand-casablanca/casablanca/

Approach and entrance

Mohammedia is a large commercial port, 13 miles north of Casablanca, which can be entered in any conditions, day or night. The port lies on the south-west side of the Bay of Fedala. Cap de Fedala [Fl (2+1)] has some very visible white oil storage tanks and can be seen from 20 miles. Ships are often moored to the north-east of the harbour entrance on the offshore oil pipeline berths. An approach line is marked

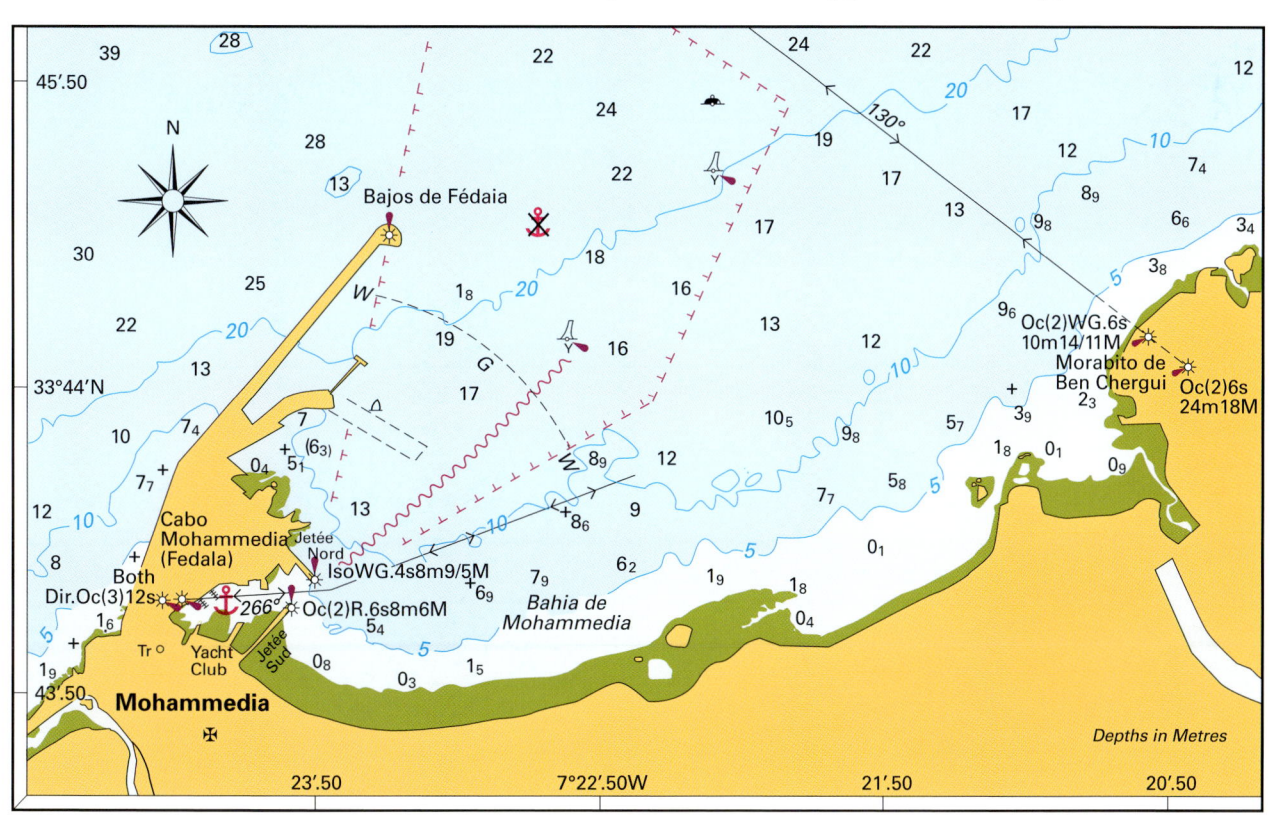

Plan 20 Mohammedia, Morocco

PASSAGES AND LANDFALLS

Mohammedia moorings looking SE towards the yacht club, which always extends a friendly welcome. Photo: Graham Hutt

by a leading line on 130°. The first leading light is on a black and white chequered pedestal [Oc (2) WG 6s]. Depths in the entry channel are greater than 5m (16ft). The entrance to the harbour is between the north breakwater, marked by a white tower with green stripes [Iso WG 4s], and the southern breakwater, marked by a white tower with red stripes [Oc (2) R 6s]. This entrance is on a leading line of two white towers with black stripes, both DirOc (3) 12s. Proceed into the inner harbour where visiting yachts are usually assisted.

Dangers

The Atlantic coast of Morocco suffers from westerly gales which shift the sandy substrate of the sea shore. Dredging does occur in the entrances to major commercial ports such as Mohammedia. Nevertheless it is wise to proceed with some caution and an eye on the depth sounder.

Radio

Port Control VHF Channel 11, Marina VHF Channel 9.

Formalities

Mohammedia is a port of entry. Officials will come to the yacht.

Berthing and facilities

The marina (33°42´.83N 7°23´.55W) has 10 visitor berths with a maximum length of 30m (98ft) and a maximum draught of 1.90m (6ft). Marine facilities include a travel lift for small yachts up to 2 tonnes and the possibility of a haul-out on a slipway.

Website: www.yachtclubdumaroc.com (French language).
Contact: Yacht Club Mohammedia, Port de Mohammedia, 20 800 Mohammedia, MAROC. Tel: 523322331
Mobile: 570467414 **Fax:** 523324977
E-mail: laser4394@menara.ma or marina.ycm@menara.ma.

Alternative marine facilities may be found in Casablanca.

Anchorage

You may be assisted to moor to the north-east of the pontoons, lying to your own anchor but with a line taken to another vessel or to the shore. Alternatively, there is usually space to anchor in 3–5m (10–16ft) just west of the pontoons.

Transport connections

There are good bus and train connections to Casablanca and elsewhere. Casablanca has an international airport.

Medical services (telephone number)

Doctor	23312480
Hospital	My Abdellah

STRAIT OF GIBRALTAR AND THE ATLANTIC COAST OF MOROCCO

Agadir
Morocco

Location:	30°25′N 09°37′W
MHWS:	3.7m
MHWN:	2.8m
Currency:	Dirham (Dh)
Time zone:	UT
Tel/fax:	Country code: 0021 Area code: 2
Language:	French and Arabic

Explore the Kasbah

Agadir is an important and busy commercial port, accessible in most conditions and offering good all round shelter. It is a popular stepping off point for the Canary Islands – Las Palmas is 353 miles distant. A new marina has been built within a waterside development which has created a very pleasant environment for visiting yachts. The marina has hosted the Transat Classique and Route du Rhum fleets in recent years. Much of old Agadir was destroyed in an earthquake in 1960 – the restored Kasbah is all that remains. The new city is modern and bustling with a produce market near to the marina and a Grand Souk to get lost in. Agadir is a good place to find a taste of the desert with a visit to the nearby tranquil oasis of Taroudannt.

Website
www.morocco.com/souss-massa-draa/agadir/

Transat Classique Fleet in Agadir. The script on the hillside beyond declares the order of allegiance: 'God, Country, King'. Photo: Agadir Maitre de Port.

PASSAGES AND LANDFALLS

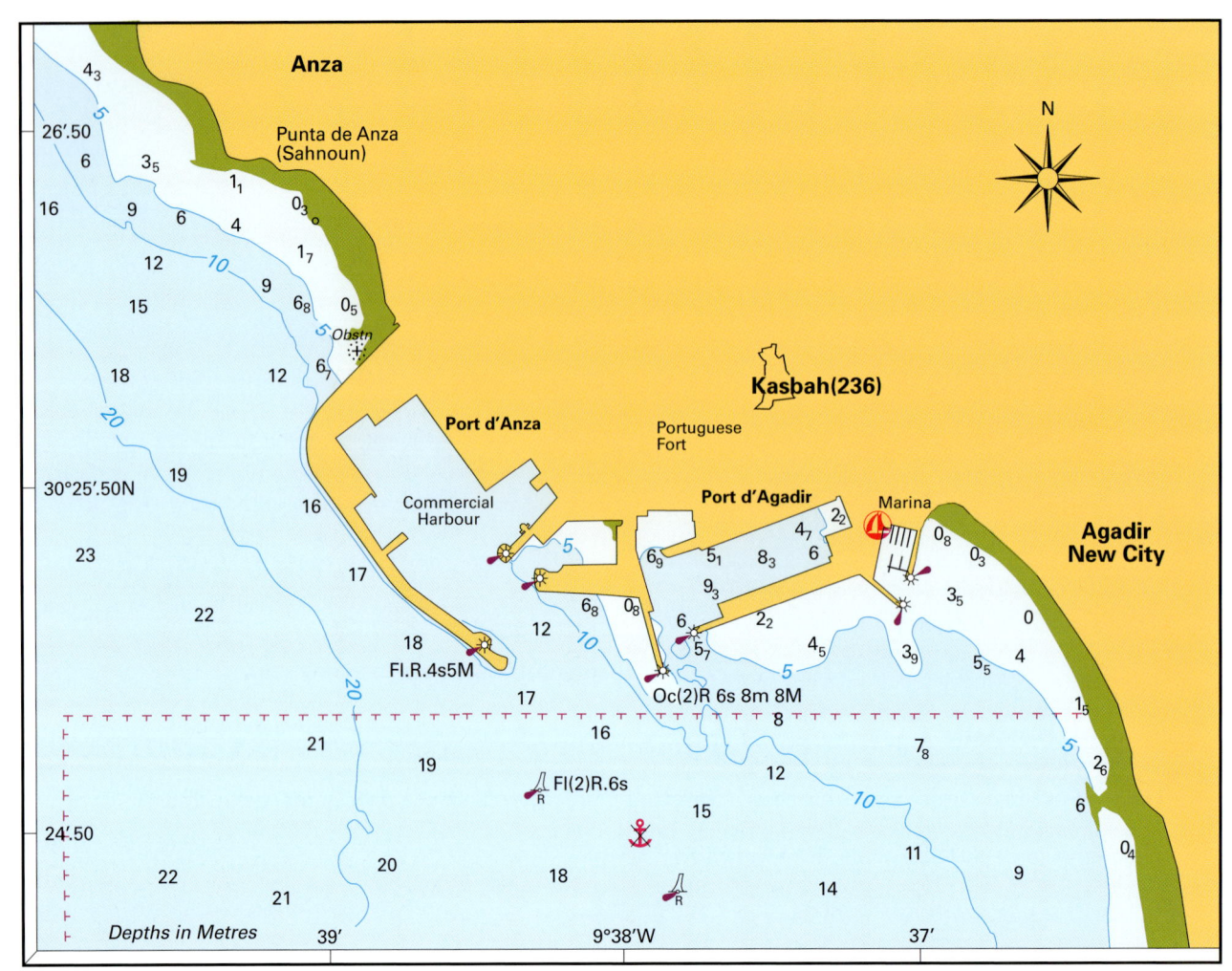

Plan 21 Agadir, Morocco

Approach and entrance

A large grain silo on the western mole of Port Anza is a prominent landmark. The southern end of the Grande Jetee breakwater [Oc (2) R 6s] marks the entrance to the Port of Agadir. Continue east towards the marina entrance which is marked with lights.

Dangers

Tunny nets may extend up to 4 miles from the shore. South of the Port of Agadir entrance, a north-east current of 2 knots has been reported. Entrance may be difficult in strong westerlies. Silting may occur, particularly after strong westerlies.

Radio

VHF Channel 09.

Formalities

Agadir is a port of entry. All formalities are conducted at the marina office on arrival.

Berthing and facilities

Marina Agadir has berths for vessels up to 30m (65ft) length and a maximum draught of 2.6m (8.5ft). Facilities include a 60-tonne travel lift and a wide range of marine services.
Website: www.port-marina-agadir.com (French)
Contact: Port de Plaisance Marina Agadir, BP 3591, Talborjt, 80 000, Agadir, Maroc.
Tel/ Fax : 528828298 Mobile: 660291701
E-mail: sogexpa@menara.ma

Transport connections

Agadir is a major centre with good travel connections and an international airport.

Medical services (telephone numbers)

| Hospital | 528841477 |
| Clinic | 528846621 |

AGADIR MOROCCO

STRAIT OF GIBRALTAR AND THE ATLANTIC COAST OF MOROCCO

Harbours in Madeira

A GARDEN OF EDEN

The Madeira group comprises Madeira Grande (Porto Santo lying some 30 miles to the north-east), the two Ilhas Desertas, and the isolated and rocky Ilhas Selvagens just over 150 miles south on the course between Funchal and the western Canaries. Only Madeira and Porto Santo are regularly visited by yachts, though both the other groups have fair-weather anchorages. Funchal was previously the primary port of call for most cruisers. However, the congested marina and roly, sometimes untenable, anchorage have resulted in Porto Santo and Marina Quinta do Lorde becoming the preferred choice for most visiting yachts.

The islands are geologically dramatic. The first glimpse of the Madeiras is likely to be of the conical peak on Porto Santo. This whole mountain is landscaped with stone wall terracing and water courses. The slopes are covered in pine

A typical levada water channel on Madeira. Photo: Harald Sammer

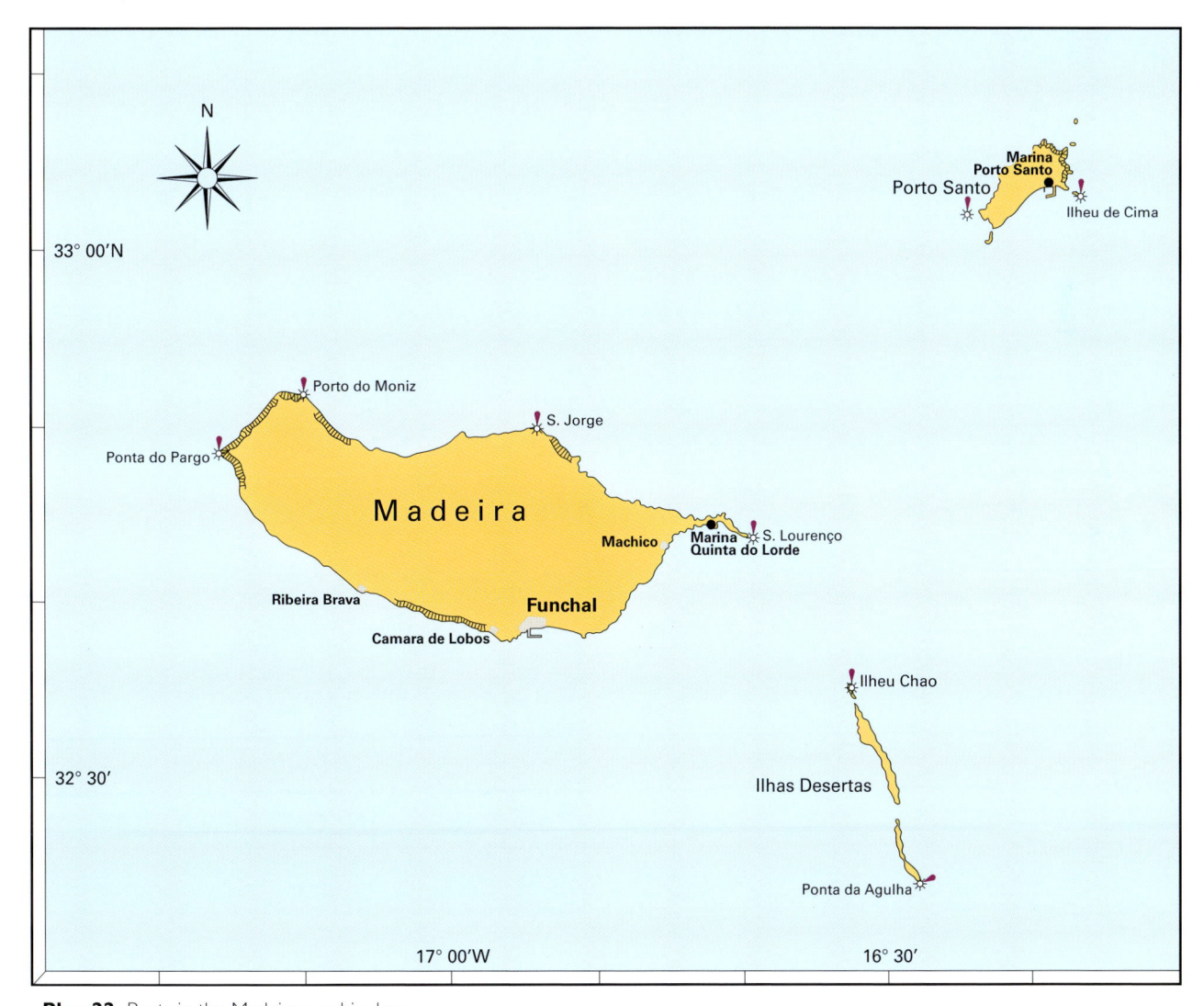

Plan 22 Ports in the Madeiran archipelago

PASSAGES AND LANDFALLS

Looking NE over the entrance to Caniçal harbour towards Quinta do Lorde with Baia da Abra beyond. Photo: Harald Sammer

trees which give off an almost intoxicating scent in the heat. Much of the rest of the island is low lying, arid and barren in summer, and fringed by a long, sandy beach. Madeira itself is spectacularly precipitous, famous for its levada water channels cut into the sides of the mountains. It is possible to walk the paths alongside some of these old canals, although many are now falling away and it is wise to be prepared for the steep and rugged terrain. Terraces all across the island produce an amazing abundance of crops including bananas and other varieties more usually associated with the tropics. The island is a botanist's delight. Funchal itself is attractively set onto the side of the island and is well worth a visit, by land if not by sea. The walk or cable car up to Monte is rewarded by the classic view down over the town. A toboggan ride back down is not for the faint hearted and you may require a glass or two of Madeira wine and a slice of Madeira honey cake to re-settle your nerves.

Fresh produce is abundant on the island and the local markets are a delight. You are bound to come across a long, pointy, evil looking fish called espada prata or black scabbard fish. These used only to be caught from Madeira, although they are now found further afield. They are deep sea fish which come closer to the surface at night when they may be caught.

WEBSITES
www.madeiraislands.travel

www.porto-santo.com

Good haul-out facilities at Porto Santo boatyard. Alternative haul-out is possible in Caniçal. Photo: Quinta do Lorde

STRAIT OF GIBRALTAR AND THE ATLANTIC COAST OF MOROCCO

12
Porto Santo
Madeira

Location:	33°03'.5N 16°19'W
Spring range:	2.2m
Neap range:	1.0m
Time zone:	UT –1
Currency:	Euro
Tel/fax:	Country code: 351 Area code: 291
Language:	Portuguese. Marina staff speak English.
Emergencies:	Tel: 112

Approach

Approaching from the north-east, Ilheu de Cima is well lit [Fl (3) 15s] and visible up to 29M. Once around this point, head up into the bay towards the harbour mouth. The marina reception berth is on the north side of the short concrete spur. Least depth alongside the floating pontoon is reported to be 3m (10ft), but there is a shallow spot off the seaward end of the spur – give this at least 15m (49ft) clearance before turning to port to come alongside.

Dangers

An underwater pipeline runs south from the southern breakwater. Entrance into the harbour may be difficult in strong south-west winds which can occur in the winter months. In these conditions a considerable surge within the harbour can strain mooring lines. The anchorage would be untenable in these conditions. Four ships' mooring buoys in the area south of the southern breakwater have now been removed.

Radio

Port Authority VHF Channel 11, 16 (call Capimarsanto), Marina VHF 09, 16.

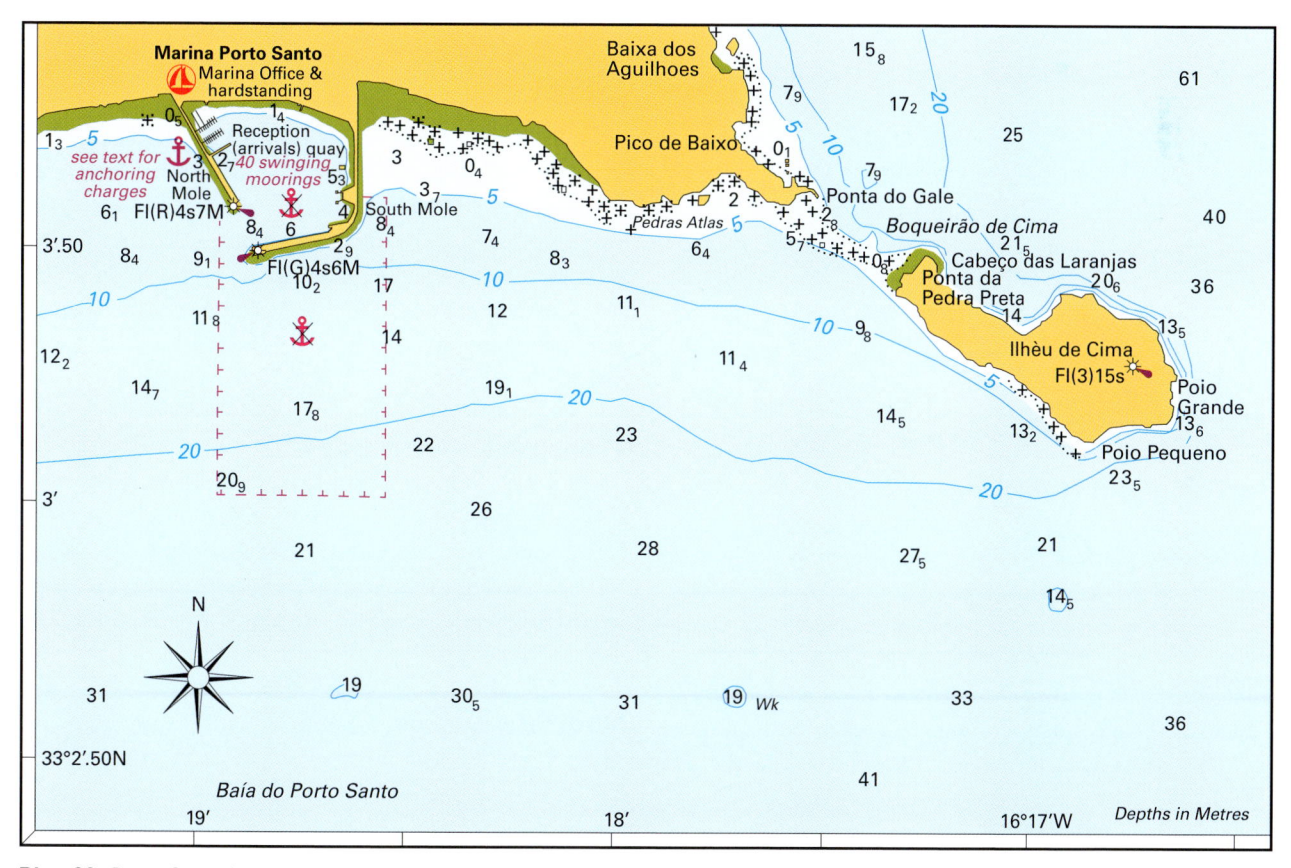

Plan 23 Porto Santo, Madeira

PASSAGES AND LANDFALLS

A gathering of cruising yachts in Porto Santo marina with the boatyard beyond. Photo: Marina Quinta do Lorde

Formalities

Madeira is part of Portugal and therefore also part of the EU. In theory, this should mean fewer formalities for EU-registered yachts arriving from another EU country, but all foreign yachts are still required to report their arrival to the relevant authorities. All paperwork is handled by the marina office and forwarded as necessary. However a visit to the Guarda Nacional Republicana (GNR) is still required if anchored off the beach. The marina office normally retains the yacht's documents until departure. Outside marina hours, visit the GNR office in the white ferry reception building, which you pass en route to the marina office. If planning to depart directly for the Ilhas Desertas or Ilhas Selvagens, the marina office can arrange for the necessary permit – allow at least 48 hours.

Berthing and facilities

Porto Santo Marina is now administered by the same company as Madeira's Marina Quinta do Lorde. It has expanded slightly to contain 140 pontoon berths for yachts up to 15m (49ft), with the possibility of larger vessels lying alongside the concrete spur in depths of around 3m (10ft). The marina sometimes becomes crowded, but advance bookings can be made by e-mail or fax. The marina offers a wide range of facilities, including haul-out and hard standing for single-hull vessels, maximum of 25 tons, 4.4m (14ft) beam, and 3m (10ft) draught.

Website: www.quintadolorde.pt Select language and marina options.
Contact: Tel: 980080 Fax: 983742
E-mail: marinaportosanto@quintadolorde.pt

Anchorage and moorings

The fore-and-aft moorings within the harbour have been removed and replaced by 40 conventional swinging moorings which are administered by the marina. Anchoring inside the harbour is no longer permitted. The traditional anchorage outside the harbour may no longer be a sensible option as daily charges, well in excess of the charges to moor within the harbour, may be levied by the Port Authority. Port Authority Tel: 982252, 982577 Fax: 982585

Transport connections

Direct flights to the European mainland. Ferries between Porto Santo and Madeira. A Spanish company, Armas Naviera (www.navieraarmas.com) runs a weekly ferry service between Portimão (Algarve), Madeira and the Canary Islands.

Medical services

Ask at Porto Santo Marina for advice about local medical services.

STRAIT OF GIBRALTAR AND THE ATLANTIC COAST OF MOROCCO

13
Marina Quinta do Lorde
Madeira

Location:	32°44′.5N 16°43′W (approach to west of entrance)
Spring range:	2.2m
Neap range:	1.0m
Time zone:	UT −1
Currency:	Euro
Tel/fax:	Country code: 351 Area code: 291
Language:	Portuguese. Marina staff speak English.
Emergencies:	Tel:112

Approach

Marina Quinta do Lorde lies about halfway along the easternmost promontory of Madeira on its south side. Leave at least half a mile clearance off the eastern end of Ponta de São Lourenço and then head westwards, remaining at least 100m (328ft) from the shore. Continue past the stratified cliffs of Baia da Abra. The marina will become visible beyond Ponta das Gaivotas; the entrance faces south-west. Visiting yachts are frequently met by the marina RIB and escorted in. Depths at the entrance are claimed to be 12m (39ft).

Dangers

In moderate north-easterly winds, heavy overfalls have been reported north-east of Ponta São Lourenço where the depth shoals from around 160m to 80m (524 to 262ft). In strong north-easterlies it would be wise to give the point at least a mile clearance. In the final approach beware of squalls 'falling off' the hills to the north, though these present no danger to yachts on pontoons.

Radio

VHF Channel 09, 16.

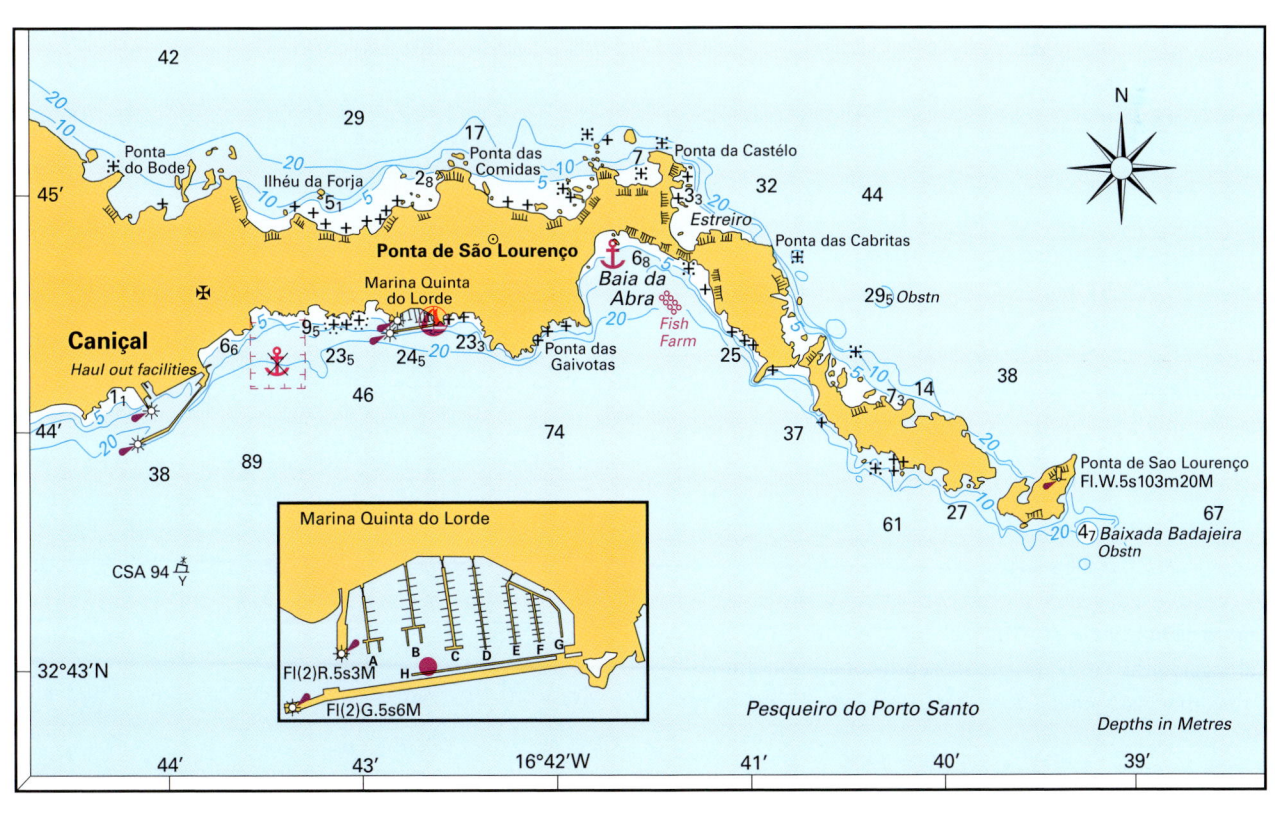

Plan 24 Marina Quinta do Lorde, Madeira

PASSAGES AND LANDFALLS

MARINA QUINTA DO LORDE
MADEIRA
13

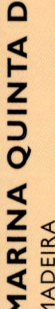

Looking down over Marina Quinta do Lorde. The visitors' berths are along the inside of the main breakwater. Photo: Harald Sammer

Formalities

Visit the marina office with all boat papers (registration documents, insurance, passports etc). The marina is now an official port of entry and forwards your information to the relevant authorities. Non-EU flagged vessels should try to give 24-hours notice of arrival, so that the correct officials can be requested to attend for clearance.

Berthing and facilities

Marina Quinta do Lorde has moorings for vessels up to 50m (165ft) and 4.5m (14ft) draught. The marina has the usual range of facilities.

Boatyard facilities and a 200-tonne travel lift are available at the nearby boatyard in Caniçal and can be booked through the marina.
Website: www.quintadolorde.pt and select language and marina options.
Contact: Tel: 969607 Fax: 960066
E-mail: marina@quintadolorde.pt

Anchorage and moorings

Baia da Abra, just to the east of Punta das Gaivotas, is a dramatic anchorage in settled weather. Foul ground, which poses an obvious threat to anchors, has been reported in the western part of the bay in depths over 10m (33ft). Right under the steep cliffs to the east and north-east the ground is clear and the holding said to be excellent.

The anchoring fees mentioned under Porto Santo may also apply to the Baía da Abra.

Transport connections

The marina is about six miles from Madeira International Airport with direct flights to the European mainland. Buses to Funchal take about two hours, but the trip is a scenic experience in itself. The Funchal bus also continues east to Baia da Abra. The marina operates a daily shuttle bus to Machico (or Caniçal) for shopping. Ferries operate between Porto Santo and Madeira. A Spanish company, Armas Naviera (www.navieraarmas.com) runs a weekly ferry service between Portimão (Algarve), Madeira and the Canary Islands.

Medical services

Ask for advice about local medical services at Marina Quinta do Lorde.

118

STRAIT OF GIBRALTAR AND THE ATLANTIC COAST OF MOROCCO

Harbours in the Canaries

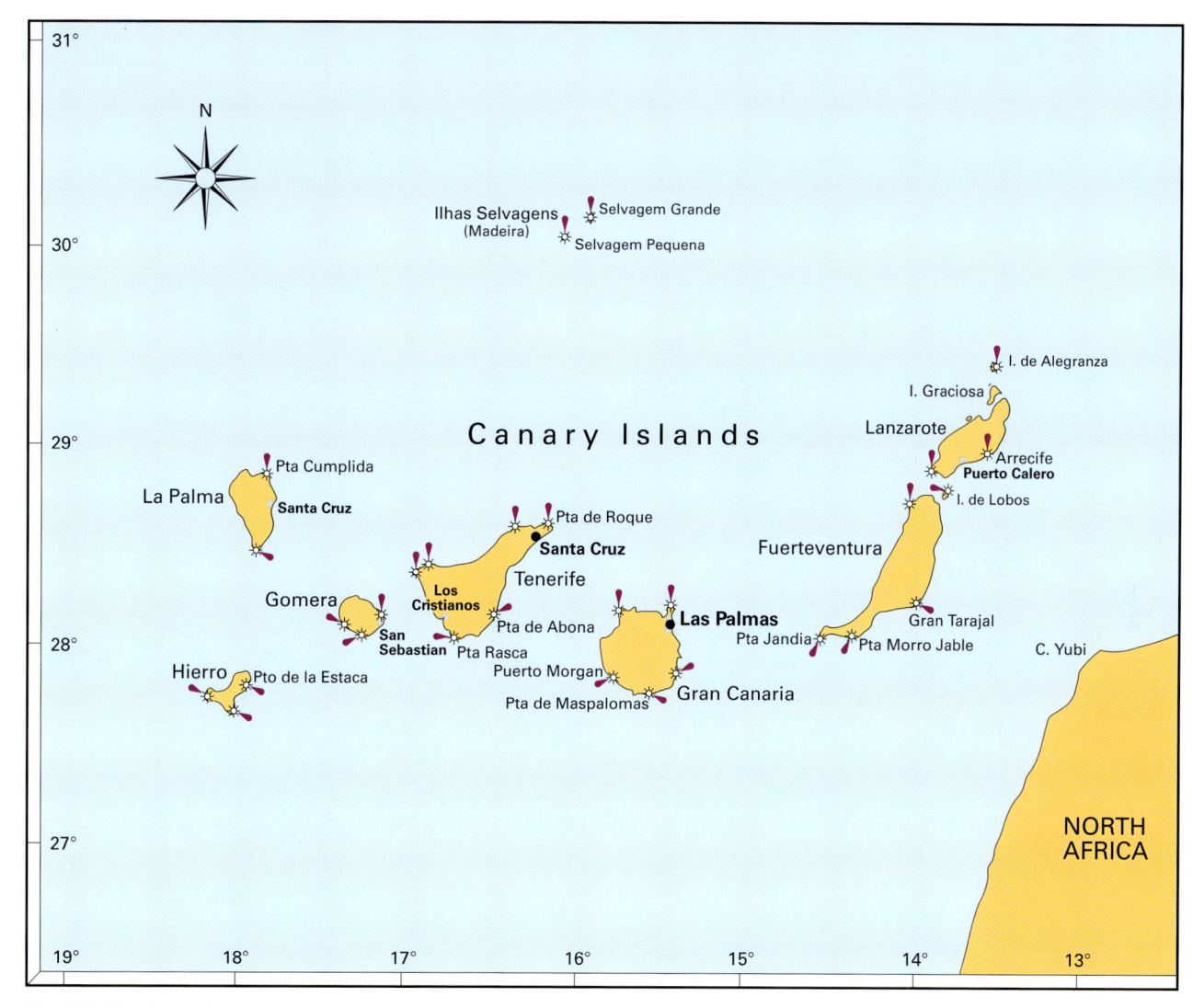

Plan 25 The Canary Islands

Rally mania

The Canaries are a popular cruising ground and pressure on facilities is intense, especially in the autumn. The annual ARC rally leaves from Las Palmas, Gran Canaria, which becomes very crowded in late October and early November in the run up to the start. If you want a marina berth during this period it is very advisable to book in advance.

Selected ports

Puerto de la Luz at Las Palmas de Gran Canaria and Marina Atlantico at Santa Cruz de Tenerife are the chosen ports for this guide because they are close to major cities with access to every facility for body and boat in preparation for the Atlantic crossing. But these are by no means the only harbours worth visiting, nor are they the only places to stock

The ARC fleet assembles in Las Palmas before the start of the 2008 rally. Photo: Graham Adam

PASSAGES AND LANDFALLS

Looking northwards from Lanzarote towards the harbour at La Sociedad on Graciosa. Photo: Mike Robinson

up or work on the boat. There are a wide variety of harbours and anchorages throughout the islands which are an intriguing cruising ground with many contrasts of scenery. If your pre-conceptions are all mass-tourism and beach resorts you will be amazed by what the islands have to offer.

Born of volcanoes

It is logical, and popular, to make a landfall at Graciosa or Lanzarote as the start to a cruise through the islands. In settled conditions, the bay at the south western tip of Graciosa is a delightful landfall anchorage. A walk to the top of the red hill overlooking the anchorage may cause you to ask 'How did all these shells get up here?' The realisation that they were once on the seabed, and that the ground has been thrust upwards by volcanic action, may be the start of a geological adventure which the Canary Islands inspire. La Sociedad has gently developed over the years. It used to be a harbour for the ferry and the fishing co-operative, but it now has its own marina with a few facilities for visiting yachts.

There are several good anchorages and marinas down the east and south coasts of Lanzarote. But don't leave this island without exploring the fantastic and extreme volcanic landscapes inland. Over a very long time the people of the island have worked with the laval rock to harvest water and nurture their crops by building countless numbers of terraces of little planting pits protected by semi-circular walls of laval rock. These structures encourage the formation of dew which then runs down to sustain the plants. Where the terraces have fallen into disrepair the prickly pears have taken over. The laval rocks have also inspired some amazing architecture which is rightly celebrated across the island. The influence of the artist César Manrique abounds.

Sahara dust

Fuerteventura is a natural progression from Lanzarote with many places to stop along the way, although yachts on a tight schedule tend to head straight across to Gran Canaria. This factor, together with the relatively small population ashore,

Extreme cultivation methods on Lanzarote. Photo: Mike Robinson

Sometimes the rain is red with Saharan dust which can cover the decks. This phenomenon is occasionally experienced as far west as the Caribbean. Photo: Mike Robinson

makes Fuerteventura a more tranquil island. The landscape is mostly barren desert with miles of sandy beaches; the sand, blown from Africa, is sometimes thick in the air.

Departure points

Beyond Gran Canaria and Tenerife are the smaller islands of Palma, Gomera and Hierro. Of the three, the marina at San Sebastian on Gomera is the most popular as a final port of call before departing for the Cape Verdes, West Africa or across the Atlantic. It is no longer permissible to anchor in the harbour. San Sebastian de la Gomera was the departure point for Columbus and his connection with the town continues to be celebrated. Relief from the dry heat of the coastal region can be found by taking a scenic bus trip across the island, up towards the central peak where pine clad slopes are often shrouded in cloud.

Hazards

One significant hazard to cruisers of the Canary Islands is the frequency, speed and merciless behaviour of the inter-island ferries. This can be particularly alarming in the approaches to some of the harbours, but you are just as likely to feel threatened by them in the open water between the islands. It is advisable to steer clear of the ferry routes as much as possible and to stay alert to their sudden arrival or departure through harbour entrances.

Unlit or abandoned *cayucos*, used by migrants attempting to reach the Canary Islands from Africa, constitute a serious hazard after dark. Many are reported on Navtex but many more go unreported. They can be 15m (49ft) long but may be low in the water or even semi-submerged.

Spanish port tax

In theory, all vessels visiting Spanish waters (including the Canaries) are liable to pay 4 euros per sq m (LOA x beam) in annual tax, which equates to 192 euros for a typical cruising yacht measuring 12m x 4m (39ft x 13ft). 20 per cent of this is payable on first entering a Spanish harbour, with a further 20 per cent due at ten day intervals until, after 50 days, the full tax – which is understood to cover port and light dues – has been paid. In the event that this charge is made, it is clearly essential to keep all receipts.

Marina Rubicon, Lanzarote. Photo: Graham Adam

PASSAGES AND LANDFALLS

14
Puerto de la Luz
Las Palmas de Gran Canaria

Location:	28°07´.7N 15°25´.4W
Springs:	2.4m Range: 2.1m
Neaps:	1.8m Range: 0.8m
Time zone:	UT
Currency:	Euro
Tel/fax:	Country code: 34 Area codes: 928 (Lanzarote, Fuerteventura and Gran Canaria) or 922 (Other islands)
Language:	Spanish. English is widely spoken.

ARC start

Puerto de la Luz becomes very crowded in the run up to the start of the ARC rally. All the various marine services also become booked up. If you plan to be in Las Palmas during this period it is necessary to make early bookings and a deposit may be payable. At other times it is usually possible to find a berth and to access services. Many cruisers choose to hire a car, sometimes sharing the hire between two or more yachts. The benefit of this is that it is much easier to do a big hypermarket stock-up. It is also a good way to explore the island which has a varied and delightful interior, well away from the marina crowds.

ARC yachts lined up along the pontoons in Muelle Deportivo de Las Palmas. Photo: Graham Adam

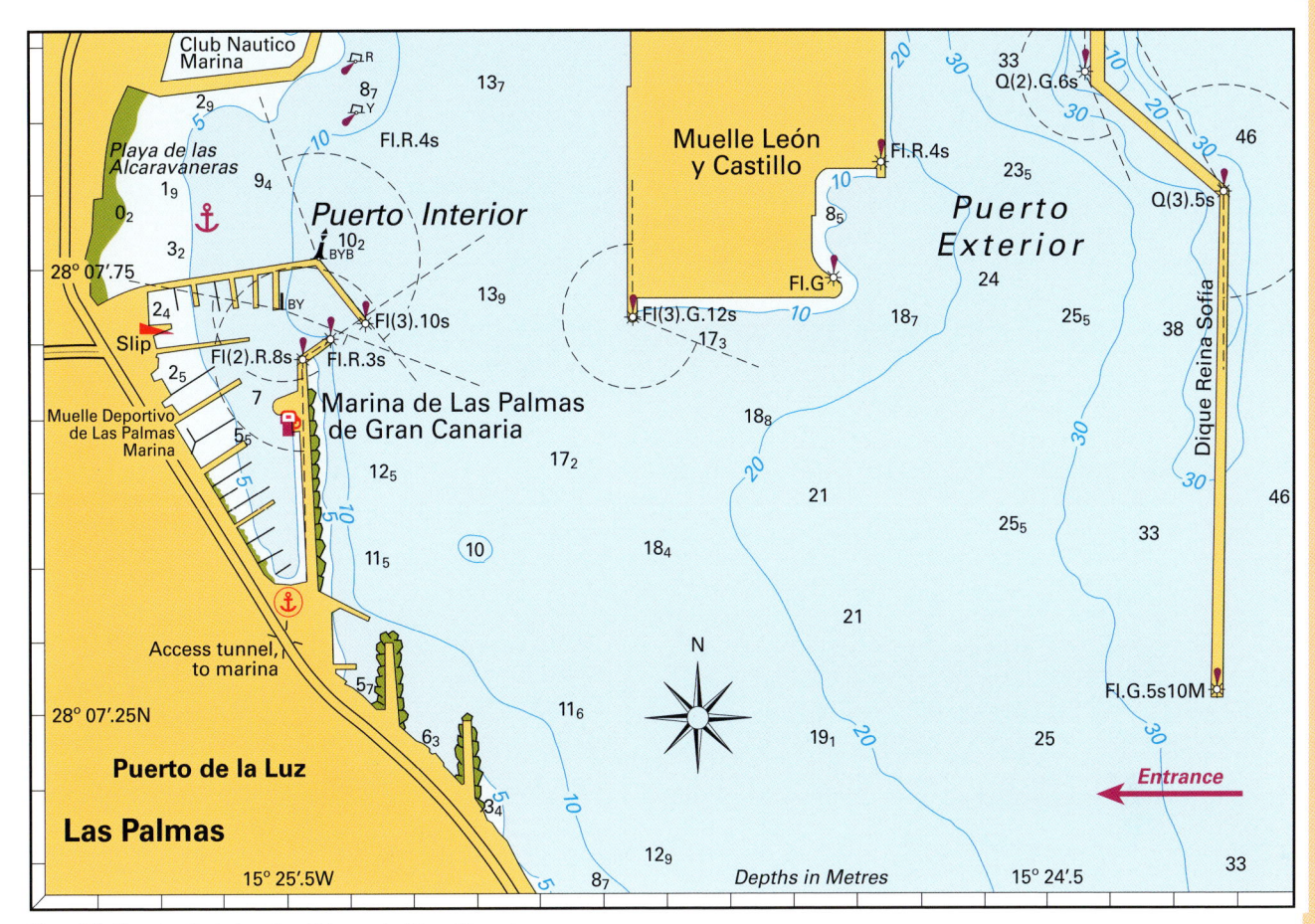

STRAIT OF GIBRALTAR AND THE ATLANTIC COAST OF MOROCCO

Plan 26 Puerto de la Luz, Las Palmas de Gran Canaria

Website
www.grancanaria.com/index4.html

Approach and entrance

The solid buildings of Las Palmas are unmistakable for many miles offshore. Head for a point half a mile south-west of the head of the Dique Reina Sofia (the main outer breakwater), keeping a good watch for commercial traffic, then turn north-west for the outer head of the marina breakwater. The Dique de Reina Sofia, has been extended south to 28°07´.3N, 15°24´.3W, and work started on land reclamation at its root. From the north, in order to avoid the harbour works detailed above, remain east of 15°23´.5W until south of 28°07´N and able to head directly for the marina entrance. If entering the harbour at night some confusion can arise because the entrance to the marina passes between two red lights. As well as the red port hand light on the northern tip of the eastern mole, a red light also marks the end of the northern breakwater – a logical necessity for ships entering the inner harbour, but confusing to small boat owners who are looking for the marina entrance. A new reception pontoon has been placed north of the Texaco fuel berth, with the relocated marina office nearby.

Puerto de Mogan, Gran Canaria. Photo: Mike Robinson

Dangers

The marina entrance shallows around the northern end of the east mole. Stay closer to the northern mole and keep an eye on the depth sounder.

Radio

Call Port Control on VHF Channel 16 or 12 (24 hours). Marina Channels 16 and 09 (0800–1400, Monday to Saturday).

PUERTO DE LA LUZ
LAS PALMAS DE GRAN CANARIA
14

PASSAGES AND LANDFALLS

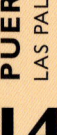

Non-ARC yachts gathered in the anchorage at Las Palmas. Photo: Graham Adam

Berthing and facilities

Muelle Deportivo de Las Palmas Marina is administered by the Port Authority and accepts yachts up to 45m (147ft) and 12m (39ft) draught. Access to a wide range of facilities includes a 60-tonne travel lift.
Website: www.palmasport.es
Marina contacts: Joaquín Blanco Torrent s/n, 35005, Las Palmas de Gran Canaria. Tel: 234960 Fax: 232378
E-mail: marina@palmasport.es

Anchorage

Anchoring is permitted north of the marina. Holding is said to be good, but a trip line might be advisable. The marina extensions have improved the shelter in the anchorage. A number of square concrete fish-cages are normally moored in the southern part of the anchorage, close to the marina's north mole. In theory they should display a low-powered yellow light at each corner, but these are reported to be unreliable and the structures pose an obvious hazard if manoeuvring at night. The anchorage is now bounded on its northern side by the private marina of the Real Club Nautico de Gran Canaria. A gap must be left clear to the south of the new marina wall to allow access to and from the beach, Playa de las Alcaravaneras.

Formalities

Report to the marina office during office hours (0700–1400 daily) with the ship's papers and passports. The marina office is now located on the marina's east mole, just north of the Texaco fuelling pontoon. Ship's papers and crew passports are held until final departure. Crew members who are leaving the Canaries by air must take their passports to the immigration office (Policia de Frontera, Tel: 264431) located at the eastern end of the main Port Authority building in the port compound.

Transport connections

Jetfoil to Fuerteventura and Tenerife plus inter-island car ferry. International airport 16km (10 miles) south of Las Palmas.

Medical services

There are several good health centres and hospitals on the islands, including vaccination clinics.

STRAIT OF GIBRALTAR AND THE ATLANTIC COAST OF MOROCCO

15
Marina Atlantico
Santa Cruz de Tenerife

Location:	28°27'.5N 16°14'.5W	
Springs:	2.4m	Range: 2.1m
Neaps:	1.8m	Range: 0.8m
Time zone:	UT	
Currency:	Euro	
Tel/fax:	Country code: 34 Area codes: 928 (Lanzarote, Fuerteventura and Gran Canaria) or 922 (Other islands)	
Language:	Spanish. English is widely spoken.	

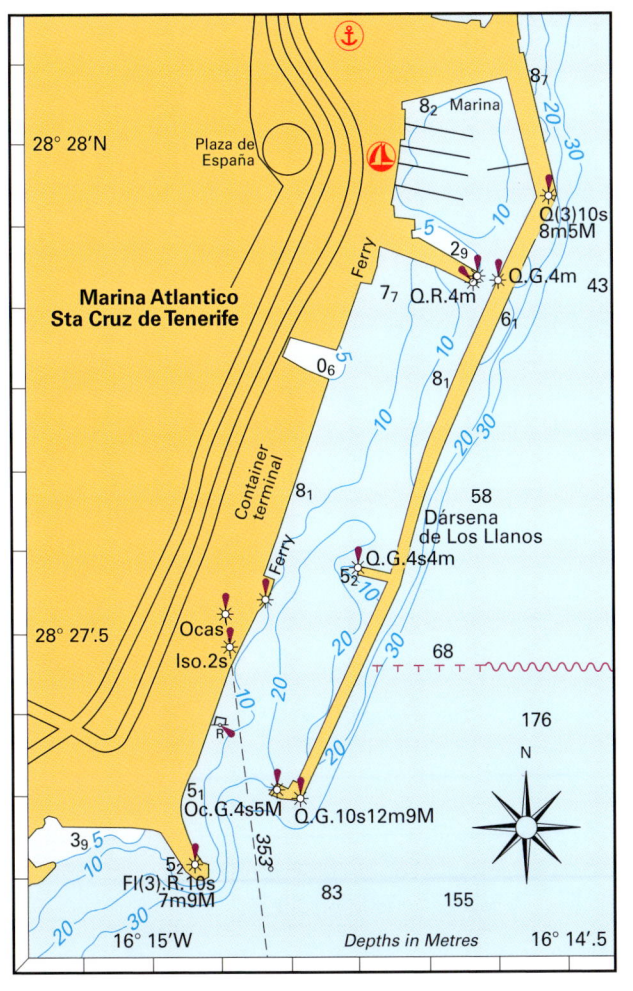

A film set

The most striking thing about Tenerife is the 3717m (12,194ft) peak of the El Teide volcano which is often clad in snow. A climb up the mountain, by any means, takes you through a progression of landscapes and panoramic views. The weird volcanic scenery towards the top has become a favourite film set for 'sci-fi' film makers. The northern end of the island is green and productive. The botanical gardens, founded in 1788, have a wonderful array of plants from all over the world. Santa Cruz has some lovely old buildings and pleasant promenades.

Websites
www.tenerife.com/
www.tenerifeguide.org/tenerife-travel-guide.asp

Approach and entrance

The Dársena de los Llanos lies at the southern end of the harbour complex, less than 1 mile north of the chimneys and fuelling berths of Puerto Caballo. Its entrance opens almost due south, with leading lights on 353°. The basin is used by commercial shipping. Contact Tenerife Port Control on VHF Channel 12 on approach.

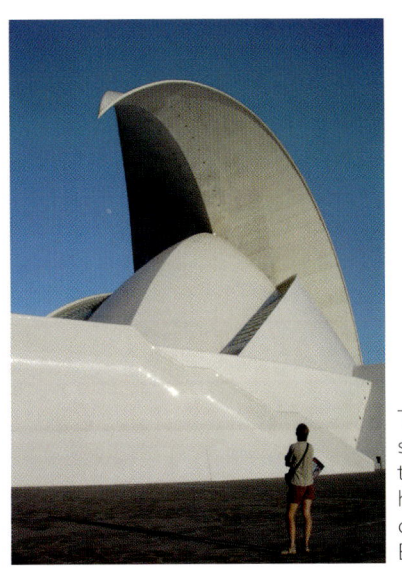

Plan 27 Marino Atlantico, Santa Cruz de Tenerife

The auditorio is a striking landmark near the entrance to the harbour at Santa Cruz de Tenerife. Photo: Barry Duckworth

125

PASSAGES AND LANDFALLS

Looking NE from the ferry terminal towards the entrance to Marina Atlantico. A yacht is leaving the marina. Photo: Barry Duckworth

Radio

VHF Channel 09, 16 (monitored 24 hours), Port Control on VHF Channel 12.

Berthing and facilities

Marina Atlantico (also known as **Marina de Santa Cruz**) is very convenient for the city. During the high season (September to December) it is advisable to reserve a berth in advance. Facilities include a 70-tonne travel lift.
Contact: Muelle de Enlace, Dársena Comercial de Los Llanos, 38180 Santa Cruz de Tenerife. Tel: 292184
Fax: 247933 E-mail: marinadelatlantico@infocanarias.com

The older Marina Tenerife, situated in the Dársena Pesquera to the north (Tel: 591247), seldom has space for visiting yachts.

Boatyard work is available at Varaderos Anaga or the nearby fishermen's co-operative.
Contact: E-mail: varaderosanaga@nauticaydeportes.com

Formalities

The port office is north of the marina, overlooking the Dársena Sur (Tel: 605472, Fax: 605481). Visit with the usual ship's papers and passports. On departure, contact Tenerife Port Control on VHF Channel 12 for permission to leave the harbour; this is because of shipping manoeuvres.

Transport connections

International and inter-island airports with regular 'feeder' bus services. There are buses around the island and ferry services to the other islands.

Medical services

There are several good health centres and hospitals on the islands, including vaccination clinics.

Yacht *Tagora*, in Santa Cruz de Tenerife, prepares for a second Atlantic crossing at the end of a circumnavigation via Panama and Suez. Photo: Lilian Duckworth

11 Cape Verde Islands, Senegal and The Gambia

| 16 | Porto Grande, Mindelo, Cape Verdes | 130 |

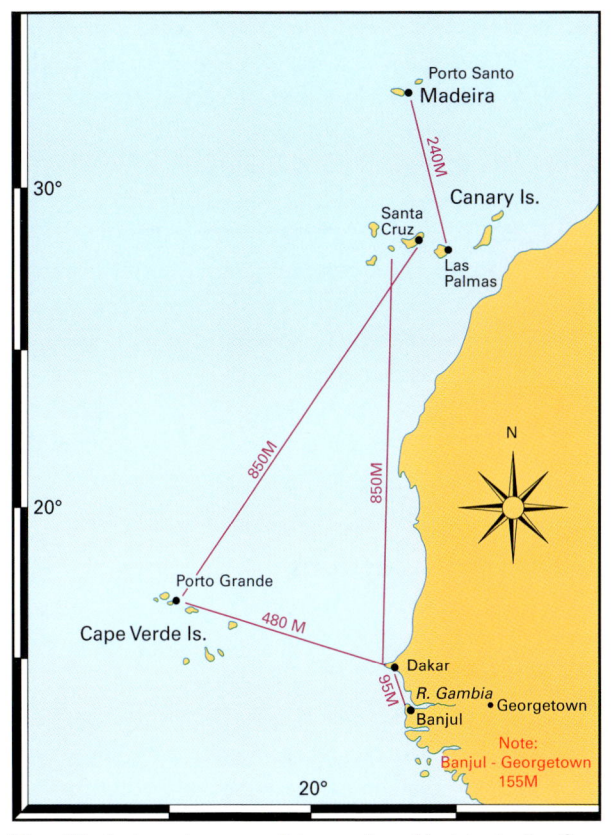

Plan 28 Ports and passage distances from Madeira to the Cape Verdes and West Africa

Making landfall on the Cape Verdes in good conditions. Visibility may be drastically reduced when the *harmattan* is blowing. Photo: Andy O'Grady

There are a number of possible routes and destinations on leaving the Canaries. The ARC fleet and many others take a relatively direct route across the Atlantic to St Lucia or one of the other Caribbean islands. Even on this route, it usually pays to head southwards to start with to pick up the trade winds, which makes the Cape Verdes an obvious port of call if you are not in a rush. For those who have a spirit for more adventure and who are happy to delay their crossing still further, a cruise to Senegal and The Gambia, either direct from the Canaries or via the Cape Verdes, will be a memorable part of an Atlantic voyage.

REGIONAL WEATHER AND PASSAGE TIMINGS

Canaries to the Cape Verde Islands

Both current and winds are likely to be favourable, with the latter becoming more reliable as you progress south. In the latitude of the Cape Verde Islands, the north-east trades blow all year round, but they are stronger in the winter when, funneled between the higher islands, they can reach gale force. In the summer months there are periods of light and variable winds and even some from south or south-east. There is no hurricane risk, though most of the storms that reach the Caribbean originate just to the west of Cape Verde. Air and sea temperatures are fairly constant throughout the year.

The *harmattan* is probably the mot significant weather disturbance to which the islands are subjected, mainly in the winter months. The *harmattan* wind blows off the African continent south of about 20°N and can carry dust up to 1000 miles offshore, occasionally right across the Atlantic Ocean to the Caribbean, dramatically reducing visibility and coating everything with a fine layer of red. At sea, whether or not visibility appears to be bad, if the wind is above 20 knots *harmattan* conditions should be suspected. Islands or other vessels may materialise out of an apparently firm horizon when only a few miles distant, so it is important to keep a good look-out.

The south-west-setting Canary Current swings further westwards by the latitude of the Cape Verde Islands. In summer, the influence of the Equatorial Counter Current may cause south- or south-east setting eddies between 10°N and 15°N, but by November or December these have usually retreated south of 10°N. Tidal range is only about 0.8m in

PASSAGES AND LANDFALLS

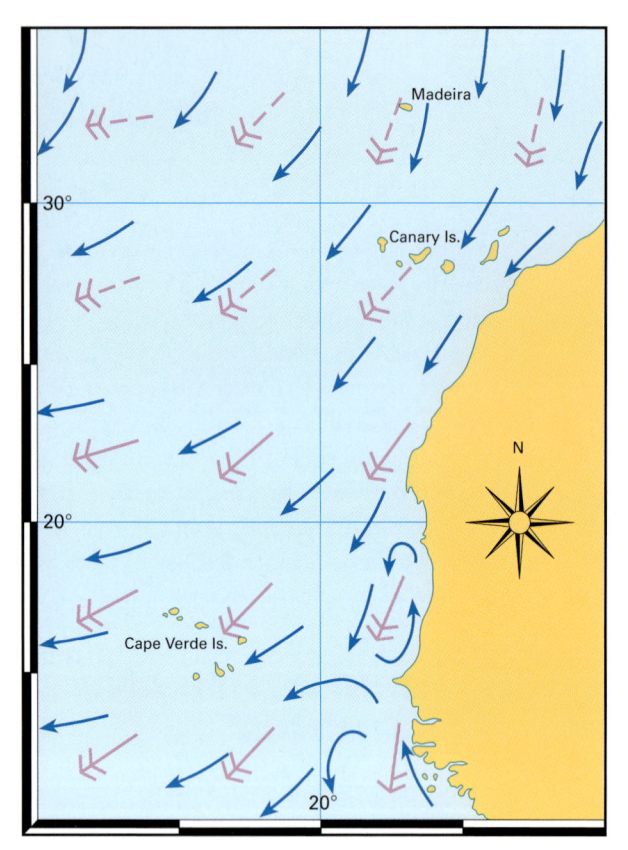

Plan 29 Prevailing winds and currents off the coast of West Africa, 10°N to 35°N, during November. Based on information from *The Atlantic Pilot Atlas*.

the Cape Verdes, so tidal streams are generally slight. However, combined with ocean currents, and when constricted between the islands, the flow may reach over 3 knots.

Cape Verde Islands to Senegal

Senegal has earned a good reputation with visiting yachtsmen. The route from Cape Verde to Dakar is so well recognised that one of the transatlantic rallies sails this way. With the prevailing north-east wind this should be an easy reach, although more easterly winds can render the passage more difficult. If your aim is to visit Dakar but not The Gambia or the Casamance it may be wise to sail first to Senegal and then call in at the Cape Verdes on your way west.

Canaries to Senegal

Once clear of the Canaries, this is likely to be a fast downwind passage, possibly even a thrilling rollercoaster ride. It pays to stay around 100 miles off Cap Blanc, partly to avoid fishing activity, but also because winds tend to die down overnight closer to the shore. This coast is rich with sea life because of an upthrust of nutrients from the ocean floor, and it is common to be escorted by huge pods of dolphins and other marine mammals. The high nutrient levels are also illustrated by extraordinary levels of phosphorescence which turn the nocturnal activities of the dolphins into an unforgettable light show.

West Africa – Senegal and The Gambia

Most of the time, the weather in West Africa is fairly kind to small craft. The traditional cruising season for the region is November to May when the doldrums, which bring the rain, humidity and storms, are further south. During this period, the trade winds are at their strongest and the weather is cooler and drier. The harmattan occurs at intervals from November to March and can cause the visibility along the coast to be very poor. This makes traditional navigation difficult in a region where the coastline is low lying and lacking natural features. In contrast the visibility becomes spectacular in the rains, especially after a storm. The rainy season brings line squalls to the area. These may contain very strong winds, but are usually of short duration. They can normally be seen in time to reef.

When the trade winds are blowing strongly, there is an associated swell which, though uncomfortable, does not create a problem unless you are attempting to enter or leave a shallow river estuary.

Navigational aids

Throughout the Cape Verdes and down the coast of West Africa, maintenance of navigation aids is poor and even the major lights cannot be relied upon. Buoys may still be in position but not be lit. It is also common for the positions of buoys to change. Do not trust even the most recent charts to be entirely accurate.

Cape Verdean mural. Photo: Andy O'Grady

CAPE VERDE ISLANDS, SENEGAL AND THE GAMBIA

The Cape Verde Islands

The Cape Verdes are becoming increasingly popular as a holiday destination. They offer an almost unique opportunity to visit a successfully developing, independent African nation with a distinct culture and friendly people. There is plenty of cruising to be had within the islands and not every overseas boat comes here in November and December only as part of a transatlantic passage. Some come earlier in the year to spend the summer cruising around the 14 islands of the group. There are only three ports of entry (or departure) for the nation: Mindelo on São Vicente, Palmeira on Ilha do Sal and Porto da Praia (the capital) on Santiago. If cruising in the islands, it would make most sense to arrive at Palmeira which is the most windward port and carry on from there, probably to the south islands first and then reaching back to the north western group to end up at Mindelo.

Further reference
The islands are well covered in *Atlantic Islands* by Anne Hammick, Imray, Laurie, Norie & Wilson.
The Lonely Planet Guide is very useful.
www.caboverde.com
www.capeverdeinfo.org.uk
www.travelguide2capeverde.co.uk
www.worldtravelguide.net

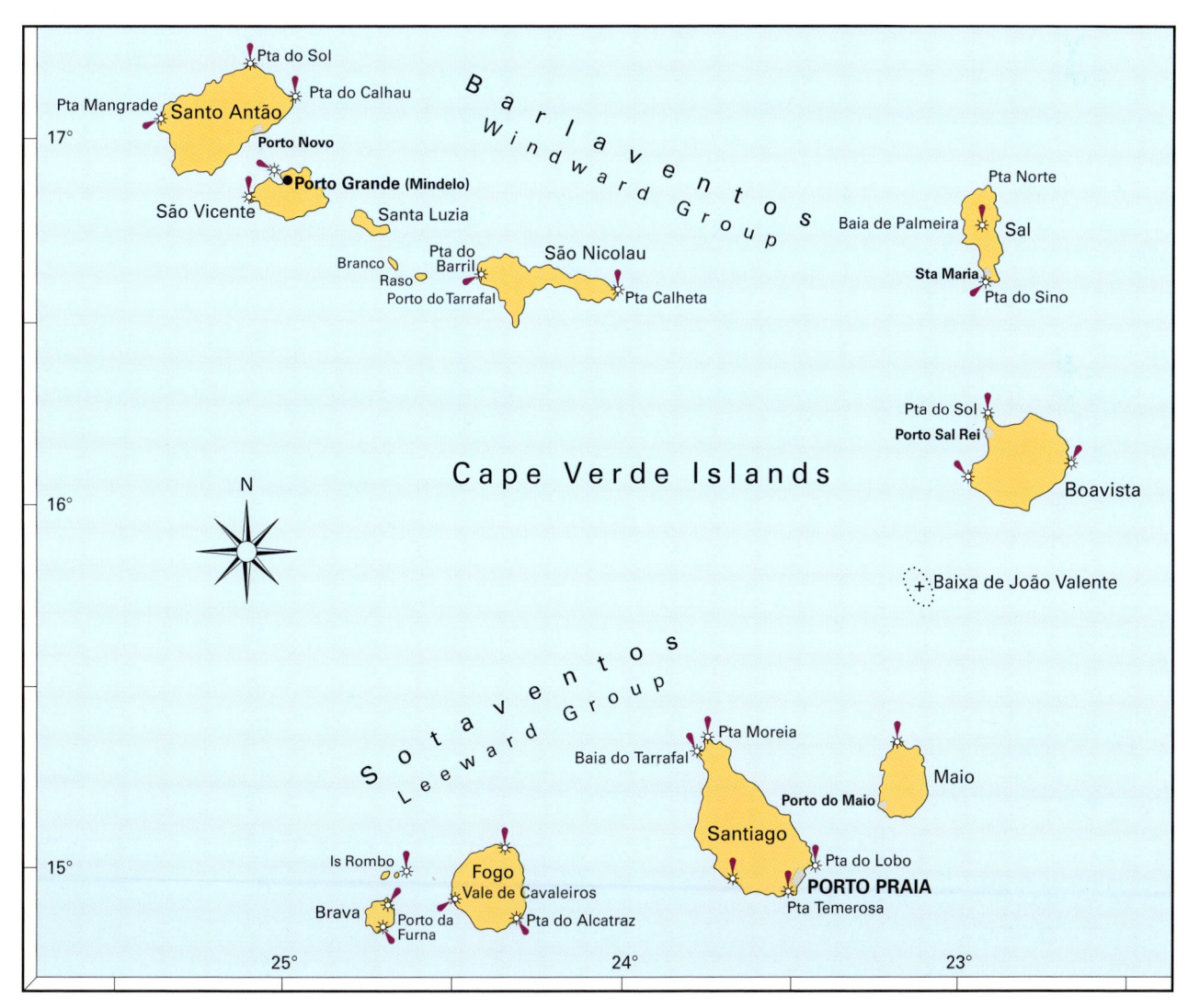

Plan 30 Ports in the Cape Verde Islands

PASSAGES AND LANDFALLS

16
Porto Grande, Mindelo, São Vicente
Cape Verdes

Location:	16°53′N	25°00′W	
Springs:	1.2m	Range:	0.9m
Neaps:	1.0m	Range:	0.4m
Time zone:	UT –1		
Currency:	Cape Verdean escudo		
Tel/fax:	Country code: 238 Area code: none		
Language:	Portuguese. (English, French and German are also spoken)		
Emergencies:	Tel: 132		

Abundant waters

After years of receiving a bad press, the Cape Verde Islands are now recognised as an interesting port of call for Atlantic voyagers. The distance to the Caribbean is reduced by 700 miles if you leave from the Cape Verdes rather than from the Canaries. Porto Grande (also known as Mindelo) is an excellent natural harbour, a port of entry, and facilities for yachts have improved dramatically in recent years.

The islands used to support some agriculture but over-exploitation, grazing by goats and deforestation turned all but the highest of the 14 islands into sandy wastelands. The sparse to non-existent vegetation ashore is contrasted by the rich marine life of the surrounding waters. The sea has always been important to their economy and, since the decline in agriculture, has become the cornerstone to any prosperity the islands have enjoyed. Since the days of Columbus they have received a large number of visits from foreign ships. First as a strategic stepping stone on the sailing route to the Americas, next as a coaling base for steamships and lately for their fishing grounds. Now yachtsmen are beginning to play their part in the economy of this little nation which is otherwise heavily dependent upon foreign aid.

Visitors often enjoy the music of Cape Verde. *Morna* is a home grown musical style, deeply rooted in African rhythm and themes but with a strong vein of Portuguese tradition and a fascinating mixture of voice, strings and drums.

Fish is abundant and superb. Fruit and vegetables grown on the higher islands are also plentiful. The local spirits

Looking northwest over Mindelo and Porto Grande. Photo: Andy O'Grady

CAPE VERDE ISLANDS, SENEGAL AND THE GAMBIA

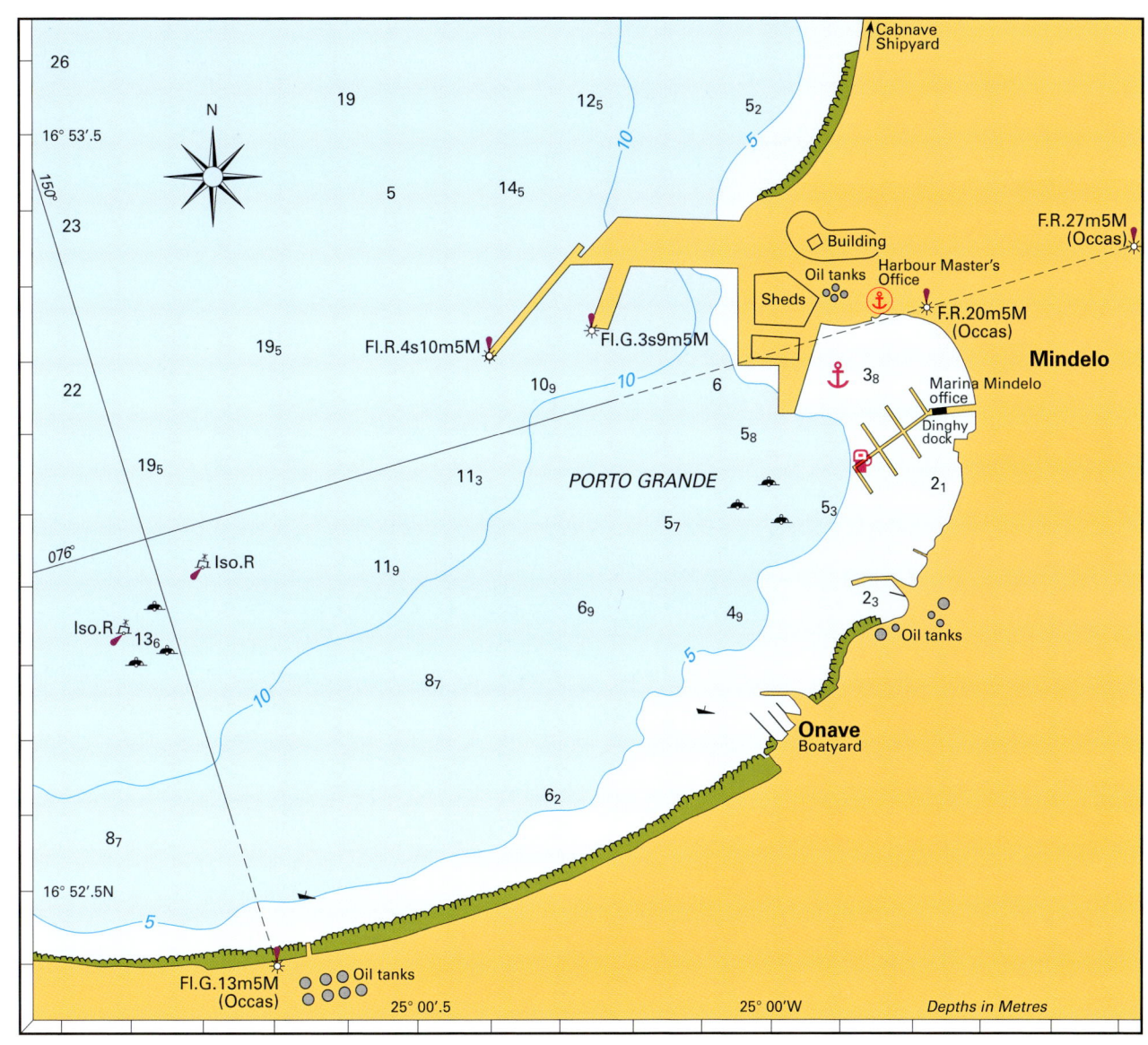

Plan 31 Porto Grande Mindelo, São Vicente, Cape Verdes

make fine drinks and good Portuguese wine is cheaply available. Apart from the importance of stocking up for the long crossing ahead, the main market is well worth a visit just for the pleasure of it. Small local supermarkets also supplement the stores.

Approach and entrance

Most yachts will approach from the north through the Canal de São Vicente. The small and rocky Ilhèu do Pássaros [Fl (3) 13s 86m 14M] is in the entrance to the bay and can be passed on either side. Note that navigation aids may not be maintained and visibility may be significantly reduced during a *harmattan*. Old shipwrecks in the harbour are being removed, but care should still be exercised as there are many commercial ships and fish-holding pens that are not lit. A night entry is possible though not recommended. Entry to the marina can be complicated by strong surges and shear winds which can make manoeuvring difficult.

Radio

VHF Channel 09.

Mindelo Marina with the anchorage in the foreground. Photo: Andy O'Grady

PASSAGES AND LANDFALLS

Looking south-east over Porto Grande from the Harbour Master's office. Photo: Andy O'Grady

Formalities

The Cape Verdean authorities take entrance and departure formalities seriously, but undertake them quickly and efficiently. It is still necessary to clear in and out of each harbour visited in the Cape Verde islands. English and French are spoken by many officials. Make sure that you take evidence of departure from the islands with you if leaving for another country. Although a Yellow Fever Vaccination card may not be required in the Cape Verdes, it is likely that you will be asked to show it at subsequent ports of call.

Berthing and facilities

Marina Mindelo is a very well-run, friendly, efficient marina, which is run in conjunction with a yacht charter business, BoatCV. More than 120 berths on six pontoons cater for vessels up to 30m (98ft) in length and 4.5m (14.5ft) draught, all bow or stern-to with a pick-up rope to a buoy. Most needs are catered for. Shore access is via the restored Cais d'Alfândega, with security gates both near the root of the jetty and onto the pontoons. Yachts can come alongside for metered water. BoatCV does not yet have a travel lift, but for those facilities that the marina cannot provide there are two shipyards, geared up for fishing boats and small ships but familiar with yachts over the years. In common with most marinas, proof of third party insurance is required.

Websites: www.marinamindelo.co

www.boatcv.co

Contact: CP 1191 – Cais Alfândega Velha, Mindelo, S Vicente, Cape Verde. Tel: 991 5878/997 2322/2300032

E-mail: mail@marinamindelo.com

info@boatcv.com

Reservations: reserve@marinamindelo.com

Anchorage and moorings

The yacht anchorage is in the north-east corner of Porto Grande Bay, with good holding in sand. Depths of 5–6m (17–20ft) in the outer part of the anchorage shoal gradually towards the beach. There are no yacht moorings and the steel mooring buoys in the outer part of the bay should be avoided. Security in the anchorage is said to have improved, though the authorities require that someone is always on board at night. Construction of the marina has inevitably encroached on the anchorage, particularly as reasonable space needs to be left around it for yachts to manoeuvre. There is a dinghy dock at the marina for which a daily charge is made, but this includes rubbish disposal (for which high fees are charged on the island).

Transport connections

There are inter-island flights or ferries to Ilha do Sal from where there are regular international flights.

Medical services (telephone numbers)

Mindelo Hospital   221-9082
Website: www.praia.usembassy.gov/med_information.html

West Africa

West Africa does not have the sort of facilities you will find in cruising grounds closer to home, making it all the more important that you, your boat and its equipment are in good order. As emphasised in Part I, self-sufficiency should be the guiding principle in all your planning. You will be over 800 miles down wind and tide of the nearest general chandlers. You will also be in a tropical environment where all forms of organic growth and corrosion will be much more of a problem.

You should also take seriously the potential health risks, particularly the threat of malaria. Ensure that you have had all the necessary vaccinations, including the Yellow Fever vaccination, and stock up with anti-malarials and antihistamine in case of reaction to bites. See Part I for more details.

Local fruit and vegetables are good and abundant in Senegal, but much less so in The Gambia and Guinea Bissau. It is generally harder to stock-up for an Atlantic crossing. The trick is to stock-up well in the Canaries, perhaps boost the stocks in the Cape Verdes and then wherever possible in Dakar and the bigger towns.

On a cautionary note; there are hippos in the rivers of West Africa and it is tempting to want to get as close to them as possible. They appear to wallow harmlessly. However, they can move surprisingly fast and can be extremely dangerous. It would be very unwise to approach closely in a small dinghy.

DAKAR

Dakar, the capital of Senegal, is about 850 miles from Las Palmas on Gran Canaria in the Canaries and about 480 miles from São Vicente in the Cape Verde Islands. It stands on a rocky promontory, and is the most visible landfall in West Africa. It is also the most westerly port on the continent. The Cap Vert light is 120m (394ft) above sea level and is visible up to 31 miles in clear conditions. The approach and entrance into sheltered water are straightforward. Yachts gather at the anchorage at Hann Bay which has a pleasant, laid-back feel to it. Ashore there is still a considerable French influence and a form of pidgin French is widely spoken. There are flight connections to France.

On arrival at any of the West African ports it is important to go ashore and find the relevant officials as soon as possible. The harbour master, customs officials and immigration officers will have an office and staff, usually in the main port. Checks against yachts which have not cleared the port's authority are certainly carried out in Dakar; elsewhere it becomes less likely, but you leave yourself open to manipulation by pseudo-officials if you have not followed the expected procedures.

Looking over the anchorage at Baie de Hann, Dakar. Photo: Ed Wheeler

Dakar to The Gambia

South from Dakar the coastline is low-lying and indistinct. River entrances tend to be shallow and may become dangerously rough if the swell is high. The tidal effects of the main rivers can continue for up to ten miles from their estuaries. The poorly maintained navigational aids make night entrances inadvisable. Some degree of overnight passage-making may be unavoidable, though the abundance of unmarked fishing nets and unlit pirogues surprisingly far out to sea are enough to jangle the nerves. The crew of the pirogues will occasionally flash a torch to warn of their presence. It is advisable to keep a good look-out.

It is about 95 miles from Dakar to Banjul, usually with wind and current behind you. It is preferable to leave Dakar in the dark and aim to reach Banjul in daylight. A heading of 160°M should allow you to pick up No 3 buoy on the River Gambia approach and take you well clear of the shallows off the coast. The Admiralty charts show a wreck close to this course at about 14° 08′N 17° 03′W. Allow for the tidal effects in your final approach – the stream runs very strongly in the lower reaches of the river and for several miles out to sea and will set you sideways very quickly. High Water at No 3 buoy is about half an hour before HW Banjul.

PASSAGES AND LANDFALLS

THE GAMBIA

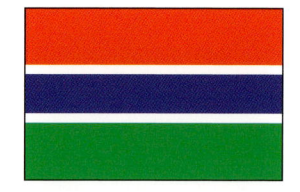

The River Gambia is an unforgettable cruising experience. It feels as if you are cruising into the heart of Africa. In fact Georgetown, which is as far as most cruisers venture, is only around 155 miles upriver but, if this is your first taste of inland Africa, it will feel more like a million miles from the familiar ocean.

Your first impression of The Gambia is likely to be the somewhat alarmingly dishevelled port area of Banjul and possibly a rather trying process of clearing in. But it is worth it! Within a few days you will have worked the tides up river into another world.

South from The Gambia

The Gambia is wrapped around by Senegal, so heading south you will once more enter French-speaking territory. Many French cruisers consider the Casamance to be the jewel in the crown of West Africa. It is not uncommon for cruisers to become seduced into prolonging a stay in this cruising ground and delaying the Atlantic crossing to the following year.

First impressions of The Gambia may be rather unappealing. Photo: Ed Wheeler

Further reference
Cruising Guide to West Africa by Steve Jones, Imray, Laurie, Norie & Wilson, is essential reading.

See also www.rccpf.org.uk for additional information on West Africa.

A short distance from Banjul but a world away. Lamin is a good place to unwind and settle into Africa. Photo: Ed Wheeler

12 Atlantic Ocean – Trade Wind Routes

For most European yachts, the trade wind Atlantic voyage generally receives the bulk of the anticipation and planning. But this crossing has not been nicknamed the 'milk run' for nothing, and it is often the most trouble-free passage of the entire circuit. Maintaining morale amongst the crew is likely to be more of an issue than anything else. Many people, years after returning from a one-year Atlantic circuit, remember the trade wind crossing as the high point of the entire cruise. For most, it will be the longest ocean passage they ever make, so it is a bonus that it is also usually one of the most enjoyable.

Even if you never spot another vessel on the crossing you will seldom be alone for long. Along with the occasional visits of cetaceans and guest appearances by flying-fish you are likely to be charmed by a number of ocean birds. Tiny little storm petrels, so at home in the midst of the vast ocean, are bound to bring a smile even to the most passage-weary.

Leaving Cape Verdes to cross the Atlantic in the trade winds. Photo: Andy O'Grady

With their little white rumps fluttering over the waves they dangle their legs down and appear to be running over the surface of the water. For this reason they are sometimes

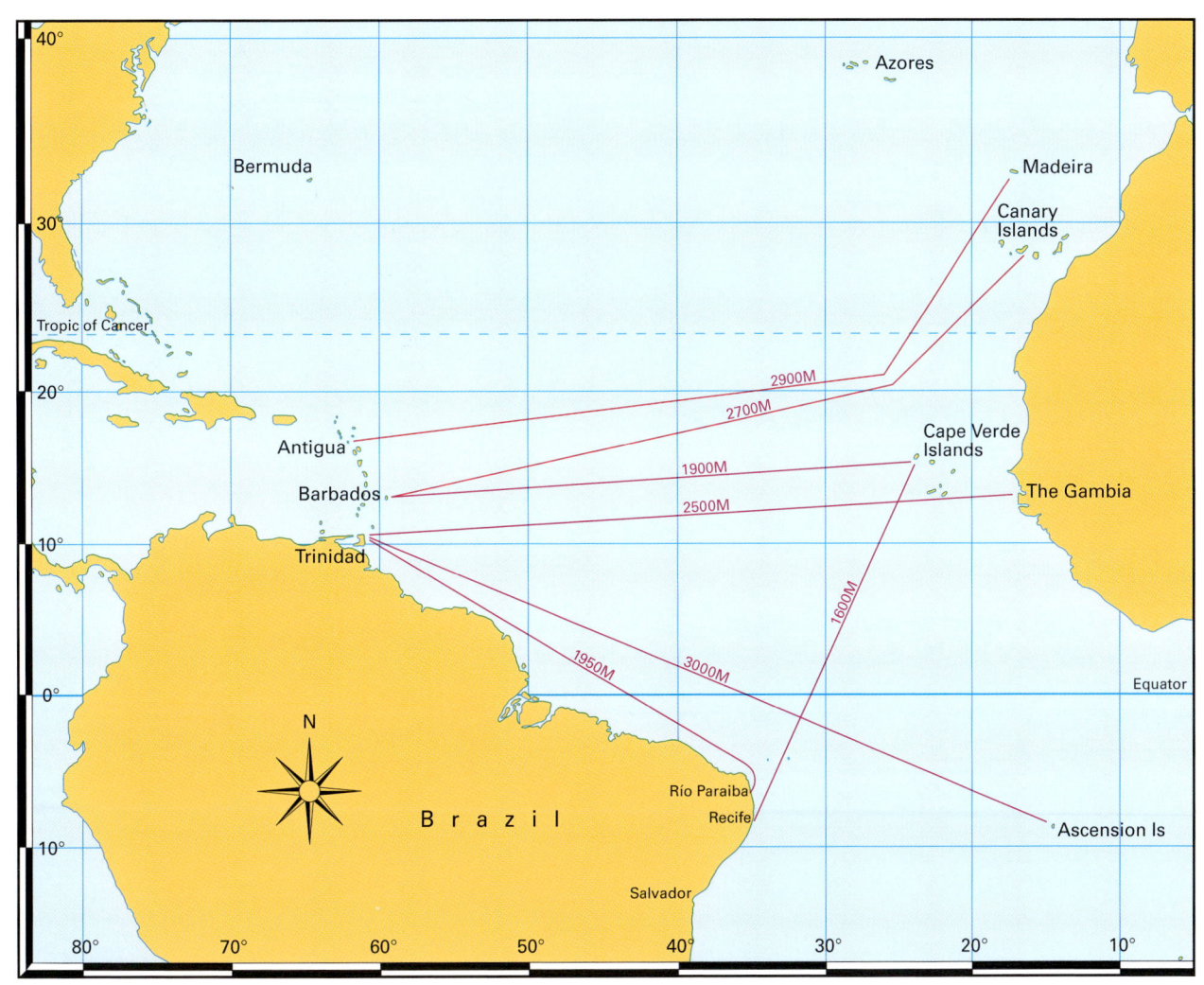

Plan 32 Typical trade wind routes across the Atlantic Ocean

PASSAGES AND LANDFALLS

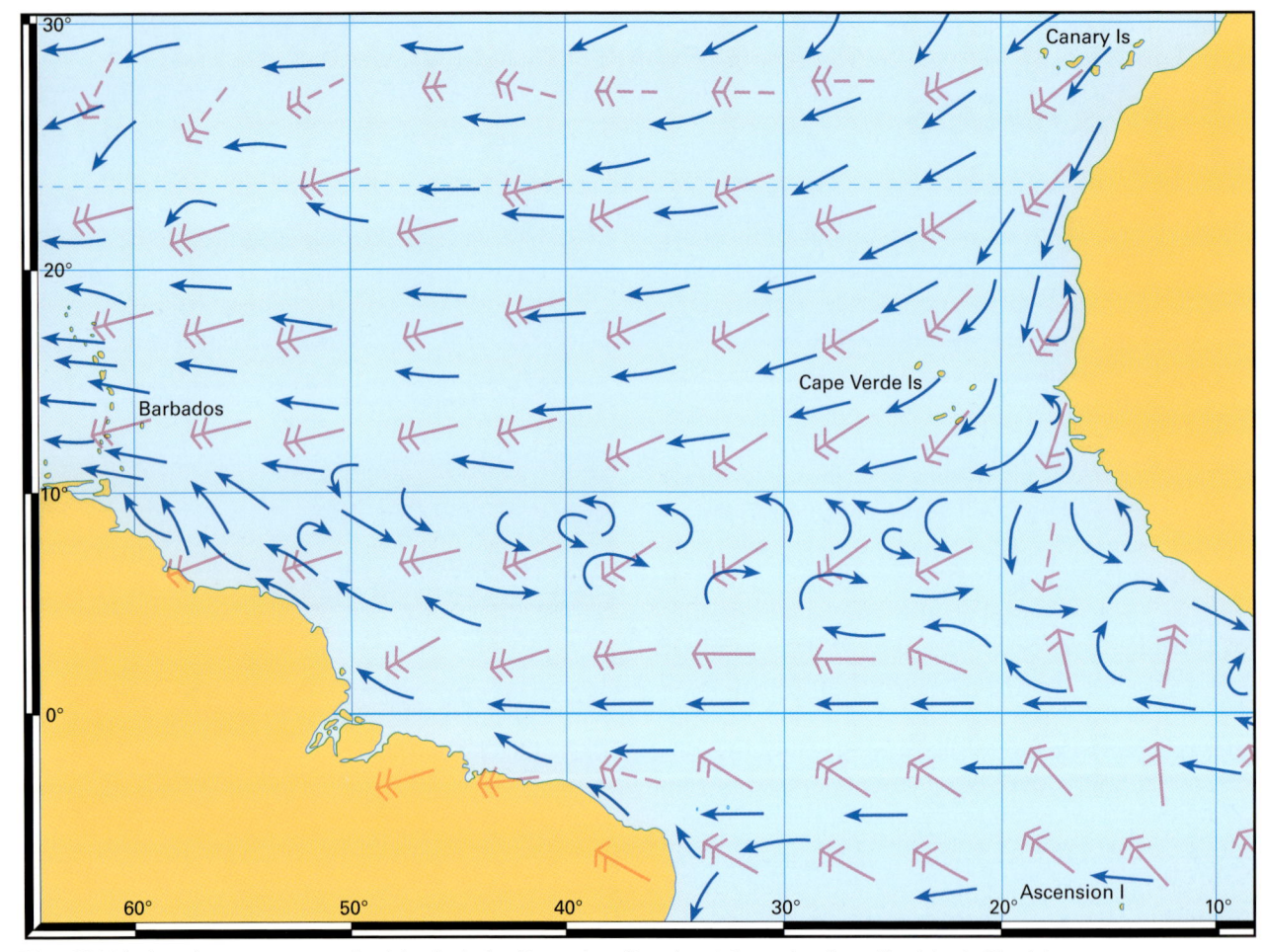

Plan 33 Winds and currents across the Atlantic during December. Based on information from *The Atlantic Pilot Atlas*

mischievously referred to as 'JC (Jesus Christ) birds'. As you close land you will start to see more birds such as the white-tailed tropicbird with its graceful white tail-streamers – many yachts are 'greeted' by these as they approach the Caribbean.

REGIONAL WEATHER AND PASSAGE TIMINGS

Best time

Mid to late November until the end of December
The majority of yachts make the trade wind crossing in November or December to give the maximum time in the Caribbean during the season. In the past, boats were accustomed to leaving the coast of Africa in October. However, over the past several years, hurricanes or tropical storms have occurred with disturbing frequency in November and even in early December. This has occurred so frequently that NOAA has extended the official hurricane season to 30 November. Winds at the end of the hurricane season are generally 15–20 knots and mostly easterly, but if you leave in mid November there is still a risk of encountering a tropical wave or depression. Troughs, rain, and thunderstorms often occur along this route in November. Seas are generally 1 to 1.5m (3–4ft). In December, winds slowly increase in speed and by the end of December are normally around 20 knots. Even when established, the trade wind does not always blow from the same quarter or at the same strength. Wind direction will vary from north-east to east. Sometimes it does not blow at all – a common occurrence at some stage of most crossings – but it rarely exceeds 25 knots.

Other times

January–March
Wind direction is predominantly north-east in the 20–25 knot range during this time period with correspondingly bigger (2–3m) seas. There may be periods of lighter winds, particularly between high-pressure cells moving to the north. Conditions are generally drier with only passing showers.

April–June
Winds will be back to the 15–20 knot range by this time. However, troughs, both at the surface or aloft, often produce squalls and rainshowers. Wind direction may vary

considerably, but is predominantly easterly. If you are heading for the Caribbean or Panama, April is the latest you should leave it so that you can be across before hurricane season starts again.

June–mid November
Attempting this passage in hurricane season is risky and likely to have light winds and rainy, squally weather from tropical waves, depressions and developing hurricanes.

Passage to Brazil

If you are heading towards Brazil, your timings are extended as tropical storms don't affect the South Atlantic. The season for this passage is October to June. In theory this passage can be made at any time of the year. In practice, between June and September the wind will be forward of the beam much of the time off the African coast south of 15°N. You would be obliged to keep close to the African coast at this time of year because of the hurricane season. Even over the equator the south-east trades will also have a more southerly tendency, not allowing you to free off very much.

OCEAN CURRENTS

The Canary Current, as it approaches the Cape Verde Islands, changes its course and changes its name. It turns increasingly westward and becomes known as the North Equatorial Current. Both its movement and its reliability tend to increase throughout the winter season, though speed at any given point cannot be predicted.

SWELL

Even an apparently calm ocean is seldom without some swell, which may suddenly increase for no apparent reason. Usually it arises from a storm many thousands of miles away and is in itself harmless. Swells running down crosswise may cause an excessive rolling motion which will damage equipment if preventative measures are not taken. When sizeable swells and locally created seas oppose each other, troublesome crests will be created, some of which may take you by surprise and find their way into the cockpit or through a hatch.

Ocean swells and the seas kicked up by more local winds can combine to create an uncomfortable motion. Photo: Mike Robinson

PASSAGES AND LANDFALLS

ROUTES: SOUTH AND WEST

Canaries or Cape Verdes to the Caribbean

The northern limit of the trade wind belt varies with the seasons – from about 30°N in summer to 25°N in winter – and also from year to year. For those leaving the Canaries without large reserves of fuel it is usually a mistake to head west too soon and to risk getting caught in the 'light 'n' variables' that predominate towards the centre of the Atlantic's massive high pressure system. On occasions, the trades become established almost as far north as the Canaries, and yachts staying near the direct route to the Caribbean make fast passages. In other years it may be necessary to go much further south to find the trades. A good general rule is to head south-south-west on leaving the Canaries, aiming to pass some 100–200 miles north-west of the Cape Verde Islands, and only turn west when you have found the trades and are at least 200 miles south of their northern limit. Once certain that you are well within the trade wind belt you can head for your chosen landfall. If you are departing from the Cape Verdes or West Africa it is likely that you will encounter the trades as soon as you have left the influence of the land.

When the trades are fully established the sky is usually speckled with rows of small puffy clouds – fair weather cumulus. Any large mass of cloud, lower and darker than the rest and coming up astern, is likely to denote a squall.

Canaries or Cape Verdes to Brazil

Cape Verdes are a great jumping-off point for the sail to Brazil. But on this passage there is a dilemma; once south of the equator, the trade winds blow from the south-east and the equatorial current is pushing west so that it is important to try and cross the doldrum belt (ITCZ) far enough to windward to be able to lay a course to the east coast of Brazil.

The doldrum belt is narrower on the western side of the ocean, but if you cross the equator too far west, you may then be hard on the wind in order to weather the north-east shoulder of Brazil. For a yacht with good range under power it may be best to stay to the east, crossing the equator east of 25°W, motor due south in the doldrums and then lay a reaching course to the destination. Yachts with better windward capability and less motoring range may prefer to cross the equator between 25°W and 30°W in the hope of still being able to lay their destination. Most boats aim for a compromise and cross at around 25–27°W. Steering southwards from the Cape Verdes should be a run but can be a bit of a rolling reach if a *harmattan* is blowing.

ROUTES: NORTH

Back to Europe from the Cape Verdes

The islands lie not far from the northbound route taken by boats heading back to Europe from the South Atlantic. It is a long fetch across the trades towards the Azores, from where most parts of Western Europe are accessible.

Brazil to the Azores and Europe

Rio Paraiba (Cabedelo) to Azores 2950M; season March to July
After leaving the coast of Brazil, try to make as much easting as possible. In the doldrums, use your engine to make further easting as well as northing. Head for a point about 5°N and 25°W. Once into the north-east trades it is then a long fetch on starboard tack towards the Azores.

Brazil to Bermuda and North America

Rio Paraiba to Bermuda 2940M
Yachts bound for the north-east North American seaboard need not make so much easting and can generally steer north until meeting the north-east trades, then they can steer for their destination.

Brazil to the Caribbean

Río Paraiba to Tobago 1931M
Venezuela and Trinidad are just outside the hurricane belt. Passages to those destinations can be made at any time of year, though the weather will be hotter and calmer with squalls in the northern summer. Along the north-east coast of South America, the trade wind is generally steady and the current favourable, so a direct course can be steered. Between August and December avoid sailing more than 50 miles off the 100m (328ft) line in order to stay out of the Equatorial Counter-current which can give adverse currents of up to two knots. The rest of the year it is possible to sail further offshore. If sailing over the continental shelf a lookout must be kept for oil platforms.

Salvador looking west over Marina Nautico and anchorage. Photo: Andy O'Grady

138

13 Landfalls in the Caribbean

17	Bridgetown/Port St Charles, Barbados	149
18	Chaguaramas, Trinidad	153
19	Rodney Bay, St Lucia	157
20	English Harbour/Falmouth Harbour, Antigua	160
21	British Virgin Islands	164

There are a number of possible landfalls in the Caribbean. Where you decide to head for will depend on a whole range of factors including planned rendezvous with friends or family, as well as your ongoing agenda. You may be planning to be somewhere for Christmas or to be in Trinidad for Carnival. You may hope to follow the Caribbean regatta circuit, or just want to pause for a pit-stop on your way to Panama and the Pacific. Where you arrive may also depend on prevailing wind direction for your passage which might persuade you to change your mind and head in towards a different point. Unless you are rallying or racing, your passage across will be more enjoyable if you are flexible about timings and your initial destination.

As with all sailing, your onward plans will be made easier if, as much as possible, you work with the winds and not against them. With this in mind it is sensible to try to make Barbados your first landfall if you would like to visit this most windward of the islands. Equally, if Tobago is on your wish list it is harder to come back out to later on. The strength and direction of the trade winds does shift during the season so, depending on when you arrive in the Caribbean, it makes sense to try to work up or down the island chains with the most favourable winds.

CARIBBEAN APPROACH AND LANDFALL

Few Caribbean islands are well lit or buoyed in terms of navigational aids. What buoyage there is throughout the islands follows the IALA B system (red right returning). There are some cardinal marks.

At night, considerable ambient light is produced by airports, hotels, domestic and street lighting. The loom over the horizon may well be your first sign of land. A night approach can be hazardous due to the number of fishing floats and unlit small fishing boats which can be found a surprising distance offshore. Any lights that are displayed by fishing boats are unlikely to be in accordance with International Regulations! If you are not rallying or racing it makes sense to adjust your speed as you close your landfall so that you can arrive in daylight.

THE CARIBBEAN ISLAND CHAIN

Preparations for a first visit to the Caribbean may produce some confusion over the names of the island groups and chains. The crescent-shaped group of relatively small islands which runs down the eastern edge and along the south of the Caribbean are the Lesser Antilles. The Lesser Antilles are made up of the Windward Islands, the Leeward Islands, the Leeward Antilles and the Netherlands Antilles. The Windward Islands are at the south and east of the chain running from Trinidad to Dominica. The

Prickly Bay, Grenada, looking north-east across the anchorage towards the small marina pontoon. Photo: David Ridout

PASSAGES AND LANDFALLS

Plan 34 Caribbean island chain

LANDFALLS IN THE CARIBBEAN

Charlotteville is a quiet and scenic landfall on the north-east corner of Tobago. Photo: Richard Woods

Leeward Islands are at the north and west end of the chain running from Guadeloupe to the Virgin Islands. The Leeward Antilles include the islands off the coast of Venezuela. The Netherlands Antilles include Bonaire and Curaçao off the Venezuelan coast, but also some of the Leeward Islands (Saba, St Eustatius, and St Martin). The Greater Antilles are made up of Cuba, Jamaica, Hispaniola (Haiti and Dominican Republic) and Puerto Rico. The Lesser Antilles, Greater Antilles and Bahamas (including Turks and Caicos) make up the West Indies. The French West Indies are Martinique in the Windwards and Guadeloupe, Saint Martin and Saint-Barthélemy in the Leewards.

THE EASTERN CARIBBEAN

References to the Eastern Caribbean may sometimes imply a geographical grouping at the eastern side of the Caribbean Sea. But Eastern Caribbean may also refer to the Organisation of Eastern Caribbean States (OECS) which is an inter-governmental grouping. The member states are Anguilla, Antigua and Barbuda, the British Virgin Islands, Dominica, Grenada, Montserrat, Saint Kitts and Nevis, Saint Lucia, and Saint Vincent and the Grenadines.

All the current OECS members are former colonies or current overseas territories of the United Kingdom. In this sense the Eastern Caribbean is more of a historical, political and financial grouping than a strictly geographical nomenclature.

CURRENCY

- In most of the islands from Grenada to Antigua, the Eastern Caribbean dollar (EC dollar) is used and the US dollar is accepted.
- Barbados, Trinidad and Tobago have their own dollars.
- All the French islands use the euro, as does Dutch St Maarten, where US dollars are also accepted.
- In both the US and British Virgin Islands, the US dollar is the official currency.

FRENCH WEST INDIES
Although not listed in this guide, there are several major yachting centres on the French islands such as Marin on the southeastern end of Martinique. The French islands are a Department of France and thereby part of the European Union. Facilities are excellent, both for yachts and more general requirements, and there are regular flights to France.

FORMALITIES

Nearly all the islands take entry and clearance procedures seriously. The authorities will wish to see clearance papers from the last port of call, and failure to produce these may

PASSAGES AND LANDFALLS

result in a fine. In some islands there is only one port of entry, in others there are several. You will usually need to clear in and out from each island before proceeding to the next one. All the ports listed in this guide are official entry ports. Procedures vary from island to island and sometimes from year to year. Local pilot books give specific details, but in general the following principles should be followed:

- Ensure that the yacht's ensign, correct courtesy ensign and the Q flag are being flown before arrival.

- In most islands it is preferable to arrive and depart during office hours. Arriving at other times may incur 'overtime' charges, even though the actual formalities may be completed during office hours.

- There may be several authorities to visit (Customs, Immigration and perhaps the harbour authority).

- There will probably be some charges to pay, both on entering and clearing, so some cash in the appropriate currency should be carried, though US dollars are normally accepted.

- If any crew members are leaving the yacht during the visit, this should be stated on entry. There will almost certainly be some formalities to be completed. Valid airline tickets may be required. If they are leaving on another yacht they will need to be transferred onto that crew list. Failure to comply with these regulations may cause considerable problems when the yacht comes to clear out.

- Generally speaking, the authorities on the islands are fair and tolerant in their treatment of yachts. However, the officials, quite reasonably, expect to be taken seriously. It will be considered discourteous if you are inappropriately dressed.

- Rudeness and incivility will lengthen the procedures, and impatience will certainly be counterproductive. Deliberate deceit or attempted bribery is likely to lead to arrest.

- The sailor who deals with the officials in the islands in the same honest and fair manner that he would adopt towards the officials in his own country is likely to encounter few problems. It is worth remembering that you are a visitor, and no country is obliged to admit you. Officials have considerable powers to make life difficult for sailors, so it is unwise to antagonise them.

Formalities in the US islands

Anyone entering the United States, other than US or Canadian citizens, must be in possession of a visa.

It is important to realise that the US Visa Waiver Scheme is only applicable to travel on commercial carriers; airlines and ferries etc. If you enter the USA by private yacht, wherever you enter, even if it is a port served by commercial carriers, you MUST have a valid visa in your passport prior to entry. The fine for arriving without a visa is $5,000 per person and entry may also be refused.

St Georges Lagoon, Grenada, from Fort George showing the marina on the left, and anchorage and superyacht berths on the right. Photo: Mike Robinson

Applications for visas have to be made at a US embassy and, in most cases, require an interview. Within the eastern Caribbean, US embassies are located in Barbados and Trinidad.

For further details on formalities in US waters see page 194.

If cruising within the British and US Virgin Islands, a useful, legal method of entry to the USVI for any boat crew or visitors who do not have visas is as follows:

- The procedure is that the boat and all crew who do have visas check out of the BVI, sail to the USVI (St Thomas or St John) and check in there with US Immigration and Customs at Charlotte Amalie or Cruz Bay.
- Those crew and visitors not having visas should travel by commercial ferry from Tortola to St Thomas/ St John and enter the USVI through the Visa Waiver Scheme.
- Evidence of a hotel booking for the first night's accommodation may be required.
- Crew then re-join the boat, having legally entered the USVI.
- It is a good idea for the crew to carry a letter from the skipper confirming that they are unpaid crew and not passengers.

REGIONAL WEATHER AND PASSAGE TIMINGS

Eastern Caribbean Islands chain

Northbound – best times
Late November until the end of December and April to June

Over the past few years, hurricanes or tropical storms have occurred with disturbing frequency in November and even in early December. This has occurred so frequently that NOAA has extended the official hurricane season to November 30.

Winds are generally south-east or easterly at 15–20 knots and seas 1–1.5m (3–5ft) at this time. Lingering weak tropical waves in November or 'between season' troughs (see Appendix B) occasionally persist but are of short duration. If moving from the south (Trinidad) to the Virgin Islands or St Martin, this is the time to move.

From April to June, winds once again become easterly to south-easterly at 15–20 knots. Precipitation increases slowly during this period and troughs with associated showers and squalls become more frequent.

Northbound – other times
End of December to March

Winds abruptly change to north-easterly 20 knots and sometimes 25 knots with seas of 2–3m (7–10ft) near the end of December. This cycle of strong winds is often referred to as 'Christmas' winds. The acceleration zones between islands

Trade wind passages between the islands can be fairly brisk. Worn sails and poorly maintained equipment can suddenly fail in these conditions. Photo: Graham Adam

PASSAGES AND LANDFALLS

St David's Marina on Grenada, looking north-west. Photo: David Ridout

often result in 3m (10ft) waves and winds into the mid 30 knot range. If you are trying to sail from St Vincent to St Lucia at this time you are likely to be hard on the wind.

Short breaks in this cycle of strong winds do occur which allow boats to move north more comfortably, though you may need to be patient to wait for these conditions. The breaks become longer by March and will then often last for several days.

June to mid-November
June is often a windy month with easterly winds near 20 knots. Tropical waves begin and gradually gain in intensity and occasionally develop into tropical depressions and hurricanes. Winds become generally light south-easterlies in July through to October, but hurricanes are significantly probable at this time. Rain and thunderstorms are frequent.

Southbound – best times
March to May
Winds become more easterly or south-easterly in the 15–20 knot range. Although it may be a windward sail between some of the northern islands, these lighter wind speeds make for good sailing. Generally this time of year is free of precipitation except for troughs which form and linger without moving for several days.

End of December to March
Travelling south during this period can be anywhere from exhilarating to delightful broad reaching. Winds are generally north-easterly 20 knots, sometimes 25 knots, with periodic lulls as high pressure cells move east.

Southbound – other times
June–July, or October to mid-December
Winds during this time-frame are often from the south-east, so in order to avoid sailing hard on the wind, it is best to wait for winds to swing east. Wind speeds (except for June, which tends to be windy), will be 15 knots or less. Precipitation will be more frequent with tropical waves and troughs passing through the area. Hurricanes are significantly probable at this time.

WIND ACCELERATION ZONES

In the lee of the islands, particularly the more mountainous ones, winds may drop off to nothing. But at various points, particularly at the northern and southern headlands of each island, the wind can accelerate very sharply. During the day it is usually possible to see from the sea state where such conditions prevail, but at night they can be a hazard and it may be wise to reduce sail in anticipation while still in the lee.

CURRENTS AND TIDES

The North Equatorial Current sets westward between the islands, often attaining a knot or more. Though tidal streams may increase or decrease the rate of flow, they are seldom strong enough to overcome it completely. It is easy to overlook this and find that you have been set a long way to leeward when sailing between the islands. Currents and tidal streams are particularly strong in some areas, notably between Grenada and Trinidad and in the Boca de Monos on the northern approach to Chaguaramas Bay, Trinidad. This area is at a confluence of ocean currents and is also affected by the flow from the Orinoco River. Dramatic changes in water colour and sea state are sometimes seen where two bodies of flow are meeting.

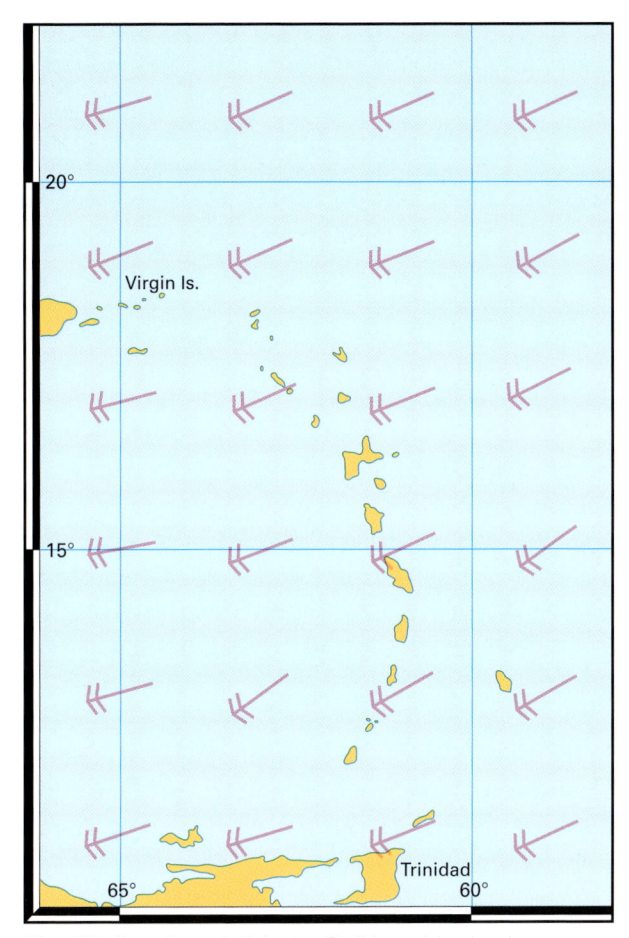

LANDFALLS IN THE CARIBBEAN

Plan 35 Prevailing winds in the Caribbean islands – January

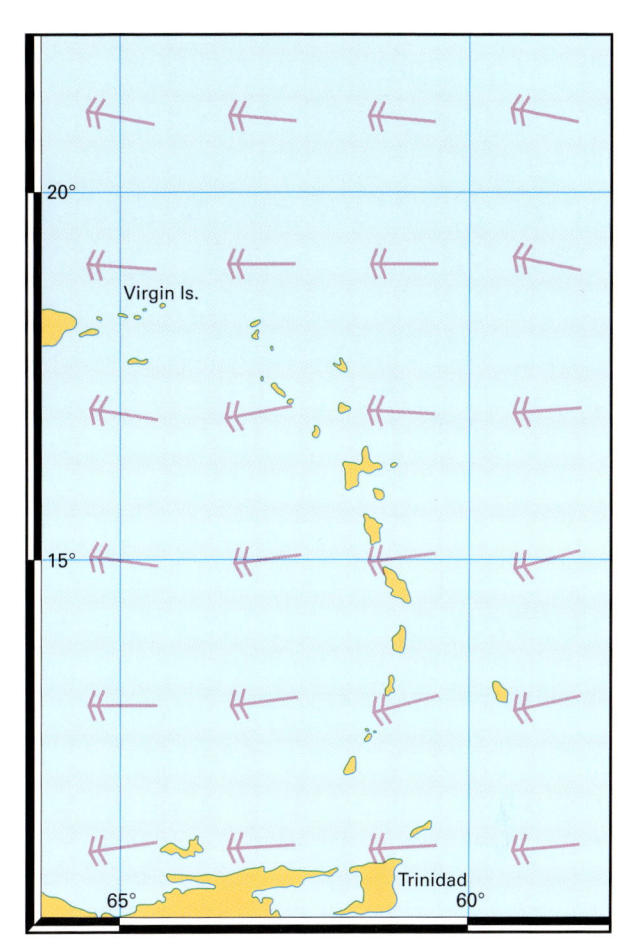

Plan 36 Prevailing winds in the Caribbean islands – May. Plans 35 to 37 based on information from *The Atlantic Pilot Atlas*

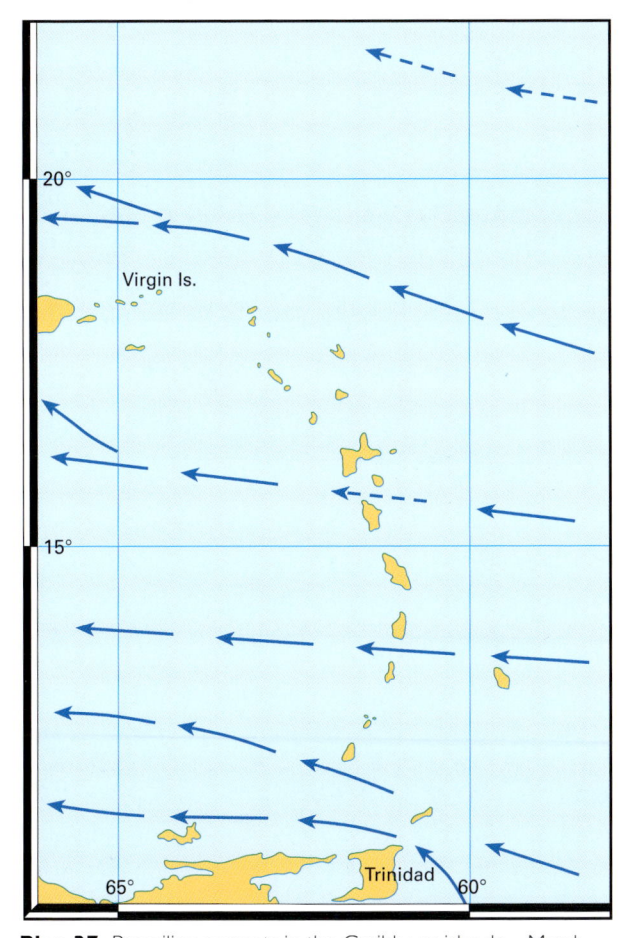

Plan 37 Prevailing currents in the Caribbean islands – March

ANCHORAGES

To those used to ever-changing winds and strong reversing tidal streams, it may go against the grain to anchor in a position protected through only half the compass or less. However, due to the constancy of the trade winds, the islands produce a reliable lee on their western coasts and many of the traditional anchorages are quite open in this direction. The best anchorages give shelter from both the wind and swell, but this is not always the case and quite often a certain amount of rolling may have to be endured. It is sometimes preferable to moor fore-and-aft into the swell.

CARIBBEAN PILOTAGE GUIDES
Chris Doyle's guides are invaluable and thoroughly recommended. They contain good aerial shots and other photographs as well as sketch maps of anchorages and harbours. They are full of good advice, built up through years of cruising the Caribbean, and all sorts of other useful information. The guides are kept updated on the web site: **www.doyleguides.com**. A useful link accesses weather services and security net information **www.doyleguides.com/advisories_page.htm**

145

PASSAGES AND LANDFALLS

Wallilabou anchorage, St Vincent. The anchorage is sometimes susceptible to a swell which can be uncomfortable. Stern lines help to hold the bows into the motion. Photo: Mike Robinson

HISTORY

When the West Indies were 'discovered' by Columbus, they were the home of the Caribs. The Caribs were warriors who had migrated up from South America and had themselves displaced the Arawaks. In most of the islands, the Caribs were wiped out within a few hundred years of European settlement, but some still live in a reserved territory on the windward side of Dominica. Nearly all the islands have small museums, but one in St John's, Antigua, is particularly notable for its comprehensive collection of pre-Columbus artefacts. The majority of the local people today are descended from the slaves who were brought over from Africa in the 17th and 18th centuries to work in the sugar plantations.

Very obvious on many of the islands are the relics of the Napoleonic era and the jostling for territory between the colonial powers. Substantial stone forts and gun emplacements overlook the more strategic harbours and anchorages.

The islands have a rich history and it is interesting to learn some of it as you visit each island in turn.

GEOLOGY

It is hard to avoid the obvious truth that many of the Caribbean islands sit on fault lines along the Earth's crust and have been produced by volcanic activity. If you didn't catch the volcano bug in the Atlantic islands, you may catch it in the Caribbean. Several of the islands are still active volcanoes, most notably Montserrat which is still coming to terms with the eruptions of the 1990s and continuing sporadic activity. During a major eruption, even vessels at sea are at risk from pyroclastic flows which can accelerate out over the surface of the water for several miles. So if you plan to visit Montserrat it would be sensible to check the latest status of activity. A more chronic problem, if you are passing downwind while the volcano is smouldering, is that of volcanic ash which is very gritty and plays havoc with winches and other mechanical workings.

It is possible to climb to the top of several of the islands' volcanoes. This is usually a long, hot, steep climb, but an amazing experience nonetheless. The Montserrat Volcano Observatory has an informative website with links about the other volcanoes in the 'Caribbean arc': www.montserratvolcanoobservatory.info/

PROVISIONING

Services and facilities for sailors throughout the eastern Caribbean are excellent, largely due to the ever-growing charter boat and tourist industries. All islands other than the very smallest now have reasonable food shops, many have large supermarkets; most sport bustling local produce markets that not only offer variety and good value, but are great fun to visit. Try out some of the local dishes like *goat roti* – delicious! Also try some of the unfamiliar tropical fruit and vegetables and ask the locals for advice on how to prepare and cook them. Cold cooked breadfruit with mayonnaise makes a good salad. Take advice about the various types of chilli pepper. Some of them are so hot that they can cause burns to your skin when cut open. If in doubt, touch a tiny piece onto your lips for a very brief second and then proceed cautiously.

Fruit delivery Caribbean style. Prices on the water are likely to be higher than in the markets ashore. Photo: Graham Adam

Rum

The production of sugar and its by-product, rum, remain integral to many of the islands. Most islands have their own distilleries and their own varieties of rum.

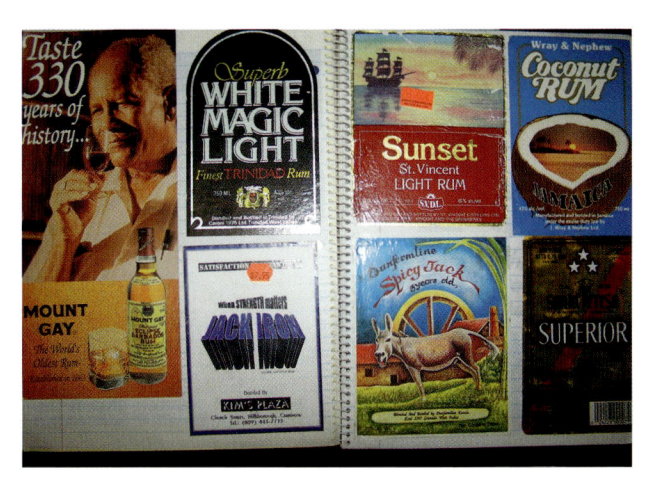

LANDFALLS IN THE CARIBBEAN

A small collection of rum labels. Photo: David Russell

A scrub-off at Peakes, Chaguaramas. Boatyard facilities throughout the Caribbean have improved dramatically in recent years. Photo: John Lytle

Manchineel trees
Manchineel trees are found throughout the Caribbean and are often marked with some kind of paint or other marker. Their fruit and leaves bear a superficial resemblance to an apple tree. In Spanish they are called 'manzanilla de la muerte' or 'little apple of death'. They are extremely poisonous and highly irritant. Avoid touching them, leaning on them, or sheltering from the rain beneath them, and definitely avoid climbing them!

Carnival day itself, the costumes, the music, the energy, the whole atmosphere are quite fabulous. Don't miss it!

Having said that, many of the other islands have their own carnivals which they are also justly proud of. Tobago's carnival includes their regatta week which, as well as being a serious race event, is a wonderful celebration of modern and traditional sailing – a real festival of wind. Later in the season Antigua Week and Antigua Classics are great fun, whether participating or spectating. Needless to say, anchorages become crowded and facilities become booked up during these events.

HAUL-OUT AND REPAIR FACILITIES

Boatyard facilities have improved dramatically in recent years. Most will be busy during the cruising season, and in particular it may be necessary to make an advance booking for a haul-out in St Lucia around the end of the ARC rally, and in Antigua around race week. It is possible that a European yacht on a one-year circuit of the north Atlantic might get away without hauling-out for antifouling, but the ban on TBT paints has made this unlikely. Even with frequent swimming to scrub, fouling on the homeward passages is likely to be severe.

SAILING FESTIVALS AND CARIBBEAN EVENTS

Arguably, the 'greatest show on earth' is the Trinidad Carnival. Carnival is not just one day, there are weeks of activity which steadily crescendo into the final week running up to the main masquerade parade on Shrove Tuesday. Carnival is celebrated on many levels. Pan bands, better described as pan orchestras, compete during staged concert evenings. The calypso tradition of political and social commentary through music is kept well alive. And on

Trinidad Carnival masquerade parade. Photo: Christine Webster

147

PASSAGES AND LANDFALLS

For many people a pan band is the sound of the Caribbean. Photo: Mike Robinson

Websites
www.gotrinidadandtobago.com/trinidad/carnival.php

Grenada Sailing Festival:
www.grenadagrenadines.com/regatta.html

Tobago's carnival celebrations include a regatta week:
www.sailweek.com/

Further north there are regattas in St Croix:
www.stcroixyc.com/

St Martin: www.smyc.com

St Thomas: www.styc.net/

BVIs: www.bvispringregatta.org/

Antigua Sailing Week and Antigua Classics are the climax at the end of the season: www.sailingweek.com
www.antiguaclassics.com/

SECURITY CONCERNS

The sheer volume of boats cruising the Caribbean, together with the sometimes enormous and blatant divide of affluence between visitors and locals, make it unsurprising that thefts do occur. Only a very small minority of incidents involve violence of any sort. Becoming fixated on security issues is almost bound to spoil your cruise, but normal security precautions should be taken, especially with dinghies and outboards. The engine and fuel tank should be locked to the dinghy and the dinghy should be locked with a wire or chain when left unattended ashore. At night, dinghies should be either locked to the boat or, preferably, hoisted out of the water.

Melodye Pompa operates the Caribbean Safety and Security Net daily at 1215 UTC on 8104 kHz USB. She also maintains a computer database of safety and security incidents. This net serves as a forum for reporting and discussing safety and security incidents throughout the Caribbean as well as for 'boat watches' for overdue vessels, navigational hazards, and other information of relevance to cruisers. It has a very wide daily audience. www.safetyandsecuritynet.com. See also Venezuela Security information at www.onsa.org.ve.

Mooring buoys at Tobago Cays. In some areas anchoring is discouraged or prohibited to protect the seabed. Photo: Mike Robinson

LANDFALLS IN THE CARIBBEAN

17
Bridgetown/Port St Charles
Barbados

Location:	13°6′N 59°38′W/13°16′N 59°39′W		
Springs:	0.8m	Range:	0.6m
Neaps:	0.7m	Range:	0.3m
Time zone:	UT −4		
Currency:	Barbados dollar		

Tel/fax:	Country code: 1-246
Language:	English
Emergencies:	Police 211 Ambulance 511

First stop – to windward of the rest

Barbados lies nearly 100 miles to the east of the main chain of islands and is a popular island on which to make a Caribbean landfall. Its welcoming loom can be seen for 40 miles or more out to sea and the final approach to the island is relatively staightforward. The island is famous for its luxury hotels and celebrity hide-aways, but it also provides a warm, Bajan welcome to ocean-weary sailors of more modest means. It may be tempting to grind to a halt on arrival, but it is worth exploring the island. Public buses provide transport through all 11 parishes but, for those who want to stretch their sea legs, the high ground around Mount Hillaby slopes down gently through rolling pastures to the wilder and more dramatic windward coast and provides some delightfully scenic walking country. Worth a visit are the botanical delights of Welchman Hall Gully and the Flower Forest. The more sporting will enjoy a pilgrimage to the historic Kensington Oval cricket ground. Those who prefer to sample the local food and drink might enjoy Bajan specialities such as fried flying fish and Mount Gay rum. Barbados hosts an international Jazz festival each January and holds several other sporting and cultural events throughout the year.

The anchorage at Carlisle Bay, Barbados. Photo: John Melling.

149

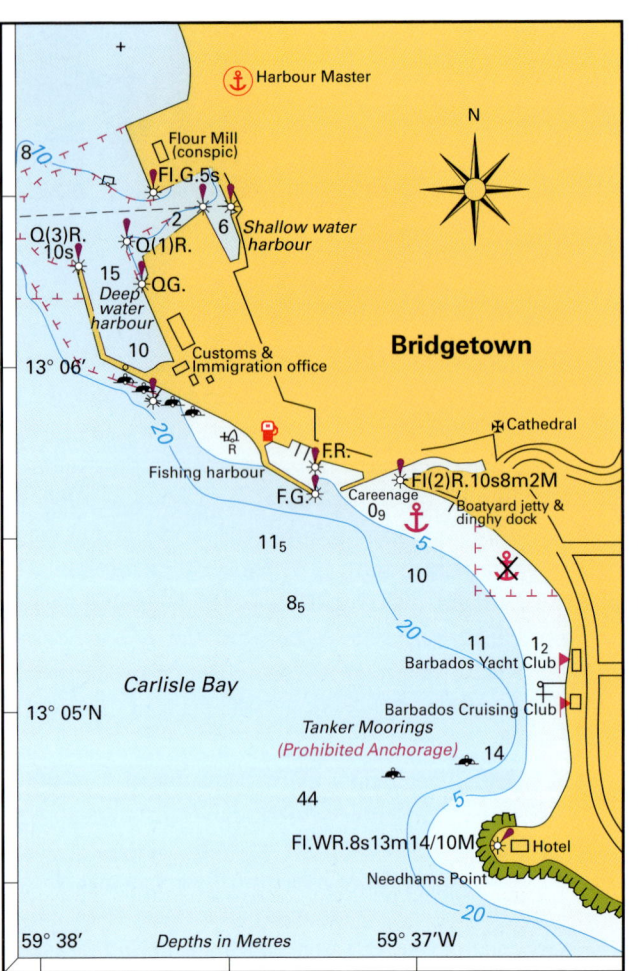

PASSAGES AND LANDFALLS

Plan 38 Bridgetown, Barbados

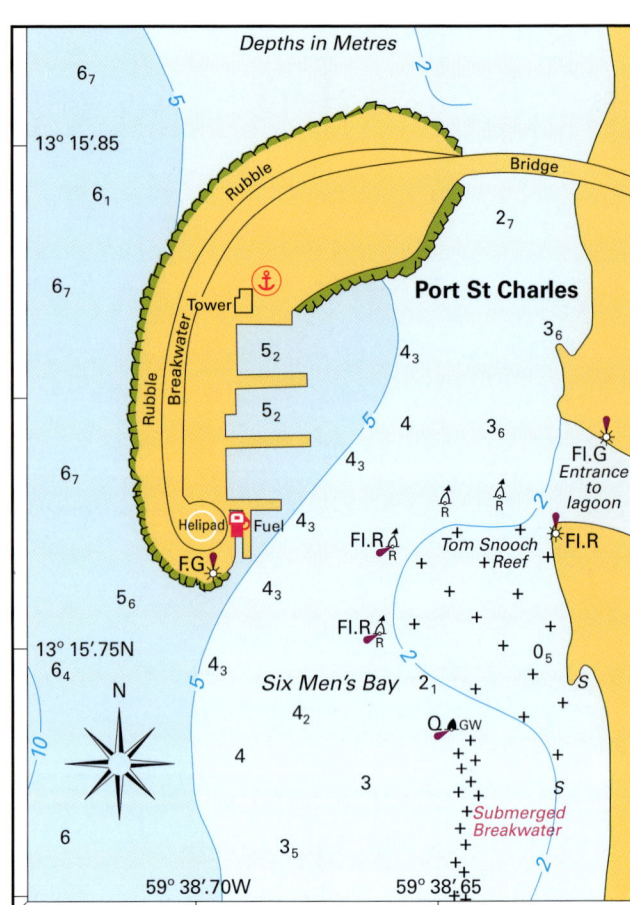

Plan 39 Port St Charles, Barbados

The US Embassy in Bridgetown is useful for anyone planning to visit the US Virgin Islands or mainland USA who has not yet arranged for a visa that is appropriate for arrival on a private yacht. See page 194 for more information.

Websites
www.barbados.usembassy.gov/
www.accessbarbados.com/index.php
www.barbados.org/
www.sailbarbados.com/
www.barbados.org/hike.htm

Approach

Barbados is relatively low-lying with only one high point, Mount Hillaby (336m (1,100ft)), in the middle of the island. If planning to clear in at Port St Charles, the preferred option for most cruisers, it is logical to approach around the north end of the island. From North Point, it is 6 miles to Port St Charles and 17 miles to Bridgetown in the lee of the land. Try to keep at least one mile clear of the land, outside the 100m contour, around the north and north-east coasts until the end of Port St Charles breakwater bears 150°

or less. The bottom drops away very sharply from 20m (66ft) to 200m (660ft).

Approaching around the south end of the island, avoid the large bank known as The Shallows which lies about four miles south-east of South Point with a least depth of 60m (200ft). This area can be very rough when a westerly swell meets an east-going current. From South Point, it is eight miles to Bridgetown.

Radio

Barbados Port Authority monitors VHF Channel 16 and uses Channel 12 as its working channel (24 hours). Port St Charles works on Channel 77. Barbados Coast Guard is the national Search and Rescue agency and watches 2182 kHz and Channel 16 continuously.

Entrance

Port St Charles The marina lies just over one mile south of the conspicuous Arawak jetty and cement works, and 0.5 miles north of Speightstown. The entrance is around a rubble breakwater with a square white tower halfway along it. The fuelling/customs jetty (18m (60ft) in length), immediately inside the end of the breakwater, is in a channel

LANDFALLS IN THE CARIBBEAN

Port St Charles breakwater, Barbados, looking NE with arrival/fuel berth seen behind the hut on the right. Photo: Port St Charles Development Co Ltd

no more than 50m (165ft) wide with a least depth of 4.3m (14ft). The shoal close to the east of the entrance is marked by a row of red buoys. Some of these buoys are lit (FL R).

Bridgetown/Carlisle Bay On approach, call Port Control on VHF Channel 12. You will be directed to secure alongside in the deep water harbour in the south-east corner where the offices are situated. This harbour is set up for large vessels and is subject to swell and surge. You may need to use a fender plank outside your fenders. It is sometimes possible to tie up outside another vessel if given permission to do so. After signing in you will be directed to anchor in Carlisle Bay, 1.5 miles to the east-south-east.

Formalities

Fly the Q flag when approaching Barbados. You can clear in at Port St Charles or at the deep water harbour on the north side of Carlisle Bay at Bridgetown. Note that you may be required to clear out, with your boat, from the same point as you clear in. Call Bridgetown Harbour Port control (VHF Channel 12) or Port Charles Marina (VHF Channel 77) as you approach. At Bridgetown you will either be given clearance to enter the harbour or, if out of hours, you may be directed to anchor in Carlisle Bay until the morning. If directed to anchor, continue to fly the Q flag and remain on your boat until you have been cleared. Customs and Immigration offices are open 0600–2200 seven days a week. Anchorage and light dues are payable on departure.

Cruising the coast

If you are planning to cruise, anchor or moor anywhere other than at your arrival port you should ask permission to do so on arrival. Customs clearance is required for cruising along the coast including from Port St Charles to Bridgetown. There are strict regulations about where you can anchor and any contravention will lead to a hefty fine. This is to protect the coral along the coast. If intending to move around, check the procedure either on arrival or through the Coast Guard on VHF Channel 16, and confirm which anchorages can be used.

Berthing and facilities

Port St Charles is a luxury development with a section of the marina reserved for yachts up to 76m (250ft). However, yachts smaller than 45m (150ft) may not be very welcome other than to clear in, re-fuel and water. Advance booking for berths is necessary. Berths within the inner basin are reserved primarily for residents and manoeuvering space is limited, however it is possible to rent an apartment with a berth. Fuel, water and electricity are available. Duty-free fuel is available on departure.
Website: www.portstcharles.com
Contact: Dockmaster, Port St Charles, St Peter, Barbados. Tel: 419 1000 ext. 2230 Mobile: 262 3759 Fax: 246 422 4646
E-mail: psc.dockmaster@caribsurf.com

Carlisle Bay Visitors are not allowed to lie in the shallow water harbour to the north of the town unless using the travel lift at Willie's. It is sometimes possible to berth in the careenage but only with permission from the Barbados Port Authority. Space in the careenage is very limited and there is often a surge which will put severe strain on warps and fenders.
Website: www.barbadosport.com
Contact: Barbados Port Inc, University Row, Bridgetown, Barbados. Tel: 430 4700/ 436 6883 Fax: 429-5384, Call Sign 8PB.

Boatyard: Willie's Diving and Marine Services is at the south end of the shallow water harbour with a 45- tonne travel lift for haul-out and boat repair. Maximum draught 2.2m (7ft). Most repair and engineering work can be arranged.

PASSAGES AND LANDFALLS

Contact: Willie's Diving and Marine Services
Tel: 424 1808/230 4271 Fax: 425-1060
E-mail: mikie@caribsurf.com

Barbados Yacht Club is an active race club which welcomes visitors and allows use of some of their facilities.
Contact: Barbados Yacht Club, Bay Street, St Michael, Barbados. Tel: 427-1125 Fax: 435-7590
E-mail: byc@sunbeach.net

For other marine services see www.doyleguides.com/barb-links.htm

Anchorage and moorings

Carlisle Bay The yacht anchorage is to the south of the careenage in 10m (30ft) or less over sand. There are wrecks and dive sites south of this area. Although in some ways a classic Caribbean anchorage, with clear blue water backed by a long sandy beach, Carlisle Bay frequently suffers from surge. Landing on the beach by dinghy can be a distinctly wet affair despite seeming deceptively normal on first approach. Make sure that any valuables are in watertight containers before taking them ashore. The Boatyard Restaurant has ten moorings in the north end of the bay and some on shore facilities including toilets and showers. A jetty has been built opposite the Boatyard Restaurant to improve dinghy access to the beach. A daily fee is charged to use this dock. The mooring buoys off the yacht clubs further south in the bay are available for residents only.

Carlisle Bay is a favourite spot for night-time music and revelry. If you are not joining in the party on the shore you may find the noise levels incompatible with an early night's sleep.

Port St Charles Anchor well clear of the entrance in 3–10m (10–30ft), in sand, avoiding the occasional coral outcrop. There are strict regulations against anchoring on coral and you should only anchor where sand is clearly visible as the substrate.

Transport connections

Buses run all over the island. Grantley Adams airport is 21km (13 miles) from Bridgetown. There are direct flights to the United Kingdom, mainland Europe, the United States and Canada. Local air services run to some of the other eastern Caribbean islands.

Medical services

The Queen Elizabeth Public Hospital is about ten minutes from the careenage on Martindales Road, St Michael. Tel: 436-6450. The small private Bayview Hospital is situated within walking distance of the Barbados Yacht Club.

The arrival berth at Port St Charles. Photo: Richard Woods

LANDFALLS IN THE CARIBBEAN

18
Chaguaramas Bay
Trinidad

Location:	10°40´.5N 61°38´W	
Springs:	1.1m	Range: 0.6m
Neaps:	1.0m	Range: 0.7m
Time zone:	UT –4	
Currency:	Trinidad & Tobago dollar	
Tel/fax:	Country code: 1-868 Area code: none	
Language:	English, but several other languages spoken	
Emergencies:	Tel: 999 (Police) 990 (Ambulance or Fire)	

An island for nature-lovers

Trinidad is a very large island with an industrial base and a large and mixed population. Its richness of traditions and histories generated by its different cultures is clearly evident during the annual carnival season. But the island has much more to offer. The high land in the north is clad with tropical forest and home to an enormous array of tropical species. The low-lying mangrove swamps further south are the perfect habitat for the amazingly irridescent scarlet ibis. The beaches on its north-eastern corner are hosts to the agonisingly slow, laborious and vulnerable process whereby turtles come ashore to lay their eggs. Watching this event is a rare privilege, as is the joyful moment when a nest hatches out and the young turtles emerge and head for the moonlit surf.

Close to Chaguaramas is the deserted island of Chacachacare where it is possible to anchor away from the crowds and go ashore onto what was once a leper colony. Many of the buildings have been encroached upon by the forest, but there is a strange sense of stepping into another time and another world.

The US Embassy in Port of Spain is useful for anyone planning to visit the US Virgin Islands or mainland USA who has not yet arranged for a visa that is appropriate for arrival on a private yacht. See page 142 for more information.

Websites
www.gotrinidadandtobago.com
www.trinidad.usembassy.gov/

A safe haven

Trinidad has developed into one of the south-east Caribbean's leading yachting centres. Its position south of the normal hurricane belt increases its appeal as a safe haven to leave a boat during the summer and makes it acceptable to most insurers. Yachting services are largely concentrated in the north-west of the island, many of them in the Chaguaramas Bay area where marinas and boatyards offer extensive facilities for haul-out, lay-up and servicing. Foreign yachts are frequently stored ashore here while their owners return home on one of the regular flights to the United Kingdom, United States and Canada. It has indeed become so popular that it is often difficult to get work done, and advance booking of a berth afloat or ashore is essential.

Security
Trinidad has gained a reputation for violent crime which is largely confined to gangs in the local community. Chaguaramas is generally considered to be reasonably safe but visitors are advised not to walk outside the boatyard and marina compounds at night and to take sensible precautions to protect themselves and their property.

Carnival time! Everyone can join the party. Photo: Christine Webster

CHAGUARAMAS BAY TRINIDAD 18

153

PASSAGES AND LANDFALLS

Hurricanes and insurance

Some UK insurers now insist that yachts being stored ashore are in one piece cradles, with tie downs to secure ground anchorage points, without covers and booms in place. Such cradles and ground anchorage points are not generally available in Trinidad. Many yachtsmen using Trinidad favour shrinkwrap covers to protect from the tropical humidity during storage, but this is not approved by some insurers.

Approach and entrance

Be aware that tidal streams can flow very strongly through the Bocas. Chacachacare Light [Fl 10s 26M] on the island of that name is the principal navigation light for the approach to Trinidad. From the north, the light should be kept well to starboard until close to land in order to counter north-westerly setting currents and prevailing easterly winds.

Yachts approaching from the north usually pass through the Boca de Monos, the most easterly of the three *bocas* (literally 'mouths'). Le Chapeau rock [Fl (3) 10s] lies on the starboard hand in the entrance, after which a course of 170° clears Têteron Rock [Fl G 4s 7m 4M] at the southern end of the *boca*. There are good depths between the islands of Caspar Grande and Gasparillo, leading directly into Chaguaramas Bay.

Shrink-wrapped at Peak boatyard, Chaguaramas. Photo: John Lytle

Yachts arriving from Venezuela generally enter the Gulf of Paria via either the Boca de Navios, east of Chacachacare Island, or south of Chacachacare Island and its two companions. Again there are no particular hazards. Approaching from the west, keep well offshore along the Paria Peninsular of Venezuela where yachts have been subjected to pirate attacks.

Formalities

Yachts arriving in Trinidad must berth immediately at the Customs Dock at Crews Inn Marina. Do not go to any

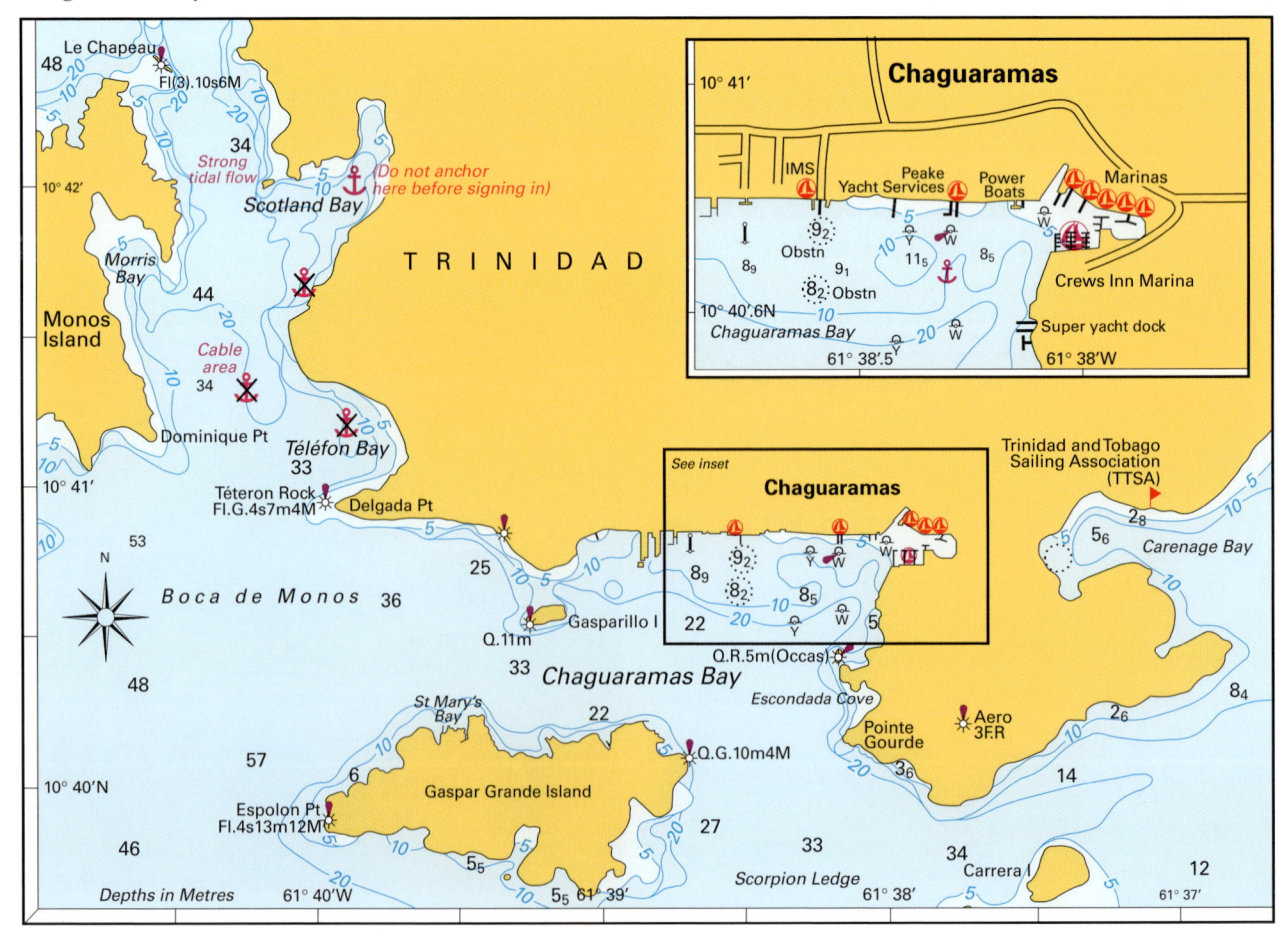

Plan 40 Chaguaramas, Trinidad

marina, mooring or anchorage before checking in with Customs, and Immigration when the latter is open. The Immigration Office is manned from 0600–1200 and 1300–1800 daily and the Customs Office is open 24 hours every day. Sizeable overtime charges are made by both offices outside normal office hours (0800-1200 and 1300-1600 weekdays only). Yachts checking out must complete immigration procedures while the Immigration Office is open, and following clearance with Customs at any time, are currently required to leave within one hour. Customs have been known to charge overtime fees during office hours if they consider that a yacht will not either have entered or left the 12-mile territorial limit during office hours. Yachtsmen are advised not to challenge officers, who are normally friendly and courteous, over what they might consider to be unusually harsh interpretations of overtime payments and leaving requirements. If they feel unfairly treated the circumstances should be reported in writing to the YSATT Office. Yachtsmen should be aware that the senior officers change every six months and that interpretation of the regulations is subject to variation.

Radio

- The National SAR Agency is the Trinidad and Tobago Coast Guard and all emergency contact is through North Post Radio on 2182kHz or VHF Channel 16. North Post Radio also operates on working frequencies 2735kHz, 3165kHz and VHF Channels 22–27. Tel: 637 9023/4474. Coast Guard direct Tel: 634 2131.
- Customs and Immigration monitor VHF Channel 16.
- VHF Channel 68 is a hailing channel for yachts and businesses but is a working channel for commercial shipping. After making contact on VHF Channel 68, yachts should switch to a working channel eg 06, 67, 71, 73.
- Crews Inn Marina monitors VHF Channel 77.
- Peakes Yacht Services monitors VHF Channel 69.
- Power Boats monitors VHF Channel 72.
- A cruisers' radio net operates daily on VHF Channel 68 at 0800 local, 1200 UTC.
- Trinidad Emergency Net transmits a weather forecast on Ham frequency 3855kHz LSB at 1030 UTC (0630 local).

Anchorage and moorings

There is a designated yacht anchorage sited in the eastern part of Chaguaramas Bay marked by large white buoys, and a hefty fine is imposed for ignoring them. Holding is patchy in sand and mud, and a chain scope of at least 5:1 is advised locally.

Trinidad and Tobago Sailing Association (TTSA) in Carenage Bay to the east of Point Gourde, has 16 visitors' moorings.
Website: www.ttsailing.org
Contact: Tel: 634 4210 Fax: 634 4376
E-mail: setsail@ttsailing.org

Trinidad and Tobago Yacht Club (TTYC) further east on Cumana Bay may be able to offer you a mooring.
Website: www.trinidadandtobagoyachtclub.com
Contact: Tel: 633 7420/637 4260 Fax: 633 6388
E-mail: ttyc@tstt.net.tt

Chaguaramas, looking NE with the anchorage in the foreground and boatyards and marinas behind. Carenage Bay can be seen top right.
Photo: Stephen Dalla Costa

PASSAGES AND LANDFALLS

The Yachting Services Association of Trinidad and Tobago (YSATT) has visitors' moorings in Chaguaramas Bay
Contact: Tel: 634 4938 Fax 634 2160 ysatt@trinidad.net
Website: www.ysatt.org

Berthing and facilities

Chaguaramas has a comprehensive collection of yacht services. The Trinidad and Tobago Boaters Directory, published annually, lists all the facilities available. Contact details can be obtained from the Yacht Services Association of Trinidad and Tobago at Crews Inn.
Website: www.ysatt.org
Contact: Tel: 634 4938 Fax: 634 2160
E-mail: ysatt@trinidad.net

Several companies of varying sizes offer berthing on the shores of Chaguaramas Bay. These include:

Crews Inn Hotel and Marina is the newest and biggest concern and caters for visiting yachts and local boats. The marina has 60 berths and can accommodate vessels up to 40m (130ft).
Website: www.crewsinn.com
Contact: Tel: 634 4384/5 Fax: 634 4175/4542
E-mail: inquiries@crewsinn.com

Power Boat Mutual Facilites (Power Boats) has 20 stern to berths for yachts up to 21m (70ft), a 50-tonne marine hoist and extensive storage facilities on site.
Website: www.powerboats.co.tt
Contact: Tel: 634 4303 Fax: 634 4327
E-mail: pbmfl@powerboats.co.tt

Peake Yacht Services has 16 stern-to berths for yachts up to 30m (100ft), a 150-tonne marine hoist and extensive storage including locked high-security compound.
Website: www.peakeyachts.com
Contact: Tel: 634 4427/4420 Fax 634 4387
E-mail: pys@cablenett.net

Coral Cove Marina and Hotel has berths for yachts up to 27m (90ft), a 60-tonne marine hoist, extensive storage and locked compound.
Website: www.coralcovemarina.com
Contact: Tel: 634 2040/634 2244-7 Fax: 634 2248
E-mail: coralcove@trinidad.net

Trinidad and Tobago Yacht Club situated four miles to the east on Cumana Bay, reserve 40 of their 80 berths for visiting yachts up to 17m (56ft)
Website: www.trinidadandtobagoyachtclub.com
Contact: Tel: 633 7420/637 4260 Fax: 633 6388
E-mail: ttyc@tstt.net.tt).

Transport connections

There are bus services, however local people and many visitors favour maxi-taxis – minibuses that operate much as regular buses would elsewhere. Like private taxis they have H number plates and may only stop at marked bus stops.

Air services: there are regular flights to US, Canada, UK and other Caribbean countries.

Medical services

There are several hospitals and medical centres in and around Port of Spain. Ask for local advice.

Carnival limbo during the greatest show on earth.
Photo: John Lytle

LANDFALLS IN THE CARIBBEAN

19
Rodney Bay
St Lucia

Location:	14°04′.5N 60°57′.5W
Springs:	0.6m Range: 0.2m
Neaps:	0.5m Range: 0.2m
Time zone:	UT −4
Currency:	EC dollar (US dollar widely accepted)
Tel/fax:	Country code: 1-758 Area code: none
Language:	English and French Patois
Emergencies:	Tel: 999 (Police)
	911 (Ambulance or Fire)

ARC landfall

Rodney Bay Marina inside the lagoon at Rodney Bay (also known as Gros Islet Bay) has become a popular Atlantic landfall over the last few years. It is the arrival port for the ARC from the Canaries and is particularly busy during December. Outside the lagoon, the bay itself, overlooked by Pigeon Island, is lined with sandy beaches backed with resort hotels. It is a large, popular and pleasant anchorage where you can enjoy swimming from your boat. Pigeon Island is worth a walk around. It is a National Landmark with a ruined fort which dates from the 18th century battles between the English and the French providing a good viewpoint. Pigeon Island is the site of the annual St Lucia Jazz Festival which is held during May.

The capital of St Lucia is Castries, a bus ride from Rodney Bay, which has a vibrant produce market and a good range of shops and supermarkets. Further south is the famous hidden anchorage of Marigot Bay and the dramatic Piton mountains, situated on the leeward side of the island. The evening symphony of tree frogs and insects is particularly memorable at Marigot Bay because you have a 'surround sound' effect. Also here, at the right time of year, you can walk up the hill and collect windfall mangoes which tumble all over the lane and verge.

Approach

Rodney Bay lies within a couple of miles of the northern end of St Lucia, one of the more mountainous of the Lesser Antilles. Although Pointe du Cap at the extreme north of the island has no outlying hazards, it is unlit and the light at Cape Marquis [Fl (2) 20s, 60m] three miles further south on the windward coast only has a five-mile visibility. Having rounded Pointe du Cap, Pigeon Island will be seen rising to over 100m (330ft) at the end of a low artificial causeway; beyond is Rodney Bay.

The entrance to the lagoon lies near the middle of the bay, between Gros Islet village to the north and Reduit Beach to the south. It is not hard to identify by daylight and is lit at night. The channel has been dredged to 4.5m (15ft) approx.

Radio

Rodney Bay Marina and Rodney Bay Marina Boatyard operate on VHF Channel 16. Channel 16 is generally monitored by a number of concerns. The Royal St Lucia Police Force is the search and rescue agency and keeps watch on 2182kHz and VHF Channel 16. They operate in

Entrance to Rodney Bay lagoon looking east. Photo: David Ridout

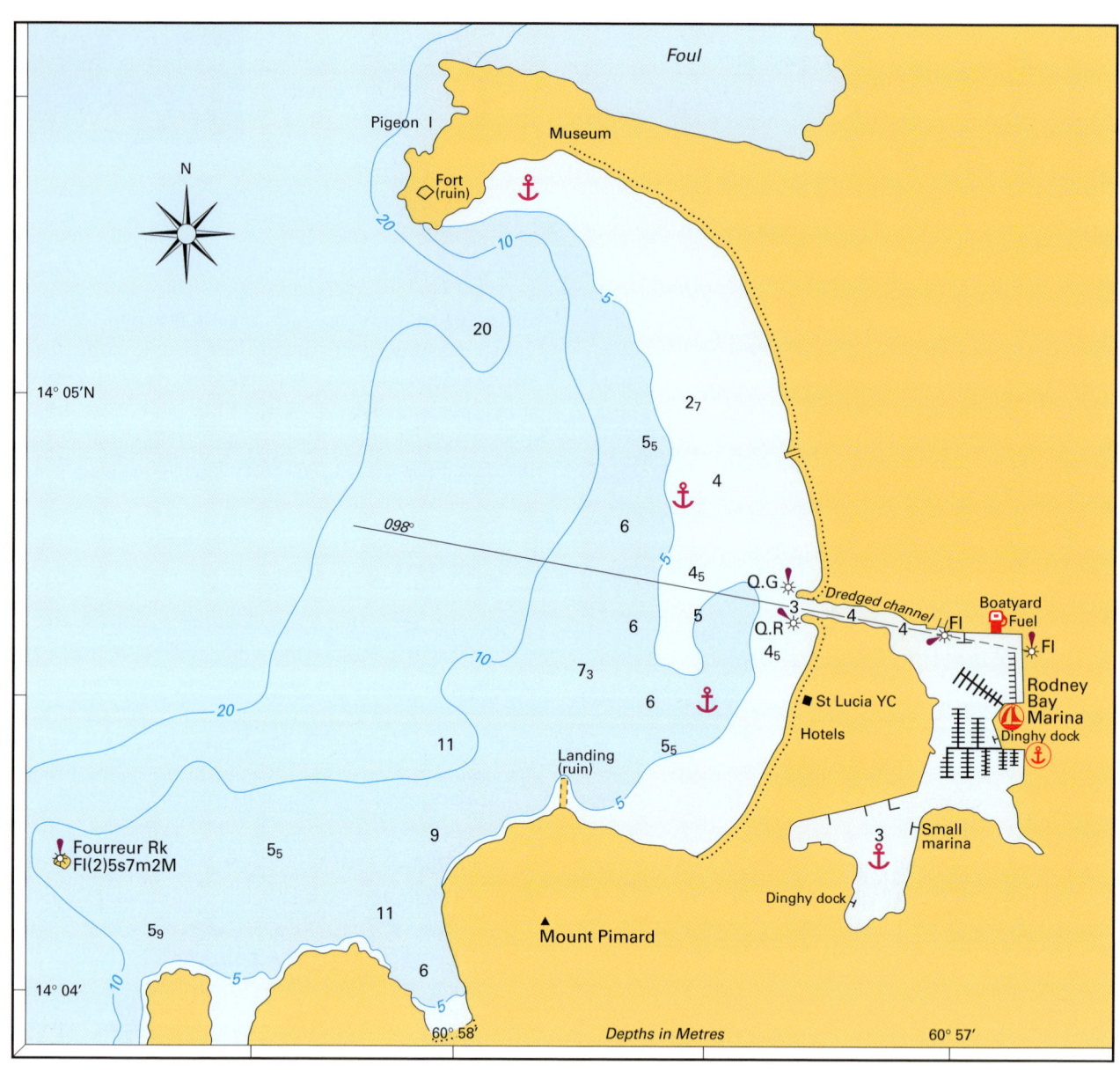

PASSAGES AND LANDFALLS

Plan 41 Rodney Bay, St Lucia

conjunction with the Maritime Rescue Co-ordination Centre in Martinique (Tel: 596 596 709292).

Formalities

Rodney Bay is one of four ports of entry in St Lucia. The offices are on the first floor of the marina buildings and opening hours are: 8–12 and 13.30–16.30 every day of the week except Friday which is: 8–12 and 13.30–18.00. There is a small overtime charge at the weekend. For stays of less than three days you can clear in and out at the same time.

Berthing and facilities

Rodney Bay Marina has completed its major re-construction and now offers excellent, large berths with a full range of facilities and services under the watch of 24-hour security guards. A certain amount of dredging has been done and a large pontoon with fingers for megayachts has been created. The marina boatyard has a 75-tonne yacht hoist. Duty free diesel is available on the fuel dock to the north of the marina berths following outward clearance.

Rodney Bay Marina looking west. Photo: David Ridout

Website: www.rodneybaymarina.com
Contact: Tel: 758 452 0324 Fax: 758 452 0185
E-mail: rbmarina@candw.lc

There is another very small marina: Waterside Landings, but that part of the lagoon has a maximum depth of 3m (10ft). They do require a valid boat insurance certificate if you wish to take a berth.
Contact: Tel: 758 452 0640 or 758 452 5241
Fax: 758 452 7448 E-mail: waterside@beachcomberltd.com

Anchorage and moorings

Anchor in the bay off Reduit Beach or south-east of Pigeon Island. Take your dinghy onto the beach or into the lagoon where you can tie up to the main marina pontoon where it joins the land. The holding in the bay is reported to be patchy. The area off Reduit Beach may be subject to swell but it is usually calmer below Pigeon Island. There is no longer any anchoring in the main lagoon. The lagoon to the south is mostly occupied by moorings for local boats.

Transport connections

There are buses to Castries and inter-island flights from Tapion airport at Vigie Cove near Castries, but long-haul carriers use Hewannora airport, adjacent to Vieux Fort at the south end of the island.

Rodney Bay lagoon looking north-west towards the harbour entrance with Pigeon Island beyond. Photo: David Ridout

Medical services (telephone numbers)

Tapion Hospital (Private, with MEDEVAC to Martinique)	4592000
Victoria Hospital	4522421
Soufriere Hospital	4547258

The anchorage underneath Pigeon Island looking south-east. Photo: David Ridout

PASSAGES AND LANDFALLS

20
English Harbour/Falmouth Harbour
Antigua

Location:	17°00′N 61°45′W
Springs:	0.6m Range: 0.3m
Neaps:	0.4m Range: 0.1m
Currency:	EC dollar
Time zone:	UT –4
Language:	English
Tel/fax:	Country code: 1-268 Area code: none
Emergencies:	Tel: 999 or 911
Rescue services:	Antigua and Barbuda Search and Rescue (ABSAR) www.absar.org Tel: 562 1234 E-mail: info@absar.org, VHF Channel 16, is a non-profit organisation devoted to search and rescue and emergency paramedic services. ABSAR works in conjunction with the Antigua Coastguard, fire and ambulance services.

Iconic views

The view of English Harbour and Falmouth Harbour from Shirley Heights is one of the iconic views of the Caribbean, and it is easy to see why Nelson approved of this spot. English Harbour still features high on the 'must visit' list for many cruising sailors. Semi-derelict until the 1950s, Nelson's Dockyard and its surrounds are now one of the busiest yachting centres in the Caribbean, particularly during Antigua Race Week and Antigua Classics run by Antigua Yacht Club in Falmouth Harbour.

Almost all the development fringing both harbours is yacht or tourist related and English and Falmouth Harbours have a comprehensive range of services for yachts. With nearly all requirements met locally it is possible to spend several weeks in this small part of Antigua without venturing more than a mile from your boat. There is always plenty going on ashore and, if you don't mind the crowds, it is a fun place to be. Some visiting yachts choose to use the same small protected anchorage favoured by the 18th-century British fleet, but others prefer the more open, breezy anchorage of Falmouth.

Sunset on Shirley Heights overlooking English Harbour with Falmouth Harbour beyond. Photo: Mike Robinson

LANDFALLS IN THE CARIBBEAN

ENGLISH HARBOUR/FALMOUTH HARBOUR
ANTIGUA
20

The approach to English Harbour, Antigua, with the Pillars of Hercules on the right. Photo Anne Hammick.

If you are not planning to cruise around the island, a bus trip to the capital, St John's, will give you more of a flavour of the island and its rolling landscape. St John's is a busy cruise ship port and has a wide range of supermarkets, shops and eateries as well as its famous international cricket ground. The pretty old town buildings used only to be overlooked by the baroque towers of the cathedral. Nowadays they are periodically completely dwarfed by some of the larger cruise ships, creating an interesting juxtaposition of images. The Museum of Antigua and Barbuda, housed in the colonial Court House (1750), has some interesting Arawak and colonial displays.

On the water, Jolly Harbour on the west coast is a less crowded alternative to English Harbour. It is a holiday village with a very well-protected harbour and good facilities for visiting yachts. If you really can't stand the crowds and adore deserted beaches, then clear in at Antigua and sail on to Barbuda, its smaller and much less developed sister island to the north.

Websites
www.geographia.com/antigua-barbuda/
www.sailingweek.com
www.antiguaclassics.com/

Approach

At one time Antigua had a poor reputation as an Atlantic landfall, not least because its vicious windward reefs are unmarked by lights of any kind. While this is still true, the bright lights of the airport in the north of the island now effectively announce Antigua's presence from afar. They appear to burn all night, and should be quite sufficient to prevent the unwary from running up on the island unawares even without GPS. If Antigua is sighted at dusk, consideration should be given to reducing speed or even heaving-to for the night, but this might be said of many Caribbean landfalls.

The entrances to English Harbour and Falmouth Bay lie almost in the centre of the south coast, and are somewhat easier to identify when approaching from eastwards than from the south. Coming in from the east in daylight, the bluff promontory of Cape Shirley [Fl (4) 20s 150m 20M] is unmistakable. This headland is the place to close the coast, and a mile or so onwards, the entrances first to English Harbour and then to Falmouth Bay will open up.

From the south the approach is straightforward, although the entrances are not always easy to pinpoint. Inland there are rolling hills, but the lower, slightly darker patch in front is Middle Ground, which separates the two entrances. On closer approach, the sandstone cliffs of Cape Shirley and Shirley Heights will be seen to terminate at their western end (Charlotte Point) in some unusual vertical columns, aptly named the Pillars of Hercules. If coming in from the south, be careful not to get set too far to the west – Middle and Cade Reefs lurk off the south-west tip of Antigua and have claimed several yachts.

Entrance

English Harbour To the north-west, the low crenellations of Barclay Point are unmistakable from nearby, while to the south-east, Charlotte Point is marked by the equally distinctive Pillars of Hercules. A reef extends north-west

PASSAGES AND LANDFALLS

from Charlotte Point directly towards Barclay Point, and the best depths will be found by keeping between half and three-quarters of the way across the gap – ie nearer to Barclay Point. The leading marks are a pair of orange boards positioned further to the north which transit on approximately 025°. Their lights [FlR 2 and 4s] should not be relied upon, and first-time entry after dark is best avoided.

Falmouth Harbour Although much larger, wide stretches of Falmouth Harbour are shallow and there are several isolated coral patches. There are leading lights [Iso and QG] on 029°, but they do not always work. As a stranger, do not enter the bay in darkness if the leading lights cannot be seen. Bishop Shoal extends nearly 0.5 miles offshore on the starboard hand soon after entering and often breaks, but the central shoal does not. Bishop Shoal is buoyed, as is the channel to Antigua Yacht Club and Falmouth Harbour Marinas [Fl R and G] but these marks should not be relied on.

There is a 4-knot speed limit in both harbours that applies to everything, including dinghies; the financial penalties for transgression are severe.

Radio

All the marinas and many yachts, businesses and taxis monitor VHF Channel 68. English Harbour Radio broadcasts a weather forecast at 0900 local time on VHF Channel 06 after an announcement on VHF Channel 68 and is helpful to visiting yachts during office hours.

Formalities

Requirements change from time to time. After entering with the Q flag hoisted, the skipper should go ashore to clear in with ship's papers, passports and previous port clearance. Currently each crew member and passenger must fill in and sign an entry document in three places (available at AYC

Plan 42 English Harbour/Falmouth Harbour, Antigua

162

LANDFALLS IN THE CARIBBEAN

The Pillars of Hercules mark the entrance to English Harbour.
Photo: Mike Robinson

Marina Office and Falmouth Harbour Marina for yachts arriving in Falmouth Harbour). These forms should be completed and then taken by the skipper to Immigration while the passengers and crew remain onboard. The combined Customs, Immigration and Port Offices are in the Old Canvas and Clothing Store in Nelson's Dockyard open 0800–1600 daily. There is currently no office in Falmouth Harbour. Dues are payable for anchoring and for a cruising permit whether or not you plan to cruise the island.

Berthing and facilities at English Harbour

Nelson's Dockyard The docks have been rebuilt in recent years with modern electricity and water installations. Yachts can berth stern-to. Some moorings have been laid for bow lines but anchors are also needed. Prior reservation is recommended.
Website: www.nationalparksantigua.com
Contact: VHF Channel 68 Tel: 481 5022/5033/5035
E-mail: natpark@candw.ag, or the Dockmaster, Tel: 464 6941

Antigua Slipway on the eastern shore is usually reserved for boats undergoing work. A few yachts may also be able to lie alongside. The yard can haul yachts up to 200 tonnes on its slipway or up to 35 tonnes on its small yacht trailer.
Website: www.antiguaslipway.com
Contact: Tel: 460 1056 Fax: 460 1566
E-mail: antslipway@candw.ag

Berthing and facilities

The marinas primarily cater for superyachts but also have space for smaller yachts.

Antigua Yacht Club Marina
Website: www.aycmarina.com
Contact: VHF Channel 68 Tel: 460 1544 Fax: 460 1444
E-mail: aycmarina@candw.ag

Falmouth Harbour Marina
Website: www.antigua-marina.com
Contact: VHF Channels 10/68 Tel: 460 6054 Fax: 460 6055
E-mail: falmar@candw.ag

Catamaran Marina has a travel lift for yachts up to 70 tonnes.
Contact: VHF Channel 68 Tel: 460 1503 Fax: 460 1506
E-mail: catamaranmarina@candw.ag

Jane's Yacht Services arrange Customs clearance for yacht parts, crew placement, a mail drop and courier service, office services, gas filling etc.
Website: www.yachtservices.ag
Contact: Tel: 460 2711 Fax: 460 3740 Mobile: 764 1297
E-mail: antyacht@candw.ag

Jolly Harbour Marina is on the west coast of Antigua. It is a full-service marina with boatyard and 70-tonne haul-out facility. The marina is part of a holiday resort with golf course and various other facilities.
Website: www.jolly-harbour-marina.com/en/index.php

Contact details for other facilities and services can be found in the *Antigua and Barbuda Marine Directory* or the online *Antigua Marine Guide* www.antiguamarineguide.com

Anchorage and moorings

English Harbour Pick any spot that offers swinging room and does not impede the channel to Antigua Slipway and Nelson's Dockyard. Some prefer the breeze and cleaner water of Freeman's Bay, some the greater convenience of being nearer the Dockyard, perhaps in Ordnance Bay on its northern side. Dinghies can be landed on the beach in Freeman's Bay or at the purpose-built dinghy landing by the boundary wall of the old Dockyard.

Falmouth Harbour Anchor where space is available but avoid the area close off the Antigua Yacht Club and Falmouth Harbour Marinas where large yachts drop their anchors and manoeuvre. Some moorings are available; call Sea Pony VHF Channel 68 or Tel 464 3164/460 1154/726 3164 E-mail: johnbentley890@hotmail.com

Transport connections

There are frequent buses (mini buses and larger) during the day to St John's starting from outside Dockyard gates and pick-up anywhere en route. International airport with regular flights to the United Kingdom, United States and Canada as well as inter-island services which link to other international flights.

Medical services (telephone numbers)

Holberton Hospital, St John's (public hospital)	462 0251/2/3/4
The Adelin Medical Centre, St John's (private clinic)	462 0866/7
Dentists in St John's.	

ENGLISH HARBOUR / FALMOUTH HARBOUR
ANTIGUA
20

PASSAGES AND LANDFALLS

21
British Virgin Islands

Springs:	0.6m	Range:	0.2m
Neaps:	0.3m	Range:	0.1m
Time zone:	UT –4		
Currency:	US dollar		
Tel/fax:	Country code: 1-284 Area code: none		
Emergencies:	Tel: 999 or 911.		

Island hopping

The Virgin Islands are an archipelago of small islands which are divided into two main groupings. The British Virgin Islands lie to the east of the group and include Anegada, Jost Van Dyke, Tortola, Virgin Gorda, and over 50 other smaller islands which are all administered as an overseas territory of the United Kingdom. At the western end of the group St Croix, St John, St Thomas, and Water Island are governed as an unincorporated territory of the United States. Further west still lie the islands of Vieques and Culebra which are sometimes referred to as the Spanish Virgin Islands. These are Spanish speaking and governed as part of the Commonwealth of Puerto Rico.

Unlike anchorages such as English Harbour, where many cruising sailors stay for several weeks, once cleared into the British Virgin Islands few yachts will stay in one harbour for long – the whole appeal is to explore by water. The islands offer wonderful cruising around easily navigable, sheltered water with many different lovely anchorages. The islands are a favourite charter destination. Road Town is the capital of the British Virgin Islands and a centre for bareboat charters, and has all facilities necessary to prepare for departure northwards. However, some skippers prefer to clear in and out at one of the other ports in the area, only visiting Road Town for essential shopping.

Approach

If coming from eastwards – ie St Martin or Anguilla – aim to arrive at dawn and enter through Round Rock Passage, between Ginger Island [Fl 5s 152m 14M] and the jumbled rocks known as Fallen Jerusalem off the south end of Virgin Gorda (unlit). Then either head north for Virgin Gorda Yacht Harbour or continue down the Sir Francis Drake Channel towards Road Town, about halfway along the south coast of Tortola.

Landfall from northwards – ie Bermuda or the United States – is more of a problem because of the dangers posed by the low-lying island of Anegada. Approach from the north-west and be certain to arrive in daylight, even if you

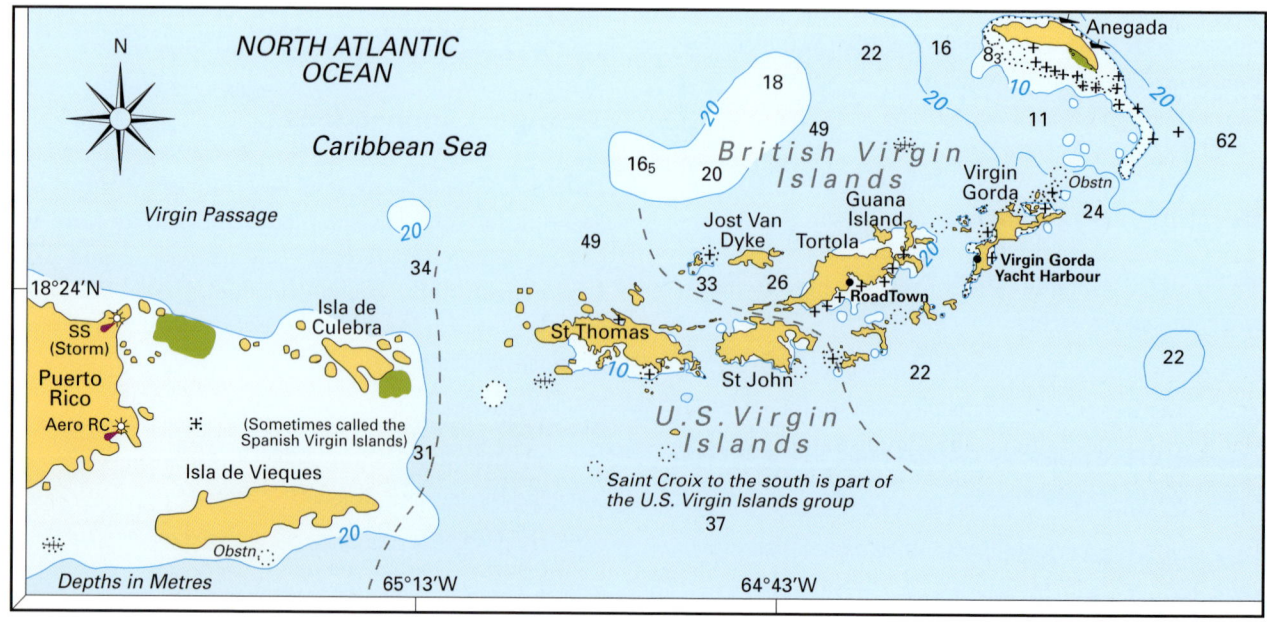

Plan 43 The Virgin Islands

LANDFALLS IN THE CARIBBEAN

Jost van Dyke anchorage, British Virgin Islands. Photo: Graham Adam

are using GPS. If coming from this direction it may be convenient to clear into the British Virgin Islands at Great Harbour on Jost Van Dyke.

Radio

VHF Channel 16 is used throughout the islands for international distress and calling. The US Coast Guard uses Channel 22A. Channels 06 and 68 are used for intership traffic and Channel 03 for weather. Road Harbour and Port Purcell use Channels 16 and 14, and Virgin Gorda Yacht Harbour uses Channel 16.

A walk-in weather centre, CARIBWX (www.caribwx.com), is based in Road Town and offers a range of weather services. Tel. 494 7559, E-mail: weather@caribwx.com

ZBVI Radio transmits a marine forecast 0805 (Mon–Sat), 0945 (Sun) and updates every hour on the half hour.

Formalities

Fly the Q flag on arrival. If wishing to clear in at Road Town it is, in theory, still necessary to anchor off the Customs dock on arrival. Go ashore to clear, taking all the usual papers plus clearance from the last port of call. In practice, it may be permissible to go on foot from a marina berth – check the current situation with the marina by radio before berthing. In Road Town the offices are on the government dock at the head of the ferry and Customs pier, in Virgin Gorda Yacht Harbour they are in the main administration block, and hours are 08:30–16:30 Monday to Friday, 08:30–12:30 Saturday. Outward clearance is valid for 24 hours, but if you admit that you intend to depart outside working hours you may well be charged overtime! Private boats are automatically given up to 30 days to cruise around the BVI; a 30-day cruising fee is charged.

See page 142 for details about entry for visitors without a prior visa.

American citizens should note that a valid passport is now required to enter the British Virgin Islands. A birth certificate plus photographic identification is no longer sufficient.

Transport connections

Frequent ferries between Road Town and Virgin Gorda. Beef Island airport, Tortola (about 16km (10 miles) from Road Town) has links with other Caribbean islands, including Antigua and Puerto Rico, but no long-haul flights. There is a convenient anchorage in nearby Trellis Bay. Virgin Gorda has a small airstrip.

Medical services

Doctors on Tortola and Virgin Gorda, hospital outside Road Town.

Virgin Island iguanas. Photo: Graham Adam

BRITISH VIRGIN ISLANDS

21

PASSAGES AND LANDFALLS

ROAD TOWN, TORTOLA

Location: 18°25′N 64°37′W

Entrance

Road Town Bay is unmistakable, with many buildings and large fuel tanks on the eastern side near the entrance. Although various shoal patches dot the entrance, all carry at least 3.6m (12ft), so can be ignored by the majority of yachts. However, avoid approaching Fort Burt Point too closely, and beware of Harbour Spit which runs south-east towards the middle of the harbour, supposedly marked by a lit buoy. If continuing into Wickhams Cay at the north end of the bay, having left the cruise ship dock to port, keep carefully to the channel – it is narrow with a distinct dogleg, but well buoyed.

Anchorage and moorings

Yachts anchor along the western shores of the outer harbour to the north of Fort Burt, with a dinghy landing at the ferry pier in the north-west corner. More protected, and with several marinas with visitors' berths, is Wickhams Cay. A notice forbidding yachts to anchor may be visible, but no one seems to take much notice, provided access to the marinas is not impeded. Visitors are also accepted in the marinas just to the west of Fort Burt.

Berthing and facilities

Village Cay Marina is on the west side of Wickhams Cay. It has over 100 slips and provides a full range of services.
Website: www.igy-villagecay.com
Contact: Road Town, Tortola, British Virgin Islands.
Tel: 494 2771 Fax: 494 2773 E-mail: VC@igymarinas.com

The Moorings/Mariners Inn to the east may have a berth available – check before arrival. Their reception pontoons are clearly marked.
Website: www.bvimarinerinnhotel.com/the_moorings.htm
Contact: MVW International Co Ltd, Wickhams Cay 2, PO Box 139, Road Town Tortola, British Virgin Islands.
Tel: 494 2333 Fax: 494 1638
E-mail: reservations@bvimarinerinnhotel.com

Tortola Yacht Services close east of The Moorings (18° 25′.8N 064° 36′.7W), has a 70-tonne travel lift with full boatyard facilities on site.

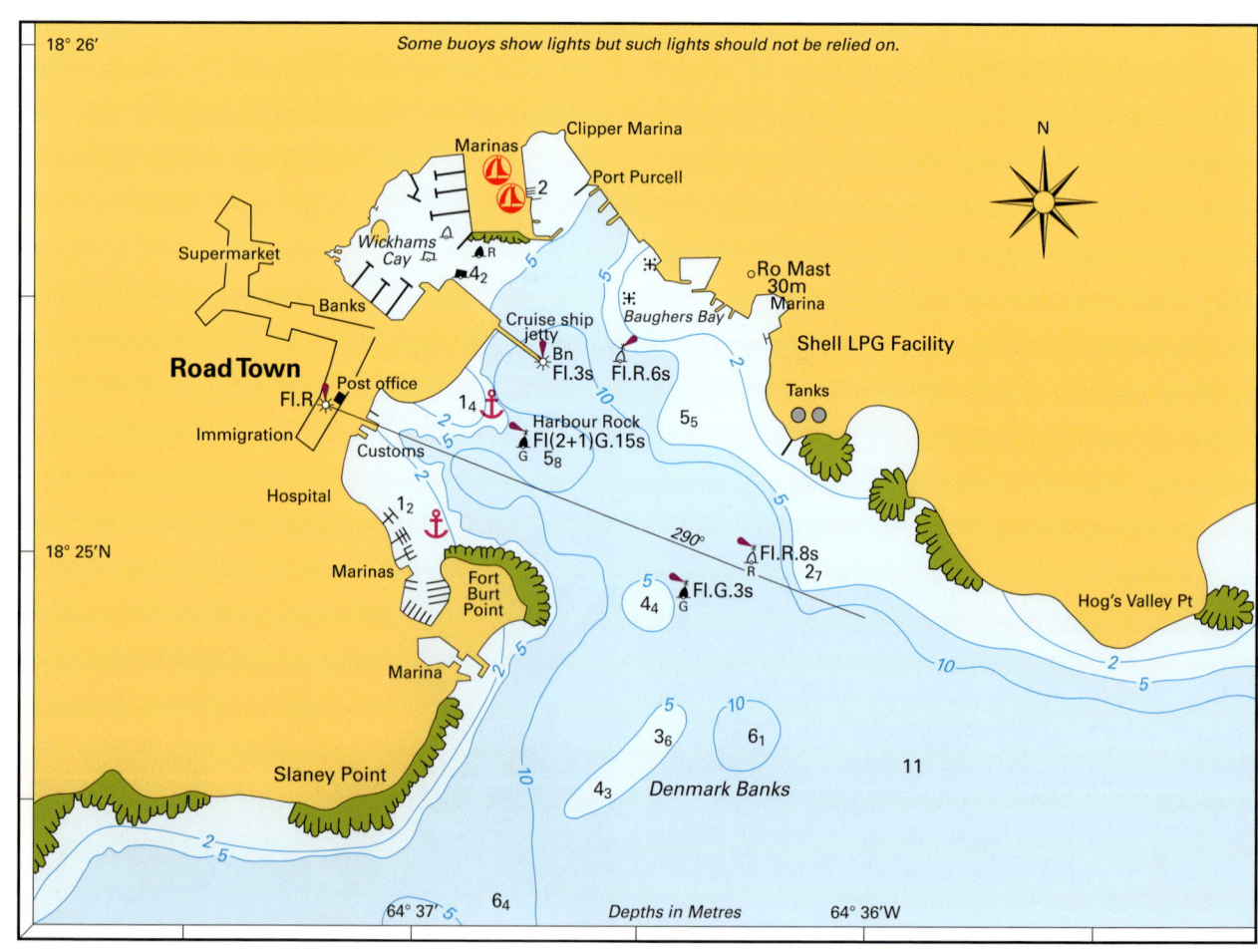

Plan 44 Road Town, Tortola, BVI

LANDFALLS IN THE CARIBBEAN

Website: www.tysbvi.com
Contact: Tel: 494 2124 Fax: 474 4707
E-mail: sales@tysbvi.com

VIRGIN GORDA YACHT HARBOUR, VIRGIN GORDA

Location: 18°27′N   64°26′W

Entrance

The marina lies north of the famous Baths on the west coast of the island. The channel is buoyed, with a sharp turn first to the south and then eastwards into the marina proper. The reception pontoon is nearly opposite the entrance and is well marked. There is little room to manoeuvre once inside, so if short on crew go in with lines and fenders ready (port side-to).

Anchorage and moorings

St Thomas Bay outside the entrance to the marina provides a pleasant temporary anchorage in 6m (20ft) or more over sand. For both safety and comfort, keep well north of the approach to the ferry pier.

Berthing and facilities

Virgin Gorda Yacht Harbour can berth over 100 yachts and has a full range of facilities.
Websites: www.paradise-islands.org/virgin-gorda/yacht_harbour.htm and www.vgmarina.biz/default.html
Contact: PO Box 1005, Virgin Gorda, British Virgin Islands.
Tel: 495 5500 Fax: 495 5706 E-mail: VG@igymarinas.com

Virgin Gorda Yacht Harbour Boatyard has a 70-tonne travel lift with full boatyard facilities and hard standing.

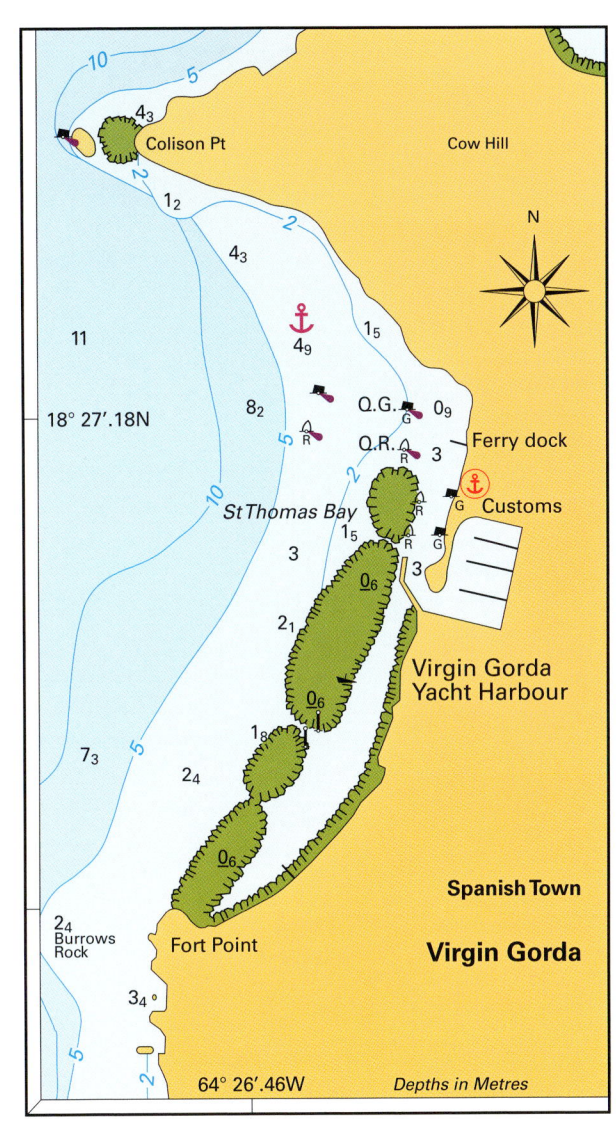

Plan 45 Virgin Gorda Yacht Harbour, Virgin Gorda, BVI

Website: www.vgmarina.biz/boatyard–services.html
Contact: Tel: 495 5500 Fax: 495 5706
E-mail: www.vgmarina.biz/amenities.html

Trellis Bay, Tortola, is a very popular anchorage for cruising yachts.
Photo: Daniel Anthony

BRITISH VIRGIN ISLANDS 21

14 Routes across the Caribbean and landfall in Panama

| 22 Colón, Panama | 173 |

Those who are only contemplating a one-year Atlantic Circuit will probably focus on the eastern Caribbean island chains. However, if circumstances allow, you may wish to explore westwards and discover the many other cruising areas around the Caribbean Sea. During Hurricane Season it is wise either to head north up the east coast of North America or to head south to Trinidad or the coast of Venezuela. From late November onwards you can continue your Caribbean explorations within the Hurricane Belt.

If you have crossed the Atlantic to the Caribbean with a view to continuing through to the Pacific you will need to head west to be in Panama by May or June at the latest for onward passages westwards. If you are heading for Panama and beyond it is worthwhile to purchase specific or specialised chandlery items at one of the major yachting centres in the eastern Caribbean.

There are two popular cruising routes to Panama from the eastern Caribbean chain; one from the north part of the chain and the other from the south. Of course, sailing direct is also an option.

THE NORTHERN ROUTE ACROSS THE CARIBBEAN

The most popular northerly route runs from the Virgin Islands along the coasts of Puerto Rico, the south coast of Hispaniola (the Dominican Republic and Haiti, including Isle de Vache) to Jamaica. Errol Flynn Marina in Port Antonio on Jamaica's north-east side is a good place to pause and stock up and change crew. From there you can then sail directly to Panama or stop at Providencia or San Andres – two offshore Colombian islands. With more time you can continue the hops from Jamaica to the Cayman Islands or Cuba, Mexico, Belize, Guatemala and Honduras. These are all increasingly popular cruising areas and worth looking into when you are setting your plans. From Puerto Vita, on the eastern end of the north coast of Cuba, it is possible to day-sail all along the north coast to the very western tip.

The reef off Belize is the second largest barrier reef system in the world and is a favourite area for divers. Like the River Gambia, the Rio Dulce in Guatemala allows you to feel as if you are cruising into the heart of a country. Deeper-draught vessels may find the entrance difficult or

Plan 46 The Caribbean Sea showing common transit routes

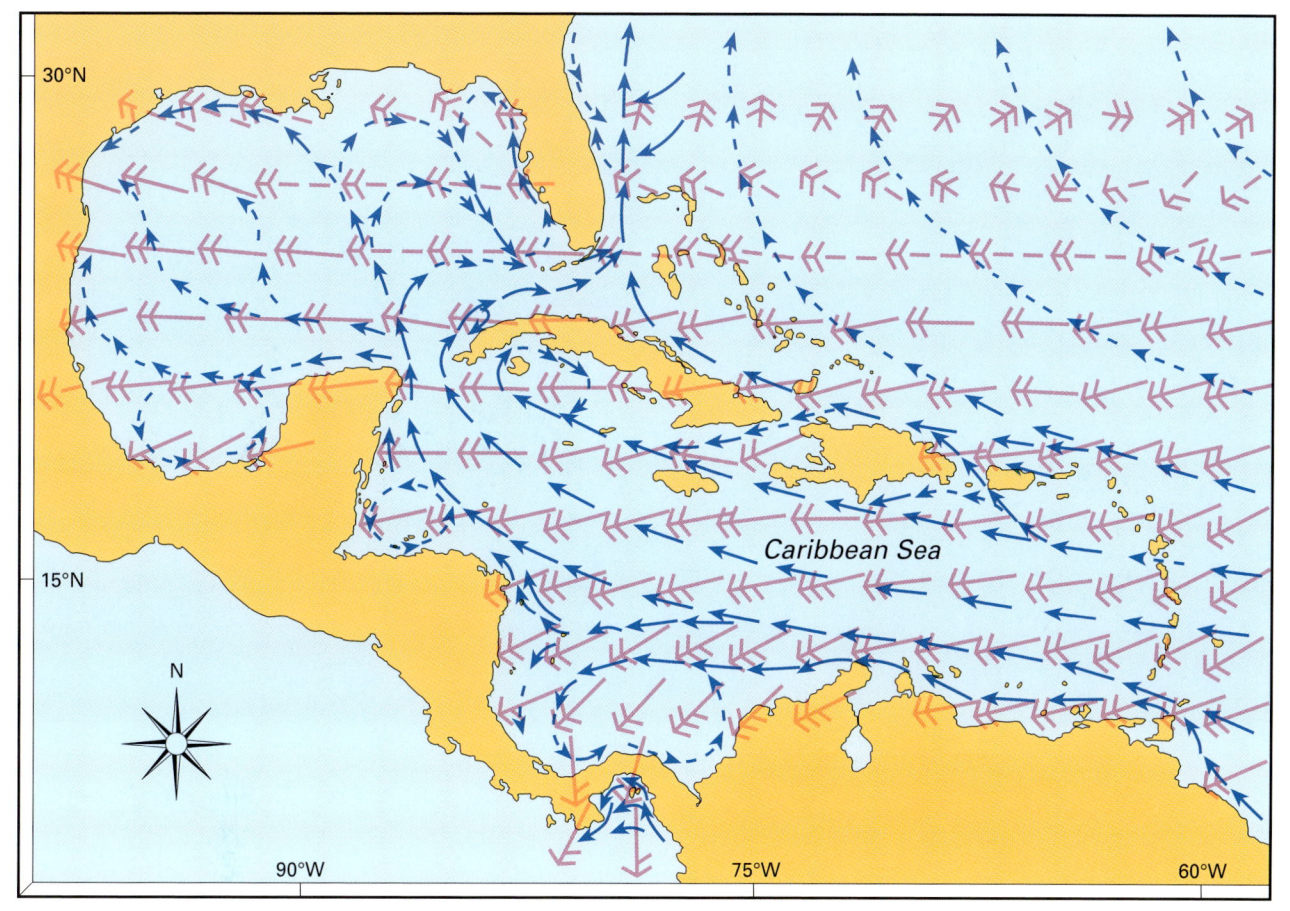

ROUTES ACROSS THE CARIBBEAN AND LANDFALL IN PANAMA

Plan 47 Winds and currents in the Caribbean Sea during March. Based on information from *The Atlantic Pilot Atlas*

even impossible, but cruising yachts with 2m (6ft) draught or less should have straightforward access.

> **Further reference**
> *Cuba: A Cruising Guide* by Nigel Calder, Imray, Laurie, Norie & Wilson
> *Cruising Guide to The Northwest Caribbean* by Stephen J Pavlidis, Seaworthy Publications
> www.dominicanrepubliccruisingguide.com/

Best times for the northern route
November and early December or from March to mid-May
Winds during these periods are light and the seas are flatter. Occasional cold fronts or dissipating weather systems sometimes bring rain or squalls, particularly along the coastal regions of the large islands, but winds are generally in the 15 to 20-knot range and blow from the easterly quadrant.

The large islands influence the wind conditions and cause local, less predictable wind patterns. Acceleration zones such as the Windward and Mona Passage are well documented. Strong winds and high seas often result.

Other times
From mid-December until March
Dry season conditions frequently produce 20 to 25-knot winds with short, steep seas which make sailing more challenging. Wind direction tends to be from the north-east. Winds from June to October tend to be lighter than 20 knots and frequently from the southeast quadrant. During this period, tropical waves, depressions and hurricanes make moving about on this route risky. The western portion of this route is subject to early season tropical system development from mid-May until the end of June. Rain, thunderstorms, and depressions make this period risky.

THE SOUTHERN ROUTE ACROSS THE CARIBBEAN

This route runs from the southern part of the island chain along the outer islands of Venezuela and the ABC Islands. There are then two alternatives for passages to Panama: to coastal-hop and visit ports in Columbia, especially Cartagena, or to head directly for Panama or the San Blas Islands. Cartagena, Colombia, is considered by many visiting cruisers to be an absolute 'must see' and worth every effort to get there. The San Blas are a slice of paradise and for many circumnavigators they are one of the lasting highlights of their extended voyaging. The more direct route from the ABC Islands to San Blas or Panama is notorious for the big seas which can pile up off the Colombian coast and create uncomfortable passage conditions.

PASSAGES AND LANDFALLS

The passage over the top of Colombia can be a real roller coaster. Photo: Mike Robinson

Further reference
Cruising Guide to Venezuela and Bonaire by Chris Doyle and Jeff Fisher, Cruising Guide Publications
The Panama Guide: A Cruising Guide to the Isthmus of Panama by Nancy Schwalbe Zydler and Tom Zydler, Seaworthy Publications

Best times for the southern route
December or April and May
Weather conditions are similar to those for the northern route, although slightly stronger winds and higher seas might be expected around the ABC Islands and off the Colombian coast. June is also possible but it tends to be a windy month with more frequent rain squalls and thunderstorms. Typical winds are easterly 15–20 knot range with seas of 1–2m.

It is also possible to make this trip during the hurricane season – June to the end of November – but tropical waves and depressions will produce squalls and thunderstorms with a significant lightning threat. Hurricanes generally move north of this route, but they may generate large swells. Winds during the hurricane season tend to be light (15 knots or less) from the south-east quadrant, but closer to Panama it is common to experience south-westerly or even westerly winds until early December. Few Panamanian anchorages are protected from the west.

Other times
Later in December through to March
This weather period is more challenging. The pressure gradient is enhanced by the combination of a semi-permanent 'thermal low' over Colombia and strong high pressure moving south and east from North America. Gale force winds are not uncommon, along with steep seas, which may exceed 6m (20ft) off the Colombian coast. Colombian ports often deny departure to yachts during this period. It is sometimes possible to move between cycles if the lower winds persist for long enough. A good strategy is to enjoy the ABC Islands and the Venezuelan offshore islands and make the trip to the western Caribbean later in the spring.

MOVING NORTH AND SOUTH IN THE WESTERN CARIBBEAN

The western Caribbean is a very diverse cruising area. Routes generally run parallel to the coastline of Nicaragua and Honduras through the offshore banks to Jamaica or west to the Bay Islands of Honduras and up the Guatemalan

The Dutch influence is evident in the architecture in Willemstad, Curacao. Photo: Richard Woods

170

ROUTES ACROSS THE CARIBBEAN AND LANDFALL IN PANAMA

The Cartagena anchorage is a tranquil reward. Photo: Mike Robinson

coast to Belize and Mexico. Weather conditions in this part of the Caribbean tend to be more challenging and timing plays a more important role in making passages.

> **Further reference**
> *Cruising Ports, Central American Route* by Pat Rains, Point Loma Publishing

NORTH FROM PANAMA

Many vessels arrive in Panama from Venezuela and Colombia or have transited the Panama Canal from the Pacific. They will often spend time in the San Blas Islands of Panama, before moving north.

Best time
April to mid May
Moving north at this time of year generally involves waiting for the wind to back into the east or better yet, south of east. Cold fronts become less frequent in early April and finally become absent from the Caribbean, stalling over the Gulf of Mexico. Winds slowly become easterly by early May, permitting a northerly course to be laid to the offshore islands of San Andres or Providencia or directly to Jamaica. From Providencia or San Andres, it is usually a good sail to the Bay Islands of Honduras or the Rio Dulce in Guatemala. This route runs through or past the various groups of cays and banks which lie off the coasts of Nicaragua and Honduras.

This is also a favourable time for leaving from the Rio Dulce, Honduras, Belize, or Mexico to travel to Cuba or the United States.

Other times
Moving during the hurricane season is risky, although the south-west Caribbean tends to escape early-season storms. Further north, in past years, early-season depressions, broad troughs and even tropical storms have made a habit of forming in late May and June. From June to November heavy rains, thunderstorms and lightning are frequent all along the coastline as far as southern Mexico. October and November are also months for late season hurricanes in the Western Caribbean.

From December to March, winds are generally north-east with typical speeds of 20 to 25 knots, which makes north or easterly progress very difficult.

The dinghy dock is a popular gathering place in Cartagena. Photo: Richard Woods

PASSAGES AND LANDFALLS

From the Western Caribbean to Florida

Best times
Late April to mid May
The routes from Mexico, Belize and western Cuba all involve gaining easting. By late April, cold fronts in the Gulf of Mexico have weakened in strength or have begun to stall in the north. Ahead of the fronts, winds tend to be easterly or south-easterly, with speeds averaging 10 to 15 knots. The location and strength of the Gulf Stream current is a major factor on these passages. The current in the Gulf Stream can run at 3 to 4 knots in a 20-mile wide band. The water temperature is much higher in the Gulf Stream than in the surrounding water. Avoid making passage when strong winds blow counter to the Gulf Stream as wind against current produces large, steep seas.

Other times
From December until early April
Frequent cold fronts penetrate well into the Caribbean during this period. Rain, gusty winds, and occasional thunderstorms are often associated with these cold fronts. Winds ahead of these fronts tend to be easterly at 15 to 20 knots. Behind the cold fronts, winds are mostly north-east 20 knots and sometimes stronger, with 2–3m (6–10ft) seas. The winds behind the fronts sometimes blow for several days until the next cold front approaches. It is possible to make a passage between fronts, depending on the strength and direction of the Gulf Stream.

MOVING SOUTH IN THE WESTERN CARIBBEAN

From Florida to the Western Caribbean

Best times
From March to mid May
Winds generally blow northeast or easterly between 15 to 20 knots. Early in the period, cold fronts may penetrate the Gulf of Mexico, shifting winds from easterly to north-easterly. Clouds and showers often accompany cold fronts.

Cruisers join locals for a San Blas dinghy race. Photo: Richard Woods

Mormake Tupu women wearing molas, a traditional design. Photo: Mike Robinson

Other times
December to March
North-east winds behind cold fronts are predominant but are stronger – in the 20 to 25 knot range. Cold fronts will be sharper and have more adverse weather accompanying them during these months.

Late May to early July should be avoided, as troughs, early-season depressions, and tropical storms often develop during this period. July and August are risky times to travel because of the possibility of tropical waves and depressions.

From the Western Caribbean to Panama

Best times
Early April to late May from Belize and the Rio Dulce
Winds at this time of year tend to be lighter and the seas calmer, although there will be occasional showers and thunderstorms. The lighter winds and smaller seas are a benefit because there is considerable easting to be made from Belize and Guatemala before rounding Cabo Gracios a Dios, the cape at the eastern end of Honduras, and turning the corner southward. This cape is called 'Thanks be to God' for good reason – it is likely to be a windward struggle to get there and you will be very thankful when you have rounded it. East and north-east winds are accelerated close to the northern coast of Honduras.

Early December until late May from Jamaica or Cuba
Winds will be typically 20 knots and more north-easterly from December until April and cold fronts will penetrate well into the Caribbean basin until late April. After that time easterly winds of 15 to 20 knots could be expected. Seas will gradually abate from 2–3m (6–10ft) to 1–1.5m (3–4.5ft) by May.

Other times
This area is best avoided from early June until mid July because early season depressions often form in this region. During hurricane season, thunderstorms are a regular occurrence in coastal areas. Short passages between tropical waves are possible. Longer voyages are best left for more favourable months. Winds tend to be lighter than 20 knots.

ROUTES ACROSS THE CARIBBEAN AND LANDFALL IN PANAMA

22
Colón
Panama

Location:	9°24´N 79°55´W
Average tidal range:	0.3m
Time zone:	UT –5
Currency:	US dollars (coins are a mix of US and local version)

Tel/fax:	Country code: 00507
Emergencies: Tel:	104 (Police)
	103 (Ambulance and Fire)

Gateway to the Pacific

Colón, on the Caribbean side of the Panama Canal, is for many cruisers the gateway to the Pacific. But it is also a popular port for yachts cruising a circuit around the Caribbean. The new marina at Shelter Bay is on land previously occupied by US forces. The fact that it is relatively 'out of town' means that a stop-over in Colón no longer causes the security concerns that it once did. Some cruisers now consider Shelter Bay to be the best venue for final preparations for the Pacific including day trips to Panama City for chandlery, but choice may be limited compared to the eastern Caribbean. The Panama Canal is one of the man-made wonders of the world. Even if you are not transiting on your own boat, volunteering as a line handler for a day is a truly memorable experience. For those who are transiting there will seem to be several bureaucratic hoops to jump through before transit day becomes a reality, but the path is a well trodden one and there will be plenty of fellow cruisers as well as helpful shore staff who will guide you through it all.

Caution
There are salt-water crocodiles in Panamanian waters, including the San Blas Islands and the canal itself.

Approach and entrance

Approach is relatively straightforward. You will be entering freighter traffic lanes for one of the busiest ports in the world and shipping traffic will increase as you close the harbour entrance.

For Shelter Bay: turn to starboard after passing through the entrance and follow the breakwater keeping the green Shelter Bay buoys on your portside. Continue to the marina

Yachts rafted up in a Panama lock. Photo: Mike Robinson

PASSAGES AND LANDFALLS

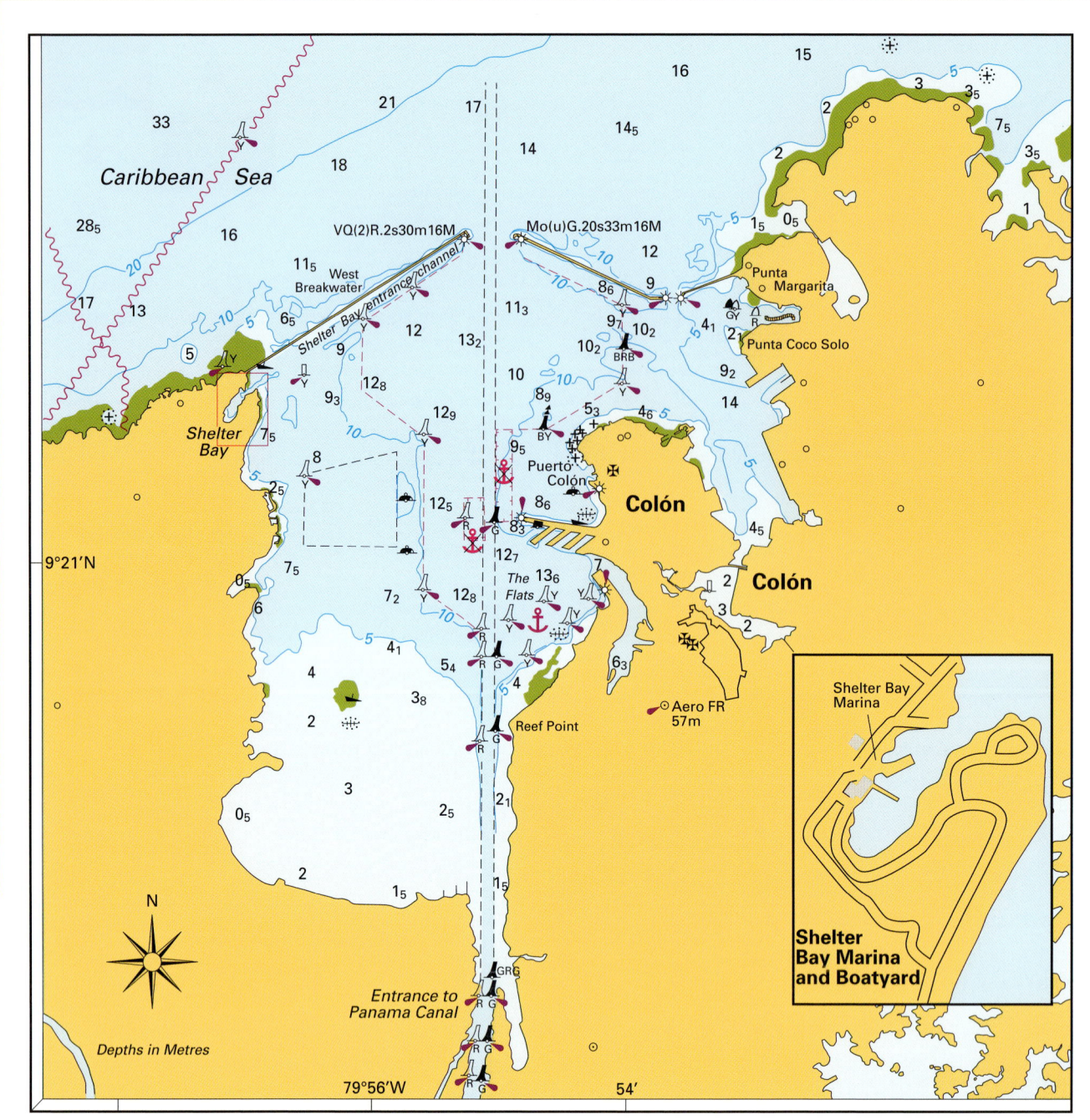

Plan 48 Colón, Panama

bay entrance. At approximately 9°22´.23N and 79°56´.864W you will see white concrete markers SB 12 Red and SB 13 Green showing the boundaries of the harbour entrance. Stay between the markers and proceed past the Coast Guard docks to the Marina.

If you are heading straight to the anchorage, continue south from the entrance to the well marked area at The Flats. Be aware of shipping movements at all times and stay clear of the main channel.

Formalities

On approaching the breakwater, call Cristobal Control (Cristobal Signal Station) on VHF Channel 12 or 16 and notify them of your presence and your intention to go to Shelter Bay Marina or the anchorage. Cristobal Control will alert other ships to your location and direct you accordingly.

Clearance procedures, and a visit by the Admeasurer if you are planning to transit the canal, can be arranged through the marina. It is also worth asking around on other yachts to find out which agents they are using and what prices they are being charged. Before entering Panama you should complete the Yachts Arrival Document for the Panama Maritime Authority from the following website: www.amp.gob.pa/atraque/CaptaCartaAtraqueYates.aspx

A 'zarpe' is required when entering Panamanian waters and a current Cruising Permit is necessary whether your boat is on the hard or in the water. A zarpe is the exit documentation that you get from the last country or port you visited. This includes internal transits within Panama, for example from the San Blas island region. The zarpe needs to be presented on arrival in in order for your cruising

ROUTES ACROSS THE CARIBBEAN AND LANDFALL IN PANAMA

Shelter Bay Marina with Colón harbour breakwater beyond. Photo: Mike Robinson

permit to be issued. You will also be given a zarpe on departure for presentation at your next country or port.

Radio

Call the marina on VHF Channel 74; a daily cruisers's net at 0730 (local) on VHF Channel 74, which is also used at other times as a hailing channel. The Panama Connection Net on 8107 kHz USB at 0830 (local) is also a useful source of information.

Berthing and facilities

Shelter Bay Marina (9° 22´.1N and 79° 57´.0W), located just inside the west breakwater in the north-west corner of the harbour, is a quiet marina with pontoon moorings. It has a range of facilities including a 100-tonne travel lift and hard standing.
Website: www.shelterbaymarina.com
Contact: Tel:507 433-3581 Cell: 507 6781-6631
Fax: 507 433-0470 E-mail: info@shelterbaymarina.com

The Flats anchorage, Colón. Photo: Richard Woods

The Panama Canal Yacht club has been bulldozed and the dinghy dock is no longer available to boats anchored on The Flats.

Anchoring

The designated yacht anchorage at Colón, known as 'The Flats', is a clearly defined area marked by buoys. The breeze keeps the anchorage pleasant and largely bug-free. The holding is good in thick, sticky mud.

Transiting

During busy periods there can be a long wait to transit the canal. Details of transit requirements can be found through the marina office and on the Panama Canal website www.pancanal.com. Once you have been admeasured and paid your Canal transit fees you may find that you have some choice on the date of transit, possibly up to 30 days, so you can continue to prepare the boat for the Pacific before transiting the Canal. Information about transiting can also be found at www.rccpf.org.uk

Transport connections

There are good bus services between Colón, Balboa and Panama City, including bus connections to the international airport. The marina runs a shopping bus service to a shopping centre every morning and afternoon which continues on into Colón and the Citibank.

Medical services

Ask at Shelter Bay Marina for advice on local services

COLÓN
PANAMA
22

15 Caribbean Islands to Florida

23	Luperon, Dominican Republic	179
24	Providenciales, Turks and Caicos	182
25	Georgetown, Great Exuma, Bahamas	184
26	Marsh Harbour, Abacos, Bahamas	186
27	Fort Lauderdale, Florida, USA	188

Heading northwards from Antigua or the Virgin Islands you have several choices of route, depending on your onward plans. Some yachts aim to make next landfall at the Azores and therefore try to shape a course to the east of Bermuda. Some yachts make direct for the North American coastline, usually south of Cape Hatteras. A more common choice is to set course for Bermuda before either heading north-west to the North American coastline or heading eastwards towards the Azores and Europe. All of these routes involve ocean passages.

An alternative is to continue the harbour and anchorage hopping and cruise Puerto Rico, the Dominican Republic, Turks and Caicos and the Bahamas before heading into the US coast and connecting with the Intracoastal Waterway. Marina Puerto del Rey (marina@marinapuertodelrey.com) at the eastern end of Puerto Rico is reputedly the largest marina in the Caribbean. Further west along the north coast is the old port and colonial city of San Juan which is well worth a visit. It is quite feasible to day-sail the whole of the route to Florida, the longest day passage being about 80 miles. There are a number of possible harbours and anchorages, but you should research the relevant information with particular regard to depths. If time is limited or draught prevents passage through the Bahamas themselves, an alternative is to sail up the Atlantic side of the chain until Eleuthera is abeam, then pass through the north-east and north-west Providence Channels and across the Strait of Florida to Miami or Fort Lauderdale.

A north-west-going current, averaging about 0.5 knots, follows the trend of the Bahamas until it merges with the Gulf Stream north of the islands. In places it may run with considerably greater speed, setting onto and across shoals and reefs, and is a good reason for avoiding passage-making after dark in this area. In the north-west Providence Channel currents are unpredictable and are very influenced by the wind. In the Florida Strait the Gulf Stream runs at 3.5 to 4 knots in midstream, rather less at the edges, so take this into account if you are heading for Miami or Fort Lauderdale.

Your choice of route will depend on your individual plans and circumstances and may be influenced by the approaching threat of hurricane season. The whole area from the Caribbean to Florida and up to Bermuda is well within the possible path of early-season hurricanes.

Up-to-date cruising guides can be more accurate and useful than some of the charts of the area, although no one source should ever be relied upon entirely.

Plan 49 Ports between the Caribbean Islands and Florida

CARIBBEAN ISLANDS TO FLORIDA

Further reference
The Turks and Caicos Guide (including the Dominican Republic) by Stephen Pavlidis, Seaworthy Publications
The Exuma Guide by Stephen Pavlidis, Seaworthy Publications
Cruising Guide to Abaco Bahamas by S J and J Dodge, White Sound Press

If you are planning to head south-east from Florida to the Caribbean read: *Gentleman's Guide to Passages South* (2001) by Bruce Van Sant, Cruising Guide Publications. Sometimes opinionated, it is nevertheless full of knowledge of the area.

REGIONAL WEATHER AND PASSAGE TIMINGS

The route via the Bahamas can often be favourable from early April when winds begin to diminish in strength. May is the transition month when cold fronts from North America cease and frontal waves from the tropical Atlantic begin. These may cause local but intense weather systems between the Virgin Islands and the Bahamas, and the Bahamas themselves often experience at least one severe storm during May.

Showers and thunderstorms become more frequent during May, as troughs form during the transition between the dry and rainy season. By mid May, developing weather systems in the Gulf of Mexico and western Caribbean should be closely monitored for rapid development and movement north. After mid May, vessels run the risk of encountering early tropical depressions and rapid development of extra-tropical cyclones along the East Coast of the US. These have become more frequent in recent years. For more information see Appendix B.

TURKS AND CAICOS TO BAHAMAS

The Turks and Caicos Islands, together with the adjoining Bahamas, form an extensive chain of rocky islands surrounded by coral reefs and sandbanks. They extend from about 21°N to 27°30´N and from 71°W to 79°W, covering an area of more than 5,000 square miles, much of it with depths of less than 1.8m (6ft). Columbus made his first landing in the New World at San Salvador in 1492. The archipelago is best cruised from south-east to north-west. Both prevailing winds and currents set this way, and for the first part of the day the sun will be aft which gives a much clearer picture of the shoals and coral heads as you eyeball your way through them.

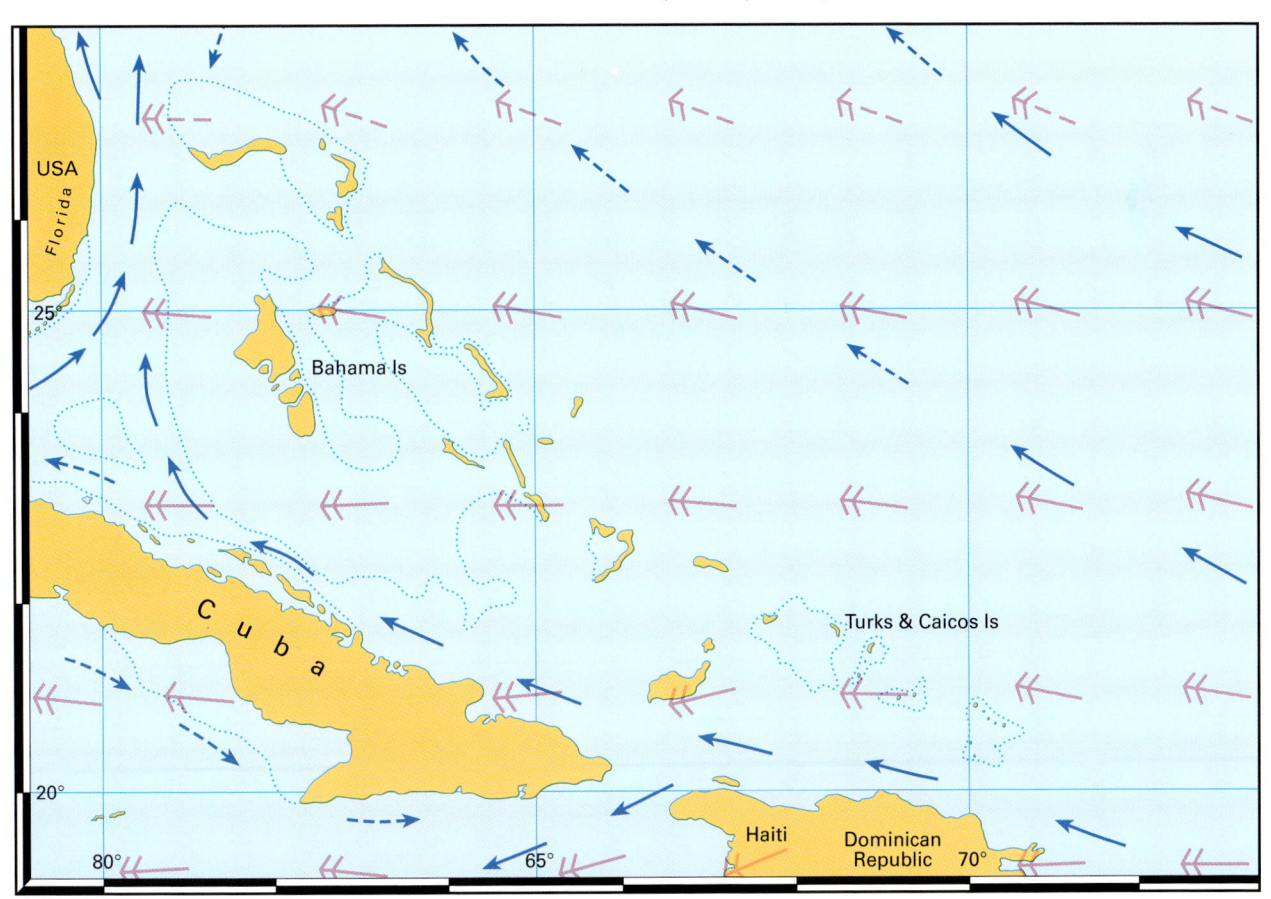

Plan 50 Prevailing winds and currents between the Caribbean Islands and Florida during May. Based on information from *The Atlantic Pilot Atlas*

PASSAGES AND LANDFALLS

The US Coast Guard stands by during a routine boarding. Photo: Richard Woods

The US Coast Guard has authority from the Bahamian government to search all vessels within their waters, regardless of nationality, and officers frequently board and search private yachts in the course of their work. This is a routine matter that should be accepted as such, and is almost invariably carried out politely and professionally.

NAVIGATION AND PILOTAGE

On the passage from Puerto Rico to Grand Turk beware the Silver Bank where depths go from several thousand metres in the Puerto Rico Trench to 2m (6ft) within quite a short space of time.

Once you are amongst the islands themselves, shallow waters dotted with coral heads and sandbanks, combined with unpredictable currents and tidal streams, all call for what is known locally as 'eyeball navigation'. It cannot be emphasised too strongly that errors in these waters may be dangerous and that the greatest care must be exercised. Yachts drawing more than 1.5m (5ft) will be constrained in the areas they can visit. Charts are frequently out-of-date or inaccurate, and markers and beacons few and far between. Those with considerable experience of the area advise as follows:

1. Avoid night passages if possible, but if you do find yourself at sea at nightfall, heave-to in open water to await daylight.

2. Navigating from east to west try to make passages across shoal waters before noon, with the sun at your back, so that you can see the submerged coral heads.

3. Avoid inter-island passages from west to east, to windward, with the sun in your eyes. If forced to go in this direction it may be safer to make an ocean passage.

4. Remember that tides and currents may not only be stronger than indicated, but may set in the opposite direction to that which is forecast. Take local advice whenever possible, especially among the skippers of fishing and inter-island trading craft.

CARIBBEAN ISLANDS TO FLORIDA

23
Luperon
Dominican Republic

Location:	19°55´N 70°56´.5W
Tidal Range::	0.5m
Time zone:	UT –4
Currency:	Dominican peso
Tel/fax:	Country code: 809
Language:	Spanish
Emergencies:	911

Merengue and bachata

The Dominican Republic is one of the largest countries in the Caribbean, famous for its *merengue* and *bachata* music. It is becoming a more popular tourist destination and a more popular cruising ground, particularly along its south coast.

The north coast is the windward coast and has fewer options for shelter, however Luperon and neighbouring Puerto Plata are useful ports of call.

Luperon harbour is 15 miles north-west of Ocean World (Puerto Plata). It is considered to be a good hurricane hole and is a popular harbour where long term live-aboard yachts tend to get stuck, despite it being rather a muddy mangrove backwater. The harbour silts up in some areas and yachts that draw more than 1.5m (5ft) will not be able to dock at the end of the lagoon. Luperon itself is a busy little town with plenty going on. A favourite yachtie haunt is Steve's Bar and Restaurant. The popularity of Luperon is leading to various shoreside developments including a new marina on the south shore, currently under construction. Puerto Plata, a scenic *guah-guah* (bus) ride to the east, is a large town with good shopping facilities. From Puerto Plata you can take a cable car to the summit of Mount Isabel with its own statue of Christ and a great view.

The docks at Luperon may not be accessible for most monohulls, but they are useful dinghy docks. Photo: Denis Webster

PASSAGES AND LANDFALLS

Websites
A useful cruising guide can be downloaded from the internet at:
www.dominicanrepubliccruisingguide.com/ see also:
www.godominicanrepublic.com/
www.thornlesspath.com/luperon.htm
www.noonsite.com/Countries/DominicanRepublic/Luperon

Entrance

The channel markers in the entrance into Luperon are not always in position and a night entrance is not recommended. Entry advice is to proceed with caution on a bearing of 180°, preferably on a rising tide so that, if you do hit the soft mud bottom, it should not be too difficult to get unstuck. Once inside, take the right hand fork to the southwest.

Radio

Both of the small marinas and many fellow cruisers stand by on VHF Channel 68. A cruisers net is run every Wednesday and Sunday morning at 0800 on VHF Channel 72.

Formalities

Officials visit the anchorage to sign yachts in. Fly your Q flag so they can find you. If possible, arrive during working hours, 0800–1700. It is illegal to land before clearance. Promised new regulations are now being implemented: Boats arriving from a foreign port can be boarded by no more than two government representatives and fees are fixed.

Anchorage

Most yachts choose to anchor and the whole harbour is dotted with various boats. Holding is in soft, silted mud and it is common for newly-laid anchors to slide through it and drag. The recommended trick is to lay out a considerable length of chain in an east-west direction and not to try to dig in the anchor immediately. After a couple of days the anchor will have sunk down into the thicker mud and can be dug in. If you arrive when the trades are very strong, try to remain on your boat as much as possible until you are sure your anchor has held. Boats often drag in the harbour during high winds, but there are usually plenty of fellow cruisers around to help.

Berthing and facilities

Luperon Yacht Club is a small marina with a modest range of facilities. Call ahead on VHF Channel 68 for pilotage advice.
Contact: PO Box 596, Puerto Plata, Republica Dominicana.
Tel: 571-8606 E-mail:info@luperonmarina.com

Marina Puerto Blanco has berths for about 15 boats and a dinghy dock.
Contact: Tel: 571 8644

There is also a dinghy dock near the town where you can obtain water. Fuel can be bought from a small fuel barge, which also sells water.

Medical services (telephone numbers)

Puerto Plata Movi-Med Ambulance
Evacuation Service   970 0707
There is a small hospital in Luperon.

Luperon looking NE towards the entrance. There has been some development around the bay since this photo was taken. Photo: Denis Webster

CARIBBEAN ISLANDS TO FLORIDA

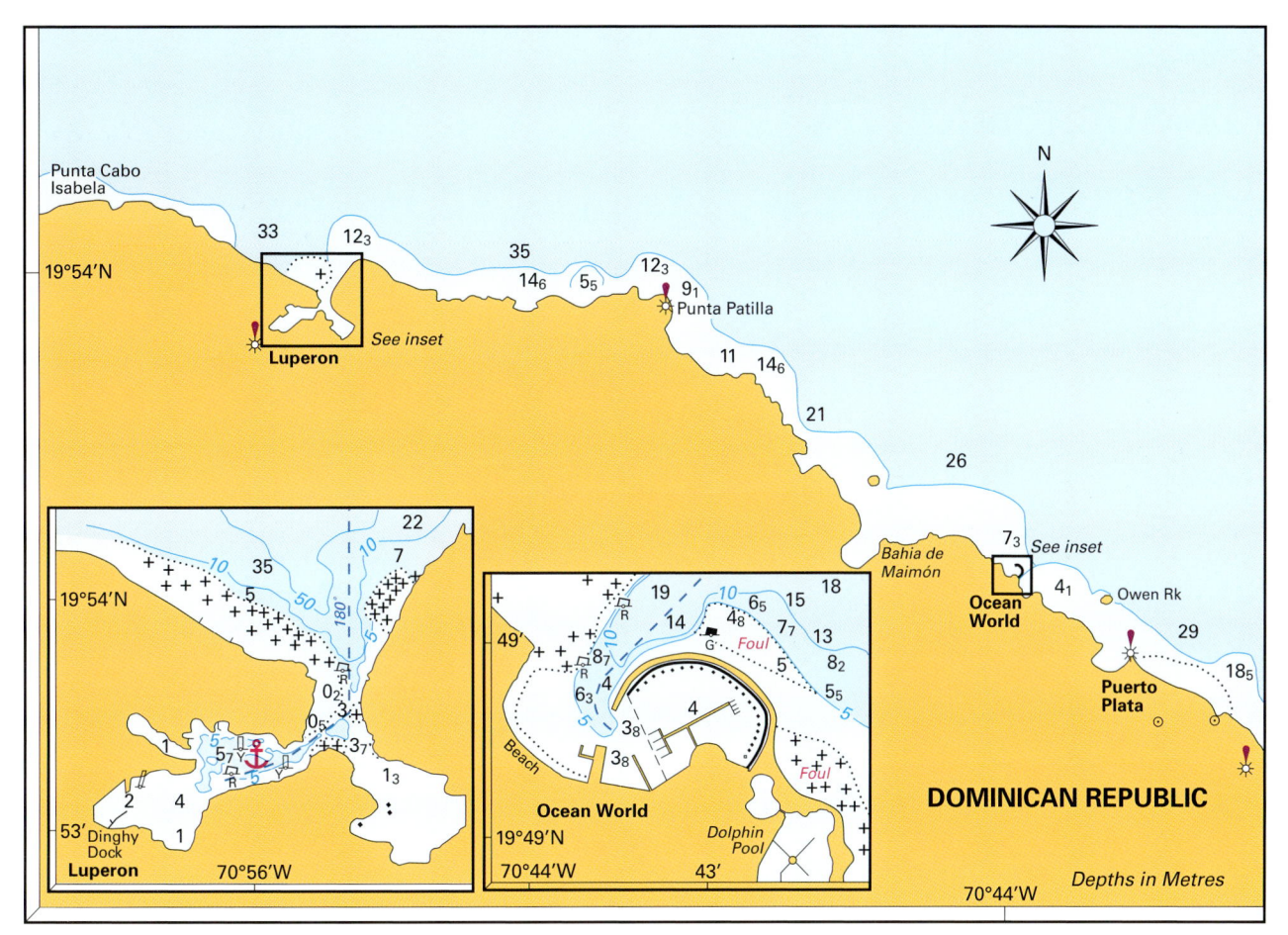

Plan 51 The north coast of the Dominican Republic with details of Luperon and Ocean World

OCEAN WORLD (PUERTO PLATA)

Sea buoy: 19°50′.095N 70°43′.535W

Ocean World is a massive tourist complex with a casino, restaurants and various other 'attractions' including a water park with performing dolphins. The water is crystal clear compared to Luperon, but it may not be as peaceful. Ocean World Marina is 2 miles west of the commercial port in Puerto Plata and 15 miles south-east of Luperon. The commercial port is not welcoming to visiting yachts except in emergencies.

Formalities

Ocean World is an official Port of Entry. Fly the Q flag and wait for officials to come to the boat as it is illegal to go ashore before clearance.

Radio

The marina responds on VHF Channel 16.

Entrance

Entry to Ocean World Marina is through a gap in the reef along a clearly marked channel approached from the north-east. A swell can build up in the marina during periods of strong north-east winds, although this is reported not to work its way beyond the superyacht berths.

Berthing and facilities

Ocean World Marina can accommodate vessels up to 76m (250ft) long in depths of at least 3.6m (12ft) and has a full range of pontoon facilities and support services ashore, though it is restricted in its haul-out services for cruising yachts. There is a fuel dock and access to some repair services.
Website: www.oceanworld.net
Contact: Tel: 970 3373 Fax: 970 7987
E-mail: roberto.tejada@oceanworldmarina.com

LUPERON
DOMINICAN REPUBLIC
23

181

PASSAGES AND LANDFALLS

24
Providenciales
Turks and Caicos

Location:	21° 44′N 72° 17′W
Maximum tidal range:	0.83m
Time zone:	UT –5
Currency:	US dollars (coins a mix of US and local version)
Tel/fax:	Country code: 649
Language:	English
Emergencies:	Tel: 999 or 911

Astronauts' landing

Providenciales is the most developed of the Caicos islands and is a good stop-off as you cruise north or south between the Caribbean and North America. There is a good range of shops in Providenciales (referred to as Provo) but they are quite spread out and you may need to use a taxi. This can become rather expensive. The traditional anchorage for clearance is Sapodilla Bay.

The Turks are very different to the Caicos and well worth visiting before you head for Caicos. Customs clearance is at the airport on Grand Turk, not at the Post Office as some guides say. There is an excellent small museum which celebrates the first US astronauts' landing

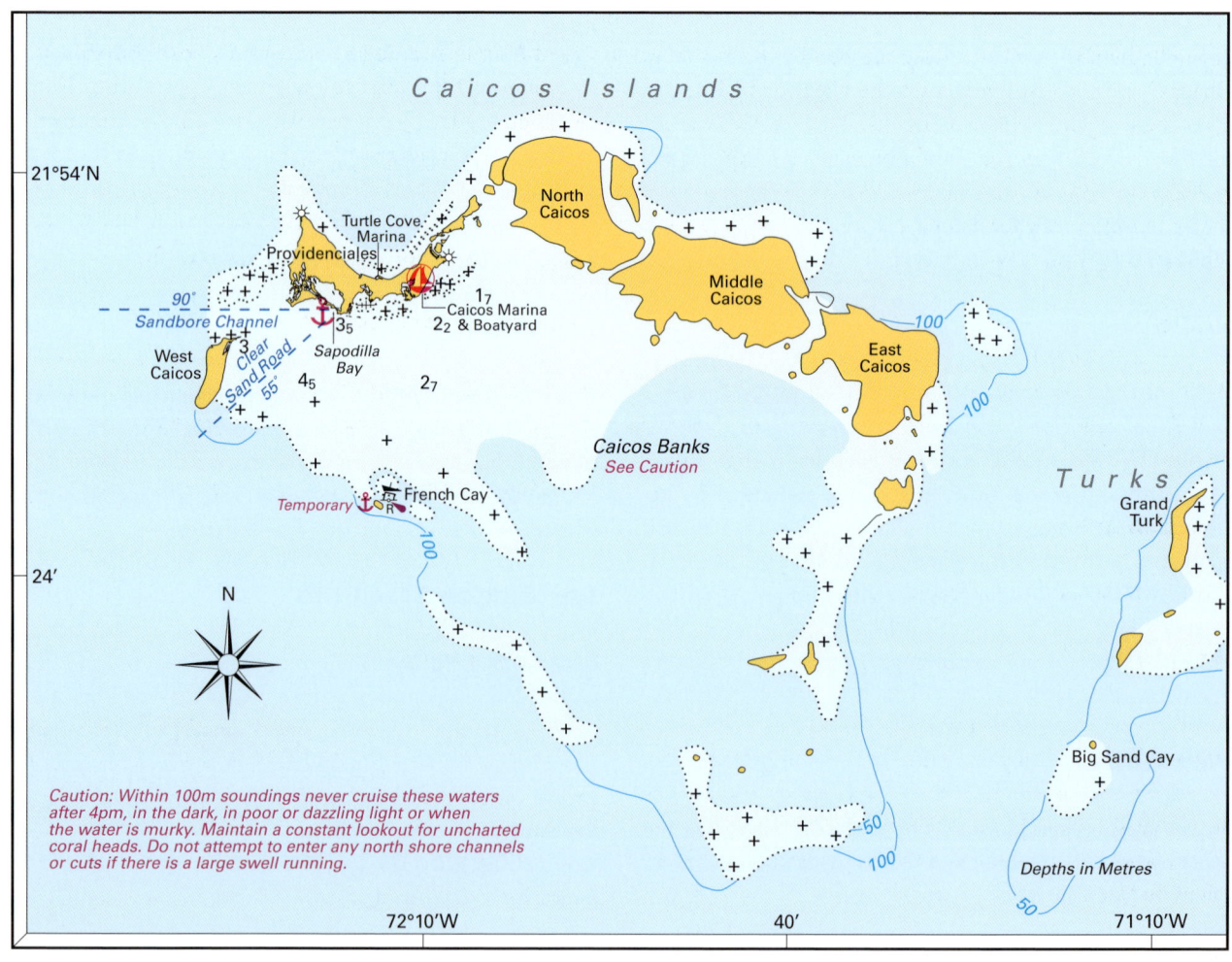

Plan 52 Providenciales, Turks and Caicos

CARIBBEAN ISLANDS TO FLORIDA

The anchorage on Grand Turk is open to the west and would be untenable in a norther. Photo: Richard Woods

on the Turks and has artifacts from a 16th century shipwreck nearby. The anchorage is open to the west and to northers.

Approach

Sapodilla Bay is approached from the west by the Sandbore Channel, from the southwest via the Clear Sand Road or from the east via the Caicos Banks. There are numerous coral heads and approach should be made early in the day with the sun behind you. Do not attempt a night approach. It is possible to anchor under the lee of West Caicos if conditions deteriorate on approach via the Clear Sand Road.

Radio

VHF Channel 68 is monitored by several local businesses as well as other cruisers. Caicos Marina and Boatyard monitors VHF Channel 16.

Formalities

Clear in at the commercial dock or at one of the marinas.

Anchorage

Most cruising boats anchor in Sapodilla Bay. The bay is reasonably well protected from the prevailing winds but suffers a very unpleasant swell which refracts around the headlands if there is any south in the wind.

In favourable conditions, a temporary anchorage can be found on the west side of French Cay.

Berthing and facilities

There are several marinas, but most of them have depth restrictions.

Caicos Marina and Boatyard is on the south coast with a minimum of 1.8m (6ft) at low water. It is a Port of Entry. Yachts up to 21m (70ft) are welcome to a limited number of berths. It has a range of facilities including an 85-tonne travel lift.
Contact: Long Bay, PO Box 24, Providenciales. Tel: 946 5600 Fax: 946 5390 E-mail: caicosmarinashp@tciway.tc

Transport connections

The international airport is near to Provo. There are flights to Florida and some of the Caribbean islands.

Medical services (telephone numbers)

Associated Medical Practices, Leeward Highway, Providenciales, Private Family Medicine and Urgent Care Center with Decompression Chamber.	
Appointments	946 4242
Fax	946 4942 or 231 0000
Doctor available 24 hours	331 4357

PROVIDENCIALES
TURKS AND CAICOS
24

PASSAGES AND LANDFALLS

25
Georgetown
Great Exuma, Bahamas

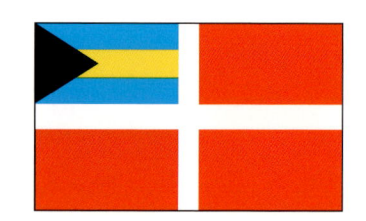

Location:	23° 30′.5N 75° 45′.5W
Maximum tidal range:	1.1m
Currency:	Bahamas dollar (US dollars also accepted)
Time zone:	UT –5
Tel/fax:	Country code: 242
Language:	English
Emergencies:	911

Snowbird destination

Great Exuma is the largest island in the Bahamas chain which fills up with hundreds of live-aboard cruising yachts over the winter. Many are the 'snowbirds' who are there to escape the North American chill. It has a busy social scene revolving around all the assembled boats, the highlight of which is a cruising regatta every March. This is the only port of entry in the Exuma chain. There are some alleged hurricane holes in the lagoons of Stocking Island, but in such a situation the area would become dangerously overcrowded with yachts.

Approach

Approach is relatively straightforward. Enter from the south-east to the south of Fowl Cay or from the north via the marked channel used by the supply ships. Note that the navigation lights may not be in working order. Sand bars across the sea bed tend to shift over time, and after storms, causing fluctuating depths.

Radio

On arrival, call Elizabeth Harbour harbourmaster on VHF Channel 16 giving name of vessel, registration number, country of origin and last port of call. This also applies if

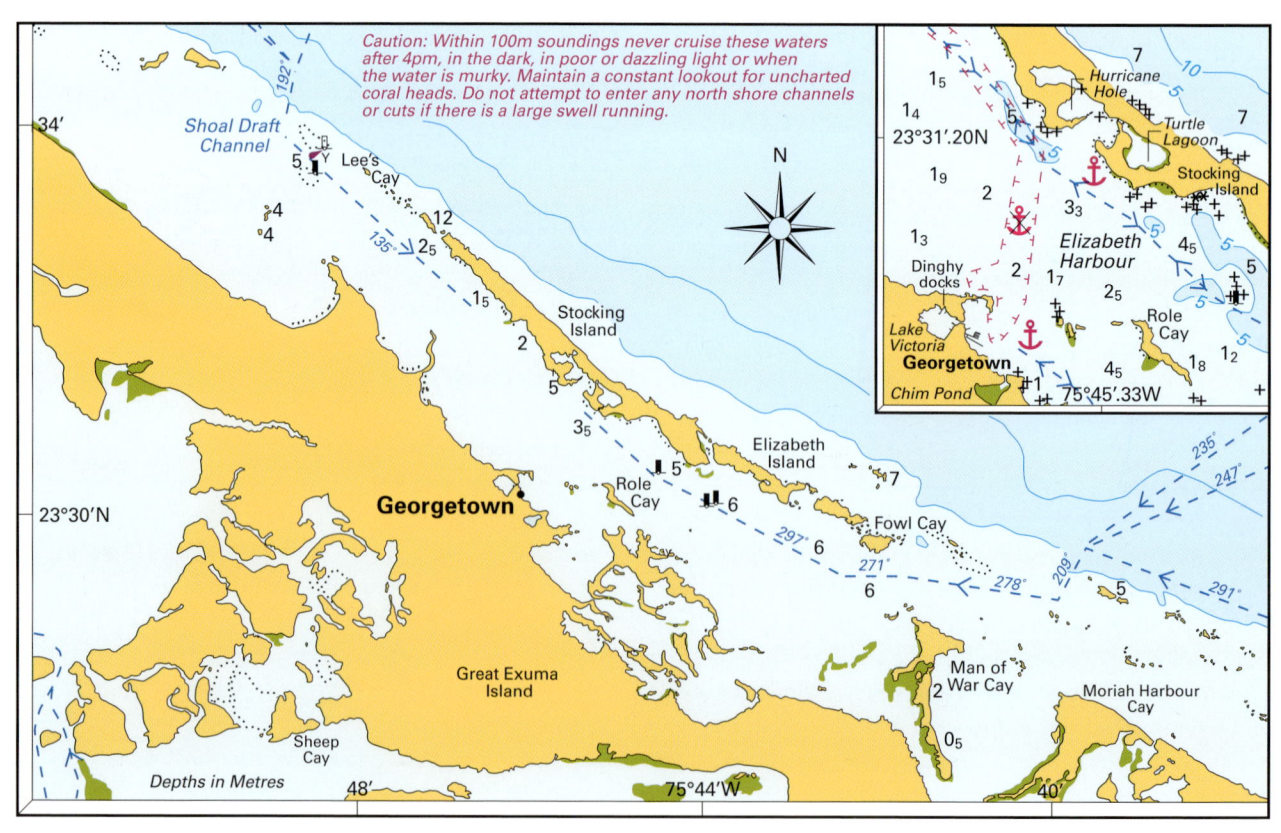

Plan 53 Georgetown, Great Exuma, Bahamas

184

CARIBBEAN ISLANDS TO FLORIDA

Administration building, Georgetown. Photo: Richard Woods

already cleared into the Bahamas. Marinas monitor VHF Channel 16. Daily Cruisers' Net on VHF Channel 68.

Formalities

Clearance must be obtained at an official entry port – prior to that, a yacht may sail through the islands but cannot anchor overnight. The Q flag should be hoisted three miles off and, in theory, everyone is expected to stay aboard until officials come out to grant clearance. In practice, it will be necessary to go ashore and complete formalities. A cruising permit will be issued, which remains valid for up to six months. There are severe penalties for not observing clearance formalities. Firearms must be declared and kept locked away until departure. Animals need valid rabies inoculation certificates. The Customs and Immigration office is in the pink two-storey building. Arrival outside of normal office hours (0900-1700 Mon-Fri) incurs overtime charges.

Anchorage

Anchor to the south of Stocking Island or off Georgetown itself, depending on your draught and available space. Anchor anywhere off the town but avoid the shipping channel that leads from the government dock to the north. Transfer by dinghy to the dinghy dock in Lake Victoria. Fuel is available with jerry cans from a small floating dock on the western shore which gives direct access to the fuel station.

Medical services

Hospitals and medical centres in Nassau. Ask locally.

Georgetown dinghy dock looking out through the bridge at the entrance to Lake Victoria. Photo: Richard Woods

GEORGETOWN, GREAT EXUMA
BAHAMAS
25

The entrance to Lake Victoria, Georgetown, giving access to the dinghy dock and a shoreside fuel station. Photo: Richard Woods

185

PASSAGES AND LANDFALLS

26
Marsh Habour
Abacos, Bahamas

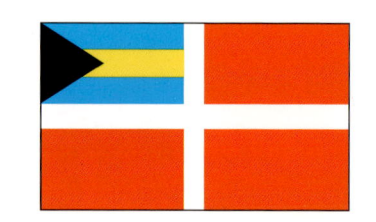

Location:	26° 33′N 77° 04′W
Maximum tidal range:	1.2m
Time zone:	UT –5
Currency:	Bahamas dollar (US Dollars also accepted)
Tel/fax:	Country code: 242
Language:	English
Emergencies:	911

Rare species

Marsh Harbour is the main town in the Abacos. It is primarily used as a stop-off for good provisioning at reasonable prices, before heading on to the outer Abaco Cays. If a weather front is coming through, many yachts head for a mooring in Hopetown, which is much better protected but can become extremely overcrowded. Marsh Harbour has a good range of facilities for cruising yachts. It is quick and easy to fly parts in from the USA but you should expect to pay significant import duties. Also expect to pay for water everywhere. Great Abaco is home to a rare parrot and the rarest breed of wild horse in the world. The Royal Marsh Harbour Yacht Club welcomes visitors, visit their website: www.RMHYC.com

Hazards

Entering the Sea of Abaco can become dangerous if there is a large swell which may be produced from distant storm systems or a cold front. The swell causes 'rages' which render the passes *im*passable.

Daily reports on weather and 'rage' conditions (see below) are available on the website: www.barometerbob.com

Approach and entrance

The south-eastern approach to the Sea of Abaco is via the passes to the north or south of Lynyard Cay. The north-western approach is via the Whale Cay Cut. This approach is the most susceptible to rages.

The entry to Marsh Harbour itself is straightforward although the anchorage is not apparent until close in. Take the marked channel which curves off to the east into the harbour, following close to the north shore. Don't be tempted to continue southwards down the main channel to the commercial dock. Anchor where draught and space allow, as far east as possible. The dinghy dock is on the south shore, west of the restaurants.

Radio

Bahamas Cruiser Net: VHF Channel 68, 0815 local time for Marsh Harbour Abaco, Bahamas.

Formalities

Coming from the south it is likely that you will have cleared in to the Bahamas at Georgetown. Coming from the US you would probably clear in at Green Turtle Cay.

Anchorage

Anchor anywhere inside the harbour. Holding is erratic – a Danforth type anchor works best on the thin 'marl' (sand over limestone). Transfer by dinghy to the dinghy dock on the south side of the harbour. The anchorage is rather open to passing fronts (northers). There are alternative anchorages around the island including Green Turtle Cay which is delightfully undeveloped and a good hurricane hole, or the very popular moorings at Hopetown with its iconic lighthouse. Hopetown becomes extremely crowded if bad weather is forecast.

Berthing and facilities

Boat Harbour Marina is outside Marsh Harbour Bay, close to Elbow Cay, and has minimum depth of 3.5m (11.5ft).

Hopetown, beneath its famous lighthouse, is well protected and very popular, especially if bad weather is forecast. Photo: Richard Woods

CARIBBEAN ISLANDS TO FLORIDA

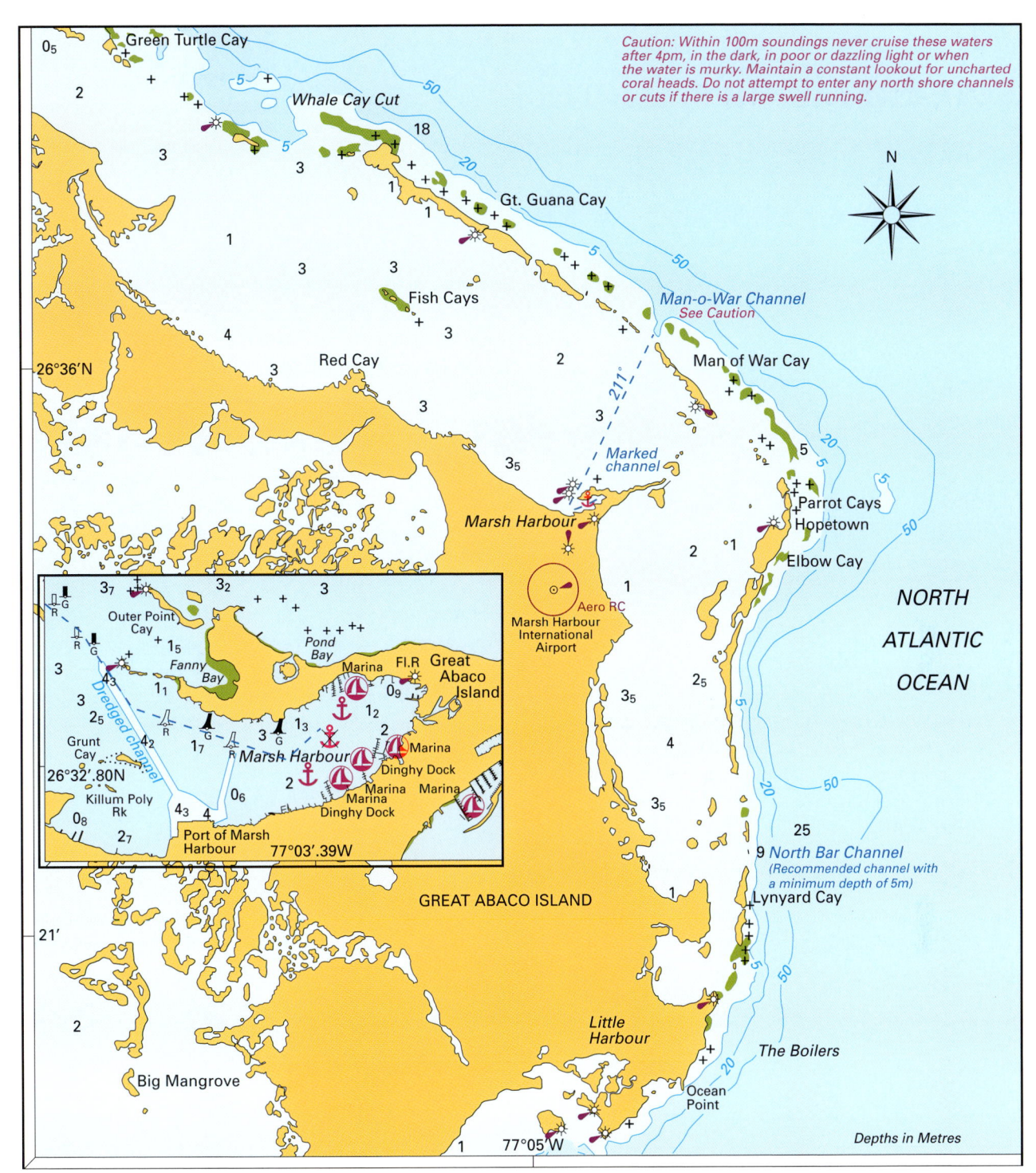

Plan 54 Marsh Harbour, Great Abaco, Bahamas

There is a full range of facilities.
Contact: Tel: 367 2158 Fax: 367 4154
E-mail: marina@abacoresort.com

Harbour View Marina has minimum depths of 2.1m (7ft) and a range of facilities.
Contact: E Bay, PO Box AB20902. Tel: 367 3910
Fax: 367 3911 E-mail: info@harbourviewmarina.com

Marsh Harbour Marina has 2.5m (8ft) at low tide and a range of facilities.

Contact: Pelican Shores, PO Box 20578. Tel: 367 2700
Fax: 367 2033 E-mail: jibroom@hotmail.com

Transport connections

There are easy air links to the USA. Ferries go to the outer cays and to Nassau.

Medical services

Hospitals and medical centres in Nassau. Ask locally.

MARSH HARBOUR, ABACOS
BAHAMAS
20

187

PASSAGES AND LANDFALLS

27
Fort Lauderdale, Florida
USA

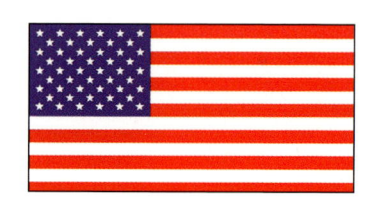

Location:	26°05′.5N	80°07′W
Springs:	0.9m	Range: 0.9m
Neaps:	0.7m	Range: 0.2m
Time zone:	UT −5	
Currency:	US dollar	
Tel/fax:	Country code: 1 Area code: (1) 954	
Language:	English	
Emergencies:	911 or US Coast Guard Station, Fort Lauderdale, Tel: 927 1611	

Sweat and dynamite

Port Everglades, Fort Lauderdale is a busy yachting centre and home to an astonishing array of superyachts with all the attendant support facilities. It is also a busy commercial and cruise ship port. Incredibly, its connection to the sea and development as a port is entirely due to man's labours and the effects of dynamite. For cruising yachts heading direct to or from the northern or western Caribbean, Port Everglades is a logical staging post. For yachts coming from the Abacos it is not such a logical port of call. In that case, West Palm Beach (48 miles to the north) or Fort Pierce are good alternative all weather ports of entry. The entrances at Fort Lauderdale, West Palm Beach and Fort Pierce all give access to the

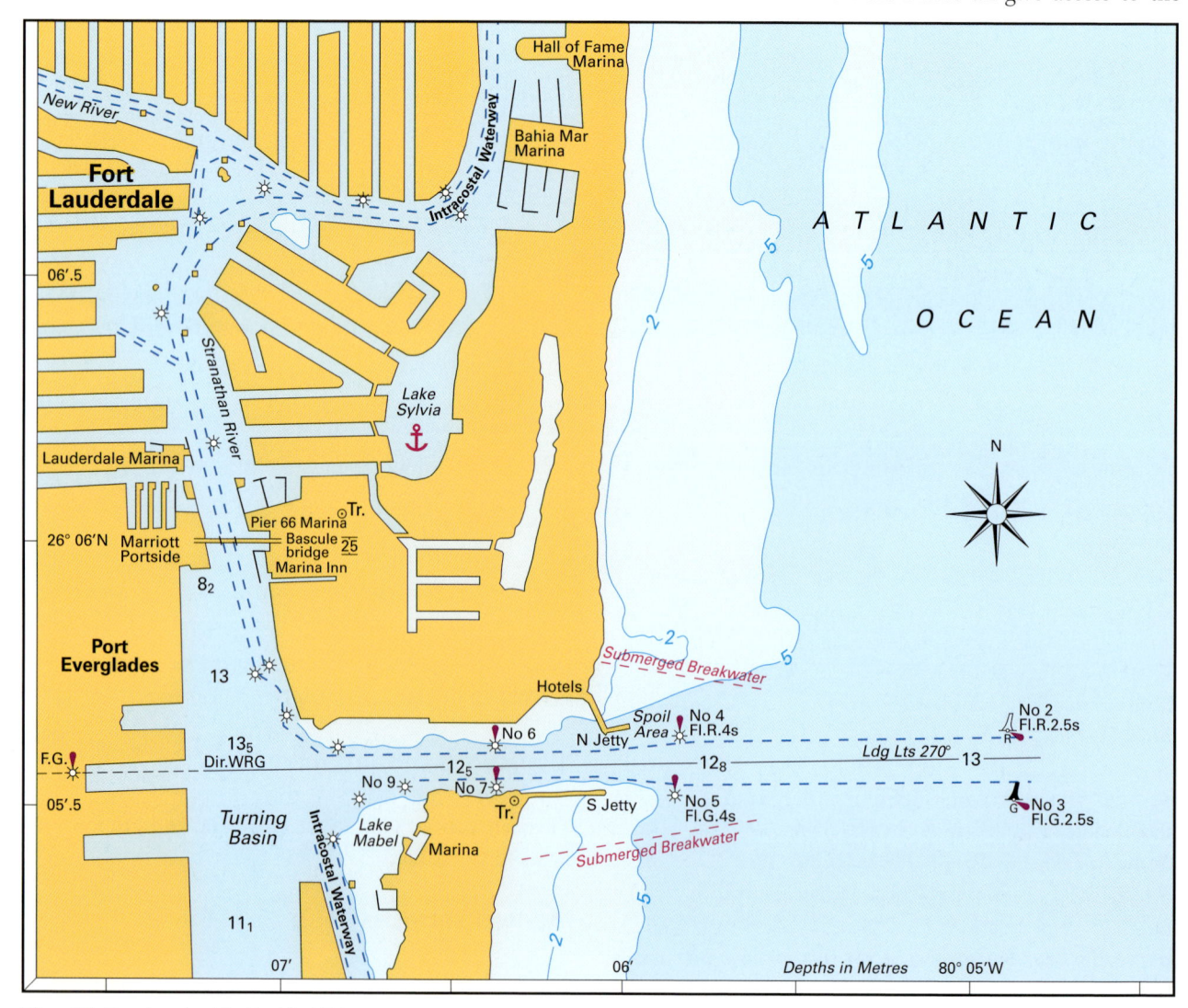

Plan 55 Fort Lauderdale, Florida, USA

CARIBBEAN ISLANDS TO FLORIDA

Entrance to Fort Lauderdale. Further out, at the start of the approach channel, the four smokestacks line up behind each other. Photo: Richard Woods

FORT LAUDERDALE, FLORIDA
USA
27

Intracoastal Waterway (see Chapter 16). If you are heading north from Fort Lauderdale, the ICW has a large number of bridges until Jupiter Point. Many yachts prefer to go out to sea for this section and re-enter the ICW at Fort Pierce.

Websites
www.fort-lauderdale-marine-directory.com/sail_only.php
www.ci.ftlaud.fl.us/marinas/index.htm
www.ci.ftlaud.fl.us/leisure.htm

Approach and entrance

The east coast of Florida shelves gently with no off-lying hazards in the Fort Lauderdale area. Four red and white striped smokestack towers are a conspicuous landmark at the entrance to Port Everglades. There is a considerable amount of traffic in and out of the entrance as well as several ships anchored off, all of which help to identify where you are. The red and white outer fairway buoy [Fl Mo (A)] lies about 1.5 miles due east of the entrance and almost on the leading line [Dir WRG and FG]. From this position the four smokestacks line up. To the north or south of the entrance channel they appear as four distinct stacks.

The first pair of channel markers: '2' to starboard and '3' to port, are about one mile offshore and from then on the relatively narrow channel, known as Outer Bar Cut, is clearly marked. Shoals and submerged breakwaters (the North and South Jetties) run from each side of the entrance out towards the channel buoys. Beware strong currents and maintain your course within the channel. Dir WRG and FG leading lights on 270° mark the fairway, the narrow white sector showing the centreline. Inside is the large Turning Basin with wharves on the western side. The marked channel turns sharply northwards and passes under a 16.7m (55ft) bridge (17th Street Causeway Bridge) to join the Stranahan River and the New River beyond. There is not much waiting space below the bridge which opens on the hour and half-hour. Currents can run strongly in this section, reaching three knots beneath the bridge.

All 'draw bridges' on the New River are on demand. Contact: Bridge Tender on VHF Channel 9 and always monitor Channel 9 for traffic reports from vessels headed up or down the river. The waterway can be extremely busy with all types of vessels. There is a two-knot tidal current in the New River which changes direction every six hours. It is best to go up the river with the tide coming out.

Note: *Bridges will not open during rush hour traffic* (Monday to Friday from 07:30 to 09:00 and in the evening from 16:30 to 18:00).

Radio

US Coast Guard: VHF Channel 16. The harbourmaster monitors VHF Channel 16 and operates on Channel 14; these two channels should be monitored by all vessels in the port. Causeway Bridge operates on Channel 09. The marinas monitor various frequencies, but all monitor Channel 16.

Formalities

See *'Formalities: the United States'* in Chapter 16 page 194. The US Coast Guard monitors all vessels entering US

189

PASSAGES AND LANDFALLS

waters and yachts are likely to be boarded at sea and searched. Fly the Q flag from offshore if arriving from abroad. You should contact the US Coast Guard initially (1 800 432 1216 or 1 800 451 0393 (24 hrs)) and then Customs and Immigration as necessary. You will probably need to take a taxi to the Customs office. The yacht may then be visited, by launch if necessary.

If you are intending to leave your boat in Florida you should apply for a Florida Sojourners' Cruising Permit to avoid paying 8 per cent Sales Tax on the value of your boat. For more information contact Florida Department of Revenue on Tel: 1 850 487 6757.

Berthing and facilities

There are a huge number of marinas in and around Fort Lauderdale but not all of them have berths for visitors (transients). The following is a selection:

Bahia Mar Yachting Center
Website: www.bahiamarhotel.com/yachting_center/yachting_center.cfm
Contact: 801 Seabreeze Blvd, Fort Lauderdale FL 33316.
Tel: 1 800 755 9558 Fax: 627 6356

Pier 66
Website: hyattregencypiersixty-six.com/marina.php
Contact: 2301 SE 17th Street, Fort Lauderdale, Florida, FL 33316. Tel: 525 6666 Fax: 728 3541

Marina Bay
Website: www.marinabay-fl.com
Contact: 2525 Marina Bay Drive West, Fort Lauderdale, FL 33312. Tel: 791 7600 Fax: 581 3909
E-mail: info@marinabay-fl.com

Hall of Fame Marina
Contact: 435 Seabreeze Blvd, Fort Lauderdale, FL 33316
Florida. Tel: 764 3975 Fax: 779 3658
E-mail: hfmarina@bellsouth.net

Las Olas Marina
Contact: Dockmaster, 240 E Las Olas Circle, Fort Lauderdale, FL 33316. Tel: 828 7200
E-mail: lekendiz@fortlauderdale.gov

New River Marina
Website: www.newrivermarina.net
Contact: 3001 State Road 84, Fort Lauderdale, FL 33312
Florida. Tel: 584 2500 Fax: 791 7522
E-mail: info@newrivermarina.net

Dockmaster
Contact: 2 South New River Dr. East, Fort Lauderdale, FL 33301. Tel: 828 5423 or (800) FTL-DOCK,
E-mail: mdomke@fortlauderdale.gov

Be aware that some of the berths in Fort Lauderdale are alongside very narrow canals where turning a yacht around could prove impossible. It is a good idea to phone ahead and check berthing details before committing to an awkward situation.

Anchorage and moorings

The city authorities provide a very limited number of moorings (many of them permanently occupied) in the bight opposite the municipal marina at Birch-Las Olas Docks about one mile north up the Intracoastal Waterway. (Call the dockmaster on Channel 09.) It is also possible to anchor here, though stays are limited to a few nights. Holding is good, but passing traffic may make for a bumpy night. Dinghies can be left at the marina. There is a yacht anchorage in Lake Sylvie (or Sylvia) to the north of the entrance. Another anchorage, at ICW 1072 miles, is to the south of the entrance, just north of Hollywood Blvd Bridge. It may not be easy to get ashore in a dinghy at either place. Most visitors head to a marina to clear in.

Transport connections

Fort Lauderdale International airport is a few miles away or use Miami International for most European flights. Facilities tend to be further than walking distance and taxis can become expensive. A bicycle is useful.

Medical services

There are several large hospitals in the area, including Broward General Medical Center, Tel: 759 7400.

Seventeenth Street Causeway Bridge inside the entrance opens on the hour and half-hour. Photo: Richard Woods

16 Landfalls on the Atlantic coast of the USA including entrances into the Intracoastal Waterway

28	Beaufort/Morehead City, North Carolina	202
29	Norfolk, Virginia	205
30	Annapolis, Maryland	209
31	New York, New York	213
32	Newport, Rhode Island	218
33	Portland, Maine	221

Your choice of landfalls on the North American coast will depend on the timings of your passages and your ongoing plans. Many yachts take a direct route to Beaufort, North Carolina where they then enter the Intracoastal Waterway (ICW) to continue north to Norfolk, Virginia and Chesapeake Bay. This route avoids Cape Hatteras. Cape Hatteras (35°15′N, 75°31′W) has a notoriously dangerous coastline, with many offlying banks and strong and unpredictable currents. The ICW runs all the way from Miami to Norfolk and with more time, depending on draught and mast height, it is possible for cruising yachts on an extended Atlantic cruise to enter the ICW further south and explore the east coast of the USA on their way north.

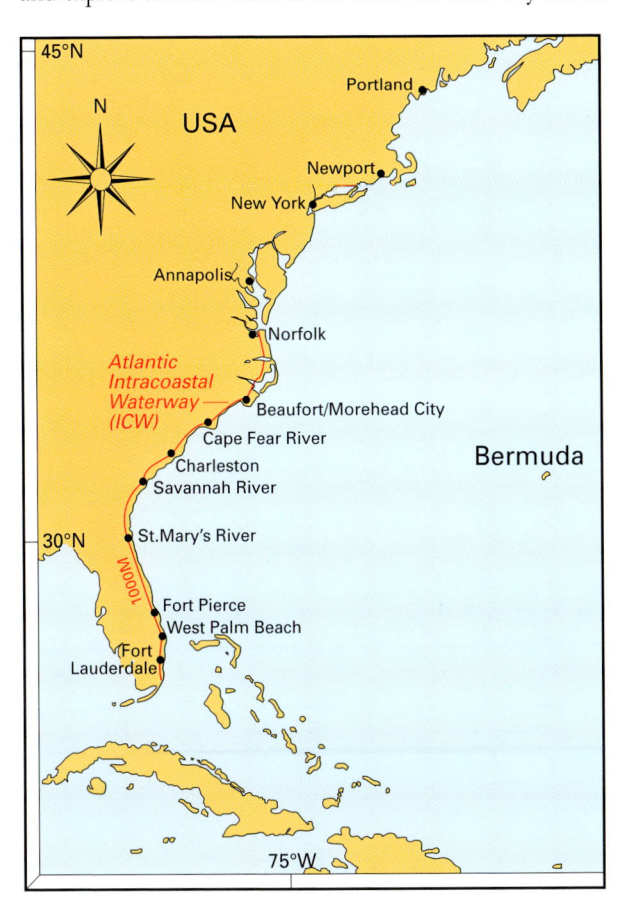

REGIONAL WEATHER AND PASSAGE TIMINGS

The continent of North America has a coastline stretching from the Tropic of Cancer to the Arctic Circle. Regional weather patterns, and particularly temperature, vary accordingly. But one of the few generalisations that can be made is that, during the summer cruising season, winds generally blow either offshore or parallel to the coast. This means that strong onshore gales, familiar to the European yachtsman, are seldom a problem. Earlier in the year, during the late winter and early spring, frequent cold fronts sweep off the coast, bringing strong northerly winds. These produce dangerous conditions in the Gulf Stream. Arriving in Norfolk in late May or early June should avoid these conditions and allow plenty of time to enjoy the summer cruising grounds further north.

Much of the Atlantic coast of the USA is fringed by a wide and relatively shallow continental shelf, with depths of 36m (119ft) or less being found 50 miles offshore in many

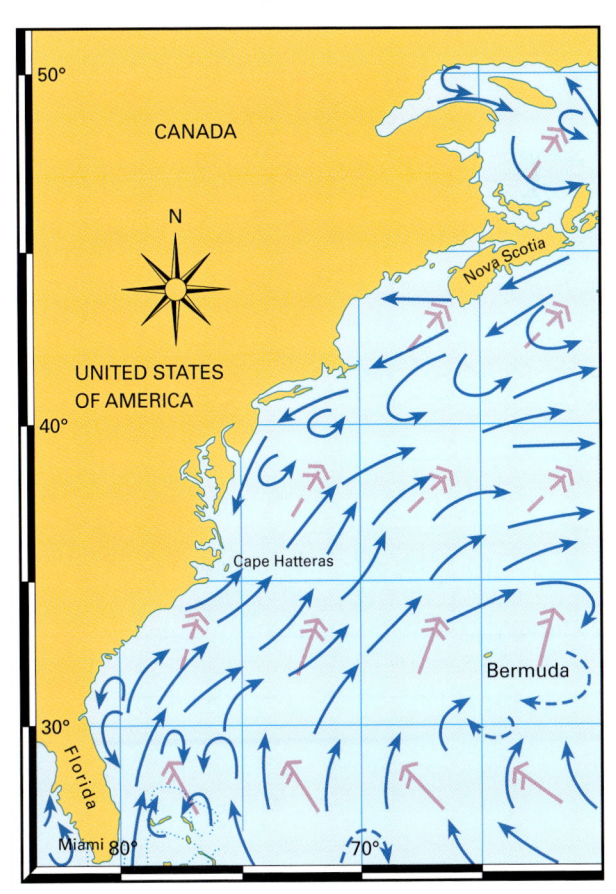

Plan 56 Ports along the Atlantic coast of the USA

Plan 57 Prevailing winds and currents off the Atlantic coast of the USA during July. Based on information from *The Atlantic Pilot Atlas*

PASSAGES AND LANDFALLS

Settled conditions on the ICW. Photo: Richard Woods

A norther comes through the same anchorage. Photo: Richard Woods

areas. Depths then drop off very suddenly to 3,000m (10,000ft) or more, and in bad weather very confused seas can result. It is important not to get caught in this area by the onset of heavy weather on approaching the coast, and equally important to make offing as rapidly as possible on departure in order to get into deep water before there is any chance of meeting heavy weather.

Within the Intracoastal Waterway

Heading north from Florida up the ICW, it is advisable to stay south of Charleston until May to avoid any late winter frosts. Heading back south it is a good idea to leave Norfolk in October. Later than this the arrival of the winter northers brings frequent periods of strong north-westerly to north-easterly winds.

Hurricanes

Much of this area is within the hurricane belt, though hurricanes rarely track beyond 40°N. The storm tracks can be unpredictable, sometimes approaching from the east or south-east and being influenced by the Gulf Stream, sometimes coming up over Florida or Georgia from the Gulf of Mexico. Greatest storm activity is usually during August and September. Along the ICW there is access to hundreds of protected hurricane holes. However it is important to find a safe spot in good time as bridges may be closed when a storm approaches in order to allow land evacuation from the area. It is also important not to underestimate the extent of the damage which can be inflicted upon an area by a passing hurricane. Even if you and your vessel come through unscathed it is possible that bridges, marinas and fuel docks may have suffered, and there is also likely to be a considerable amount of debris in the water. See comments on hurricanes on page 68 and in Appendix B.

Fog

Fog is common on the coast of Maine and in the region of the Grand Banks. It is most prevalent in spring and summer, and can be expected on about ten days in each month. The fog is caused by the cold Labrador Current bringing Arctic water south in a narrow stream almost to the latitude of Cape Hatteras. As the cold water encounters the warm air, it literally steams, giving rise to the notorious fogs of the Newfoundland Banks, Nova Scotia and Cape Cod. Poor visibility along the European coastline is often associated with high pressure and therefore light winds or calms. This is not the case off the American and Canadian coasts where thick fog allied with winds of 20–30 knots is not unusual. North of about 40°N, poor visibility is a frequent problem. In the summer there is a 20 per cent likelihood of less than two miles visibility in all areas north of Block Island, increasing to a 40 per cent likelihood of less than two miles visibility off Nova Scotia and Newfoundland. Radar is a definite advantage in these waters.

Ice

The Labrador Current is also responsible for carrying icebergs south past Newfoundland, but only very

Manoeuvring in fog can be a regular event as you head further north up the east coast of the USA and Canada. Photo: Jenny Franklin

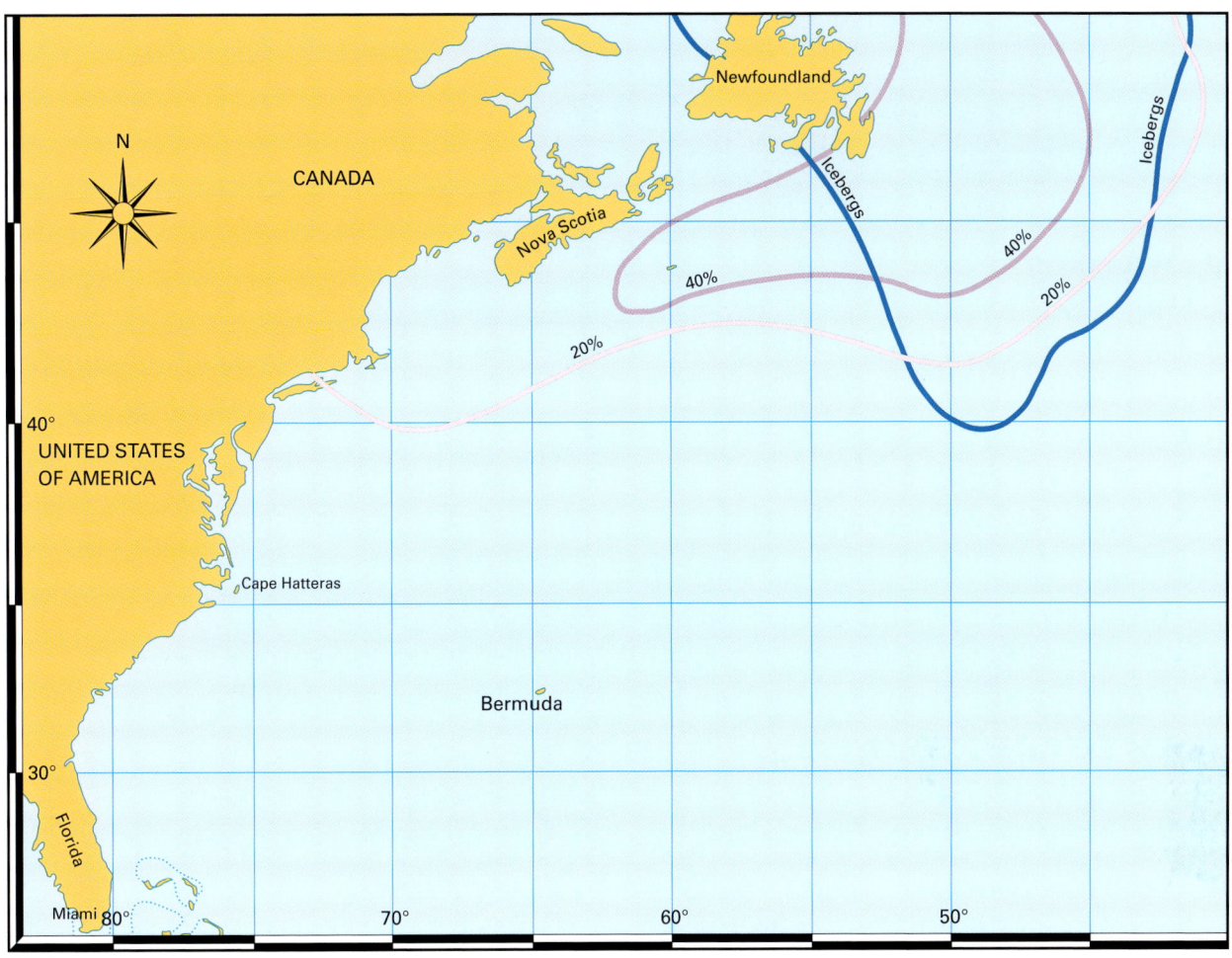

Plan 58 Iceberg limits and the percentage chance of encountering fog off the North American coast in July. Source as Plan 57

occasionally do bergs reach as far south as 40°N before melting; their range being most widespread in April and May and shrinking throughout the summer. There is some evidence that global warming is changing this pattern, but the occasional rogue berg which comes further south is usually well tracked and its position broadcast. There can be a concentration of bergs east of Cape Race, where the big ones go aground on the Grand Banks. As the season progresses and the icebergs begin to melt, they float off and move further south, finally reaching the northern edge of the Gulf Stream where they disperse and melt completely. Ice is therefore most prevalent in the northern and eastern parts of the Grand Banks early in the year and on their southern side later on. The International Ice Patrol co-ordinated by the US and Canadian Coast Guard services broadcasts daily reports of the location and drift of bergs. See also Chapter 18.

TIDES AND TIDAL STREAMS

Tidal influence varies enormously along the North American coast, from only 1.3m (4.2ft) in Florida to the massive 15m (49ft) tides of the Bay of Fundy. The appropriate tide and tidal stream tables should be consulted.

The Gulf Stream

Further south, the warm Gulf Stream parallels the coast, running at up to 4 knots in the Florida Strait but slowing as it fans out into the Atlantic. When strong northerly winds oppose the north-east setting current, particularly vicious seas can form, which have been responsible for the loss of more than one yacht. Satellite surveillance now enables the position of the stream and its associated eddies to be known with accuracy. The Gulf Stream is carefully monitored by the US Coast Guard who give regular voice and text updates of the co-ordinates of the speed and position of the middle of the Gulf Stream at various latitudes, and the position of major established eddies. The broadcasts also indicate the position of the West or Cold Wall which is the line of demarcation between the Gulf Stream and the Labrador Current. The Cold Wall is normally very noticeable because of the change in water temperature and in colour – the cold Labrador Current is light green, whereas the warm Gulf Stream is a deep blue.

The Labrador Current

The Labrador Current flows south around Newfoundland and Nova Scotia. Where it meets the Gulf Stream, the

PASSAGES AND LANDFALLS

Labrador Current divides. One part forces a passage down between the Gulf Stream and the North American coast continuing south-west along the coast before petering out around the latitude of the Chesapeake. The other part turns eastward and combines with the Gulf Stream to form the North Atlantic Current.

SHIPPING

The Grand Banks and the waters off Nova Scotia are popular fishing grounds for fleets of trawlers and coastal fishing boats. A sharp lookout should be maintained for them, and also for both nets and lines of pots marked by floats, which may be found well offshore. The gear itself will be submerged so the buoy is the only danger. The main concentrations of shipping may be expected off Cape Race, the approaches to Halifax, the Nantucket Light Vessel, and to the north of Cape Cod where the routes to Boston and the Cape Cod Canal will be crossed.

NANTUCKET SHOALS

The Nantucket Shoals stretch more than 30 miles south-east of Nantucket Island and have a least depth of 1.25m (4ft) causing them to break in bad weather. Strong tidal streams set over the Shoals, and though they can be crossed in calm weather via the marked channels this is not advised. Many yachts on passage from Europe or coming up from Bermuda make landfall at the Nantucket Shoals Lanby (40°30′N 69°26′W), 50 miles south-east of Nantucket Island. Nantucket Shoals Lanby carries a 13-mile range light standing 13m (43ft) above sea level, and is also equipped with a horn. Care must be taken in the vicinity of the Lanby as it also marks the separation zone for the shipping lanes in and out of New York. If heading northwards from here, either close the coast at Buzzards Bay and traverse the Cape Cod Canal, or head north-east from the Lanby to shape a course between Nantucket Shoal and Georges Bank, where oil rigs may be encountered.

FORMALITIES: THE UNITED STATES

Anyone entering the United States, other than US or Canadian citizens, *must be in possession of a visa*.

It is important to realise that the US Visa Waiver Scheme is only applicable to travel on commercial carriers: airlines and ferries etc. If you enter the USA by private yacht, wherever you enter, even if it is a port served by commercial carriers, you MUST have a valid visa in your passport prior to entry. The fine for arriving without a visa is $5000 per person and entry may also be refused.

Applications for visas have to be made at a US Embassy and, in most cases, require an interview. Interviews are by prior appointment after completing an application form and paying the application fee. Depending on the particular Embassy, the time required for the application and interview process may be several weeks. It is normally best to make the application in your home country, but applications may be made at any US Embassy. Visas, when issued, are normally valid for 10 years and are for multiple entries. A valid visa in an expired passport is still valid if presented with a new, valid, passport. Full information is available on US Government websites: travel.state.gov/visa/visa_1750.html

When asked why you need a visa you must state that you will be visiting the USA by private sailing vessel and that the Visa Protection Scheme is not applicable to such visits. Many US Immigration officials are unfamiliar with their own regulations and it is not unknown for them to advise you that a visa is not necessary. Be firm, polite and diplomatic if this happens.

Guests picked up within the USA, will normally have entered by commercial airline within the Visa Waiver Scheme and will obtain a visa on entry. Provided they are not aboard the yacht when the yacht enters, they do not need visas as above.

Yachts entering the United States should be aware that US Customs agents handle both yachts and large ships. There is no simplified procedure specifically for yachts. It is necessary to clear in at a designated port of entry. Normally, clearance is carried out at any public access berth (such as a municipal pier or marina dock), or at a yacht club jetty. If in doubt, the local Coast Guard will advise on procedure. Yachts are expected to seek clearance immediately upon arrival, and most foreign yachts are then boarded for inspection. While US Customs agents have been known to board yachts at sea, this is very rare. A Coast Guard boarding at sea has nothing to do with inward customs clearance, which must still be completed after arrival. Unless the entire crew are US citizens, an Immigration officer will normally accompany a Customs officer to the arrival inspection. Ship's papers, clearance from the previous port and a crew list will be required. Firearms must be registered upon arrival, and only hunting and sporting firearms may be brought in without restriction. Individual state firearms' laws also apply, and these may be more restrictive.

While fresh perishable foods (especially fruits and vegetables) may not be imported, it is rare for agriculture inspectors to visit yachts unless animals are aboard. Animals do not need rabies certificates if arriving from rabies-free countries, but will otherwise require them, and rabies does exist in some of the Caribbean islands. Pet birds will be put into quarantine. There are also restrictions on various animal products from declared endangered species – few yachts are likely to have furs aboard, but many people may have bought souvenirs of tortoise or turtle shell jewellery, scrimshaw on whalebone or ivory, or simply have picked up some coral.

LANDFALLS ON THE ATLANTIC COAST OF THE USA

Returning with the catch as the sun rises. Photo: Richard Woods

Foreign yachts (not US or Canadian) of most nationalities, including those from Britain and EC countries, are required to obtain a cruising permit on first entry. This permit, which exempts the yacht from further clearance while in US waters, remains valid for one year and may not be renewed until after expiry, and then only after the vessel has left US waters for at least 15 days and returned. Note that 'US waters' for this purpose include Puerto Rico and the Spanish Virgin Islands but not the USVI. A condition of the cruising permit is that yachts notify US Customs when they move from one Customs port sector to another. Notification is simple and may be made by calling the toll-free number 1 800 973 2867 or any local Customs office. The regulation regarding reporting movement between ports may be interpreted differently in different reporting areas. You may need only to report on entry into each new area, but you may be asked to report in every time you move port, even within the reporting area. The cruising permit renewal regulations may impose restrictions on the cruising plans of yachts wishing to remain in US waters for more than one year. This should be taken into account when planning your cruise – the most convenient foreign countries to go to on expiry are Canada, Bermuda or the Bahamas.

There is no specific requirement for any vessels to clear outwards, though it may be wise to do so since the authorities of most other countries will wish to see evidence regarding date and port of departure. Also, on leaving the USA, the white stub of the I-94 card in the passport should be returned to US migration. Failure to do so may cause difficulty on next entry. The I-94 form can be returned by post – ask for the correct mailing address when you clear in.

THE US COAST GUARD

Confusion can sometimes arise over the role and responsibilities of the US Coast Guard, which has a much wider brief than the British service of the same name. Whereas the British Coastguard is largely land-based, the

PASSAGES AND LANDFALLS

US Coast Guard is very active afloat. Its responsibilities include policing its own and nearby international waters for drug smugglers (in the course of which private yachts are frequently boarded and searched), the maintenance of navigational aids, and generally ensuring that all vessels proceed in an orderly manner. Unlike Britain, where lifeboats are the responsibility of the Royal National Lifeboat Institution, in the United States the Coast Guard also runs its own search and rescue vessels and aircraft. They will respond if a vessel is in immediate danger, but where there is no risk to life or craft, the Coast Guard will usually turn the job over to private contractors for commercial assistance – which is likely to be expensive.

The US Coast Guard monitors VHF Channels 16 and 22A, the latter being their working channel. Except in an emergency, initial contact should be made on 22A. European yachts should note that it is illegal to call the Coast Guard (or anyone else) on Channel 16 solely for a radio check.

The Coast Guard is also responsible for small craft safety, and if your boat is boarded by them they are likely to inspect the safety equipment carried. Almost certainly the Coast Guard will board you between the Bahamas and the USA. They have to ask permission but it is advisable to give it or you will probably be subjected to a prolonged search when you get to shore. The list of requirements includes several items not normally found aboard European yachts. The Coast Guard will check on lifejackets (not buoyancy aids) in dinghies and have fined foreign cruisers for not wearing them. Dinghy navigation lights are also checked. In theory, foreign yachts are governed by exactly the same regulations as US-registered ones; in practice, a reasonable approach is usually taken and, provided the authorities are not antagonised, a well-equipped ocean cruiser should have few problems. Once inspected you will be given an inspection certificate which is valid for 6 months so you don't get boarded again. (See regulations for sewage discharge placards given below.)

Sewage disposal and discharge placards

The Federal government has charged the US Coast Guard with the inspection of sewage disposal arrangements on yachts. The rules in US waters are an amalgam of Federal, State and local regulations. Many yacht harbours have been designated 'No Discharge Areas', where disposal of even treated sewage is strictly prohibited. Local harbourmasters or State marine police are usually responsible for enforcing the regulations. Holding tanks can be emptied via a deck fitting at pump-out stations at many marinas and yacht clubs, or the tank may be discharged overboard when the yacht is well clear of the harbour. Heads without holding tanks must show evidence of being secured from use while in harbour – it has been suggested that a cable tie securing the discharge seacock in the shut position would suffice. A portable chemical toilet is usually acceptable.

All vessels cruising within US waters are required to adhere to US regulations appertaining to discharge overboard of oil and garbage. US vessels are required (and foreign vessels are recommended) to post in a prominent position two placards summarising these regulations. These placards, each measuring about 9in x 6in are obtainable from yacht chandlers in the UK or by mail order from the USA. The US Coast Guard always look for these 'Discharge labels' and can fine the owner for non-compliance.

PROVISIONING

Access to supermarkets in the USA can be problematic for a visiting yacht as most of the supermarkets are several miles out of town. Taxis are sometimes required, although many marinas will offer a courtesy car and it is not uncommon to be lent a car by warm-hearted locals.

> **Floating casinos**
> Several areas of the east coast of the USA have floating casinos. These tend to leave port at about 19-00 local time and return at about midnight. They look like cruise ships but have erratic courses. Don't assume that once one has passed it is no longer a danger. It may well turn round.

LANDFALLS ON THE ATLANTIC COAST OF THE USA

The Intracoastal Waterway

The Atlantic Intracoastal Waterway (ICW) is nearly 1100 statute miles of dredged, navigable canal running just inland, parallel to the coast, all the way from Miami, Florida up to Norfolk, Virginia. Even if you are not planning to travel the whole of the ICW it makes sense to take a short cut from Beaufort (NC) to Norfolk. This scenic route has the benefit of allowing you to avoid the notorious Cape Hatteras and offlying shoals. Most sailing yachts under auxiliary engine will make around 50 miles along the ICW in a day. Progress is indicated by mile markers. Night passages are not recommended. Progress is sometimes tidally dependent, may be affected by the number of other boats, and is also influenced by the number of bridges and locks and by the manoeuvres of commercial barges. A number of fast motor boats use the ICW, although there are speed restrictions (6 knots) along much of it in order to protect the manatees. If you are new to the ICW you should be aware that there is an increasing risk of encountering alligators the further south from Cape Hatteras you travel.

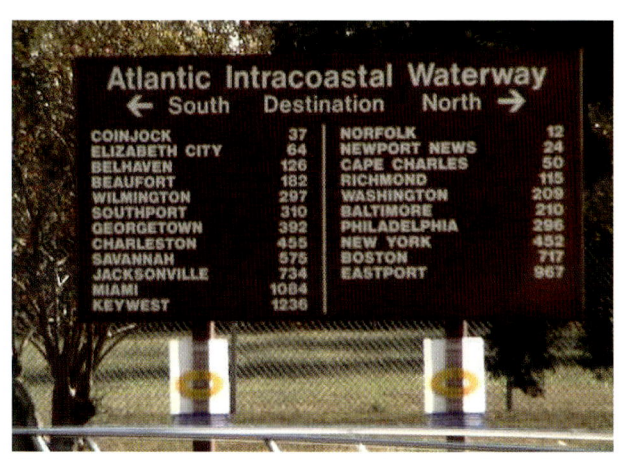

ICW mileages are clearly signed all along its length. Photo: Richard Woods

Depending on the prevailing weather conditions, it is quite feasible to use sections of the ICW interspersed with coastal passages at sea.

> **Charts**
> Anyone considering using the ICW should obtain up-to-date charts and pilotage information, particularly for the entrances into the ICW. *The Intracoastal Waterway Chartbook* (editors John and Leslie Kettlewell) is a very useful source of information.

Depths

The federal project depths for the ICW are 12ft (3.7m) from Fort Pierce, Florida all the way to Norfolk. However, in some areas considerable shoaling has occurred and passage is only possible by working with the tides. Yachts drawing more than 8ft (2.4m) should probably avoid the ICW.

Bridges

There are more than 80 opening bridges between Miami and Norfolk as well as several fixed bridges. The official lower limit for fixed bridges is 65ft (20m), but there is one in Miami with a clearance of 56ft (17m). Clearance heights are subject to some change depending on water levels. Most of the bridges have clearance gauges. Opening bridges usually have specified opening times and are controlled by bridge tenders who can be called on VHF Channels 09, 13 or 16.

Locks

There is one lock in Great Bridge, Virginia which is easy to negotiate with only a couple of feet of fall. There are deeper locks on the Dismal Swamp alternative route – a section which cries out to be explored for its name alone, although too shallow for boats drawing more than 6ft (1.8m).

Anchorages and marinas

There are hundreds of great anchorages all the way up the ICW. There are also several marinas, although these become full quite quickly during the season. The Skipper Bob guides: *Anchorages Along the Intracoastal Waterway* and *Marinas Along the Intracoastal Waterway* are considered essential reading by many ICW users. They give details of anchorages and free docks, marina and yard facilities and prices as well as a great deal of other useful information.

> **Website**
> www.skipperbob.net/publications.htm

Buoyage

The channel marks on the river inlets leading into the ICW are 'red, right, returning' (IALA B). Within the ICW, red marks are to starboard when heading south. A number of marks and aids are used along the ICW including leading lines or ranges. Not all of the marks are lit and some of the supposedly lit ones are not maintained.

Entrances into the ICW from the sea

There are many entrances into the ICW although many of them are not recommended for a visiting yacht as they require local knowledge due to shifting shoals around the channel. Most of the inlets, even those designated 'all

197

PASSAGES AND LANDFALLS

ICW Dismal Swamp lifting bridge. Photo: Richard Woods

weather' become rough or even dangerous when onshore winds meet an outgoing current. Shoals around any of the entrances may create large areas of breaking seas in heavy weather or if a large swell is running. It would be unwise to close the coast in these conditions. Some entrances are protected by long submerged piers which may extend a considerable distance out to sea and it is advisable to study the relevant charts thoroughly before attempting an entrance for the first time.

Several of the entrances into the ICW are considered to be 'all weather' inlets. These are marked channels, many of which are used by commercial or naval shipping. Heading north from Fort Lauderdale some useful all weather inlets are as follows:

Florida

West Palm Beach (Lake Worth Inlet) You will need to take a taxi to clear in. This is one of the few places along the US coast where it is possible to walk to the shops, including a

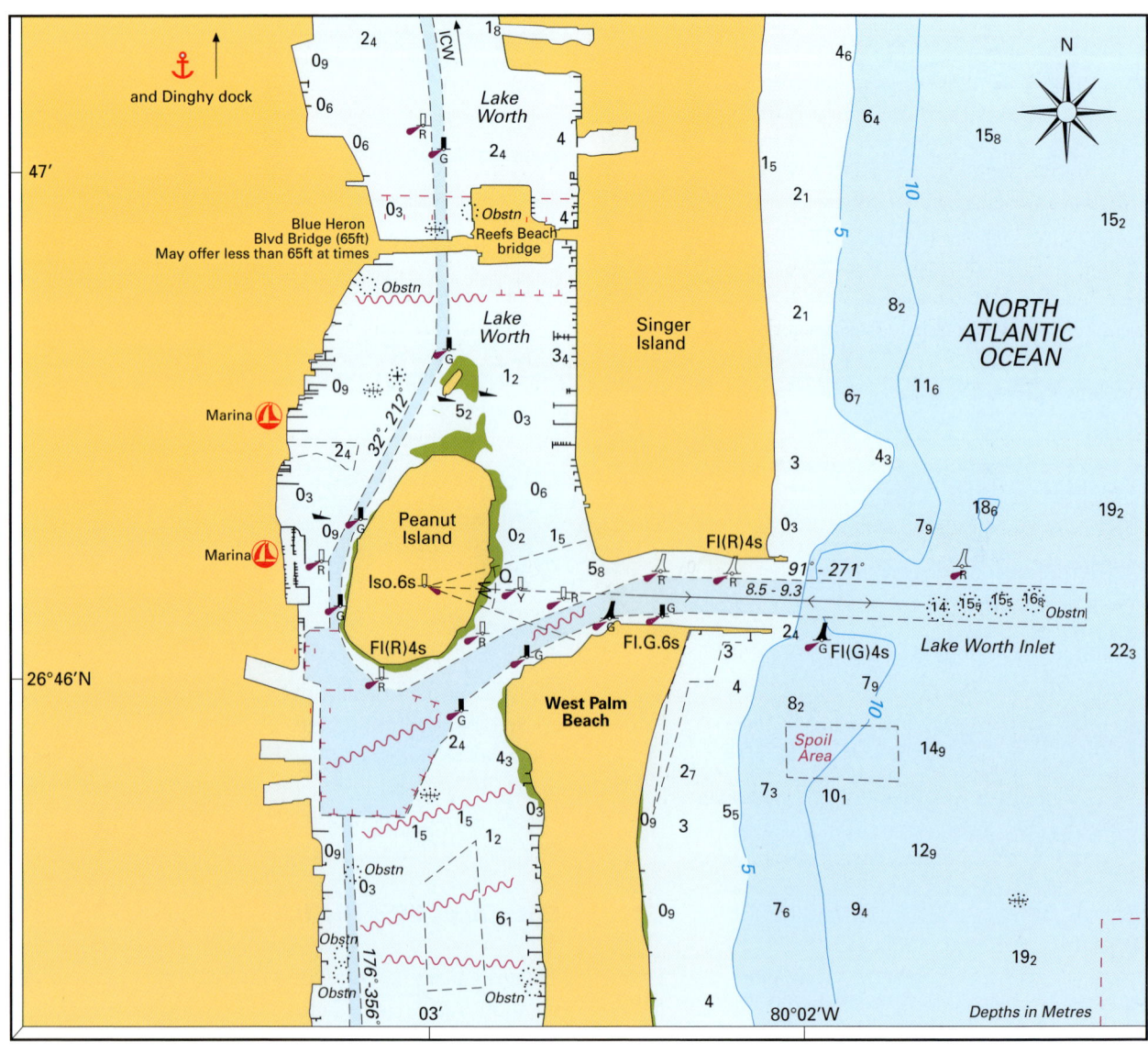

Plan 59 Entrance to West Palm Beach, Florida, USA

LANDFALLS ON THE ATLANTIC COAST OF THE USA

A typical ICW free government dock. Photo: Richard Woods

West Marine chandlery. The supermarket is just across the street from the dinghy dock so you can take the trolley to your dinghy. There is plenty of anchoring room in good holding. The disadvantage of entering the ICW at West Palm Beach is that the section from here to Jupiter Point has a testing number of bridges to negotiate.

Fort Pierce From The Abacos to Fort Pierce uses the Gulf Stream to best advantage and is a smoother passage. The entrance is straightforward. Once inside there are several marinas and a small anchoring area. It is a taxi ride to the airport to clear in where Formalities are very straightforward. Entering the ICW here avoids the worst section of bridges. The Indian River and the stretch of Waterway 120 miles north of Fort Pierce is one of the most attractive sections of the ICW.

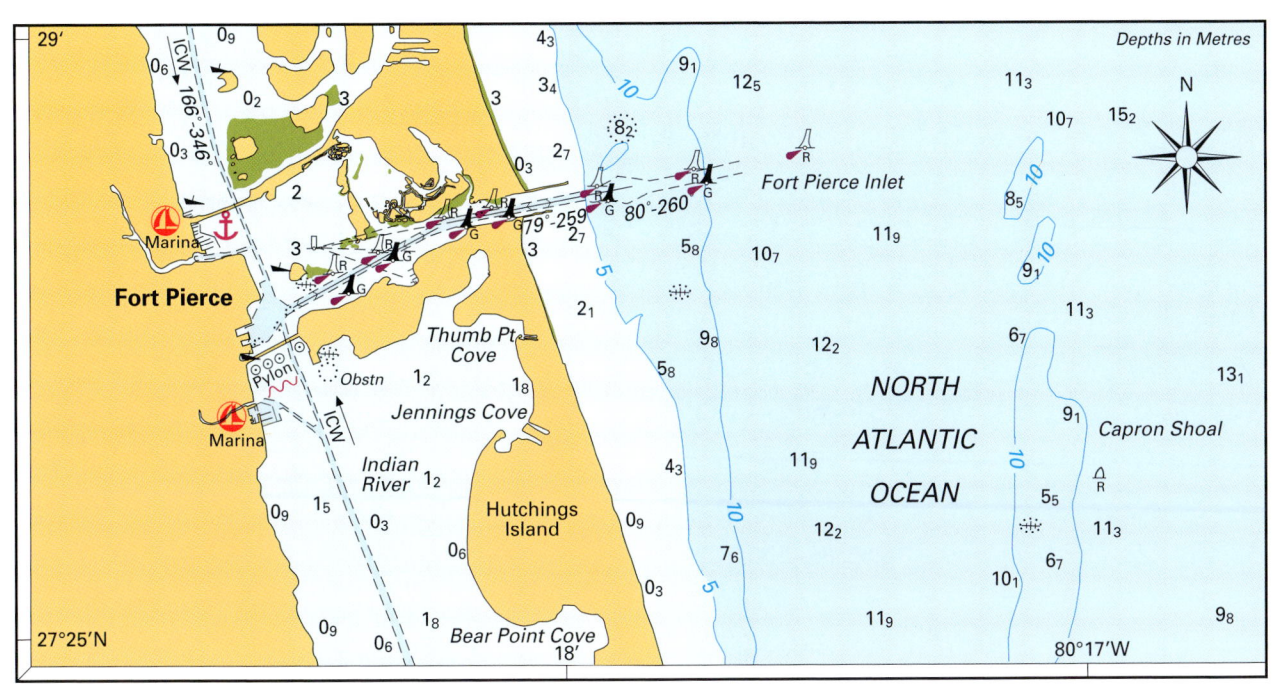

Plan 60 Entrance to Fort Pierce, Florida, USA

199

PASSAGES AND LANDFALLS

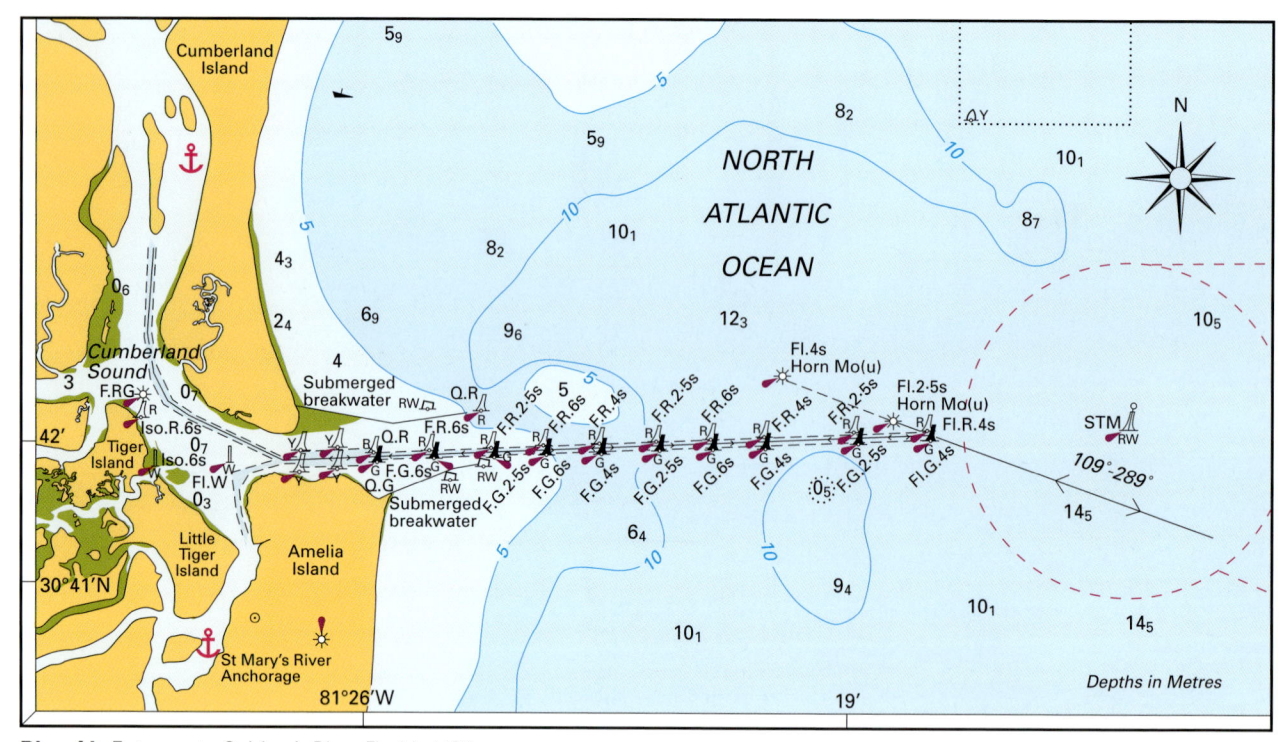

Plan 61 Entrance to St Mary's River, Florida, USA

Cape Canaveral Entrance and Barge Canal This is an interesting stop-off along the ICW. Titusville/Cocoa Beach is a good place for watching rocket launches from Cape Canaveral or the Kennedy Space Centre. It may not be such an ideal entrance for foreign yachts not yet cleared into the USA.

Cape Marina (28° 24´N, 80° 37´W), VHF Channels 16 and 68, provides transient dockage and a full range of facilities.
Website: www.capemarina.com/
Contact: Tel: 321 783 8410 Fax: 321 799 3271
E-mail: capemar@aol.com

St Mary's River This is the US Trident submarine base. Be aware of naval traffic and maintain a VHF watch. Exclusion zones apply around the submarines. There are long breakwaters at the entrance but the entrance channel is extremely well lit. Beware strong currents in the entrance and in the anchorages. Yachts heading north commonly exit the ICW at St Mary's and sail up the coast to Charleston or further because the Georgia section of the ICW is very shallow and contorted.

Georgia

Savannah River (South Carolina/Georgia border). This channel is excellent but subject to strong currents. It is the only ICW inlet with an entrance and marinas suitable for megayachts.

South Carolina

Charleston Entrance This is one of the best inlets, but heavily used by commercial shipping and naval vessels. The breakwaters guarding the entrance extend over two miles out south-eastwards towards the edges of the channel and the inner portions of them are submerged. Do not be tempted to cut the corners. If you are planning to head north on the ICW there is an anchorage just to the north of the Ben Sawyer Bridge. The ICW section north of Charleston, particularly the Waccamaw River, is very pleasant and rural. If you are planning to spend some time in Charleston, head west from the entrance along the southern channel, past Fort Sumter (where the first shots were fired, triggering the start of the American Civil War) to the marinas and anchorage off Charleston itself.

Use a tripping line when anchoring. This tree trunk was hauled up from the Alligator River. Photo: Richard Woods

LANDFALLS ON THE ATLANTIC COAST OF THE USA

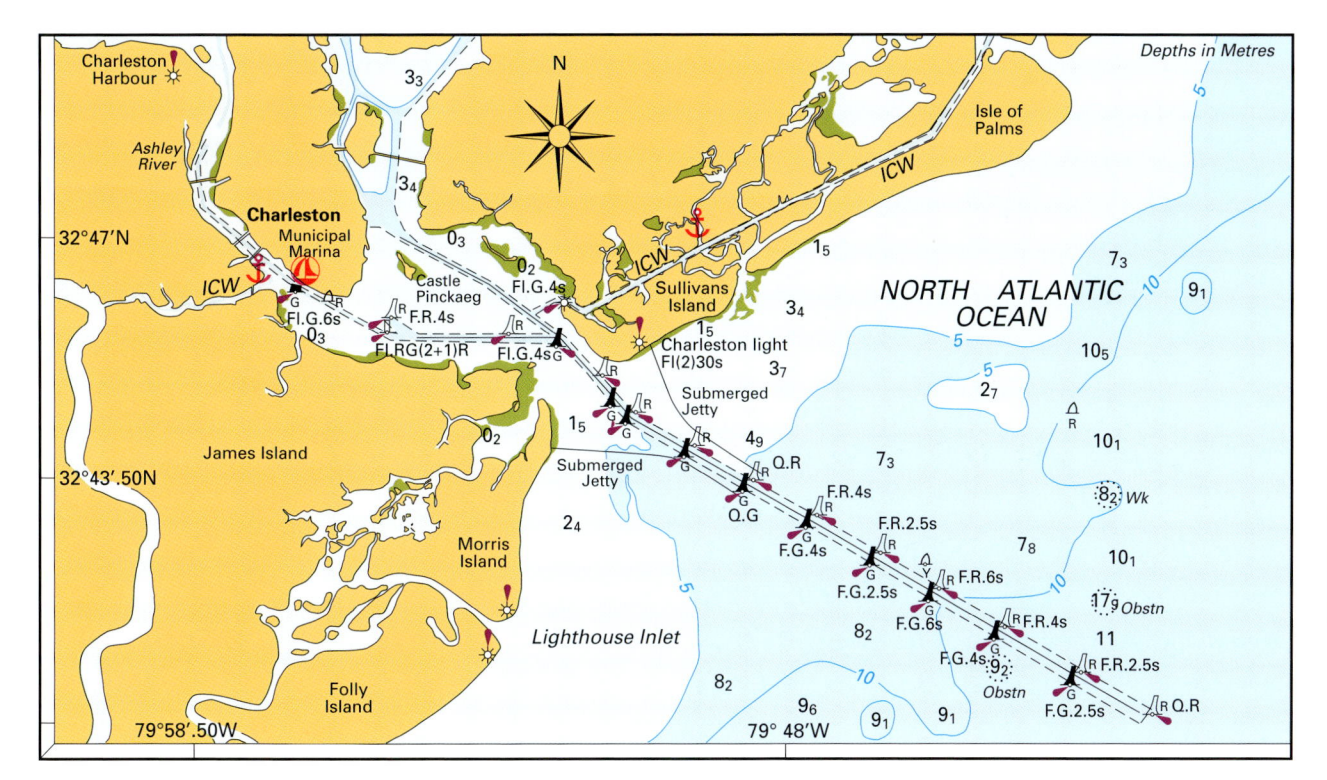

Plan 62 Entrance to Charleston, South Carolina, USA

North Carolina

Cape Fear River This is a safe all-weather entrance, although it is best to enter at slack water. The marinas or anchorages to the west of the entrance channel are a good place to sit out bad weather or wait for a flood tide to take you further north within the ICW.

Beaufort Inlet (North Carolina) and **Norfolk** (Virginia) are major ICW inlets and covered in detail as reference ports on the pages that follow.

Motoring weather – but it is possible to sail on some sections of the ICW. Photo: Richard Woods

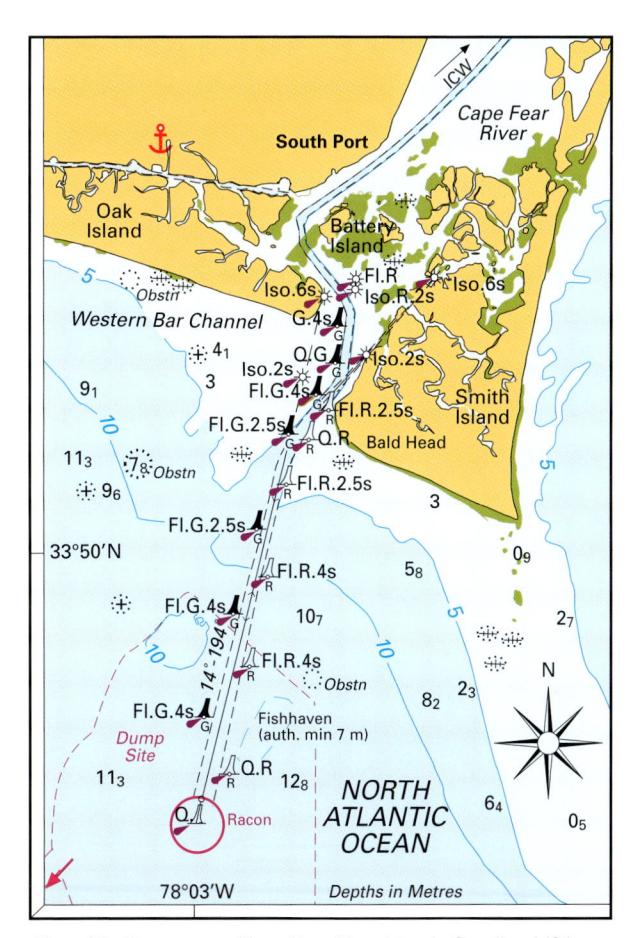

Plan 63 Entrance to Cape Fear River, North Carolina, USA

201

PASSAGES AND LANDFALLS

28
Beaufort/Morehead City
North Carolina, USA

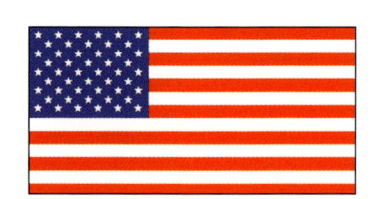

Location:	34°43′N	76°42′W
Springs:	1.0m	Range:	1.0m
Neaps:	0.9m	Range:	0.7m
Time zone:	UT –5		
Currency:	US dollar		
Tel/fax:	Country code: 1	Area code: (1) 252
Language:	English		
Emergencies:	911		

Websites
www.beaufort-nc.com
www.beaufortnc.org/default.aspx
www.ncmaritime.org

Approach and entrance

Final approaches to Beaufort Inlet are protected from the east and north by Cape Lookout, about 10 miles to the south-east. Cape Lookout has dangerous offlying shoals extending 10 miles to the south-south-east and should be given wide clearance. The powerful Cape Lookout light [Fl 15s 48m 25M] is about 1.5 miles north of the point itself. The outlying shoals are well buoyed. The coast to the west of Beaufort Inlet runs on an almost east/west axis, with good depths within 0.5 miles or less of the shore.

The long, buoyed Beaufort Inlet Channel is one of the safest on the coast. It begins at the red and white BM seabuoy [Fl Mo (A)] which is almost seven miles offshore. The channel is marked with leading lights on a bearing of 011°. Off Shackleford Point the second leading line is on a bearing of 340° which leads up Fort Macon Reach and into the well-buoyed Morehead City Channel. Fort Macon to

Beaufort (pronounced bow-fort as in bow and arrow) and its twin town of Morehead City are popular either as a stop along the Intracoastal Waterway or as an entry point or exit point for passaging yachts wishing to avoid Cape Hatteras by taking the inland route. Beaufort NC is not to be confused with Beaufort SC (pronounced Bew-Fort) – the home of Forrest Gump. Beaufort is often referred to as the US 'gateway to the Caribbean' – from here it is commonly a four-day sail to the Bahamas, five to Bermuda, and between seven and ten days direct to the Virgin Islands. The North Carolina Maritime Museum on Front Street, Beaufort, is worth a visit and is very welcoming towards visiting sailors.

Beaufort, North Carolina, looking south-west towards the entrance to Taylor Creek from the maritime museum. Photo: Richard Woods

LANDFALLS ON THE ATLANTIC COAST OF THE USA

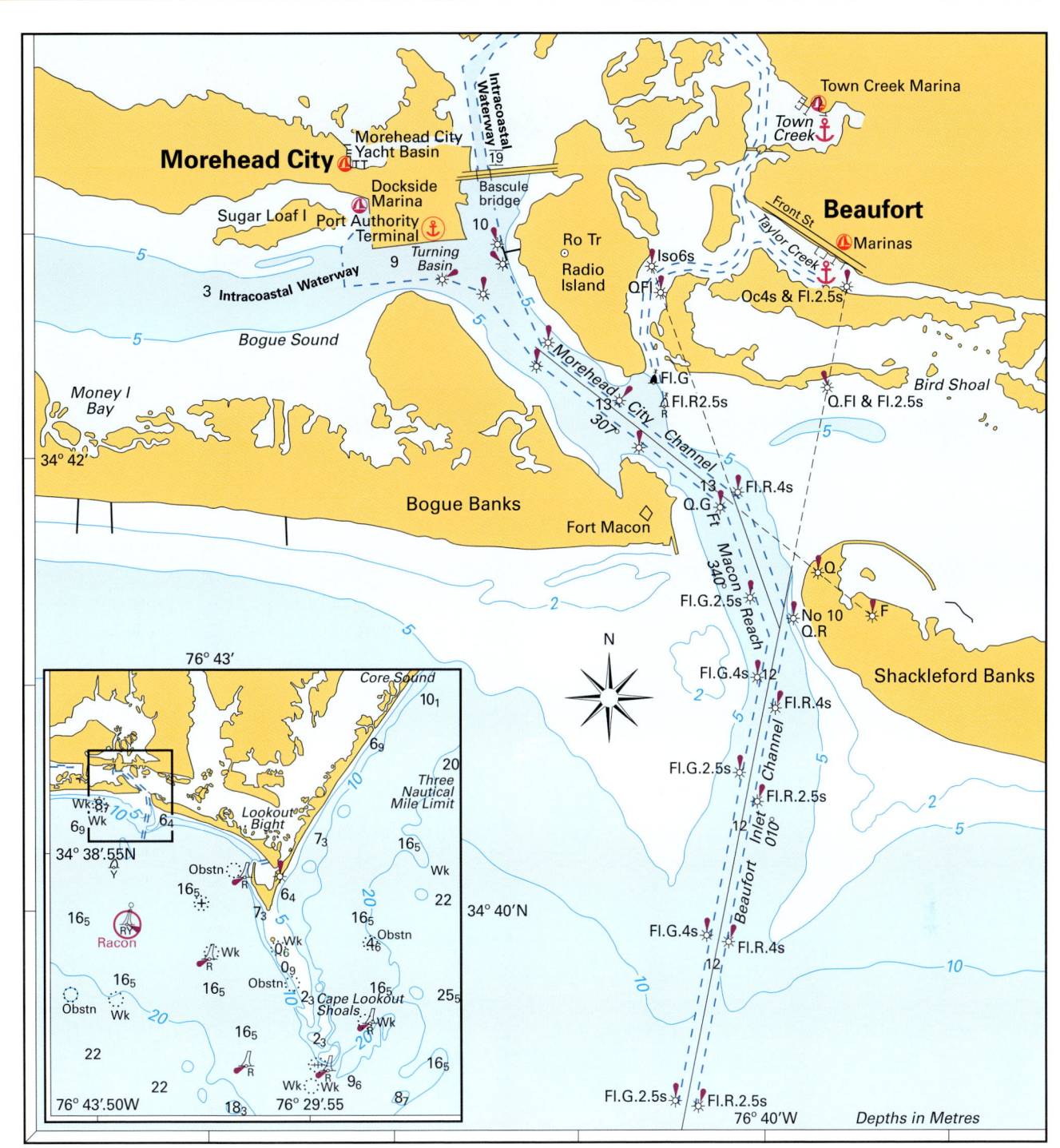

Plan 64 Beaufort/Morehead City, North Carolina, USA

port is unlit. If making for Beaufort, once in the Morehead City Channel look for red pillar buoy R2 [Fl R 2.5s] and the nearby marker G1 [Fl G 4s 4.5m 4M], after which the channel is buoyed to starboard. Tidal streams in the Beaufort Inlet Channel may run at 2–3 knots and an opposing wind will cause steep seas. In the vicinity of the Port Authority Terminal the stream can reach more than 4 knots at springs.

Radio

The Coast Guard monitors VHF Channel 16 and operates on Channel 22A. Port operations monitor VHF Channel 16 and work on Channels 10, 13, 14 and 16. All the marinas monitor VHF Channel 16 during daylight hours.

Formalities

See 'Formalities: the United States' at beginning of Chapter 16. The US Coast Guard monitors all vessels entering US waters, and yachts may be boarded at sea and searched. Fly the Q flag from offshore if arriving from abroad. You should contact the US Coast Guard initially (1 800 432 1216 or 1 800 451 0393 (24 hrs)) and then Customs and Immigration as necessary. You will probably need to take a taxi to the Customs office. The yacht may then be visited, by launch if necessary. A cruising licence, valid for one year, is issued to a foreign yacht at the first port of call.

Berthing and facilities

There are many marinas in the area, but those with most visitors' berths are listed below.

Downstream of the bridges on the Beaufort side:
Beaufort Docks is on the north side of Taylor Creek and has a wide range of repair facilities.
Contact: 500 Front Street, Beaufort, NC 28557 United States Tel: 252-728-2503.

Downstream of the bridges on the Morehead City side:
Dockside Marina is just to the west of the Port Authority Terminal.
Contact: 301 Arendell Street, Morehead City, NC. Tel/Fax: 247 4890.

Through the bridges on the Beaufort side:
Town Creek Marina is reached via a bascule road bridge which opens on the hour and then at 20 minute intervals. There is a 50-tonne travel lift with full service boatyard
Website: www.towncreekmarina.com
Contact: Tel: 728 6111 Fax: 728 4053.

Through the bridges on the Morehead City side:
Morehead City Yacht Basin is approached via a bascule bridge which carries the railway and is normally open unless a train is due, and a fixed bridge with 20m (65ft) air height.
Website: www.mcyachtbasin.com
Contact: 208 Arendell St, Morehead City, NC 28557.
Tel: 726 6862 Fax: 726 1939
E-mail: dockmaster@moreheadcityyachtbasin.com

Jarrett Bay Boatyard is a few miles up the Intracoastal Waterway and can lift boats up to 220 tons and 50m (165ft) with all the attendant facilities.
Website: www.jarrettbay.com
Tel: 728 7100 Fax: 728 2607.

Typical architecture in North Carolina. Photo: Richard Woods

Anchorage and moorings

The two best anchorages are on the south side of Taylor Creek, in a marked area opposite the Beaufort Docks, or in Town Creek to the north of Beaufort, through the bascule bridge. The latter anchorage is quieter, but still convenient for the town. Choose a spot clear of the main channel and use a bahamian moor in the strong streams. There is a public dinghy dock opposite the post office on Front Street, Beaufort. Unfortunately there are no shops within walking distance.

Transport connections

National airport at New Bern, 64km (40 miles) away.

Medical services

There is a hospital in Morehead City. Doctors and dentists are in both Morehead City and Beaufort.

A tranquil North Carolina anchorage on Pamlico Sound, ICW. Photo: Richard Woods

LANDFALLS ON THE ATLANTIC COAST OF THE USA

29
Norfolk
Virginia, USA

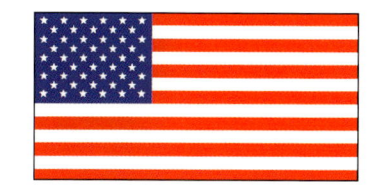

Location:	36°51′N 76°18′W	
Springs:	0.9m	Range: 0.9m
Neaps:	0.7m	Range: 0.7m
Time zone:	UT −5	
Currency:	US dollar	

Tel/fax:	Country code: 1 Area code: (1) 757
Language:	English
Emergencies:	911

The world's largest naval base

Norfolk lies at the mouth of the Elizabeth River. This marks the northern end of the Intracoastal Waterway where it emerges into the entrance to the Chesapeake Bay. Most yachts passing through Norfolk will be either joining or leaving the ICW. Although yachtsmen generally refer to the area as Norfolk, several of the marinas and facilities are actually in Portsmouth, on the west bank of the Elizabeth River. Hampton Roads is always very busy with commercial and naval shipping. The Norfolk naval base is the largest in the world. Tours of the base are run daily in summer. There is a wonderful maritime museum in Newport News which is to the northern side of Hampton Roads on the east bank of the James River. Be prepared to feel the need for a repeat visit to see everything you miss the first time. Historic Jamestowne, the site of the first permanent English settlement in America, and the Williamsburg re-enactment village are further up the James River.

If you are heading south down the ICW be aware that, just south of Norfolk, the ICW splits into the Virginia Cut route and the Dismal Swamp. The Virginia Cut is faster and is the preferred route for powerboats. The Dismal Swamp is older, some of it surveyed by George Washington, and it is not always open. During the summer it closes during

The Dismal Swamp section of the ICW, south of Norfolk, may be too shallow for some yachts. Photo: Richard Woods

NORFOLK, VIRGINIA
USA
29

205

PASSAGES AND LANDFALLS

Plan 65 Approaches to Norfolk, Virginia, USA

droughts when the water is used for fire-fighting. Even when it is open it may be too shallow for some yachts.

Websites
www.mariner.org/visitor-information
www.norfolkvisitor.com/norfolknavy
historicjamestowne.org
www.history.org

Approach and entrance

Norfolk is very busy with commercial and naval ships with the added complication of a number of opening bridges across the waterways. The approach from the Atlantic is via the Chesapeake Channel between Cape Charles [Fl 5s 55m 24M] on the northern shore and Cape Henry [Mo (U) WR 20s 50m 17/15M] to the south. Just west of Cape Henry the Thimble Shoal Channel branches off towards Hampton and crosses through the Chesapeake Bay Bridge Tunnel. This is a well-buoyed channel about three miles from the southern shore. Strong currents can run in this area, sometimes exceeding 3 knots, so particular care must be taken in the vicinity of the bridge supports. The Thimble Shoal Channel continues a further six miles west-north-west towards Old Point Comfort [LFl (2) W/R 12s 16m 16/14M] and the northern end of the Hampton Roads Bridge Tunnel which links Norfolk to Hampton. Fort Wool [Fl 4s 8m 8M] marks the southern side of the channel into Hampton Roads.

LANDFALLS ON THE ATLANTIC COAST OF THE USA

Formalities

See 'Formalities: the United States' at beginning of Chapter 16. The US Coast Guard monitors all vessels entering US waters, and yachts may be boarded at sea and searched. Fly the Q flag from offshore if arriving from abroad. You should contact the US Coast Guard initially (1 800 432 1216 or 1 800 451 0393 (24 hrs)) and then Customs and Immigration as necessary. You will probably need to take a taxi to the Customs office. The yacht may then be visited, by launch if necessary. A cruising licence, valid for one year, is issued to a foreign yacht at the first port of call.

Norfolk Port Authority c/o Virginia Port Authority, 600 World Trade Centre, Norfolk, Virginia 23510. Tel: 804 623 8000.

Berthing and facilities

There are numerous marinas around Norfolk and Portsmouth, with more at Hampton on the north bank. Marinas with good facilities for visitors (transients) include:

Willoughby Harbor Marina 36° 57´N 74°17´.69W is located on the north side of Willoughby Bay about four miles from Norfolk city centre, near the southern end of the Hampton Roads Bridge Tunnel. It is some distance out of town, but there are good facilities locally and a courtesy car may be available. A current of up to two knots can flow in the marina basin. There is a boatyard next to the marina.
Website: www.willoughbyharbormarina.com
Contact: 1525 Bayville St, Norfolk, VA 23503. Tel: 583 4150.

Waterside Marina is much closer to the city centre on the Norfolk shore and is an all-transient facility with 50 berths, capable of taking megayachts up to 120m (400ft).
Website: www.watersidemarina.com
Contact: 333 Waterside Drive, Norfolk, VA 23510.
Tel: 625 3625 Fax: 623 8477
E-mail: dock@watersidemarina.com

Tidewater Yacht Marina has 325 berths for vessels up to 30m (100ft), a hundred of them reserved for visiting yachts, and is situated right opposite Waterside Marina and the Norfolk city centre. Facilities include a 60-ton travel lift and 25m (80ft) enclosed wet slip.
Website: www.tyamarina.com
Contact: 10 Crawford Parkway, Portsmouth, VA 23704.
Tel: 393 2525 Fax: 393 7845, Toll Free (US Only): 888 390 0080

Anchorage and moorings

There are several possible anchorages convenient to Norfolk and Portsmouth. A popular choice is at ICW, mile 0 at

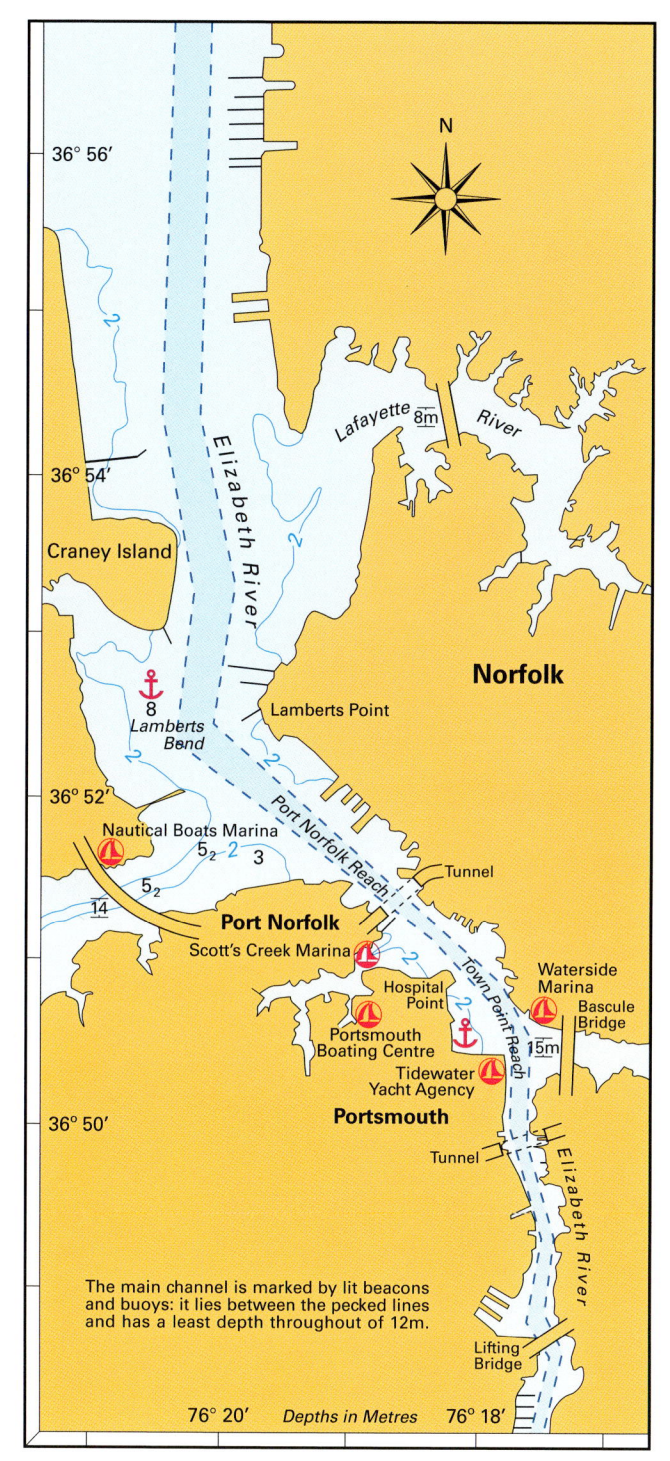

Plan 66 Norfolk harbour, Virginia, USA

Continue south-west from the Hampton Roads Bridge Tunnel, past the narrow but well-marked channel for Willoughby Bay, and on down Entrance Reach. Norfolk Harbor Reach then leads south past the Naval Base into the Elizabeth River. The entire area is extremely well buoyed.

Radio

Both Coast Guard and harbourmaster monitor VHF Channel 16. All the marinas listen on VHF Channel 16 and many also use Channel 68.

PASSAGES AND LANDFALLS

NORFOLK, VIRGINIA USA — 29

A yacht passes under one of the Norfolk lifting railway bridges. Photo: Jetti Matzke

Hospital point in 4.0m (13ft). This is convenient for dinghy trips to the town centre and shops, but it's very noisy here. It is also possible to anchor on the west side of the channel opposite Lamberts Point in about 8.0m (26ft) or just south of Lamberts Point. The Ocean Marine water taxi covers the inner harbour from 0700 daily. An alternative anchorage in good holding is in Willoughby Bay, but this is also noisy from the Navy helicopters working and is exposed to west winds.

Transport connections

Local and airport buses. Two ferries link Portsmouth and Norfolk from 0700 daily. Norfolk International airport is a few minutes away.

Medical services

Several hospitals and numerous doctors and dentists. Ask locally.

Evening sun catches the autumn colours on the ICW. Photo: Richard Woods

208

LANDFALLS ON THE ATLANTIC COAST OF THE USA

30
Annapolis
Maryland, USA

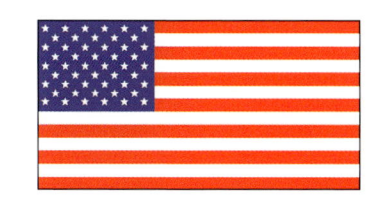

Location:	38°58´.5N 76°29´W	
Springs:	0.3m	Range: 0.2m
Neaps:	0.3m	Range: 0.2m
Time zone:	UT –5	
Currency:	US dollar	
Tel/fax:	Country code: 1 Area code: (1) 410	
Language:	English	
Emergencies:	911	

October Boat Show

Annapolis, Maryland, is 140 miles north of Norfolk on the western shore of Chesapeake Bay. It was briefly the capital of the United States and has been the state capital since 1695. Many of the homes of the early settlers have been restored and are open to visitors. The town, with its rich heritage, is very popular with tourists. It is also a major yachting and sailing centre with a full range of marine and general facilities.

Annapolis is the home of the United States Sailboat Show and the United States Powerboat Show, which run consecutively for two weeks during October. Much of the land between Spa Creek and College Creek is occupied by

Looking ESE over Annapolis. College Creek is in the foreground, Spa Creek centre right and Back Creek are just visible. To the left can be seen Greenbury Point with radio masts. Photo: David Wallace.

209

PASSAGES AND LANDFALLS

Plan 67 Annapolis, Maryland, USA

the United States Naval Academy. The Tourist and Visitors' Information Booth are in the same building as the harbourmaster, to the east of City Dock; it is open from 1 April to 1 November and will provide all tourist information during normal business hours. *The Port Book*, which is produced annually and covers Annapolis and the eastern shore of Maryland, lists marine, tourist and travel services, bridge opening times, etc. and is available free of charge from the harbourmaster's office.

Annapolis is a good place to leave the boat to visit Washington DC. It is possible to sail up the Potomac River to Washington, but it is likely to be a two-day motor in both directions.

Website
www.ci.annapolis.md.us

LANDFALLS ON THE ATLANTIC COAST OF THE USA

Looking west up Spa Creek, Annapolis. Photo: Richard Woods

Approach and entrance

Annapolis lies on the south-west shore of the Severn River where it broadens out into the Chesapeake Bay. Approach from the Chesapeake Bay is straightforward. For Spa Creek, follow the buoyed channel up the Severn River to marker HP [Fl 6s 6M], then head north-westerly to Spa Creek. Marker HP is at the eastern edge of a very shallow area which extends all the way to the shore. For Back Creek, which has a minimum depth at the entrance of 3.0m (10ft), turn to port before the HP marker and head south-westerly for the FlG 4s marker which you leave to port at the entrance to Back Creek. Back Creek is deepest along its northern shore, so beware of straying to the south of the buoyed channel until the marinas are reached.

Caution
There is little tidal range even at springs, and heights are affected by wind as much as by lunar forces – a strong north-westerly breeze will reduce the water level in the Bay by as much as 1.0m (3ft).

Radio

The harbourmaster monitors VHF Channels 16 and 09 and uses others, principally Channel 17, for communication. The marinas generally use one or more of Channels 16, 17, 71, 72 and 74. The water taxi that serves Back Creek and Spa Creek monitors Channel 68.

Formalities

Annapolis is NOT an official Port of Entry. Visiting sailors should clear Customs and complete appropriate formalities elsewhere before sailing up Chesapeake Bay. The harbourmaster (Tel: 263 7973) has an office close to the east of the City Dock, welcomes visiting yachts enthusiastically and will assist in any way he can.

Berthing and facilities

Within the city limits are several marinas which offer many berths for transient vessels. All provide the usual services and some have boatyards on site. Some of the marinas are listed below. For more possibilities visit **www.noonsite.com**

Back Creek marinas north shore:
Horn Point Harbor Marina
Website: www.hornpointharbor.com
Contact: Horn Point Harbor Marina, 105 Eastern Ave, PO Box 4358, Annapolis, Maryland 21403. Tel: 263 0550 Fax: 571 0320 E-mail: info@hornpointharbor.com

Mears Marina
Website: www.mearsannapolis.com
Contact: 519 Chester Avenue, Annapolis, Maryland 21403. Tel: 268 8282 Fax: 268 7161.

Back Creek marinas south shore:
Annapolis Landing Marina
Website: www.annapolismarina.com/index.html

ANNAPOLIS, MARYLAND
USA
30

PASSAGES AND LANDFALLS

Contact: 980 Awald Drive, Suite 500, Annapolis, Maryland 21403. Tel: 263 0090 Fax: 263 9109
E-mail: ALMarina@earthlink.net

Port Annapolis Marina
Website: www.portannapolis.com/aaa/index.html
Contact: 7074 Bembe Beach Road, Annapolis, Maryland 21403. Tel: 269 1990 Fax: 269 5856
E-mail: office@portannapolis.com

Bert Jabin's Yacht Yard
Website: www.bjyy.com
Contact: 7310 Edgewood Rd, Annapolis, MD 21403.
Tel: 268 9667 Fax: 280 3163.

Spa Creek marinas north shore:
Annapolis Yacht Basin
Website: www.yachtbasin.com
Contact: 2 Compromise Street, Annapolis, MD 21401.
Tel: 263 3544 Fax: 269 1319.

Spa Creek marinas south shore:
W & P Nautical
Website: www.wpnautical.com
Contact: 222 Severn Avenue, Annapolis, MD 21403.
Tel: 268 7700 Fax: 268 7750 E-mail: judy@wpnautical.com

Annapolis City Marina
Website: www.marinas.com/annapoliscitymarina/
Contact: 410 Severn Avenue, Annapolis, MD 21403.
Tel: 268 0660 Fax: 268 1761
E-mail: dockmaster@annapoliscitymarina.com

Anchorage and moorings

There are several possible anchorages around Annapolis but holding is variable. Anchorage may be found in Back Creek, the upper reaches of Spa Creek, and Weems Creek which is further north up the Severn River. There is a deep anchorage along the south side of the Naval Academy. College Creek to the north of the Academy, although within the city limits, is unsuitable as an anchorage.

Weems Creek anchorage lies above the first of the highway bridges crossing the Severn River. Vertical clearance is 22.8m (75ft). The creek entrance is on the port side, indicated by a red and green marker labelled 'WC'. A bascule bridge crosses Weems Creek about 0.5 miles from its mouth but there are anchoring depths of around 4.5m (15ft) downstream of the bridge. It is a quiet anchorage with very limited access to the shore, though it is possible to land at the end of Tucker Street on the south-eastern shore, from where it is a one-mile walk to a small shopping centre.

The harbour authorities maintain 59 moorings in Spa Creek; 40 downstream of the bridge for yachts of no more than 13m (43ft) or so, and 19 beyond it in St Mary's Cove for yachts less than 11m (36ft) overall. The city moorings are white with a blue stripe and a number, and are allocated on a 'first come, first served' basis. The harbourmaster patrols the moorings during daylight hours. Dinghies can be left for no charge at the end of every street running down to the water. You can also leave a dinghy at the head of City Dock which is in the heart of the main shopping area for the city.

Transport connections

The Jiffy Water Taxi (Tel: 263 0033) operates from the City Dock and serves Spa Creek, Back Creek and the Severn River. It listens on VHF Channel 68. Local bus service plus longer-distance routes. Baltimore–Washington International airport, which provides national and international services, is about 45 minutes away and can be reached by shuttle service or public transport.

Medical services

The hospital at Anne Arundel Medical Center in downtown Annapolis is about five minutes from Spa Creek.

Annapolis waterfront houses. Photo: Richard Woods

LANDFALLS ON THE ATLANTIC COAST OF THE USA

31
New York
New York, USA

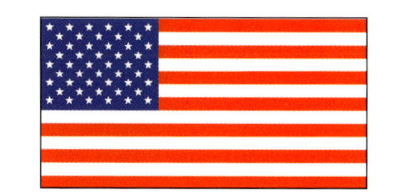

Location:	40°39′N 74°03′W
Springs range::	1.8m
Mean range::	1.5m
Time zone:	UT −5
Currency:	US dollar
Tel/fax:	Country code: 1 Area code: (1) 212 (other codes are given where appropriate)
Language:	English
Emergencies:	911

Approaching the Statue of Liberty. Photo: Richard Woods

New York, New York

The thought of sailing up into the heart of New York and past the Statue of Liberty is one that will thrill many visitors to these waters. New York is a Port of Entry, a departure port and a good stop off during a cruise up the coast. It is also the southwestern gateway to Long Island Sound which is the major summer yachting area of the east coast of the USA.

The geography of New York can be confusing to the first time visitor. New York City itself is on Manhattan Island, but is just one of many interconnected urban areas. New York City is within New York State, but is not the state capital.

New York Harbour is an extremely busy commercial thoroughfare. Commercial shipping, ferries, tugs and sightseeing boats all compete with you for space on the water. Do not attempt to enter these waters without a reliable engine. Surprisingly, amidst all the apparent chaos, it is possible to find a marina berth or mooring right in the heart of this great city – a great base from which to explore all the attractions ashore.

It is also the starting point for yachts setting out to complete the Great Circle Route. This route follows the Hudson River to Waterford where it joins the Erie Canal. The Erie Canal links to the Oswego Canal which gives access to Lake Ontario and the Great Lakes. From there it is possible to join into the top of the Mississippi and cruise southwards through the heart of the USA to the Gulf Coast. There are variations to the route, but for at least some of it you will need to un-step the mast.

Further reference
www.nyc.gov
New York State Canal system:
www.nyscanals.gov/exvac/boating/index.html
Skipper Bob Guides: *The Great Circle Route*

Approach and entrance

Approaching from the south or east it makes sense to stop off at Atlantic Highlands before heading up into New York. This enables you to plan your entrance to New York according to the tides. If you are planning to head through to Long Island Sound up the East River you will need to plan carefully as streams run very strongly.

Atlantic Highlands is tucked in to the west of Fort Hancock. There is a marina and a large anchoring area protected by an extensive mole. From here, head north across the bay and under the Verrazano Narrows suspension bridge. Continue upstream past the container port and anchored ships. You should then see the Statue of Liberty which you leave to port.

If you are heading for Long Island Sound, turn to starboard around the north end of Governors Island and under the Brooklyn Bridge into East River. This will take you past the end of Wall Street and the United Nations with the Empire State Building clearly visible behind. The East River runs under several fixed bridges with substantial

213

PASSAGES AND LANDFALLS

Plan 68 New York, New York, USA

clearance. Once clear of the Throgs Neck Bridge you are into Long Island Sound and have access to a number of anchorages and marinas. Heading west it is possible to anchor in Flushing Bay off La Guardia airport to wait for the tide.

If you are heading for one of the marinas or moorings on the Hudson River, continue up the west side of Manhattan past Ground Zero.

Radio

Both Coast Guard and harbourmaster monitor VHF Channel 16. All the marinas listen on VHF Channel 16.

Formalities

See 'Formalities: the United States' at beginning of Chapter 16. The US Coast Guard monitors all vessels entering US waters, and yachts may be boarded at sea and searched. Fly the Q flag from offshore if arriving from abroad. You should contact the US Coastguard initially (1 800 432 1216 or 1 800 451 0393 (24 hrs)) and then Customs and Immigration as necessary. You will probably need to take a taxi to the Customs office. The yacht may then be visited, by launch if necessary. A cruising licence, valid for one year, is issued to a foreign yacht at the first port of call.

LANDFALLS ON THE ATLANTIC COAST OF THE USA

Heading down the East River beneath the bridges towards the Statue of Liberty. The currents can run extremely fast here.
Photo: Richard Woods

Port Authority of New York-New Jersey, 225 Park Avenue South, 18th Floor, New York, New York 10003-1604.
Tel: 435 7000.

Berthing and facilities

There are numerous marinas and a full range of facilities in and around New York City. Some of the marinas with berths reserved for visitors (transients) heading north are listed below:

Liberty Landing Marina is a 600-slip full-service marina on the lower Hudson River, opposite Ground Zero, with a spectacular view of Manhattan. It has a service department at Morris Canal Basin, West End with a 60-tonne travel hoist.
Website: www.libertylandingmarina.com/
Contact: 80 Audry Zapp Drive, Liberty State Park, Jersey City, NJ 07305.
Tel: 201-985-8000 Fax: 201 985 9866/201 985 8908
E-mail: info@libertylandingmarina.com

Marina at Chelsea Piers (40° 44.7´N 74° 00.7´W) lies on the Manhattan shore of the Hudson. It has 60 slips (max length 100m [300ft]) with 20 reserved for transients. Reservations are required.
Contact: Tel: 336 7873 Fax: 824 4092

The West 79 St Marina is located in the heart of Manhattan north of the Empire State Building and is a great base from which to explore ashore. It is a good starting point for the Great Circle Route. It is located on the Hudson River, Riverside Park, Manhattan.
Website: www.nycgovparks.org/facilities/marinas/10
Contact: Tel: 496 2105, VHF Channel 09.

Minneford Marina is located on the east side of City Island, which is in Long Island Sound, to the east of the Throg's Neck Bridge. It has 500 berths for vessels up to 30m (100ft) and a 45-tonne travel lift and short or long term haul-out facilities. The marina warmly welcomes visiting yachts and monitors VHF Channel 77.
Website: www.minnefordmarina.com/index.php
Contact: Tel: (718) 885 2000 Fax: (718) 885 2015

Anchoring

This is not advisable between the Verrazano Narrows Bridge and La Guardia airport or in the Hudson River within the city. Once through Throg's neck into Long Island Sound you are spoilt for choice. The anchorage off La Guardia is useful, but very noisy and should only be considered as a temporary stop.

Transport connections

There are regular harbour ferries. It is a major transport hub with three international airports, bus and train links.

Medical services

An array of services are available. Ask locally.

PASSAGES AND LANDFALLS

Plan 69 New York to Cape Cod showing approaches to New York, Newport and the Cape Cod canal

Outer approaches to New York and Newport

Heavy concentrations of shipping are likely to be encountered on the approaches – fishing vessels around the various banks, and commercial traffic en route to New York, Narragansett Bay and Boston. The approaches are well marked and entrance is possible both day and night. The entrance to Narragansett Bay itself is well lit, with lights also marking Buzzard's Bay [Fl 2.5s 19m 17M] 16 miles to the east, Point Judith [Oc (3) 15s 20m 16M] 6 miles to the south-west, and Block Island south-east [Fl G 5s 80m 20M] 18 miles south-southwest. All have fog signals.

Approaching from the north-east, the coast and islands between Cape Cod and Newport are low-lying with areas of shoal water. The area is very prone to fog and it can be difficult to identify the coast. Most yachts approaching from this direction will use the Cape Cod Canal, which leads into a dredged channel at the north-east end of Buzzard's Bay. Beware of the strong currents which run through the canal at up to seven knots and the railway bridge across the canal which may be closed on your approach. If you are transiting the canal, there is a pleasant anchorage at Onset Bay on the Buzzard's Bay end. A middle route, through Nantucket Sound and Vineyard Sound, is possible but not recommended.

If you are coming from the south-east or south it is advisable to make first landfall at Nantucket Shoals Lanby. This keeps you well south of the shoals themselves and ensures an exact position from which to close the land. If coast-hopping, Block Island is a useful stop off before Newport. It can sometimes be very crowded but is well worth a visit.

LANDFALLS ON THE ATLANTIC COAST OF THE USA

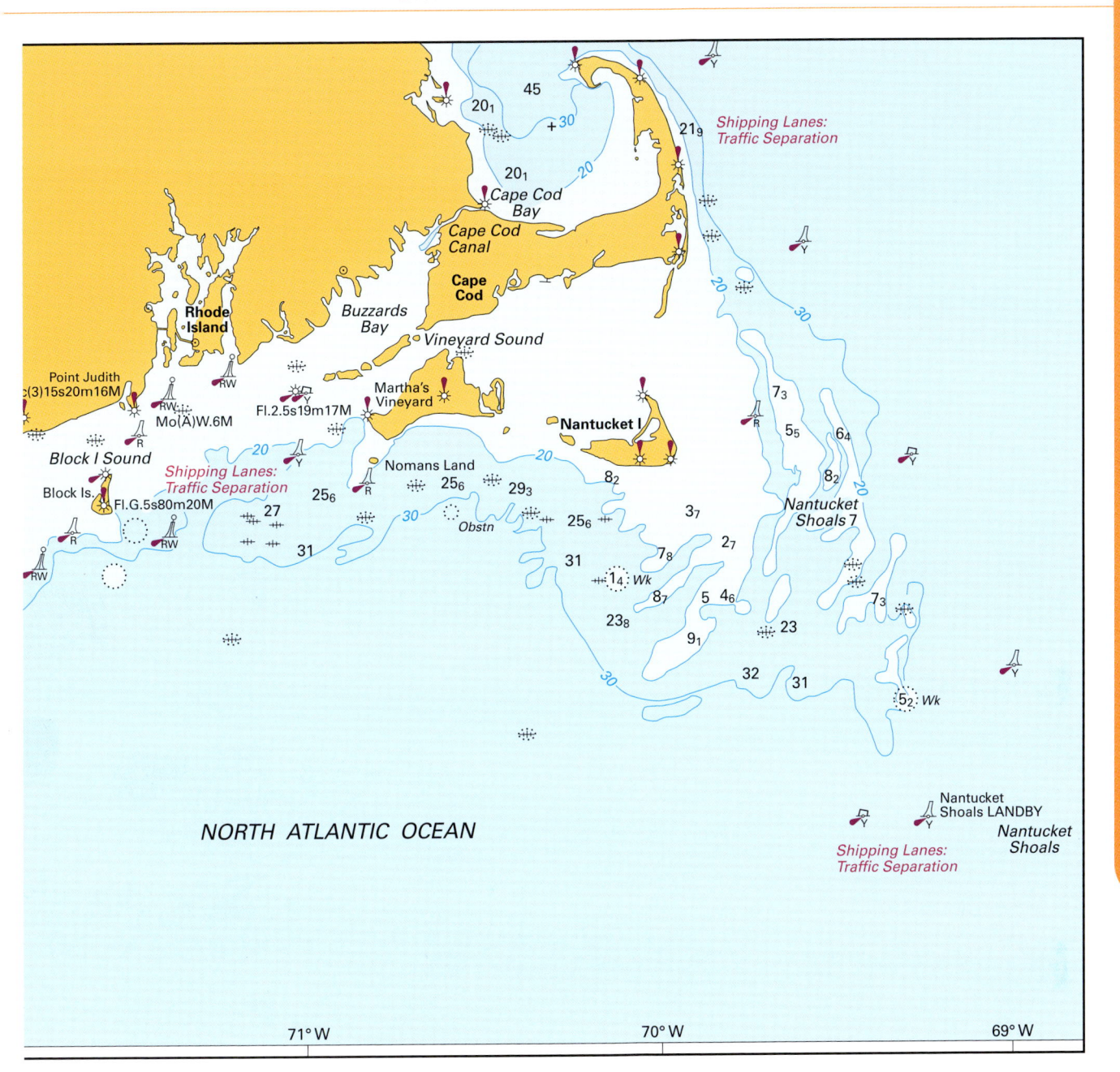

APPROACHES TO NEW YORK AND NEWPORT
USA

There are dozens of anchorages all along both shores of the Sound. Mystic Seaport, Block Island and the Peabody Museum of Natural History at Yale are all must-sees.

Mystic Seaport, Long Island Sound.
Photo: Richard Woods

217

PASSAGES AND LANDFALLS

32
Newport
Rhode Island, USA

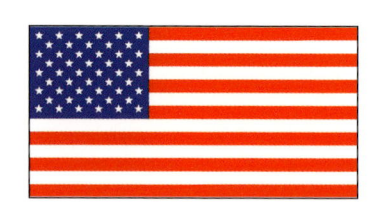

Location:	41°29′N 71°19′.5W
Springs:	1.2m Range: 1.2m
Neaps:	0.8m Range: 0.8m
Time zone:	UT –5
Currency:	US dollar
Tel/fax:	Country code: 1 Area code: (1) 401
Language:	English
Emergencies:	911

America's Cup History

Newport, Rhode Island, lies to the east of the main entrance channel to Narragansett Bay. It has long been an important yachting centre and for many years was the venue for the America's Cup races. It is also the destination of the single-handed transatlantic races run from Plymouth, UK, and a favourite landfall for yachts heading north from Bermuda. The city and its environs have a rich heritage and there are plenty of interesting historical sites to visit ashore. The Visitors' Information Center at 23 America's Cup Avenue is worth a visit, as is the Fort Adams complex across the harbour.

Website
www.gonewport.com/

Entrance

Heading in towards Newport, make for the red and white Narragansett Bay entrance buoy [Fl 4s Mo(A) and Racon B]. From Narragansett Bay entrance buoy, steer 026° to give Castle Hill [Iso R 6s 12m 12M] good clearance to starboard. This should also leave Brenton Reef whistle buoy [Fl R 4s] to starboard and take you well clear of Brenton Reef and the many fish nets in the area.

The channel to Newport lies between Beavertail Point [Fl 9s 20m 15M] to the west and Brenton Point to the east. Although the rock cliff is very bold, it is essential to leave Butterball Rock bell buoy to starboard. The buoy marks a barely awash shoal south-west of Castle Hill. From Castle Hill follow the buoyed channel and then turn in towards Newport Harbor itself, following the buoyed channel that leads between Fort Adams and Goat Island.

Looking NW across Newport Harbour from the New York Yacht Club. Fort Adams is the building at the extreme left.
Photo: Miles Bidwell (OCC)

LANDFALLS ON THE ATLANTIC COAST OF THE USA

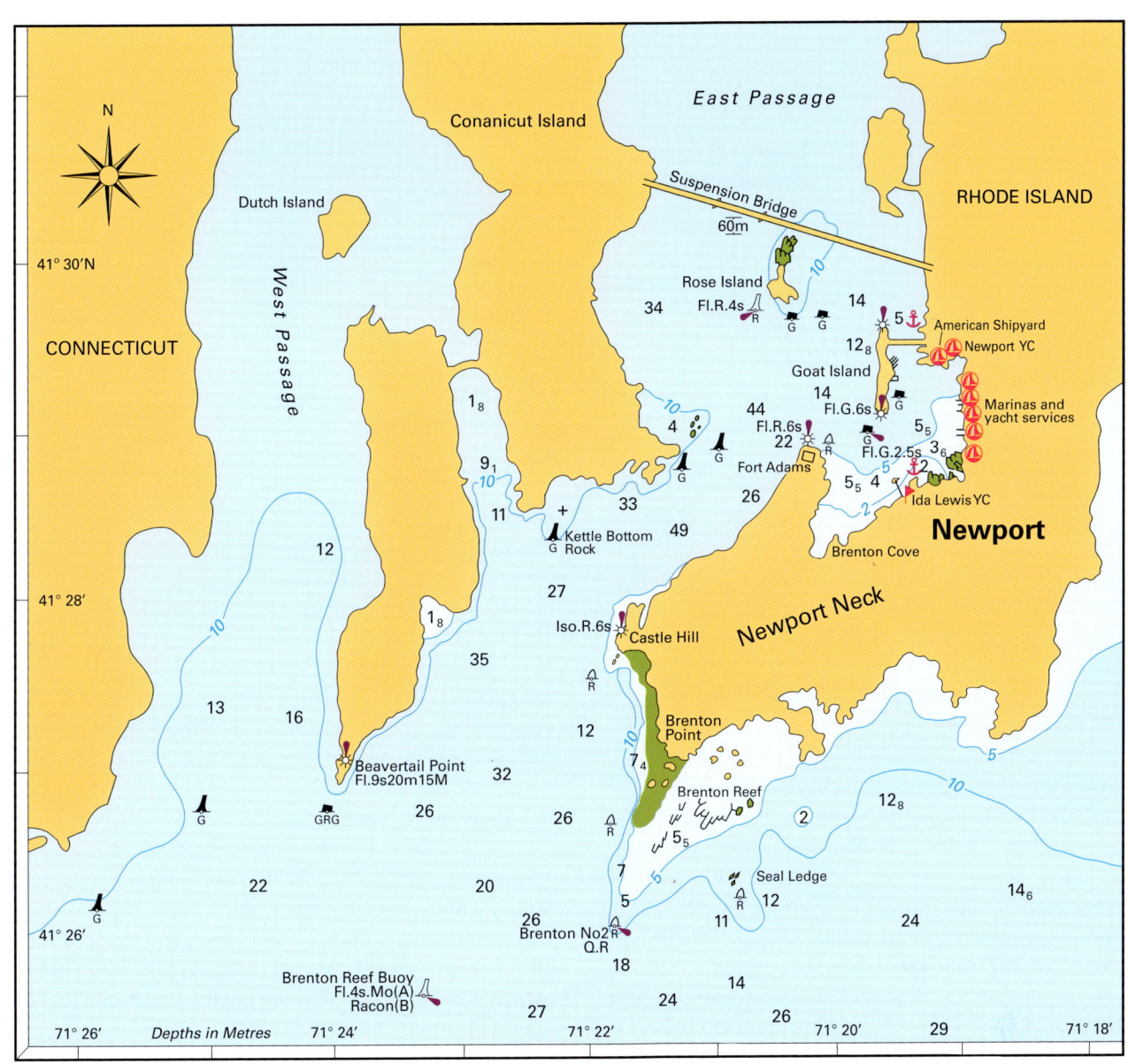

Plan 70 Newport, Rhode Island, USA

Radio

Castle Hill Coast Guard station maintains a 24-hour watch on VHF Channel 16, but can also be called direct on Channel 22A. The harbourmaster monitors Channel 16, but communicates on Channel 14. The marinas use Channel 09 and 11, with Oldport Marine's launch listening on Channel 68.

Formalities

See 'Formalities: the United States' at beginning of Chapter 16. The US Coast Guard monitors all vessels entering US waters, and yachts may be boarded at sea and searched. Fly the Q flag from offshore if arriving from abroad. You should contact the US Coast Guard initially (1 800 432 1216 or 1 800 451 0393 (24 hrs)) and then Customs and Immigration as necessary. You will probably need to take a taxi to the Customs office. The yacht may then be visited, by launch if necessary. A cruising licence, valid for one year, is issued to a foreign yacht at the first port of call.

Harbourmaster: (Tel: 848 6492) will assist with information and advice.

Anchorage and moorings

The yacht anchorages in Brenton Cove at the south-western corner of the harbour and at the northern end between Goat Island and the town waterfront are now occupied by moorings. Most transient yachts now anchor either just north of the Ida Lewis Yacht Club or north of the causeway to Goat Island. Everywhere you may struggle to find anchoring room. Beware of the reef to the north-east of the yacht club. The harbourmaster maintains 20 moorings available on a first come, first served basis, but there is seldom one free. Others are controlled by Oldport Marine Services (Tel: 847 9109 or VHF Channel 68). They also run

PASSAGES AND LANDFALLS

an excellent launch service between 0800 and midnight which will pick up and deposit passengers anywhere in the harbour for a modest fee. Otherwise, try Brenton Cove Moorings (Tel: 849 2210). Alternatively, the Ida Lewis Yacht Club (Tel: 846 1969 or VHF Channel 78A) may have a visitors' mooring available. Dinghies can be left at the Municipal Dock or the Ann Street Pier.

Berthing and facilities

There are many marinas in the Newport area with a complete range of marine and general facilities. Some of those with berths for visitors (transients) are listed below. For more possibilities visit www.noonsite.com

American Shipyard has a marine railway and can take vessels up to 80m (260ft).
Website: www.americanshipyard.com
Contact: 1 Washington St, Newport RI 02840.
Tel: 846 6000 Fax: 846 6001 VHF Channel 09
E-mail: info@americanshipyard.com

Bannister's Wharf Marina has 24 boat slips for transients and a range of facilities. It is located in the centre of Newport.
Website: www.bannisterswharf.net/
Contact: America's Cup Ave, Newport, RI 02840.
Tel: 846-4500 Fax: 849 8750 E-mail: bwdocks@aol.com

Casey's Marina has seasonal and transient dockage available with haul-out facilities at Spring Wharf, PO Box 187, Newport, RI 02840.
Contact: Tel: 640 4458/848 5945 Fax: 849 0281/849 9209

Newport Shipyard is the oldest of the yachting facilities and is a full-service yard and marina.
Website: www.newportshipyard.com

Contact: Tel: 846 6002 Fax: 846 6003
E-mail: dockoffice@newportshipyard.com

Newport Marina
Website: www.newportmarina.com/
Contact: 1 Lees Wharf, Newport, RI 02840-3419.
Tel: 849 2293 Tel/Fax: 849-9503   VHF Channel 09
E-mail: info@newportmarina.com

Newport Yachting Center Marina
Website: www.newportyachtingcenter.com/marina/overview.htm
Contact: 20 Commercial Wharf, Newport, RI 02840.
Tel: 847 9047 Toll Free: 800-653-3625   VHF Channel 09
E-mail: reservations@newportyachtingcenter.com

Oldport Marine
Website: www.oldportmarine.com
Contact: PO Box 141, Newport, RI 02840.
Tel: 847 9109 Fax: 846 5599 VHF Channel 68

West Wind Marina
Website: www.westwindmarina.com
Contact: One Waite's Wharf, Newport, Rhode Island 02840.
Tel: 849 4300 Fax: 847 0862 E-mail: WestWindRI@aol.com

Transport connections

There are buses to Providence, Rhode Island, with rail connections to Boston and New York. Flights from Providence or Boston to international destinations.

Medical services

Newport Hospital (Tel: 846 6400), and many doctors and dentists.

Castle Hill lighthouse on the approaches to Newport. Photo Jim Mcelholm.

LANDFALLS ON THE ATLANTIC COAST OF THE USA

33
Portland
Maine, USA

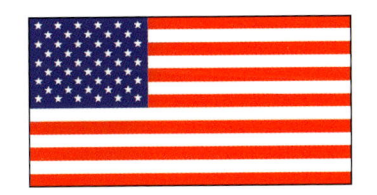

Location:	43°39′N 70°13′W
Spring range:	3.3m
Neaps range:	2.4m
Time zone:	UT −5
Currency:	US dollar
Tel/fax:	Country code: 1 Area code: (1) 207
Language:	English
Emergencies:	911 Coastguard Tel: 799-1680

Gateway to Maine

Portland is Maine's business, financial and retail capital and is the largest city in the state. It is perched on a peninsula, jutting out into island-studded Casco Bay. Most visiting yachts use Portland as a good base at which to provision and make repair before heading off for one of the many anchorages around the islands of Casco Bay or on up the coast of Maine. The harbourmaster has an office in the Chamber of Commerce building near the public landing. He and his staff welcome visiting yachts and will assist in any way they can. The Chamber of Commerce (Tel: 596 0376, Fax: 596 6549) provides general tourist information. The Portland Head Light is the oldest lighthouse on mainland USA.

Websites
www.portlandmaine.com

www.boatmaine.us/ for information about sailing the coast of maine

www.portofportlandmaine.org/directory.html for a marine directory

Typical Maine anchorage. Photo: Richard Woods

PORTLAND, MAINE
USA
33

221

PASSAGES AND LANDFALLS

Hazards

The tidal range becomes steadily more extreme as you sail northeast from Portland until you reach the Bay of Fundy which has the largest tidal range in the world. The whole area is prone to fog and radar is essential. Throughout Maine, thousands of lobster pot buoys are a major hazard and a rope cutter on the propeller shaft is highly advisable.

Approach and entrance

If you have been coast-hopping northwards you will notice a sudden and dramatic change from the low lying, sandy shoreline to one of rocky outcrops and islands. There are several off-lying rocks and shoals in the outer approaches to Portland. Closing the coast from the south-east, leave the Portland Head Light [Fl 4s 31m 24M] to port and Ram Island Ledge Light to starboard [Fl (2) 6s 23m 8M] and head up the buoyed channel. Leave Spring Point Ledge light and Bug light to port. The historic Fort Gorges on Diamond Island ledge to the west of Little Diamond Island is a conspicuous landmark on the east side of the main channel. Before reaching Fort Gorges turn to port and head across to the anchorage on the north side of the Fore River or head up the river to one of the marinas.

Radio

Harbourmaster: VHF Channel 09 and 16.

Fort Gorges on Hog Island Ledge is a conspicuous landmark in the entrance channel. Photo: Stephen Bradnock

Formalities

See 'Formalities: the United States' at beginning of Chapter 16. The US Coast Guard monitors all vessels entering US waters, and yachts may be boarded at sea and searched. Fly the Q flag from offshore if arriving from abroad. You should contact the US Coast Guard initially (1 800 432 1216 or 1 800 451 0393 (24 hrs)) and then Customs and Immigration as necessary. You will probably need to take a taxi to the Customs office. The yacht may then be visited, by launch if

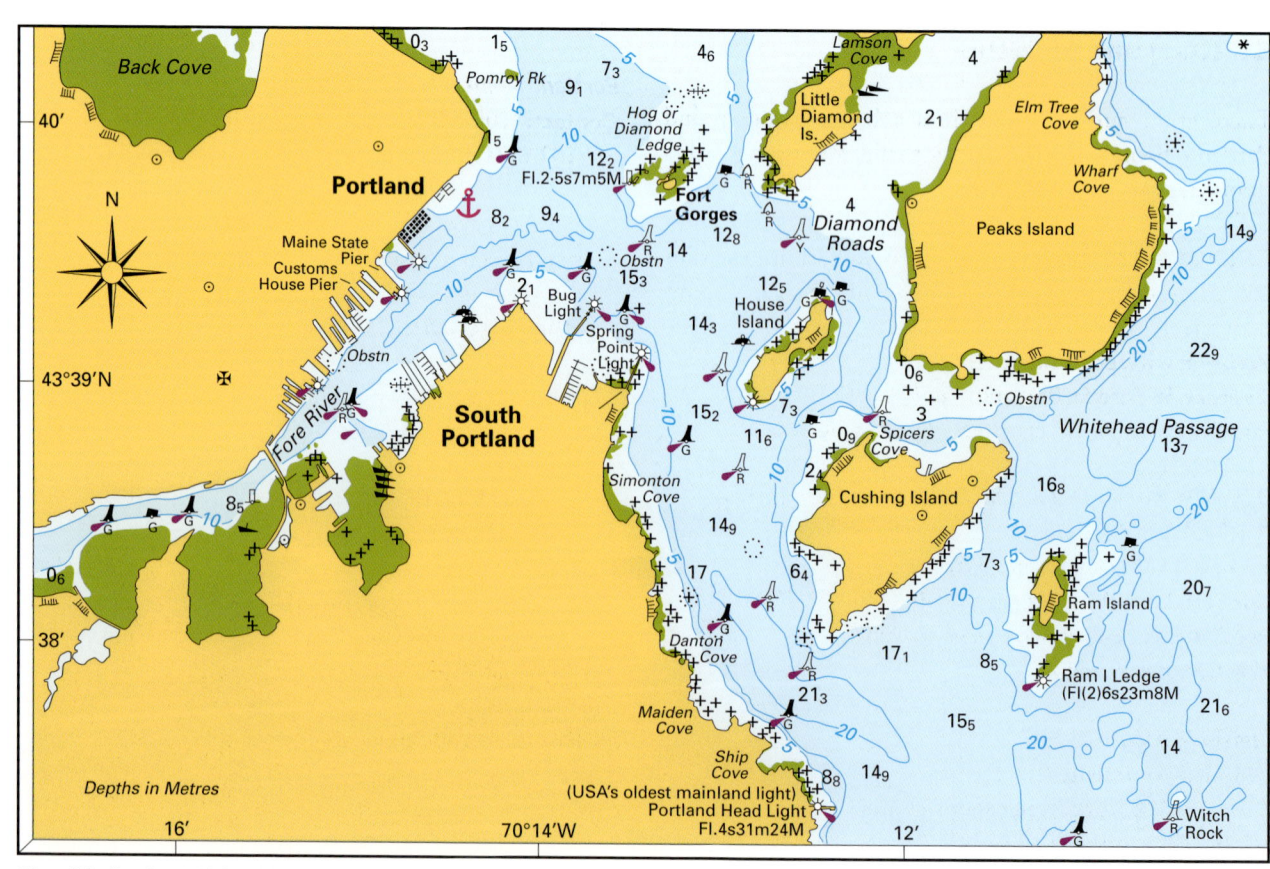

Plan 71 Portland, Maine, USA

Looking south past Spring Point Light with Portland Head Light beyond. Photo: Stephen Bradnock

necessary. A cruising licence, valid for one year, is issued to a foreign yacht at the first port of call.

Harbourmaster: Portland Harbor Commission, Tel: 772 8121.

Berthing and facilities

There are a number of marinas and boatyards around Portland. Some of those offering berths for visiting yachts (transients) are detailed below.

Portland Yacht Services close to the Old Port has 128 slips including 18 transient moorings and a full service boatyard with travel lift.
Website: www.portlandyacht.co
Contact: 58 Fore St, Portland. Tel: 774 1067
Fax: 774 7035 E-mail: marina@portlandyacht.com

DiMillo's Old Port Marina is located in the heart of Portland's Old Port.
Website: www.dimillos.com/marina/
Contact: Long Wharf, Portland, ME 04101. Tel:773 7632
Fax: 773 4207 E-mail: info@dimillos.com
VHF Channel 09 and 71

Sunset Marina
Website: www.sunset-marina.com
Contact: 231 Front Street, South Portland, Maine 04106.
Tel: 767 4729 Fax: 767 4721 VHF Channel 09, 12 or 16
E-mail: info@sunset-marina.com

South Port Marine
Website: www.southportmarine.com/marinab.htm
Contact: 14 Ocean Street, South Portland, ME 04106.
Tel: 799-8191 Fax: 767-5937
E-mail: marina@southportmarine.com
VHF Channels 16 and 78

Portland Yacht Haven
Contact: 100 Kensington St, Portland. Tel: 842 9000,
Fax: 842 9274 E-mail: info@yachthavenportland.com

Chandlery is available from, amongst others, the Hamilton Marine Discount Store: www.hamiltonmarine.com/

Anchorage and moorings

The anchorage at East End should really only be considered a temporary stop-off.

Transport connections

Portland International Jetport is within a few miles of the centre of Portland. Portland is on the network of public bus and rail services. Ferry services link the islands and connect to Nova Scotia.

Medical services (telephone numbers)

Maine Medical Center,
22 Bramhall Street,
Portland, Maine 04102   (207) 662-0111 871-0111

17 Passages in the middle latitudes of the North Atlantic – including landfalls in Bermuda and the Azores

Crossing the northern Atlantic from west to east is generally considered to be more pleasant than heading westwards, due to the likelihood of favourable winds for most of the passage. There are a variety of possible routes from the United States or Canada to the United Kingdom and Europe. Most cruising yachts aim to cross via Bermuda and the Azores. Others make the passage direct, usually keeping north of Bermuda and the Azores and making maximum use of the North Atlantic Current.

34	St Geroge's, Bermuda	230
35	Porto das Lajes, Flores, Azores	237
36	Horta, Faial, Azores	239
37	Ponta Delgada, São Miguel, Azores	242

WEATHER PATTERNS AND ROUTE TIMINGS

The various routes are discussed as separate sections but there is considerable cross-over of information between all the routes.

In the middle latitudes, weather patterns are dominated by the prevailing westerly and south-westerly winds which are created by low pressure in the north and a relatively stable mid-Atlantic high pressure system to the south. This high pressure typically encompasses Bermuda and the Azores throughout the summer, but in some years may remain further south than usual, allowing the passage of depressions also to track unusually far south. Less frequently,

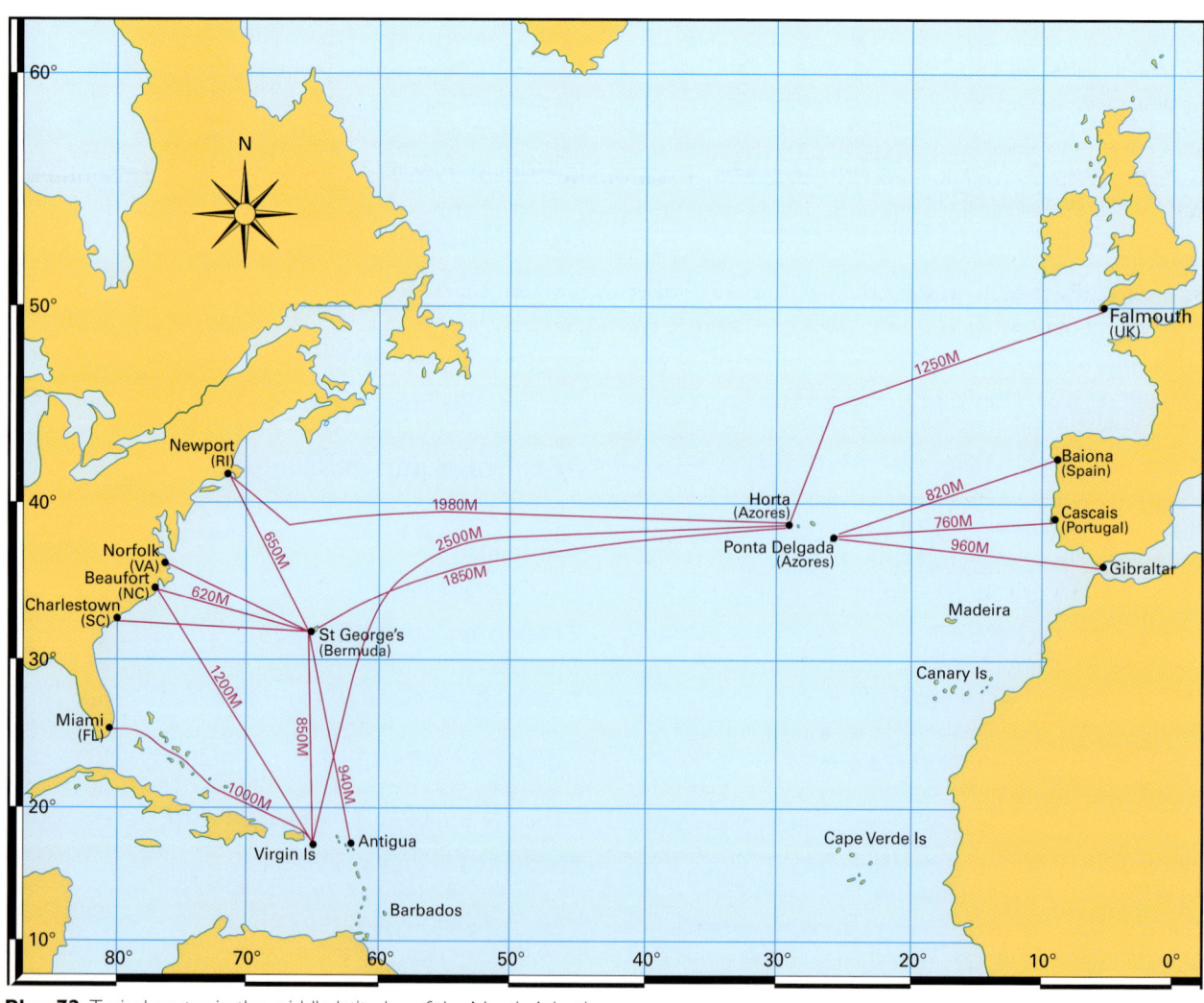

Plan 72 Typical routes in the middle latitudes of the North Atlantic

224

PASSAGES IN THE MIDDLE LATITUDES OF THE NORTH ATLANTIC

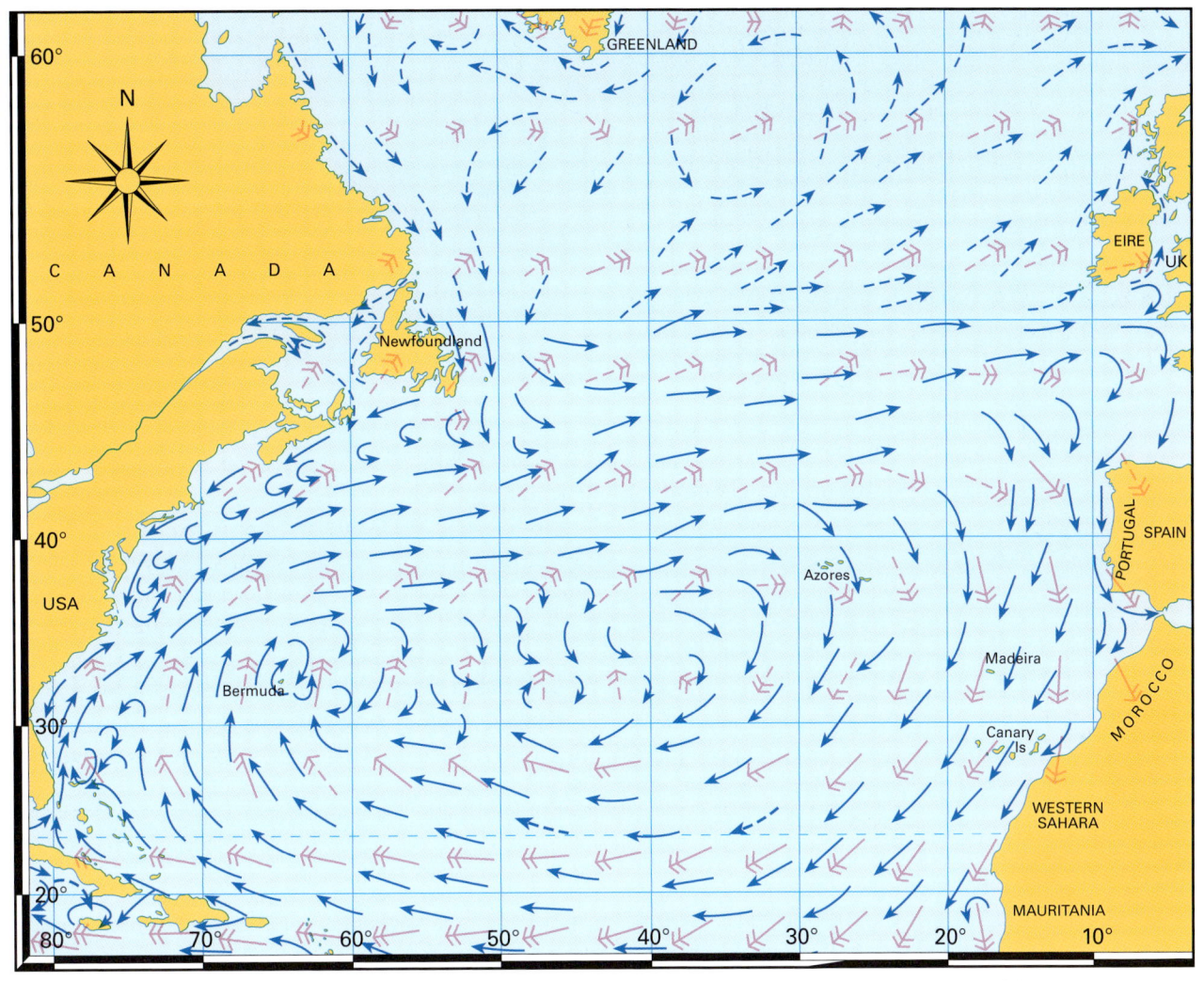

Plan 73 Prevailing winds and currents in the North Atlantic for June. Based on information from *The Atlantic Pilot Atlas*

associated cells of high pressure form and persist further north, giving light winds and calms over large areas of the North Atlantic for weeks at a time. Short-term weather over the entire area is dominated by the west-to-east passage of Atlantic depressions as they move from North America towards Europe over the top of the Azores High. These give rise to a repeating pattern of rapidly changing conditions. Winds veer and pressure drops as the depression approaches. South-westerly winds then establish for a time, accompanied by heavy rain as the warm front passes. A sudden wind shift into the north-west often accompanied by sharp, squally showers indicates the cold front coming through. These showers clear to give blue skies and good visibility. Such Atlantic depressions are usually less intense and move more slowly in the summer months, generating less powerful winds than during the winter. The chance of encountering a gale is always greater in northern latitudes than further south, but is everywhere much reduced between mid-May and mid-August. Hurricanes rarely track beyond 40°N 60°W, but the possibility should be borne in mind and it is always worth keeping an eye on their status and track. Unfortunately, visibility off the coasts of Canada and the northern United States is at its worst in the summer, and the iceberg limit is also at its greatest extent. However, these drawbacks are far outweighed by the almost certain promise of lighter winds.

CARIBBEAN TO BERMUDA

Best time
Mid April to mid May

Most cruising yachts leave the Caribbean in April or May in order to be well clear of the danger zone before the start of the hurricane season in June. Departure in good time also enables yachts to reach their next cruising ground on the North American or European coasts at the best time of year. The route to Bermuda usually involves waiting for favourable winds. Winds will gradually shift from north-east 20 knots to a more favourable easterly 15 to 20 knots during this period. They may even shift south of east as progress is made northwards, with a high probability of light variables or calms later in the passage, depending on the position of the Azores High. Some motoring may be

PASSAGES AND LANDFALLS

Calms are common on the route between the Caribbean and Bermuda. Photo David Ridout

required. The passage between the Virgin Islands and Bermuda traverses the western edge of the Sargasso Sea – technically, this is not a sea at all, but the static area around which the vast North Atlantic current systems sweep. Large carpets of brown Sargasso seaweed are likely to be encountered. A north-west going current of about 0.5 knots can be expected until within 100 miles of Bermuda, after which it will vary in both speed and direction.

Before departure, monitor the Atlantic storm tracks as low pressure areas leave the US coast. If sailing direct to the US, ensure that the storms are passing to the north of your planned route. Atlantic storms migrate north as the summer progresses.

BERMUDA TO PORTS NORTH OF NEW YORK

The route lies within the hurricane belt, so aim to make a landfall before the end of June if possible. Winds in that month are likely to be south or south-westerly for much of the passage, although occasional cold fronts move eastwards off the American continent and bring strong west or north-west winds, often accompanied by driving rain. Particularly unpleasant or even dangerous seas will be produced where the wind runs against the Gulf Stream. Currents are likely to be variable until around 35°N where the full force of the Gulf Stream will be encountered. Between Bermuda and Newport this sets east or north-east at up to 1.5 knots. The width of the main stream varies from a mere 20 or 30 miles to 300 or more. The last 100 miles or so of the passage will be affected by the cold Labrador Current. The northern edge of the Gulf Stream, where it meets the cold Labrador Current flowing south-west, is typically marked by a wall of fog.

CARIBBEAN TO BEAUFORT, NORTH CAROLINA

This should be another largely downwind passage, with south-easterly winds veering into the south and a 2.5- knot current following the trend of the coast. If sailing the rhumb line course in May or June there is an outside chance of encountering a hard blow, but a far greater likelihood of experiencing calms – particularly during the mid portion of the passage. Plenty of fuel should be carried. The alternative is to sail a dog-leg, shaping a course to a point near 28°N 37°W before swinging northwards, in order to avoid the edge of the central Atlantic high pressure system with its associated light winds and calms. If taking the direct route towards Beaufort, North Carolina, take into account the effects of the Gulf Stream.

CARIBBEAN DIRECT TO THE AZORES

The direct distance from the Virgin Islands to the Azores is about 2200 miles. The recommended route is 300 or 400 miles longer, shaping a course to pass within 200 to 300 miles of Bermuda before swinging north-eastwards. The direct, Great Circle, course passes through the large area of high pressure that dominates the central Atlantic where light and variable winds are almost guaranteed. It should only be attempted by yachts able to make good progress in very light winds or able to carry fuel for at least 1,000 miles. Even those taking the more traditional route are likely to encounter some calms and carrying plenty of fuel is advisable. In some years the passage may take a yacht with limited range under power as much as 35 days. When it is

PASSAGES IN THE MIDDLE LATITUDES OF THE NORTH ATLANTIC

The anchorage in St George's Harbour. The Customs House is behind the yachts on the right hand side. Photo: David Ridout

calm it is likely to be extremely hot. Water consumption will be noticeably greater than on previous passages and this should be allowed for.

UNITED STATES TO BERMUDA

Best time
Early April to mid-May
Timing depends on your departure point from the East Coast. Storm tracks have begun to move further north by late March, reducing the possibility of northerly gales, and by leaving in May you are more likely to be clear of Bermuda before the onset of the hurricane season. The further north your departure point from the United States, the more likely the probability of head winds. At this time, south-west winds of 15 to 25 knots tend to alternate with stronger winds from the north or north-east. But there may be periods when the Azores High will establish its presence as far east as the North American coast bringing lighter easterly or south-east winds against which you can make progress. Strategies for departure usually involve waiting for favourable winds with no northerly component to cross the Gulf Stream, and then gaining easting as winds permit to approximately 68°W before turning south. The high pressure ridge at this time of year may be interrupted periodically by troughs or weak cold fronts permitting periods of sailing even along the ridge line.

Other times
Mid November to mid December
The traditional snowbird routes from the East Coast to the eastern Caribbean almost always involve waiting for weather. Winds and seas tend to be ramping up at this time of year. Cold fronts are becoming stronger and the gale tracks moving further south. Crossing the Gulf Stream is necessary from any point of departure and monitoring the location of the stream, eddies and forecast wind is essential. Strategies involve picking favourable conditions for crossing the Gulf Stream and a forecast for reasonably benign conditions to allow the vessel to get south of the North Atlantic gale track. Departures are risky at this time of year

Looking across to Pico from Faial in the Azores. Photo: John Aldridge

227

PASSAGES AND LANDFALLS

because of late season hurricanes and tropical depressions. Developing Atlantic storms are also frequent features.

Hurricanes

The corridor between Bermuda and the US coast is a hurricane track, those later in the season tending to run further inshore than early-season hurricanes, which have a statistically greater chance of approaching Bermuda itself. The speed and track of hurricanes become more predictable as they develop and meteorologists are usually able to give accurate predictions for the US – Bermuda corridor. The peak of the hurricane season is usually between July to September. So, departure eastward from Bermuda should be made by mid-June, with close attention to weather forecasts.

Currents

On departure from the North American Coast, the Labrador Current will work in your favour, whereas the Gulf Stream will be working against you and it will pay to cross it as quickly as possible. Although the Routeing and Pilot Charts show the Gulf Stream in this area to run at 1 to 1.5 knots, it may eddy more strongly in some areas. When winds oppose the Gulf Stream, dangerous seas can be created. Avoid crossing the Gulf Stream in strong northerlies.

BERMUDA TO THE AZORES

There are two choices regarding this passage. The first is to head north-east to around 39°N before turning due east for the Azores. Unless a major cell of high pressure has formed much further north than is usually the case, this should put you in the belt of the westerlies with a favourable current. The longer distance is offset by the likelihood of better winds, but there is an increased chance of gales which are common in these latitudes, particularly in May and June. Alternatively you can take a more southerly course. On this route the likelihood of calms is considerably greater and current will be much less predictable, but the chance of gales is correspondingly less. This route is likely to require long periods of motoring. The Azores are well known for the extensive calm that often surrounds them so, whichever route you choose, enough fuel should be kept in reserve to motor the last 100 or so miles.

UNITED STATES OR CANADA DIRECT TO THE AZORES

This is a common choice for yachts leaving from the Chesapeake Bay or further north. From south of New York it should be possible to sail a Great Circle course, and enjoy favourable winds and currents most of the way. From further north the standard procedure is to head south-east to make a good offing and get clear of the Labrador Current with its attendant fogs. From around 40°N you can head direct for the Azores, though some skippers may prefer to continue a little further south (see the comments above). The first part of the passage will be within the hurricane zone, and it would be wise to be east of 55°W before mid-June.

AZORES TO NORTHERN EUROPE

It is often necessary to leave the Azores under engine, and if fuel is limited, the wind is most likely to be found more quickly by motoring due north. Even if leaving with a good wind, every opportunity should be taken to make northing until at least 45°N, aiming to cross it near 20°W. It may be necessary to work even further north before reaching the westerlies but, once you have found them, a direct course from this position should make the most of these favourable winds and the easterly-setting current, avoiding the south-east set towards Spain and Portugal. If at all possible, landfall should be made before the end of August. The coasts of northern Europe are notorious for the severe gales that often come through early in September.

AZORES TO SPAIN, PORTUGAL OR GIBRALTAR

There is a good chance of this being a pleasant passage, with northerly winds and a south-going current, both of which

The abundance of colourful flowering plants and trees make the Azores a delightful landfall. Photo: John Aldridge

PASSAGES IN THE MIDDLE LATITUDES OF THE NORTH ATLANTIC

Horta Marina can become very crowded at peak times. Photo: David Ridout

are apt to be quite strong. As the chance of north-easterlies increases on closing the coast, it would be wise to keep well to windward of the intended destination, to avoid a last minute slog against both wind and current. If continuing direct to Gibraltar, beyond Cape St Vincent, the winds may be variable but the current will tend towards the Straits as there is a permanent surface flow into the Mediterranean caused by the high rate of evaporation from the Mediterranean basin. There are busy shipping lanes off the coasts of Spain and Portugal and through the Straits of Gibraltar. Be aware of the Traffic Separation Schemes. See Chapters 9 and 10 for more details.

PASSAGES WESTWARD

Any passage westward across the Atlantic in the higher latitudes involves a lot of windward sailing, adverse currents, fog, ice and a strong likelihood of frequent gales. On the other hand, a middle route via the Azores and Bermuda puts you into hurricane territory. Ideally, landfalls on the American coast south of 40°N should be made before the end of June. A possible alternative is the Viking Route (see Chapter 18).

EUROPE TO THE UNITED STATES OR CANADA VIA AZORES AND BERMUDA

Headwinds and an adverse current are inevitable for much of this passage. Yachts with a good range under power may consider motoring a course along the ridge of high pressure that normally lies between Bermuda and the Azores. Extensive calms and flat to glassy seas can be expected on this route, and it will be very hot. Timing and route planning for this passage are easier than they used to be due to better weather forecasting. Resist heading north of 38°N until south or south-east of your landfall to reduce the time spent in fog over the Grand Banks.

WEATHER OVER BERMUDA

Weather in Bermuda is influenced by the position of the Azores high, the Gulf Stream, and the weather systems on the eastern seaboard of the United States. Bermuda is not in the trade wind belt. In June and July, when the majority of yachts pass through, an average of 15–20 knots from the south-west may be expected, though a sudden increase to 30 or 40 knots may accompany the passage of a frontal wave moving from the American coast. The islands lie well within the hurricane belt and passage-making yachts should endeavour to be out of the area by the end of June.

Temperatures vary from around 17°C (62°F) in February to 28°C (82°F) in August. Currents in the vicinity are unpredictable, though a northerly set is the most common. The islands lie within a few hundred miles of the eastern wall of the Gulf Stream, which frequently sets up large eddies, and though currents seldom exceed 0.5 knots, they may reverse direction within a matter of days.

PASSAGES AND LANDFALLS

34
St George's
Bermuda

Location:	32°22′.5N 64°40′.5W
Springs:	1.1m Range: 0.9m
Neaps:	0.9m Range: 0.5m
Time zone:	UT −4
Currency:	Bermudian dollar (US$ accepted)

Tel/fax:	Country code: 1-441
Language:	English
Emergencies:	Tel: 911

Better than Heaven?

Mark Twain once famously declared 'You can go to heaven if you want to, I'll stay here in Bermuda.' Bermuda was first sighted by the Spanish explorer Juan de Bermúdez in 1503. It was later the location of the shipwreck of Sir George Somers who, together with the entire crew, survived to colonise the island. It is Britain's oldest colony and its culture is a mix of colonial heritage and African influences. It is self-governing and has its own currency, the Bermuda dollar. Its economy is closely linked to the American tourist trade, and the US dollar is interchangeable with the local currency.

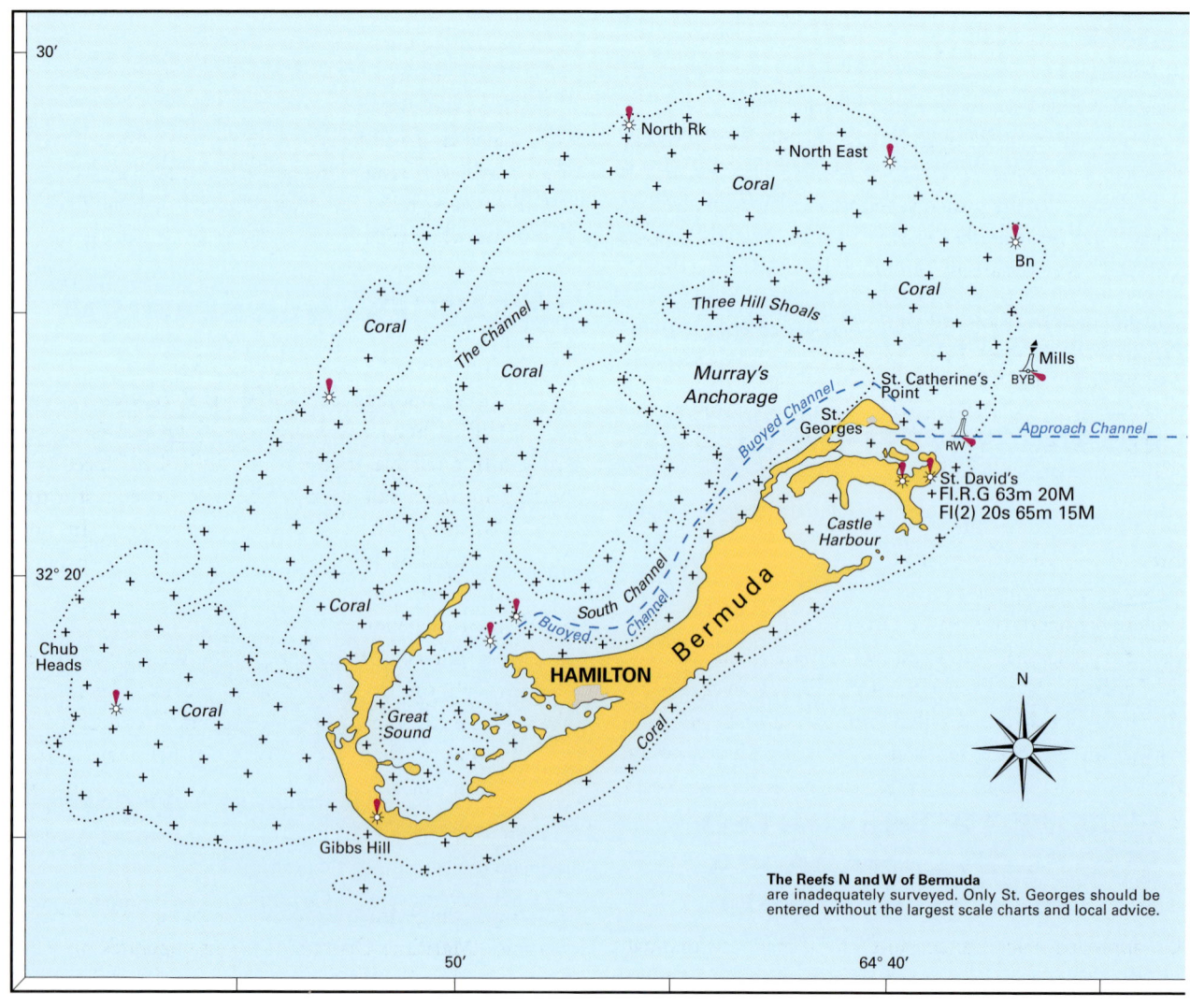

Plan 74 Bermuda

Bermuda entrance – Town Cut Channel looking west, on the approach to St George's. Photo: David Ridout

The island actually consists of a low-lying group of around 180 small coral reefs and islets, the larger of which are linked by bridges or causeways. St George's, the Port of Entry, is Bermuda's second town, considerably smaller than the capital, Hamilton. But distances are such that travel is easy between the two. Bermuda is a sophisticated island with a range of shopping facilities. However, almost everything is imported, making food and other stores extremely expensive. Canned foods are available, but variety may be limited as great reliance locally is placed on chilled and frozen foods. For the yacht without refrigeration, this creates a problem, since chilling fruit or vegetables badly impairs their keeping properties. It may be possible by asking around to find some locally grown vegetables and locally laid eggs which have been neither washed nor chilled. All slipping and repair services are available though similarly costly.

> **Further reference**
> www.bermudatourism.com
>
> *Bermuda Yachting Guide* by Jane and Edward Harris, Bluewater Books & Charts

There is some interesting cruising to be had around Bermuda, with many isolated and attractive anchorages, although most visiting yachts tend to stay in St George's and explore overland. A 20-page information sheet for visiting yachts is published twice a year by the Bermuda Department of Tourism (PO Box HM 465, Hamilton HM BX, Bermuda). This gives detailed information on buoyage and navigation, clearance, facilities, and so on and will be sent free on request. Alternatively it is available on line at www.bermudatourism.com/pdf/2006yachts_info.pdf

Approach and entrance

On approach, take into account a local magnetic anomaly, which may increase the variation by up to 6°. Due to the reefs that extend up to 10 miles off the north-east, north and west coasts of Bermuda, the only safe approach is from the south or south-east of the group. Here the coast is very steep-to, with the 200m (650ft) sounding lying within one mile of the coastline in places. Yachts will be called by Bermuda Harbour Radio on VHF Channel 16 as they approach the islands. This station can often be received as far as 80 miles off. Channel 16 should be monitored throughout the approach to St George's as the harbour will be closed during the movement of large cruise liners through the narrow cut at its entrance. St George's harbour is situated at the extreme eastern end of the island and is approached via a well-buoyed channel, one branch of which leads north-west around the island towards Hamilton, and the other through the Town Cut Channel into the harbour. A red and white pillar buoy [Mo(A) 6s] 2.3 miles east of the island marks the entrance to the channel. The powerful St David's Island light [F RG 63m 20M and Fl (2) 20s 65m 15M] lies about one mile to the south.

Arrival into St George's is very straightforward and C-map accurate. Buoyage follows the IALA B system as used in the United States. Although the Town Cut is narrow, entry with a reliable engine is not difficult. If faced with beating in under sail, it might be wise to request a tow, which Bermuda Harbour Radio can arrange. In poor visibility, including heavy rain squalls, the Harbour Radio can monitor your progress on radar. The Town Cut and its approaches are generally well lit and a night approach in otherwise fair conditions should not present problems. Alternatively you can anchor off St David's Head. Once through the cut, the harbour opens out. If entering after dark, keep watch for anchored yachts, which may be unlit, and take care not to stray south out of the dredged channel.

Radio

The VHF range from Bermuda is around 60–80 miles. Bermuda Maritime Operations Centre operates on VHF Channels 16 or 27, 2182 or 4125 kHz USB or Tel: 441 297 1010, Fax: 441 297. All vessels must contact Bermuda

PASSAGES AND LANDFALLS

Plan 75 St George's, Bermuda

Harbour Radio on VHF Channel 16 from 30 miles inwards and before entering the buoyed channel, with an ETA, when instructions about Immigration and berthing will be given.

Formalities

Bermuda Maritime Operations Centre (www.rccbermuda.bm/portal/server.pt) has a Yacht Pre-arrival Information Questionnaire which you should complete and return by Fax: 441 297 1530 or E-mail: dutyofficer@marops.bm

The Maritime Operations Centre acts as a combined Rescue Co-ordination Centre, Vessel Surveillance Centre and Coast Radio Station. The questionnaire enables them to respond more quickly and effectively in any emergency and also speeds up the entry procedures on arrival. If you have not completed the questionnaire there may be a lengthy process of questioning over the VHF as you approach the island.

Entry must be made at St George's where you should go alongside the Customs dock at the eastern end of Ordnance Island. Out of hours you may be directed to anchor in Powder Hole anchorage to the north of Brooks Island. The Q flag should be flown when entering and until pratique has been granted, after which boats may proceed to Hamilton or elsewhere. Onward clearance prior to departure is also from St George's.

Visitors are normally allowed to remain for an initial period of three weeks, but if a longer stay is desired, application must be made to the Department of Immigration. If

PASSAGES IN THE MIDDLE LATITUDES OF THE NORTH ATLANTIC

Bermuda Customs House dock on Ordnance Island. Photo: David Ridout

any crew members are leaving or joining in Bermuda, the immigration authorities should be contacted well in advance, preferably several months ahead. Various forms must be completed without which it is unlikely that a single airline ticket to the island could be purchased. Firearms, including flare pistols and spear guns, must be declared and may be impounded until departure or placed under seal aboard. Medically prescribed drugs must also be declared. There are severe penalties for the possession of illegal drugs.

Further useful information can be found at www.bermudayachtservices.com/index_files/page0007.htm

Anchorage and moorings

The main yacht anchorage is north of the dredged channel and east of Ordnance Island in depths of 2–5m (7–17ft). Holding is good, but there are various old chains and other snags littering the bottom and a trip line may be advisable. Larger yachts will find greater depths in the southern part of the harbour, but it is a long dinghy ride ashore. Dinghies can be left at the steps inside Ordnance Island.

Berthing and facilities

Bermuda Yacht Services provides a range of services for visiting yachts including marina berths. They manage the dockside moorings around St George's. Berthing alongside a number of wharfs around the harbour is generally on a strictly 'first come, first served' basis. Some wharves are reserved for shipping and berthing a yacht on any of the commercial quays is prohibited.
Website: www.bermudayachtservices.com
Contact: Tel: 297 2798
E-mail: mark@bermudayachtservices.com

St George's Dinghy & Sports Club (32°22′45N, 64°40′05W) is a small marina which welcomes visiting yachts.
Website: www.stgdsc.bm
Contact: 24 Cut Road, St George's GE03. Tel: 297 1612.

Captain Smokes' Marina is a small marina in St George's at Godet & Young Ltd on McCallans' Wharf.
Contact: Tel: 297 1940 Fax: 297 1813
E-mail: voatley@northrock.bm

There are various other marinas and yacht facilities around the island including haul-out yards and repair facilities.

Transport connections

There are regular buses to Hamilton, Ireland Island at the west end of Bermuda, and elsewhere. Daily air services fly to the United States, Canada and Europe.

Medical services (telephone numbers)

King Edward VII Hospital, Paget East, outside Hamilton	236 2345

ST GEORGE'S
BERMUDA
34

PASSAGES AND LANDFALLS

The Azores Group

WHALES AND VOLCANOES

The Azores have sometimes been regarded simply as a convenient place to break the Atlantic passage. But the islands are a pleasant and interesting cruising ground which warrants at least two or three weeks planned into your cruising schedule. Some yachts returning from an Atlantic circuit maintain that their stay in the Azores was the absolute highlight of all the island groups. Recent and ongoing harbour developments have increased the number of all-weather ports and there are also many less well-protected bays and harbours where a yacht can lie at anchor in settled conditions.

The nine islands lie in three distinct groups stretching over more than 300 miles of ocean, and show surprising diversity in terms of both landscape and populace. All the islands are of volcanic origin, and ancient caldeira craters are a common feature. Only Pico retains its original cone, with the dramatic 2,351m (7713ft) summit being visible at 50 or 60 miles in clear weather. The volcanic soil gives rise to a wonderful abundance of plants. Visitors frequently comment on the hedges of vivid blue hydrangeas and the electric blue of the morning glory, which is considered a serious weed on the islands because of the delight with which it rampages through the landscape.

The islands are a centre for whale-watching and there is an excellent whale museum on Pico which has a full-size sculpture model of the silhouette of the largest sperm whale ever caught in the Azores. There is also a viewing platform with an unobstructed view over waters where sperm whales come within a mile of the shore.

Food shopping has improved considerably in recent years, though many of the smaller towns still offer little more than the basics. Most islands have markets and the locally grown fruits and vegetables are excellent. Particularly good cheese is also produced, notably on Pico and São Jorge. A major re-stock can be achieved at Ponta Delgada, Horta, or Praia da Vitoria, where there are supermarkets and a full range of food shops.

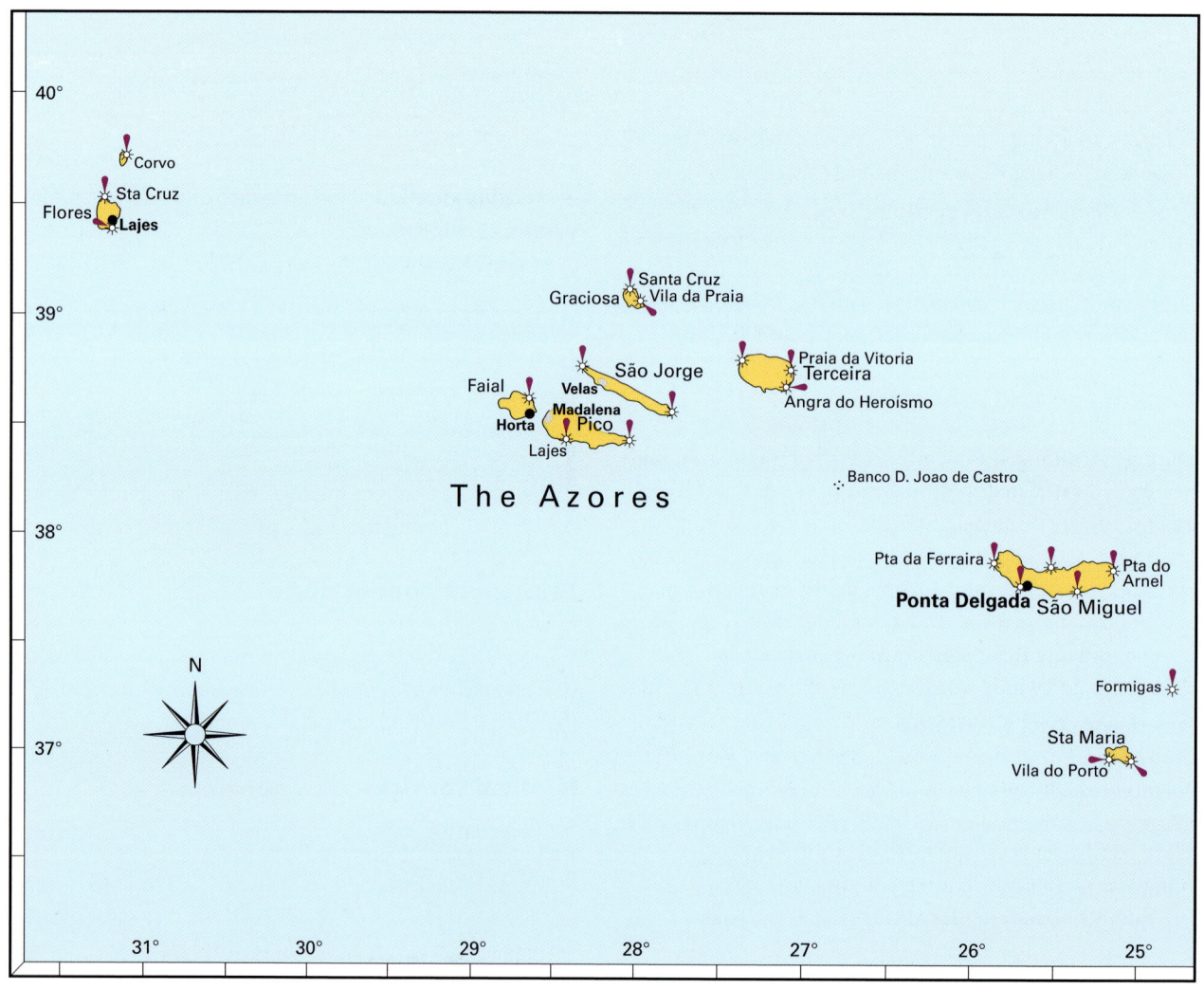

Plan 76 Ports in the Azores archipelago

234

PASSAGES IN THE MIDDLE LATITUDES OF THE NORTH ATLANTIC

Praia da Vitória outer harbour. Photo: David Ridout

Praia da Vitória Marina. Photo: David Ridout

Local festivals, such as the Sanjoaninas festivities at Angra de Heroísmo in Terceira during the third week of June, can lead to serious congestion in marinas and anchorages. If planning to attend it is wise to arrive early if possible. No Azorean marinas accept advance reservations.

Most Azorean marinas are the responsibility of Portos dos Açores SA. Their website (see below) carries news about the latest harbour developments as well as prices, a directory of facilities and some good photos. The marina at Praia da Vitória (Terceira) belongs to the local Câmara Municipal (town or city council).

Websites
www.bienal-baleias.org/malcolm/index.php
www.destinazores.com/en/index.php
www.marinasazores.com

WEATHER IN THE AZORES

During the sailing season, effectively from June until mid-September, the climate is dominated by the Azores High. In most years this becomes strongly established, resulting in prolonged periods of light winds or calms, but sometimes the High remains weak so that windier, more changeable weather predominates as it does during other seasons. There is some evidence that global warming may be causing more changeable and windy weather during the summer months. Winds between south-west and north are the most common throughout the year, but almost every other direction is likely to be experienced at some time. As in Atlantic Europe, south-easterly winds usually foretell an approaching front. There is a six per cent likelihood of calms between June and August, decreasing to four per cent in September.

Summer temperatures typically rise to around 23°C, though heat-waves can occasionally produce a sizzling 30°C for days at a time. However, nights can feel chilly, particularly to those who have spent the previous months in the tropics. Visibility is generally good, though southerly winds may produce hazy conditions that limit the field of view to five miles or so while still apparently giving a sharp horizon. This is particularly common around the western islands of Flores and Corvo, and can be most misleading.

Ocean swell can be a factor when picking an anchorage, as it frequently runs in from the west even when winds are light. The most protected harbours are usually on the east or south of each island.

CURRENTS, TIDES AND TIDAL STREAMS

The Azores are affected by the branch of the North Atlantic Current which sets south-east towards the Iberian coast and later becomes the Canary Current. Flow in open waters

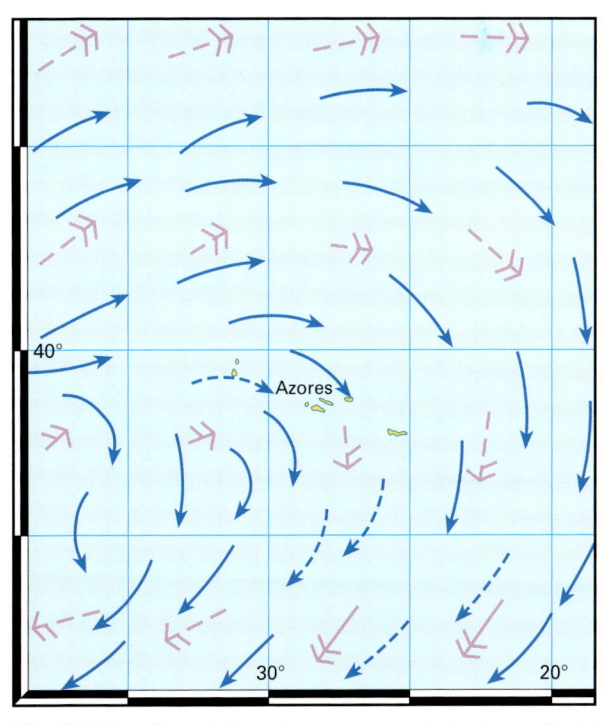

Plan 77 Prevailing winds and currents around the Azores for July. Based on information from *The Atlantic Pilot Atlas*

PASSAGES AND LANDFALLS

Entrance to the little harbour at São Jorges. Photo: David Ridout

seldom exceeds half a knot, but this may double around the ends of the larger islands and, when ocean and tidal currents combine, races may form. Tidal range is relatively small throughout the Azores and nowhere exceeds 1.8m (6ft). However, streams can run with surprising speed and may reach two knots in the Canal do Faial between Faial and Pico. Tides set north or north-east on the flood, south or south-west on the ebb.

APPROACH AND LANDFALL

Approach to the Azores is straightforward, and neither Flores nor Faial, the two most popular landfall islands for transatlantic yachts, have any serious outlying hazards. The usual course is to skirt their southern coasts, and if approaching Faial in darkness it should be noted that the Vale Formoso lighthouse at its western end is widely regarded as being considerably less powerful than stated, with a range of nearer five miles than the claimed 13 miles. Yachts approaching from Europe often make landfall on São Miguel which again is steep-to. Buoyage follows the European IALA A system, which is opposite to that found in North America and the Caribbean.

LONG-STAY TAX

All yachts spending more than 183 days in Portuguese waters, including the Azores, are liable for a 'long-stay' tax. The tax is calculated using a formula based on displacement in metric tonnes, engine capacity and age. Non-payment can, in theory, lead to a fine of around 150 euros, though the tax is often poorly publicised. A certificate and receipt are issued on payment, valid for one year from the date of arrival in Portuguese waters.

PASSAGES IN THE MIDDLE LATITUDES OF THE NORTH ATLANTIC

35
Porto das Lajes, Flores
Azores

Location:	39°22.5´N 31°09.5´W
Mean spring range:	1.2m
Mean neap range:	0.5m
Time zone:	UT −1
Currency:	Euro
Tel/fax: Language: Emergencies:	Country code: 351 Portuguese Tel: 112

Island of flowers

As its name suggests, Flores is an island of flowers. Its steep terraces fringed with hydrangeas leave a lasting impression. It is the most westerly island in the Azores and is often the favoured landfall for yachts which have taken one of the more northerly routes across the Atlantic in the mid-latitudes.

Stretch your sea legs and explore the lakes and waterfalls on the island. Santa Cruz is the main town on the island and has a modest range of facilities including an airport and hospital. The Festival of San Joao is celebrated in Santa Cruz during the last week of June and the Festa do Emigrante is celebrated in Lajes in the middle of July. There are plans for a marina development within Lajes harbour and construction work is under way. A new slipway has already been completed. The current guess as to when the whole project will be completed is sometime during the summer of 2011.

Website
www.azores.com/azores/flores.php

Approach and entrance

The approach is relatively straightforward, although it would be preferable to arrive in daylight. Remaining at least one mile off shore until closing the harbour entrance should

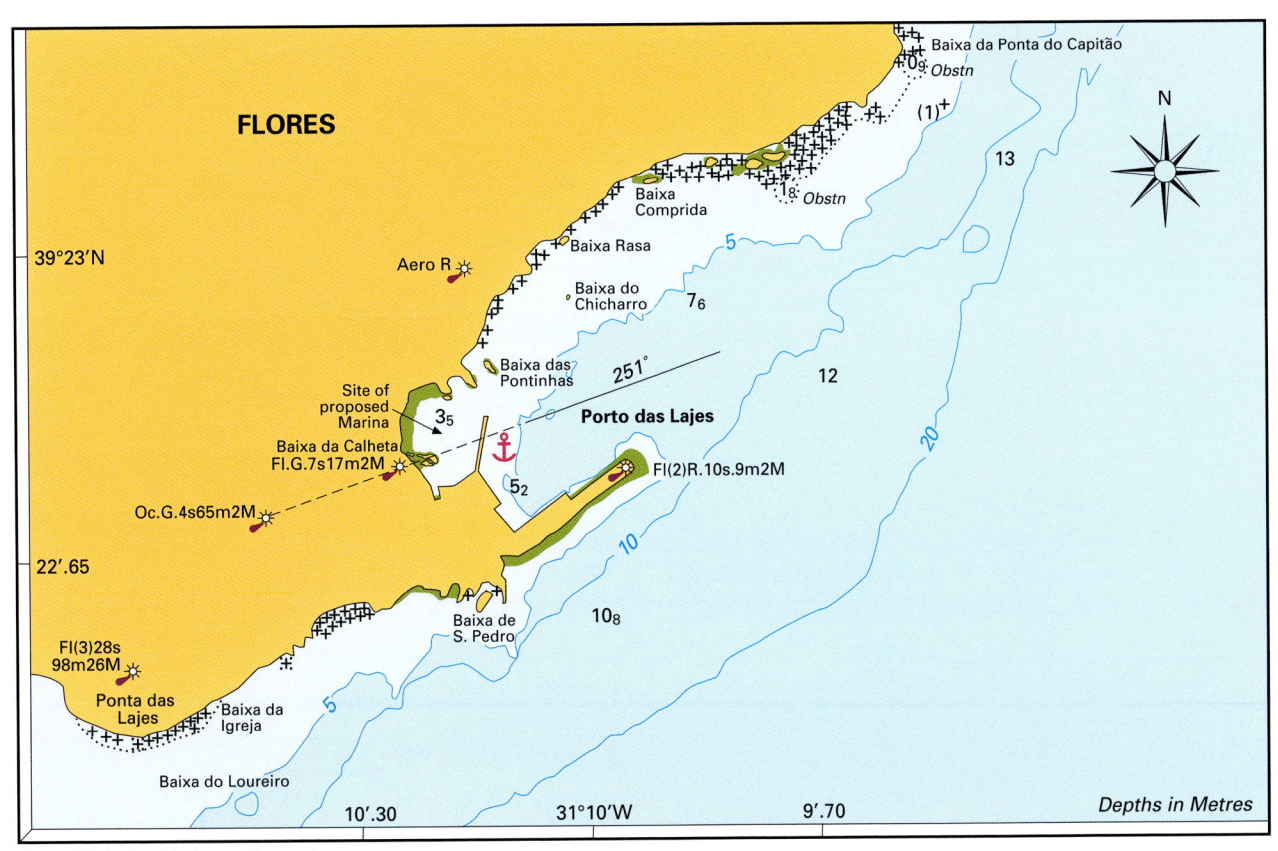

Plan 78 Lajes Harbour, Flores, Azores

237

PASSAGES AND LANDFALLS

Flores harbour showing the marina development inside the inner breakwater, November 2009. Photo: APTO SA

keep you clear of any hazards. When approaching round the south of the island, beware the breaking rocks half a mile south of Ponta da Rocha Alta. Keep a 50m (164ft) clearance around the end of the harbour breakwater which has underwater boulders extending around it. While construction of the new marina is continuing it would be wise to enter the harbour itself with some caution. The harbour entrance is marked by a white post and light [Fl(2)R10s 9m 2M]. The light may not be working.

Radio

VHF Channel 16 and 23.

Formalities

Fly the Q flag on arrival. The Portuguese courtesy flag should also be flown, and many visiting yachtsmen like to hoist the blue, white and gold Azorean flag beneath it. Although Santa Cruz is the official Port of Entry for the island, port officials visit Porto das Lajes several times a day to check-in any visiting yachts. They may alert you to their presence by beeping their horn or flashing their lights. Formalities are usually carried out on the quayside by the Guarda Nacional Republicana (GNR), Policia Maritima and an Immigration officer but you may need to go and find the officials in their offices in town. The maritime police are next to the library.

Berthing and facilities

Until the new marina is completed there is likely only to be limited space to moor alongside at the quay, and quayside mooring is only permitted when a ship is not expected. There is a 40-tonne static crane on the quayside, although if you need to haul-out you may be better doing it at one of the main facilities on Horta, Terceira or São Miguel.

On completion, the new marina will have a fully serviced pontoon with space for 10 yachts over 10m (30ft). There will be further pontoon space for 66 smaller vessels and marina offices and facilities on the quay.

Clube Naval das Lajes das Flores is the local Yacht Club which welcomes visiting yachtsmen. Tel: 292 592 542.

Anchoring

Anchorage inside the harbour is sheltered and usually quite comfortable, although the harbour is sometimes susceptible to swell working its way around the island. Anchor in 5–12m (17–40ft) on sand, gravel and rock. The area for anchoring is likely to be affected to some extent by the marina construction. In previous years, dinghies have been tied up to the wharf steps by the boat ramp closest to town.

Transport connections

A ferry service linking Flores to the other islands runs once a week during the summer months. Limited flights are available from the airport.

Medical services

There is a hospital in Santa Cruz. Ask locally for medical services.

PASSAGES IN THE MIDDLE LATITUDES OF THE NORTH ATLANTIC

36
Horta, Faial
Azores

Location:	8°32′N 28°37′.5W		
Springs:	1.6m	Range:	1.2m
Neaps:	1.2m	Range:	0.5m
Time zone:	UT −1		
Currency:	Euro		
Tel/fax:	Country code: 351 Area code: 292		
Language:	Portuguese		
Emergencies:	Tel: 112		

In the wake of Joshua Slocum

Horta is the only town of any size on Faial, with a history reaching back to the mid-15th century. The harbour is probably the best in the islands and has been a favourite with sailors since Joshua Slocum visited in 1895 – he commented then on the friendliness and hospitality of the local people, and things have changed little since then. No visit to Horta would be complete without a drink in the famous Café Sport which has been run by the Azevedo family for three generations. Neither would it be wise to tempt the fates by neglecting to add a painting, or at least the yacht's name, to the thousands that cover the harbour and marina walls. Many famous yachts feature here.

Work has started on a new north breakwater. On completion, the ferry and cruise terminals are to be moved to a new quay off Praia da Conceição, north of the town, allowing the southern part of the harbour to be further developed for yachts and fishing vessels. Berthing for superyachts – most of which currently lie alongside the commercial breakwater – will also be upgraded.

The Gruta das Torres (Grotto of the Towers), a few kilometres from Madalena, is now open for several hours each day and is well worth a visit. Check opening times at the tourist office in Horta, then ask directions or get a taxi once in Madalena.

Approach and entrance

Horta lies near the south-east corner of the island, facing Pico across the Canal do Faial. The stated range of the light

View over Horta harbour looking south. Photo: David Ridout

PASSAGES AND LANDFALLS

HORTA, FAIAL AZORES — **36**

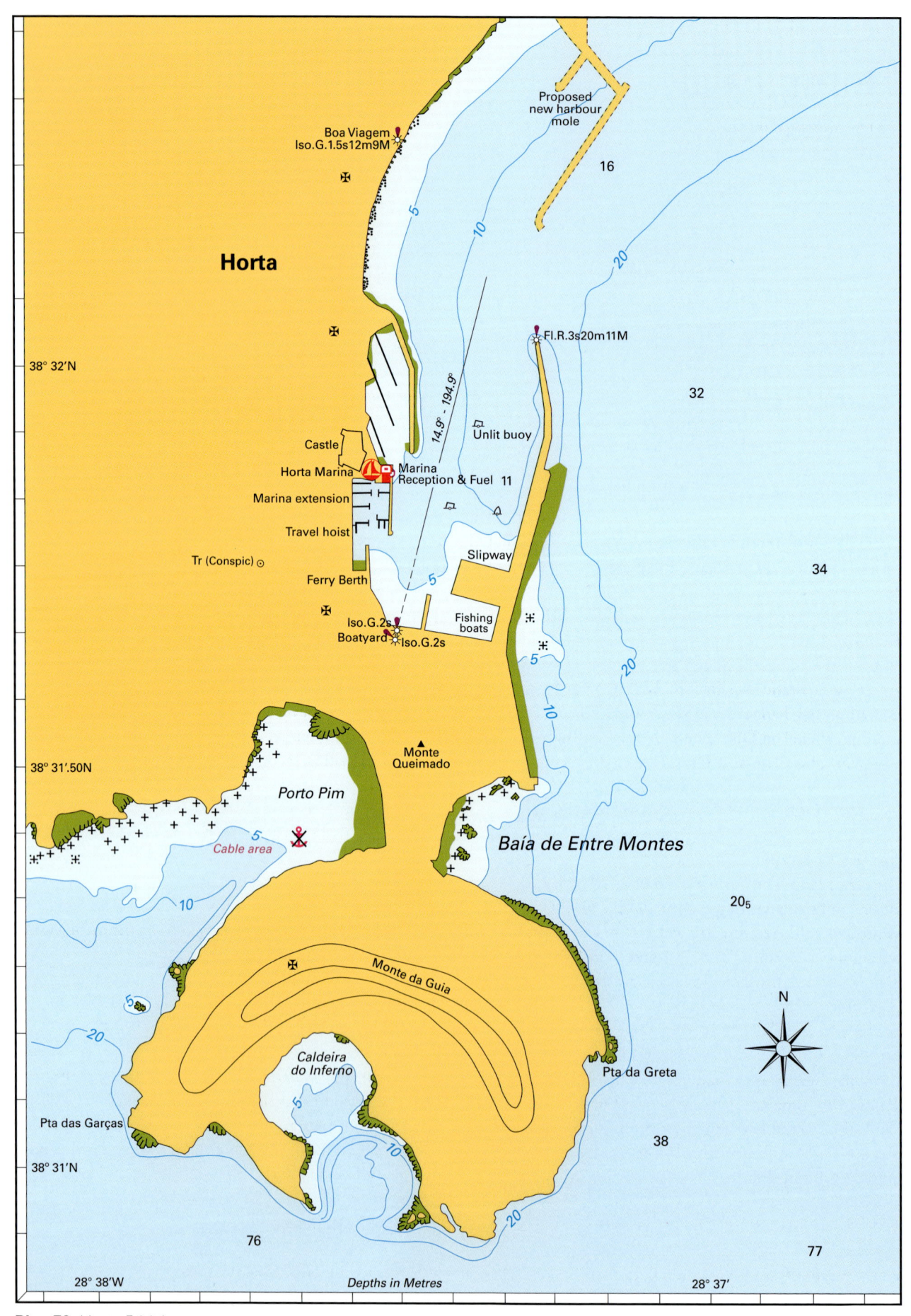

Plan 79 Horta, Faial, Azores

at Vale Formoso [LFl (2) 10s 113m 11M] near the western tip of the island is optimistic and may be nearer to five miles. The only other major light is at Pta da Ribeirinha [Fl (3) 20.5s 131m 12M] on the east coast north of Horta. Faial has few offlying dangers and the coast may safely be closed to within half a mile or so. If approaching from the southeast, the Baixa do Sul (7.0m (23ft) depths – also known as Chapman's Rocks) should be avoided if any sea is running. Lights and buoyage follow the European IALA A system.

An experimental marine farm has been established in the Canal do Faial, centred on 38°32´.5N 28°33´.9W. Although 6m (20ft) below chart datum, vessels should give generous clearance both to it and to its associated (and apparently unlit) bright blue buoys.

If approaching from westwards, Horta harbour will not be seen until the last headland is rounded, when a course can be steered directly for the breakwater head which has good depths close in. However, avoid rounding it too tightly – the Pico ferry leaves at speed and tends to cut it fine. At night the breakwater light will probably be seen first, as the light of Boa Viagem tends to be overshadowed by town lights. The marina entrance is not lit. Visiting yachts should secure to the reception/fuel berth on the western side of the entrance until assigned a berth.

Radio

Coast Radio Station operates on VHF Channels 16, 24, 25, 26 (Autolink Channel 25, DSC Channel 70). Radionaval is now operational on DSC: MF MMSI 002040200. Harbour communications are on VHF Channel 10 and 16.

Formalities

Fly the Q flag on arrival unless coming from another Azorean island. The Portuguese courtesy flag should also be flown, and many visiting yachtsmen like to hoist the blue, white and gold Azorean flag beneath it. The Azores are an autonomous region of Portugal and therefore part of the EU. In theory, this should mean fewer formalities for EU-registered yachts arriving from another EU country, but in practice this represents such a small percentage of total arrivals that it is likely all yachts will be expected to follow the same clearance procedures. It is necessary to visit the Policia Maritima and Alfandega (Customs), whose offices flank that of the berthing master on the reception quay. Report to the officers again before departure, taking the receipted marina bill.

Berthing and facilities

Horta Marina is a busy but well-run marina with a good range of facilities. The majority of yachts are allotted finger

Horta Habour looking north over the ferry berth. Photo: John Aldridge

pontoons, with the larger ones rafting up inside the mole. Fuel is available alongside. The boatyard has an 18-tonne travel lift; it is capable of rough but serviceable repairs to steel, aluminium and wood, but not so good for major GRP repairs.
Website: www.marinasazores.com (click on Horta Marina).
Contact: Marina da Horta, Cais de Santa Cruz, 9900-017 Horta. Tel: 391693 Mobile: 0936 6491292 Fax: 393986
E-mail: hortamarina@aptosa.com

Mid-Atlantic Yacht Services (MAYS) can be found opposite the root of the marina mole and provides a full range of services to visiting yachts.
Website: www.midatlanticyachtservices.com
Contact: Call 'Mid Atlantic' on VHF Channel 77
Tel: 391616 Fax: 391656 E-mail: mays@mail.telepac.pt

Anchorage and moorings

Anchoring in the harbour is allowed when the marina is full. There are some privately owned moorings.

Transport connections

There is a circular bus route around the island. The tourist office will supply a timetable on request. There are ferry services several times daily to Pico, and also to the other islands of the 'central' group – details are available from the tourist office. Daily flights go to Lisbon and the other islands. All United Kingdom flights are routed via Lisbon.

Medical services

There is a hospital outside the town.

PASSAGES AND LANDFALLS

37
Ponta Delgada
São Miguel, Azores

Location:	37°44′N 25°39′W	
Springs:	1.7m	Range: 1.4m
Neaps:	0.6m	Range: 0.6m
Time zone:	UT –1	
Currency:	Euro	
Tel/fax:	Country code: 351 Area code: 296	
Language:	Portuguese	
Emergencies:	Tel: 112	

An outstandingly beautiful island

Ponta Delgada is the largest town in the Azores, with the best shopping and provisioning in the group. It is a busy naval and commercial harbour and hosts visiting cruise ships. The island of São Miguel is outstandingly beautiful, with spectacular lakes and hot springs. Take the time to explore a little during your stay here. The new cruise ship terminal, Portas do Mar, and the adjacent marina formally opened in early July 2008, increasing marina berths in Ponta Delgada to 670 berths. Visiting yachts generally appear to be berthed in the new section. There have been problems with swell and wash entering the new marina even when the harbour appears calm, but a breakwater pontoon has now been positioned off its western edge, which will hopefully

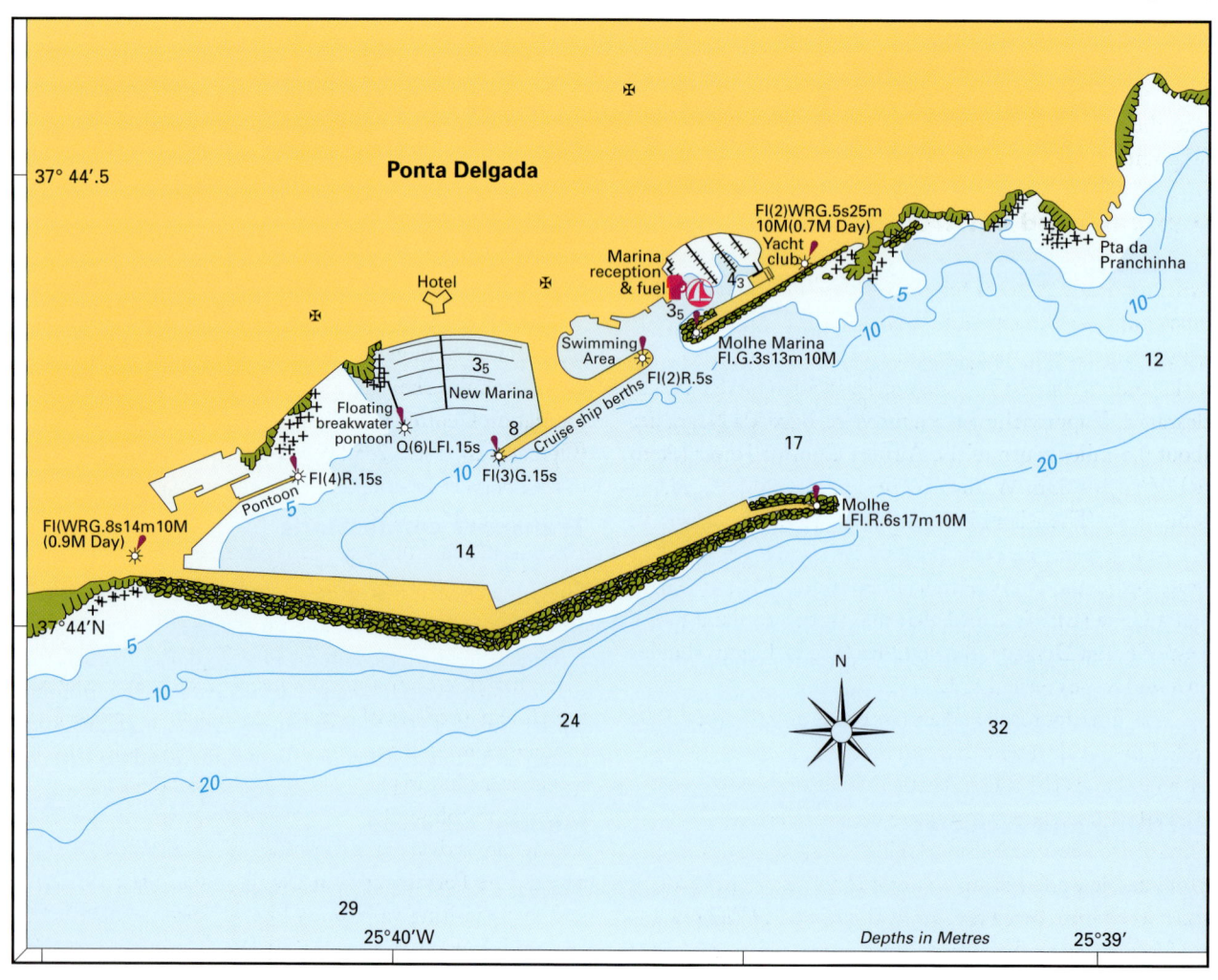

Plan 80 Ponta Delgada, São Miguel, Azores

Ponta Delgada, Azores: looking south across the marina to the main breakwater (note rubble extension to breakwater end). Photo: Nigel Wollen.

cure the problem. Ponta Delgada is the obvious jumping-off point for yachts bound for the Iberian peninsula.

Approach and entrance

Much of São Miguel is high and often visible from many miles away. The coastline is largely steep-to, with few off-lying dangers, but many of the headlands are fringed by rocks and all should be given at least 500m (0.25 miles) clearance. If approaching from the west, Baixa da Negra lies about 0.5 miles south of the Airport Control Tower [Aero AlFlWG 10s 83m W28M/G23M] and should be given a wide berth. The island is relatively well lit, with powerful lights at Pta da Ferraria [Fl (3) 20s 106m 27M] at its western end and Pta do Arnel [Fl 5s 66m 25M] to the east. Santa Clara [LFl 5s 26m 15M] marks the headland to the west of Ponta Delgada. Banco Dom João de Castro shoal is now said to be charted at 12m (39ft).

The final approach and entrance is straightforward. The end of the breakwater is marked by a 5m (16ft) white tower with red bands [Fl R 6s 17m10M]. The old marina mole is marked with a white round tower with green bands [Fl G 3s 13m10M]. The cruise ship terminal is marked by a red and white banded pillar at its east end [Fl(2) R 5s 3M], and a green and white banded pillar at its west end [Fl(3) G 15s 3m 3M]. The new floating breakwater pontoon is marked at its southern end by a south cardinal pillar [Q(6)Fl 15s 3M].

Rubble fringing the end of the old marina mole may be marked by some unlit, small, green conical buoys. The swimming area opposite the new marina area is cordoned off by a string of unlit, small red buoys.

Radio

Coast Radio Station operates on VHF Channels 16, 24, 25, 26 (Autolink Channel 23), The Maritime Rescue Co-ordination Centre: Tel: 281777 (Emergency), Tel: 205227 (Operations), Fax: 205239, E-mail: mrcc.delgada@mail.telepac.pt gives weather bulletins and navigational warnings on Channel 11 at 0830, 2000. The marina monitors VHF Channels 16 and 09.

Formalities

The Azores are an autonomous region of Portugal and therefore part of the EU. In theory this should mean fewer formalities for EU-registered yachts arriving from another EU country, but in practice it is likely that all yachts will be expected to follow the same clearance procedures. Fly the Q flag on arrival unless coming from another Azorean island. The Portuguese courtesy flag should also be flown, and many visiting yachtsmen like to hoist the blue, white and gold Azorean flag beneath it. All but the largest yachts are required to go to the reception berth at the entrance to

PASSAGES AND LANDFALLS

The new marina in Ponta Delgada in 2008. Photo: L M Correia

the old marina basin in order to visit the marina office, Customs and Immigration. The entrance to the old marina is considerably narrower than it was previously. All officials have offices in the marina area. The skipper should visit the Policia Maritima bearing ship's papers, passports and insurance documents, and will be advised of the other officials to be seen. Report to the officers again before departure, taking the receipted marina bill.

Anchorage and moorings

Anchoring anywhere inside the harbour is strictly prohibited. In the event of engine failure, contact the marina for assistance.

Opening celebrations for the new marina in Ponta Delgada in 2008. Photo: L M Correia

Berthing and facilities

Marina de Ponta Delgada is a recently expanded marina with a good range of facilities including a 25-tonne travel lift. For information about the marina including a plan, prices and facilities go to www.marinasazores.com and click on Ponta Delgada.
Contact: Marina de Ponta Delgada, Av Infante D Henrique, Apartado 113, 9500 Ponta Delgada.
Tel: 281510 Fax: 281 311 E-mail: marinapdl@apsm.pt

All boatyard and repair facilities are to remain around the old marina, so skippers of yachts needing such services should ask to be berthed there if possible.

Clube Naval de Ponta Delgada (CNPD) is the yacht club situated next to the marina. It is very welcoming and helpful to visiting yachts.
Contact: Tel: 23005 Fax: 26383 E-mail: info@cnpdl.pt

Transport connections

There is a good bus network, obtain a timetable from the tourist office. Daily flights go to Lisbon and the other islands and there are international flights from Ponta Delgada to London Gatwick one or two days a week.

Medical services

A hospital is situated near the harbour, plus there are several medical centres.

18 Passages and landfalls in the higher latitudes of the North Atlantic

38	Halifax, Nova Scotia, Canada	250
39	St John's, Newfoundland, Canada	254
40	Stornoway, Isle of Lewis, Scotland	257

North of 50°N, yachts transiting eastwards or westwards between Europe and North America face the likelihood of encountering severe weather. In the past these waters have been the domain of transatlantic races and a handful of experienced and hardy cruisers. But there appears to be an increasing interest in northern passages and landfalls, so it seems pertinent to outline some of the possibilities which lie therein. You do not need a steel ice-breaker to venture into these waters, indeed Contessa 32s appear well-suited to the task. But you do need to give due consideration to all the potential hazards and to the advice of those who have ventured before you. Be well prepared for storms and cold.

Ice at sea is a significant risk for any yacht, but on most routes you may only encounter the occasional isolated iceberg. A good look-out is essential, and given the prevalence of fog, radar is strongly recommended.

Further information
RCCPF Faroe, Iceland and Greenland, published by Imray is a 'must read' for anyone who is considering northern waters. It is very important that the up-to-date supplement is downloaded from the Imray website www.imray.com. Also recommended is a study of the surface currents and the distribution of ice and icebergs in UKHO Arctic Pilots Vol II and Vol III.

Note that magnetic variation differs as you cross the Atlantic, rising to more than 20° of westerly variation near 50°W. The amount of variation fluctuates slowly, rates varying from place to place. Ocean passage charts show isogonic lines, linking places with equal variation, and also give details of annual changes.

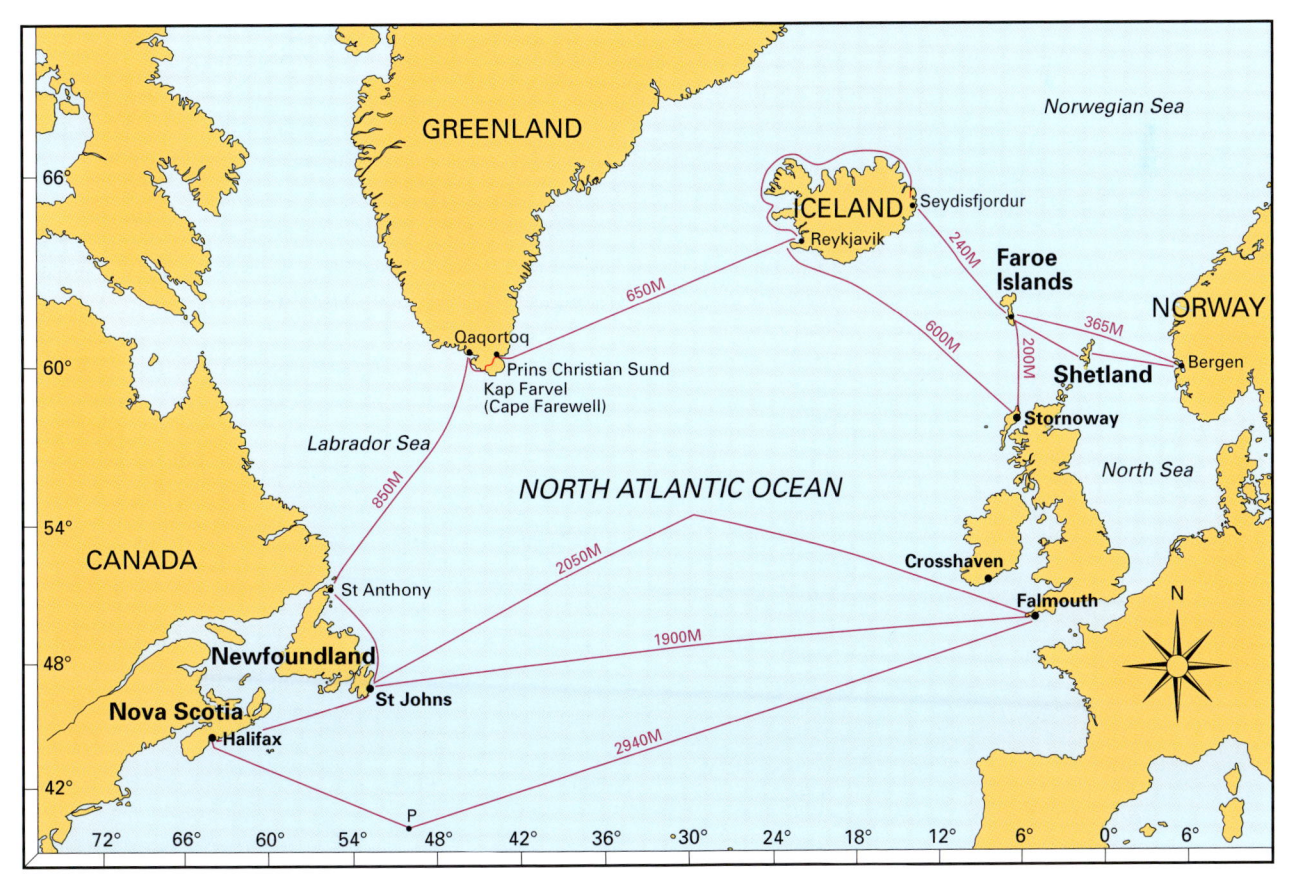

Plan 81 Ports and passage distances in the higher latitudes of the North Atlantic

245

PASSAGES AND LANDFALLS

ICE REPORTS

The extent of sea ice cover varies within and between seasons and any information about ice limits can quickly become out-of-date, particularly in strong winds. There are various possible sources of information, all of which should be treated with due caution. The Danish Meteorological Institute publishes ice charts for Greenland on their website (see below); these are also broadcast from Skamlebaek as Radio-fax. The information is provided by Iscentralen (Ice Central), the office based at Narsarssuaq in south-west Greenland, who also provide an ice advisory service by telephone or radio. The area west of 54°W is covered by the Canadian Ice Service.

The US NOAA National Ice Centre website (see below) carries ice charts for the Arctic and Greenland. See the national snow and ice data centre website given below.

The US Coast Guard, International Ice Patrol monitors iceberg danger near the Grand Banks of Newfoundland and provides the limits of all known ice to the maritime community. The IIP does this by sighting icebergs (primarily through airborne Coast Guard reconnaissance missions), plotting and predicting iceberg drift using a model, and, every 12 hours during the ice season, estimating the 'limit of all known ice'. This limit, along with a few of the more critical predicted iceberg locations, is broadcast by radio stations and made available on line as an 'Ice Bulletin'. Twice daily, a radio facsimile chart of the area, depicting the limits of all known ice, is broadcast. The IIP broadcasts its products during the time of year that icebergs threaten shipping. This varies, but usually begins in February and ends in July. Go on their website (see below) and click on 'Announcement of Services' for current broadcast times and frequencies. Click on 'Latest ice Limits' for current information either as text or in chart format.

The 'limit of all known ice' tends to err on the side of caution and encompasses some areas which may have very few icebergs. This report on its own may not necessarily warrant a change of course.

Websites for ice reports
www.dmi.dk
www.ice-glaces.ec.gc.ca
www.natice.noaa.gov
www.nsidc.org/arcticseaicenews/
www.uscg-iip.org/General/mission.shtml

UNITED STATES OR CANADA DIRECT TO EUROPE VIA THE MID-LATITUDES

The mid-latitudes, as far as this passage is concerned, may be defined as a track passing south of Sable Island and the Newfoundland Grand Banks but well north of the Azores

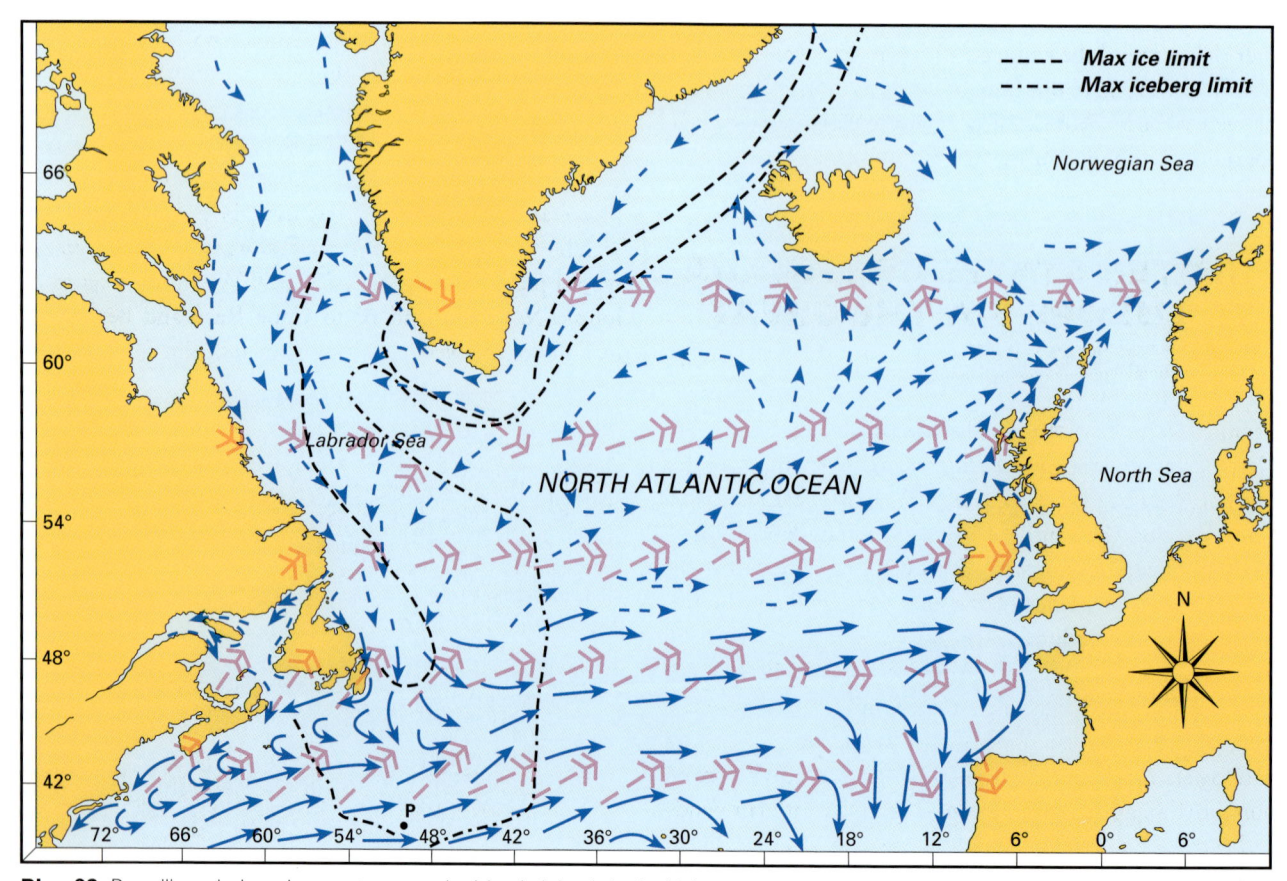

Plan 82 Prevailing winds and currents across the North Atlantic in the higher latitudes during June. Maximum limits of ice and icebergs are shown. Based on information from *The Atlantic Pilot Atlas* and *Arctic Pilot Vol II*

246

PASSAGES AND LANDFALLS IN THE HIGHER LATITUDES

Fog and ice make radar a priority in these waters. Photo: Mark Hillman

high pressure system. If the yacht is lying west of Cape Cod, the choice is either to sail south of the Nantucket Shoals or transit the Cape Cod Canal and leave from further north.

Fog, ice and shipping lanes will influence the course chosen, but an arbitrary waypoint P (40°N 50°W) is a reasonable way to start. Up-to-date weather and ice reports may make it possible to shift this point further north to reduce the distance sailed, but the track may then coincide with the main shipping routes. If ice is reported particularly far south, it may be wise to head further south. From 50°W a Great Circle course can be sailed for most European destinations. Winds will be predominantly westerly, but may veer right around the compass as depressions pass through. West of 30°W, up to one knot of north-easterly current may be experienced, but both the strength and northerly component diminish further east.

UNITED STATES OR CANADA TO EUROPE VIA THE GREAT CIRCLE ROUTE

From anywhere in the north-eastern United States the Great Circle route to northern Europe runs close past the coast of Nova Scotia (well inside Sable Island) and thence to Cape Race on the southern tip of Newfoundland. This is likely to be a predominantly downwind passage, but there can be a high incidence of fog, and there will also be the weak adverse Labrador Current on this part of the route. St John's Harbour, 60 miles north of Cape Race, makes a good final port for provisions and stores. From Cape Race or St John's you can shape a direct Great Circle course. Icebergs and fog are a risk until around 40°W. East of 40°W normal northern Atlantic conditions can be expected with fair winds and current, but there is a good chance of at least one severe gale and correspondingly big seas if crossing this far north.

EUROPE TO THE UNITED STATES OR CANADA VIA THE NORTHERN ROUTE

Any passage westward across the Atlantic in the higher latitudes involves a lot of windward sailing, adverse currents, fog, ice and a strong likelihood of encountering frequent gales. Whatever latitude you choose, this passage is, according to one connoisseur, 'a long thrash to windward with a permanently foul tide'. Winds will mainly have a westerly component, and there is a high probability of heavy weather as Atlantic depressions track across. The northern route is unusual amongst cruisers but common to entrants in various transatlantic races because it offers the potential of a fast passage, but it is likely to be cold and stormy. The accepted wisdom for this crossing is to close-reach on whichever is the making tack towards your objective. A typical point to head for is 55°N 30°W and then on to St John's, Newfoundland or to Cape Race and beyond. If making for the west coast of Greenland, aim for a point at

Prins Christian Sund Icefall. Photo: Mark Hillman

PASSAGES AND LANDFALLS

least 150 miles to the south of Kap Farvel (Cape Farewell) before turning north. A lot of heavy, multi-year, drift ice (*storis*) is brought down from the Arctic Ocean on the East Greenland Current in a narrow band and is carried around Kap Farvel, often as late as July. This southern point of Greenland is also another 'Cape of Storms' because winds are squeezed and accelerated between the Atlantic lows and high pressure over Greenland. Boats have been knocked down as far as 140 miles south of the cape.

Onboard radar is considered essential for the northern route. The combination of drift ice and icebergs, often coupled with fog, as well as heavy shipping on the coasts of north America, mean that without radar, a yacht would need to be fully crewed to maintain a constant watch. And although in the northern summer there is virtually constant daylight, towards the end of the crossing it is likely that nights will get longer and icebergs show no lights! Although it is not certain that all ice will show up on radar, multi-year *storis* does usually show up and sometimes even low-lying 'growlers'. Icebergs, being deep-keeled, are carried by the current, whereas bergy bits and growlers tend to be wind driven and therefore lie downwind of icebergs. So by passing to windward of the icebergs, you should also avoid the bergy bits. Another reason for having radar is that without it, even with a GPS, navigation in areas where there are cliffs and craggy islands can be quite stressful in fog. Your instinct may be to get out of the opposing Gulf Stream and into the favourable Labrador Current as soon as the ice situation permits, but this will mean heading into the worst of the fog. Cape Race has a 40 per cent incidence of less than two miles visibility in July.

THE 'VIKING ROUTE' BETWEEN EUROPE AND NORTH AMERICA VIA FAROE, ICELAND AND GREENLAND

Cruising in the North Atlantic is not the dream of most sailors, whatever their level of experience. However, for some of those who have ventured into these waters, the rewards of sailing north of 60°N surpass all other cruising experiences. A logical path across the top of the Atlantic has been well beaten over the centuries. From the east, the route follows the Norse migrations of the 10th century and before them St Brendan and the Celts. The western end is the domain of the Inuit. Either heading eastwards or westwards across the northern Atlantic, with access to good weather forecasts and ice reports, and with time and prudence on your side, it is possible to experience an enjoyable and memorable cruise. The fact that the Arctic sea ice is reportedly receding year on year may open up some of the previously ice-bound regions to create even more possibilites for the adventurous.

From Norway at the eastern end of the route, the first stepping stone is to Shetland. From Shetland, or from the coast of Scotland, the first step is to Faroe. From Faroe you sail on to Iceland. In fair conditions, each of these passages is only two days sailing and each destination is a new cruising ground. The onward passages between Iceland and Greenland, Greenland and Labrador or Newfoundland are a few days longer, but they are still much shorter passages than direct routes between North America and Europe. On

The route through Prins Christian Sund narrows may be impassable if the ice has not retreated sufficiently. Photo: Mark Hillman

any passage in the high north there is a likelihood of encountering heavy weather, but in June and July the long day length is a friend. If you are lucky you will sometimes be able to make use of the easterly winds that blow over the top edge of low pressure systems passing to the south.

The Scottish coast

Boats passing round the north of Scotland, should have no problems provided they are well clear of Rockall (57°37′N 13°41′W). The St Kilda Island group and the Flannan Islands, 40 miles and 20 miles off the west coast of the Outer Hebrides, should not pose a threat, but Sula Sgeir (59°06′N 6°11′W) and North Rona (59°08′N 5°50′W) could be close to the route and are hazards to be avoided in bad weather. Both are lit.

The passage through the Pentland Firth, between the north Scottish coast and the Orkney islands, should not be attempted in strong winds or poor visibility. Coming from the north-west, shelter can be sought in the lee of Lewis by passing round the Butt of Lewis to Stornoway on the east side. Stornoway is an official Port of Entry with good facilities for yachts. Under no circumstances should the Sounds of Harris or Barra be attempted by a stranger in other than ideal conditions. If approaching the southern end of the islands, pass at least three miles clear of Barra Head to avoid the strong tidal stream and heavy overfalls. The best haven in the south is Castlebay, Barra. When anchoring in Scottish waters, beware of kelp; a heavy anchor should be used.

Faroe

The Faroe Islands are an archipelago of 18 islands lying close together on the 62nd parallel. They are carpeted with green, though mostly denuded of trees, and are characterised by their steep cliffs separated by deep but narrow channels. These channels force the tidal flow into potent rips and races, causing widespread overfalls around the islands. The capital of Faroe is Tórshavn on Streymoy, where visiting yachts will find all the usual facilities of a large harbour town plus ferry links and access to international flights. However, the strong tidal streams may make Tórshavn a problematic point of arrival. With this in mind, many yachts make landfall in Trongisvágsfjørður on the east coast of Suðuroy. The approach is straightforward and, if the wind is not funnelling down the fjord, an initial safe anchorage can be found in 5-8m (16–26ft) sand on the west side of Tjaldavíkshólmur. Tvøroyri harbour is a Port of Entry; it is completely secure and has good facilities.

Iceland

When sailing from the Faroes to Iceland you should consider whether or not you plan to cruise around the coast. The south-east coast is low-lying, shallow and dangerous, with no harbour or shelter at all for 150 miles between Hornafjörður and Vestmannaeyjar (note that Hornafjörður/Höfn is not a safe, first port of call due to difficult navigation on account of the strong tidal streams and continually shifting sandbanks). If your cruising time is restricted, Vestmannaeyjar harbour on the north side of Heimaey in the Vestmann Islands (on the south-west corner of Iceland) is an excellent point of arrival. From there it is straightforward to sail to the capital, Reykjavík, and tour the surrounding area. If you are planning a more extensive cruise around Iceland, and are approaching from Faroe, it may make more sense to use Seyðisfjörður on the east coast as a point of arrival. This is a first class harbour and a Port of Entry. Ferries from Europe terminate here and it is possible to enter the harbour under virtually any conditions, even dense fog under radar.

Greenland

The west coast of Greenland is a cruise in itself. By August, the ice has usually retreated from most of the potential anchorages in the south-west of Greenland, opening up a stunning cruising area. In some years it is possible to enter Prins Christian Sund to the east of Kap Farvel and then sail through the interconnected fjords to emerge on the south-west coast although cruising this route should be considered a bonus. Sailing from St John's towards Qaqortoq should be possible in July because, to the south of the Davis Strait, the sea is virtually ice-free. But from either direction you should monitor ice reports before planning a landfall at Qaqortoq as the entrance can remain completely blocked by heavy drift ice, known as *storis*, until late July. Harbours up the west coast may open much earlier; it is wise to keep your plans flexible to allow for ice and weather.

Heading towards Europe from Greenland it is wise to complete the trip by the end of August or mid-September, though boats have done it safely later than this. Erik the Red had his homestead at Brattahlið near Narsarsuaq Airfield, about 30 miles from Qaqortoq.

Newfoundland

If you are heading from south-west Greenland westwards, the nearest good harbour in Newfoundland is St Anthony. This is close to the only known Norse settlement in North America at L'Anse aux Meadows and makes an interesting point of arrival, particularly if you are set on completing the Norse Experience. The first survey of the area was by Captain James Cook aboard HMS Grenville in July 1763. Most yachts prefer to head 150 miles further south to St John's; a major harbour with all facilities and good communications. Vessels should call 'St John's Traffic' on VHF Channel 11 or 14 about two miles from the entrance to obtain clearance for entering and to avoid meeting a large container ship head on in the narrows.

PASSAGES AND LANDFALLS

38
Halifax
Nova Scotia, Canada

Location:	44°38′N 63°34′W		
Springs:	1.8m	Range:	1.5m
Neaps:	1.0m	Range:	1.0m
Time zone:	UT −4		
Currency:	Canadian dollar		

Tel/fax: Country code: 1   Area code: 902
Language: English and French
Emergencies: Tel 911

Welcoming seafarers since 1749

Halifax is the capital of the Canadian province of Nova Scotia. It is a large commercial port and a naval base, and an official Port of Entry. Yachting activity is largely centred in the North West Arm, a long narrow bay branching off just inside the main entrance, and in Bedford Basin north of the city. The city was settled by the British in 1749 and it has been a permanent settlement ever since. It has a rich maritime heritage and several historic sites are worth visiting including the star-shaped Citadel. Pier 21 gives an insight into what it must have been like to arrive here as one of the many thousands of immigrants who came here in the 1900s. Halifax undertook the grisly task of sending ships to recover bodies after the sinking of the Titanic and some of the city's graveyards are the final resting place of victims of the disaster.

Websites
www.halifaxinfo.com/
www.portofhalifax.ca/index.html

Hazards

Sable Island (43°55′N 59°50′W) lies just under 100 miles off the coast of Nova Scotia and should be given a wide berth. With its strong and unpredictable currents and shoal water it is a graveyard for ships. In the southern part of Nova Scotia a strong in-draught has been reported in the vicinity of Cape Sable. Oil rigs may be encountered in the area. Nova Scotia is subject to considerable periods of fog during the summer months, particularly with onshore winds. In

Halifax: the North West Arm with the Royal Nova Scotia Yacht Squadron moorings on the left. Photo: John Gibb.

PASSAGES AND LANDFALLS IN THE HIGHER LATITUDES

HALIFAX, NOVA SCOTIA
CANADA
38

Plan 83 Halifax, Nova Scotia, Canada

251

PASSAGES AND LANDFALLS

poor visibility it is wise to exercise caution when closing the coast.

Approach

The coastline of Nova Scotia is rugged and hilly with many inlets. Off-lying rocks and small islands extend up to five miles from the coast in places. These are usually all well marked, but working lights and fog signals should not be relied upon in poor conditions. If approaching from west of 63°30´W, beware the area of shoal water and isolated rocks off Pennant Point and Sambro Island. In bad weather the sea breaks fiercely.

The final approach to Halifax is between Chebucto Head to the west and Devil's Island off Hartlen Point to the north-east. Chebucto Head is a 30m (100ft) headland of whitish granite with a light [Fl 20s 49m 14M] shown from a white tower. Devil's Island light flashes [Fl 10s 16m 13M]. Portuguese Shoal and Rock Head Shoal lie in the approaches and are well buoyed. There are numerous other buoys and leading lights in the final approach. If entering at night, the leading lights at George's Island and Dartmouth will be useful (but keep a careful watch for shipping). Enter the harbour between Sandwich Point and McNab's Island. Shipping generally uses one or other of the tracks indicated on the plan, and as there is good water outside the channel, yachts may do better to keep further west. The only possible hazard is a 2.0m (7ft) patch about 0.5 miles south-east of Sandwich Point.

Radio

'Halifax Traffic' operates a Vessel Traffic Management System for all vessels over 20m (65ft) and will advise smaller craft on the proximity of shipping. It monitors VHF Channel 16 and works on Channels 12 and 14 (Channel 14 for traffic to seaward of Chebucto Head, Channel 12 in the harbour itself). The harbourmaster uses Channel 65A. The Canadian Coast Guard monitors Channel 16, and works on Chanels 26 and 27. In addition, a continuous weather forecast is broadcast on Channel 21B. The Royal Nova Scotia Yacht Squadron and other marinas and yacht clubs use Channel 68.

Formalities

Fly the Q flag from offshore if arriving from abroad. On arrival call Canadian Customs Control on 1 888 226 7277 (toll free 24hrs), with all yacht and personal details to hand. They will want to know the yacht's exact location and will then issue a Report Number. Local Customs will then visit the yacht to stamp the passports of non-US or Canadian nationals. All weapons, firearms and alcohol must be declared. There is a total ban on retaining hand guns on board. Restricted goods may be brought into Canada if an appropriate permit, certificate, licence, or other specific required documents have been issued, and if the goods meet certain safety standards. Controlled goods include endangered species of animals and plants and any item made out of them.

Berthing and marinas

Opposite the northeast corner of McNab's Island:
The Canadian Forces Sailing Association/Shearwater Yacht Club is located on the Dartmouth side of the harbour, tucked behind McNab's Island and well sheltered from the elements. Marina facilities include showers, laundry and a bar (open Wednesday and Friday evenings, Saturday and Sunday afternoons).
Contact: Box 280, Shearwater, NS, B0J 3A0. Tel: 469 8590 Fax: 469 0639 E-mail: syclub@psphalifax.ns.ca

In the North West Arm:
Royal Nova Scotia Yacht Squadron is located at the entrance to North West Arm in Halifax harbour and is particularly welcoming to visiting yachtsmen. It has a good range of services including a marina and boatyard with haul-out and shore storage up to 20 tons. Fuel dock, pump-out.
Website: www.rnsys.com
Contact: 376 Purcell's Cove Rd, Halifax, NS B3P 1C7, Canada. Tel: 477 5653 Dockmaster: 477 2595 Fax: 477 2595
E-mail: rnsysboatyard@ns.sympatico.ca

Armdale Yacht Club is at the head of the North West Arm in Halifax harbour at 40 Purcell's Cove Road, Halifax. This is relatively close to town. There are several large grocery stores within walking distance and a bus service runs into the town. The club welcomes visiting yachts and provides a range of facilities including safe anchorage, moorings and a fully serviced marina with a 20-tonne boat hoist (up to 45ft/14m).
Website: www.armdaleyachtclub.ns.ca
Contact: PO Box 22105, Bayers Road Postal Outlet, 7071 Bayers Road, Halifax, Nova Scotia, Canada B3L 4T7.
Tel: 477 4617 Fax: 477 0148
E-mail: office@armdaleyachtclub.ns.ca

There are two yacht club marinas in Bedford Basin which is north of the harbour through the narrows:
Dartmouth Yacht Club is on the east side of the Basin about 1.5 miles past the Narrows. The Dartmouth Yacht Club is close to the largest industrial park in Atlantic Canada. A wide selection of useful services and equipment for visiting yachts is available including fuel dock, chandlery, repairs and provisions.
Website: www.dyc.ns.ca
Contact: Dartmouth Yacht Club, 697 Windmill Rd, Dartmouth, NS, B3B 1B7. Tel: 468 6050 Fax: 468 0385
E-mail: dyc@dyc.ns.ca

Bedford Basin Yacht Club is at the head of the Basin about three miles past the Narrows and has a range of facilities. The clubhouse is open Sunday, Wednesday, Friday and Saturday afternoons and evenings.
Website: www.bbyc.ns.ca
Contact: 377 Shore Drive, Bedford, NS B4A 2C7.
Tel: 835 3729 Fax: 835 2047
E-mail: bbyc@ns.sympatico.ca or manager@bbyc.ns.ca

Halifax waterfront:
The Maritime Museum of the Atlantic used to offer free berthing for up to three days on a pontoon just south of SMCS Sackville and CSS Arcadia. Most of the waterfront is now managed and berths are charged. There are very limited facilities for visiting yachts and the berths are subject to the wash from passing vessels.

Further west along the coast of Nova Scotia from Halifax:
Shining Waters Marine is at the head of St Margaret's Bay (44° 39′30N, 63° 54′42W). It has a full service marina, chandlery, boat storage facility and repair service and is only 30 minutes from Halifax International airport.
Website: www.shiningwaters.ca
Contact: Shining Waters Marine, Tantallon, Nova Scotia B3Z 2P3. Tel: 826 3625, 800 687 1469
E-mail: admin:shiningwaters.ca or marina@shiningwaters.ca

Anchorage and moorings

Anchorage and moorings are available off Shearwater Yacht Club north of McNab's Island and off the yacht clubs in the North West Arm and in Bedford Basin. If entering the North West Arm at night or in poor visibility be aware that there are a large number of yacht moorings and anchorage is prohibited inside a 'no wake corridor' which runs up the central third of the entire length of the inlet. Anchoring is allowed outside this centre corridor clear of any moorings. Beware of a rocky shoal patch 60m (200ft) off the western end of Melville Island when approaching Armdale YC. Anchoring is not permitted in the main harbour between McNab's Island and Point Pleasant or in an area below the first bridge.

Transport connections

There are harbour ferries. A local bus route connects the area, including the North West Arm. Halifax is served by the Canadian National Railway system. The main bus and train stations for the national network are near the southern end of the docks. The international airport is 35km (22 miles) north of the city and has flights within Canada and to the United States and Europe. The airport shown on the plan is for the Services.

Medical services

There are a number of hospitals and medical centres in Halifax and Dartmouth. Ask locally for contact information.

PASSAGES AND LANDFALLS

39
St John's
Newfoundland, Canada

Location:	47°34′N 52°42′W	
Springs:	1.3m	Range: 1.0m
Neaps:	1.0m	Range: 0.5m
Time zone:	UT –3.5	
Currency:	Canadian dollar	
Tel/fax:	Country code: 1 Area code: 709	
Language:	English	

In the wake of Marconi

St John's sits on the eastern side of the Avalon Peninsula. The peninsular is almost a separate island, attached by a narrow isthmus to the south-eastern corner of Newfoundland. St John's is the capital and principal commercial port of Newfoundland and is landlocked and well sheltered. It is the oldest English-founded city in North America and has a rich maritime history. Cabot Tower, which sits on the top of Signal Hill overlooking the town, was built in 1897 to commemorate the 400th anniversary of John Cabot's discovery of Newfoundland and Queen Victoria's Diamond Jubilee. An

Plan 84 St John's, Newfoundland, Canada

PASSAGES AND LANDFALLS IN THE HIGHER LATITUDES

St John's, Newfoundland: looking west through the inner entrance. The yacht pontoon is central on the far side, to the left of the red building.
Photo: Department of Fisheries and Oceans

old hospital building near to Cabot Tower is the site where Marconi received the first transatlantic wireless transmission in December 1901. St John's was the departure point for another historic first – Alcock and Brown's successful transatlantic flight in 1919. It continues to be the departure or arrival point for many similar adventures, including yachts crossing the Atlantic by one of the northern routes. Newfoundland has strong Celtic links and there is a lively musical culture – try one of the many Irish pubs in St John's.

Website
www.stjohns.ca/index.jsp

Hazards on approach

The approaches to Newfoundland lie in one of the foggiest areas in the world. However, it is often clearer as you approach within a few miles of the shore. Icebergs carried south by the Labrador Current are seasonally prevalent. Virgin Rocks, and the nearby Eastern Shoals, which lie 100 miles east of Cape Race are a potential hazard on the approach. (See photo on page 71.) Offshore to the east of Newfoundland, the current sets southerly at about 1 knot, but it runs westerly around Cape Race. Be aware of the currents and tides, particularly a strong northerly eddy close in to the south coast of Newfoundland which has caused many vessels to be swept up into the bays along this southern coast. The barren coastline is generally very steep, rising directly to 60m (200ft) in many places. Hills of 150m to 250m (500ft to 800ft) back the shoreline which can be confusing when you are trying to identify the harbour entrance. The bluff coastline can also result in squally winds or wind shadows when close inshore. Vestal Rock, with a depth of 3.7m (12ft), lies 65m (215ft) south-east of South Head. In thick weather it is possible to mistake the entrance to Quidi Vidi harbour (one mile further north) for that of St John's. Quidi Vidi has no lighthouses or fog signals.

Large ships entering and leaving through the narrow harbour entrance are monitored and controlled by St John's Traffic. They will need to know when you are within 12 miles of the harbour.

Approach and entrance

The shore is generally steep-to and clear of underwater rocks, and in thick weather can be approached using the depth sounder. The 40m (130ft) line lies between 0.2 and 0.5 miles offshore. Sugarloaf Head, four miles north of St John's, has a conspicuous, 168m (550ft) high, sheer cliff face. It appears wedge-shaped when seen from north of north-east, but as a truncated cone from east-north-east round to the south-east. There are a number of radio masts close to the south of it. Cape Spear, 3.5 miles south-east of St John's, is an 80m (260ft) high promontory, projecting north-eastward from the coast. A light is shown [Fl (3) 15s 71m 20M] from a 10.7m (35ft) white tower, with an old light structure about 200m (660ft) to the south-west.

The final approach to St John's harbour is between North and South Head and is straightforward. North Head is a steep headland of 72m (240ft) rising up to Signal Hill to the north-west, topped by the conspicuous Cabot Tower. A light [Fl R 4s 26m] is shown from a mast at the entrance. South Head is marked by Fort Amherst Light [Fl 15s 40m 13M], on a square white tower. There is also a fog horn. Enter between the two headlands on a course of 276°. There are daymarks and leading lights [F G 29m and F G 59m] on this bearing, but they are difficult to identify. The twin towers of the Roman Catholic Cathedral break the skyline on the outskirts of the city – the rear light (itself mounted on a church tower) is just to the north of these towers and almost level with their bases. If the leading line cannot be identified, continue on 276° until through the narrows, observing the

ST JOHN'S, NEWFOUNDLAND
CANADA
39

buoys that mark shoals on both sides of the channel. Once inside, the harbour opens up to the south-west.

Radio

St John's Radio monitors VHF Channel 16 and broadcasts weather forecasts and ice reports. A Vessel Traffic Management System is administered from Signal Hill and should be contacted on VHF Channel 11 or 14 as 'St John's Traffic'. The Canadian Coast Guard monitors VHF Channels 16 and 26. In addition, a continuous weather forecast is broadcast on VHF Channel 21B.

Formalities

Fly the Q flag from offshore if arriving from abroad. When you are about 12 miles from the approach channel to St Johns Harbour, call 'St Johns Traffic' on VHF Channel 11. Customs is located on the 6th floor of the Canada building. On arrival, the skipper should go ashore alone to call Canadian Customs Control on 1 888 226 7277 (toll free), with all yacht and personal details to hand – registration number, last port, names and dates of birth of all crew, etc. This number is in operation 24 hours a day. They will want to know the yacht's exact location and will then issue a Report Number. They will inform local customs who will visit the yacht to stamp the passports of non-US or Canadian nationals. Note that all weapons, firearms and alcohol must be declared and that guns, particularly handguns, may be confiscated and held ashore.

Berthing and facilities

There is pontoon berthing for yachts just south of the leading line opposite the entrance and just to the south of a large red building adjacent to the pilot boat berth. Alternatively, a berth may be found in the small boat harbour in the south-west of the port. There are no services on either of these berths. The harbour is quite polluted, and care should be taken when handling lines that have been in the water.

The Royal Newfoundland Yacht Club in Conception Bay on the western shores of the Avalon Peninsula, 40 miles by sea from St John's, welcomes visiting sailors and has a 50-tonne travel lift.
Website: www.rnyc.nf.ca
Contact: PO Box 14160, Station Manuels, Conception Bay South, NL. A1W 3J1. Tel: 834-5151 Fax: 834-1413
E-mail: manager@rnyc.nf.ca

Anchorage and moorings

The harbour is busy and anchoring is only allowed under the direction of the harbourmaster. There is good holding in mud. The harbourmaster's office is on Water Street.

Transport connections

Daily bus service to Port-aux-Basques (14 hours) for the ferry to Sydney, Nova Scotia. St John's airport has direct flights to the United Kingdom as well as links within Canada and the United States.

Medical services

There are three large hospitals in the city, plus many doctors and dentists.

Looking east from the yacht landing towards the narrows at the entrance to St John's. Photo: Paul Heiney

40
Stornoway, Isle of Lewis
Scotland, UK

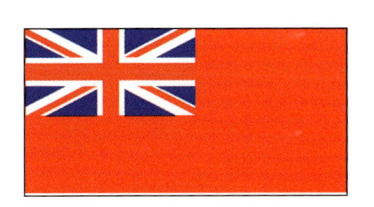

Location:	58°11′.5N 06°22′W
Springs:	4.8m Range: 4.1m
Neaps:	3.7m Range: 1.7m
Time zone:	UT
Currency:	Pounds (£) (Note: Scottish banknotes are issued in Scotland but may not be generally accepted elsewhere in the UK)
Tel/fax:	Country code: 44 Area code: (0)1851
Language:	English, Gaelic is also spoken

Sheltered haven

Stornoway is a well-sheltered natural harbour on the east coast of the Isle of Lewis. It is a logical point of arrival or departure for anyone taking the Viking Route across the Atlantic. Although primarily a commercial and fishing harbour, Stornoway welcomes visiting yachts. It may be difficult to find a space in the inner harbour during July when the Maritime Festival, Hebridean Celtic Festival and Highland Games take place. Lews Castle is a prominent local landmark with very pleasant grounds to walk around, giving some lovely views over the harbour and town. If you explore further afield you may be lucky enough to spot some of the golden eagles that are native to the island. The facilities for provisioning and repair are relatively modest in Stornoway, but most things are available if you take local advice.

Websites
www.reedsalmanac.co.uk/media/432.pdf
www.stornowayhistoricalsociety.org.uk/features/castle
www.sailhebrides.info
www.hebceltfest.com
www.lewishighlandgames.co.uk

Approach and entrance

During the day, the large sheds on Arnish Point are a good landmark. The Beasts of Holm at the east side of the

Stornoway inner harbour showing the yacht pontoons to the left and Poll nam Portan anchorage in the distance. Photo: Clyde Cruising Club

PASSAGES AND LANDFALLS

Plan 85 Stornoway, Isle of Lewis, Scotland

entrance are marked by an unlit green beacon. There is a conspicuous memorial on Holm Point to the north of the Beasts. A rock to the north of Arnish Point on the west side of the entrance is marked with a buoy [QR]. North of Arnish Point, on the opposite shore, Sgeir Mhor Inaclete reef is marked by an unlit beacon. At night a series of sector lights lead you into the harbour. Follow the white sectors of Arnish Point light [Fl WR 10s 17m 9/7M], Sandwick light [Oc WRG 6s 10m 9M], Stoney Field (astern) [Fl WRG 3s 8m 11M] and No1 Pier [Q WRG 5m 11M].

Radio

Stornoway Port Authority VHF Channel 16; Harbourmaster Channel 12.

Formalities

All vessels must call the Harbourmaster on VHF before entering the harbour. All visitors must report on arrival to the Harbourmaster, Stornoway Port Authority, Tel: 702688, E-mail: information@stornoway-harbour.com

Entry requirements are waived in the case of an EU registered yacht arriving direct from another EU country. In the case of a non-EU registered vessel, or if arriving from a non-EU country or with non-EU nationals aboard, hoist the Q flag and the courtesy flag if appropriate.

Foreign flag vessels or vessels with foreign crew on board must clear immigration through the Port Authority and immigration at Aberdeen Airport. Complete Form NDP(Y), obtainable from the harbour office and fax it to Immigration

Lews Castle, Stornoway. Photo: Clyde Cruising Club

Aberdeen on 01224 214340. Telephone 01224 722890 for further instructions. Customs clearance should be carried out via the National Yacht Line Tel: 0845 7231110.

Berthing and facilities

A small marina at the very northern end of the inner harbour has eight visitors' berths for yachts up to 12m (40ft). Yachts drawing more than 1.5m (5ft) should manoeuvre with caution as depths shallow off from 3.3m (11ft) to less than 1.5m (5ft) in some areas. Larger or deeper draught yachts can tie up alongside the Cromwell Street Quay, or Esplanade Quay (on the north wall to the left of the marina symbol).

Anchorage and moorings

Space available in the marked anchorage in Poll nam Portan may be restricted by a number of moorings. Do not anchor in the fairway to the inner harbour. The anchorage can become uncomfortable if a south easterly swell finds its way in.

Transport connections

There are flights to Inverness, Aberdeen, Glasgow and Edinburgh and ferries to Ullapool on the mainland. Buses go around the island.

Medical services

There are a number of services available, including the Western Isles Hospital in Stornoway (Tel: 704704) and the Health Centres (Tel: 703145 and 704888).

OBAN

Further south, on the Scottish mainland, Oban Marina offers a full range of facilities including haul-out and storage. Oban Marina (56°25′N, 5°30′W) lies on the shore of Ardantrive Bay, on the east side of Kerrera Island, right opposite Oban itself. It is accessible at all states of the tide and has a full range of facilities including pontoon berths, re-fuelling berth, 50-tonne travel lift and hard standing. Trains from Oban give easy access to Glasgow where there are national and international connections by rail, bus or plane.

Website: www.obanmarina.com
Contact: Oban Marina Ltd Tel: (0)1631 565333
Fax: (0)1631 565888 E-mail: info@obanmarina.com

THE ATLANTIC CROSSING GUIDE

Appendix A

AMERICAN CHARTS

NOAA's (US Government) entire suite of over 1,000 nautical charts is available for free as Raster Navigational Charts in the BSB format. Commercial electronic charting software is required to use them. Weekly digital updates are also available. Go to: www.nauticalcharts.noaa.gov/staff/charts.htm Click on 'Chartviewer' then click on 'Atlantic Coast' then click on 'Catalogue'.

Nearly all NOAA paper charts are available in Print on Demand (POD) format. Charts are fully corrected up until the time of purchase. Purchase through OceanGrafix at www.OceanGrafix.com

Traditional paper charts are also available on line via the website or through an agent. Agents are listed on the website.

IMRAY CHARTS AVAILABLE FOR YACHTS CRUISING THE NORTH ATLANTIC

For further information about Imray nautical charts (paper or digital), books and software visit www.imray.com/chart_i_diag_search.cfm

Electronic (digital) chart updates are available at www.imray.com/digital_index.cfm

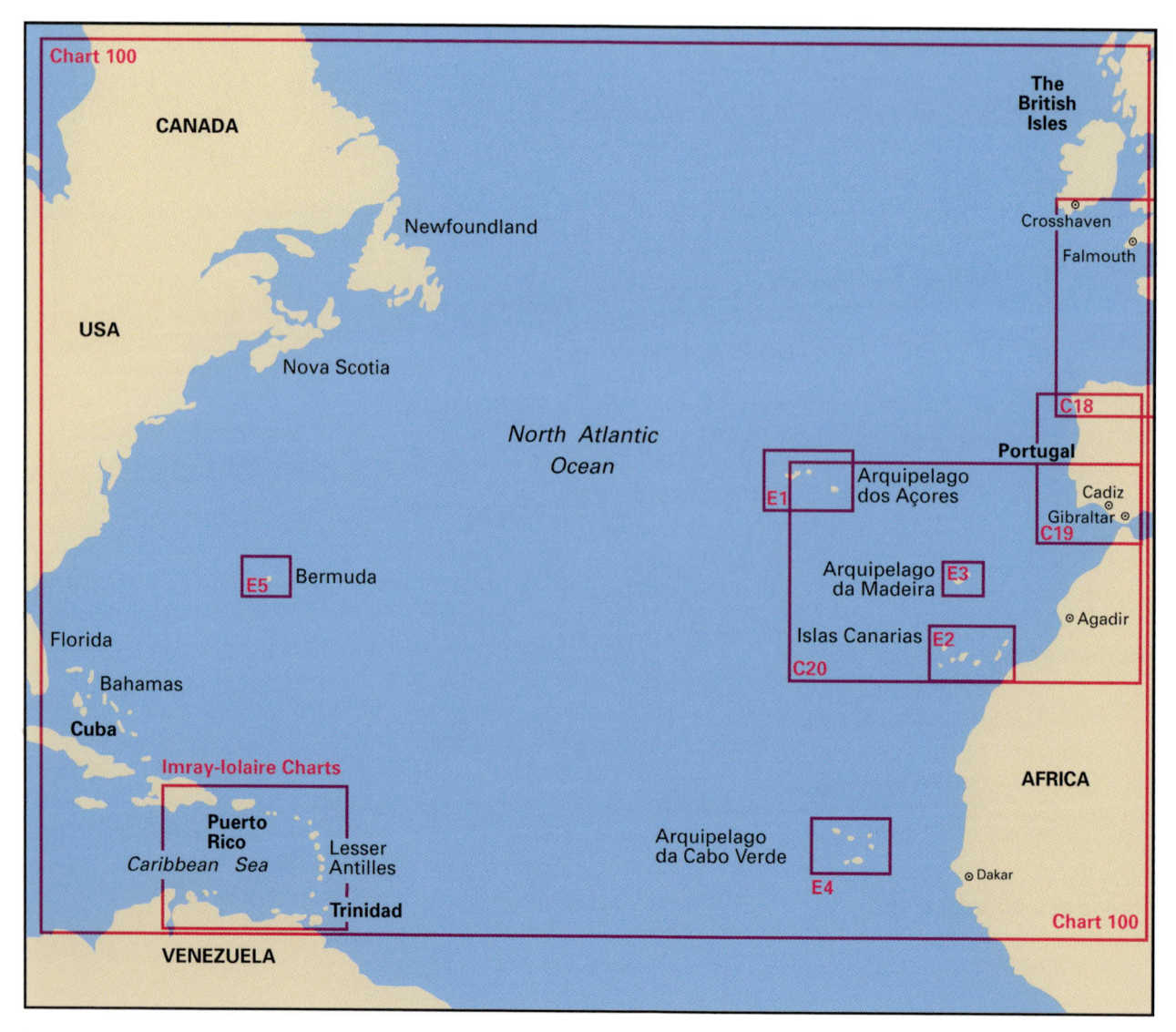

Imray charts for the North Atlantic, passages and island groups. Reproduced with permission from Imray, Laurie, Norie & Wilson Ltd

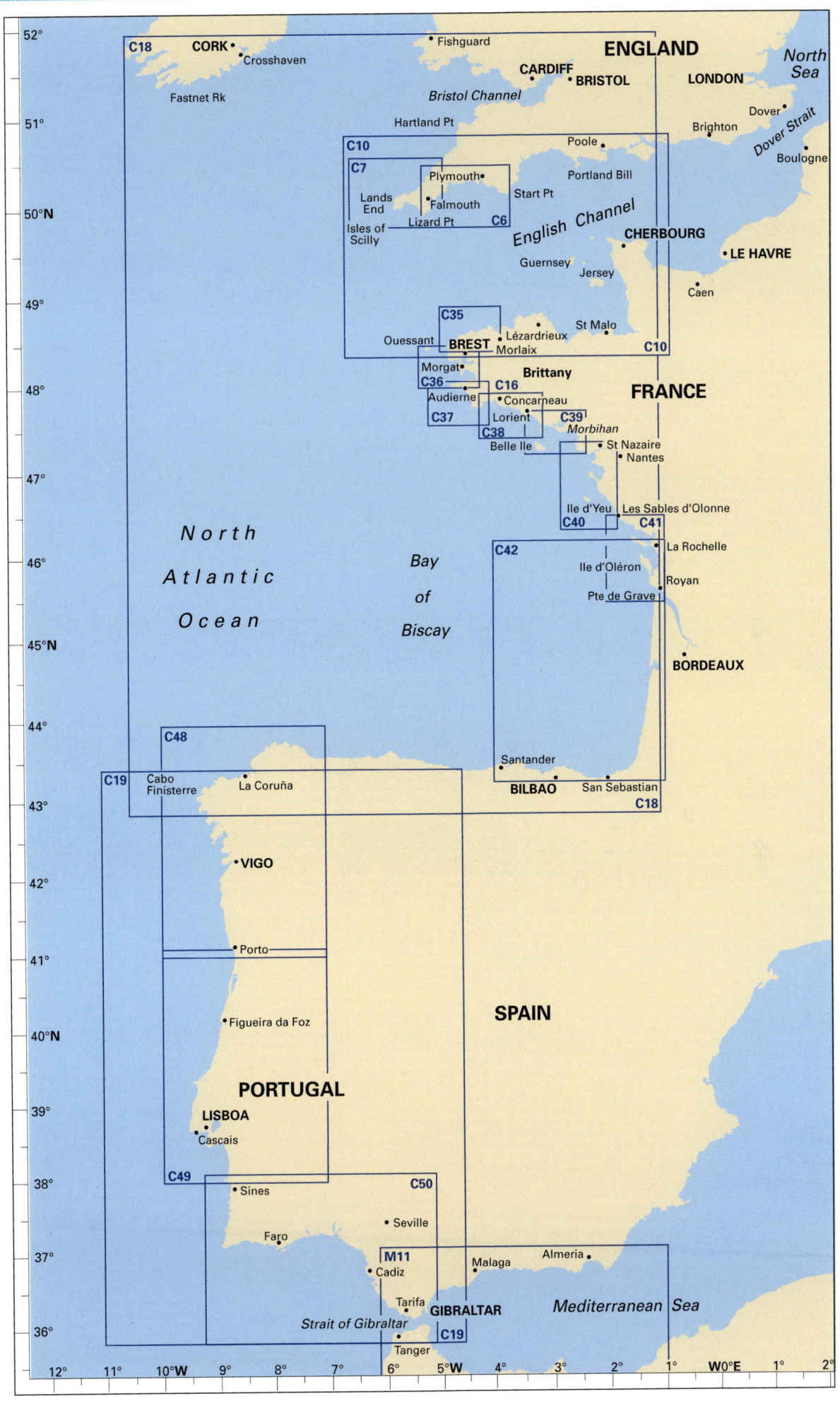

Imray charts for the Atlantic coast of Europe, passages and some of the port charts. Reproduced with permission from Imray, Laurie, Norie & Wilson Ltd

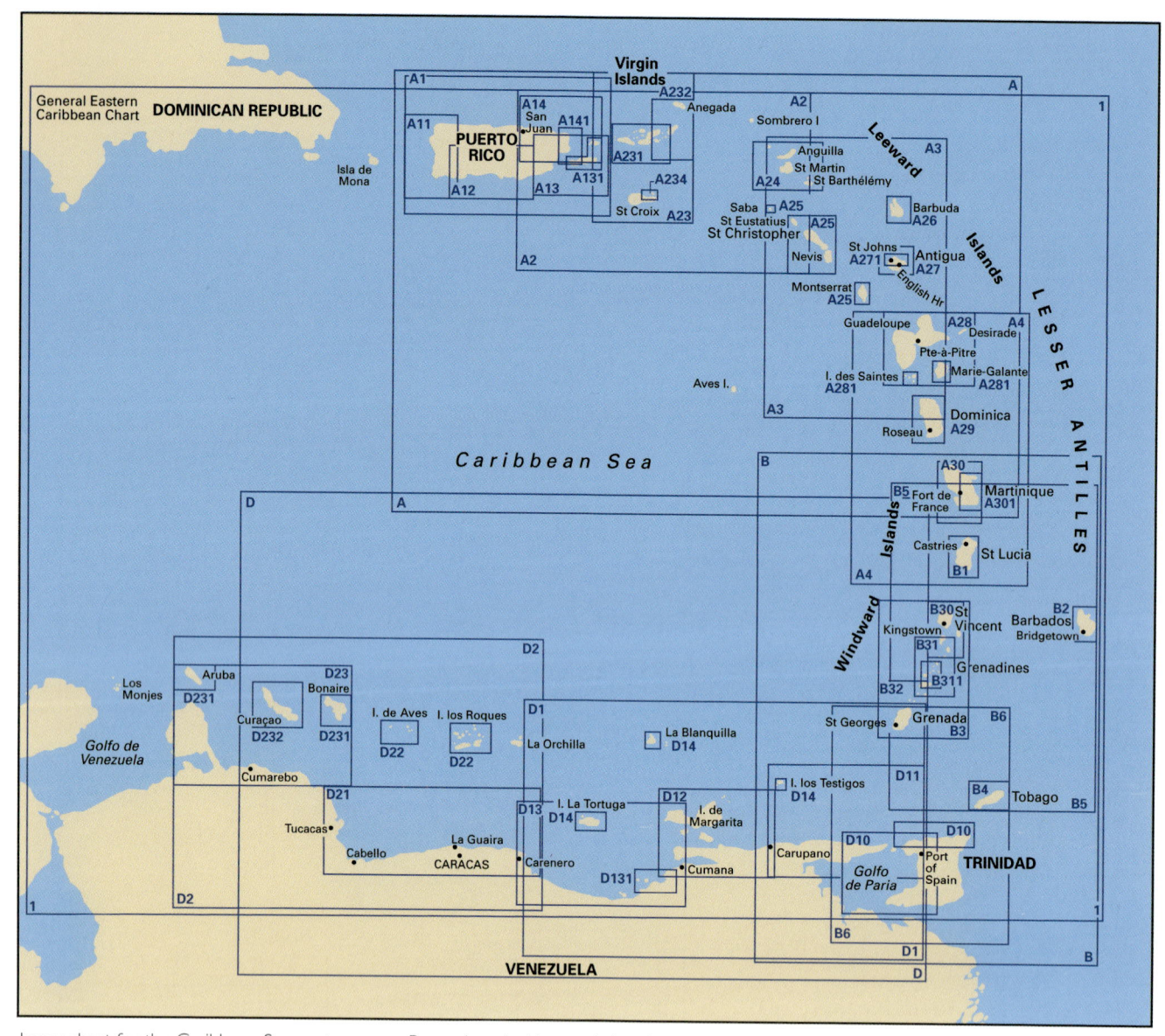

THE ATLANTIC CROSSING GUIDE

Imray chart for the Caribbean Sea, eastern area. Reproduced with permission from Imray, Laurie, Norie & Wilson Ltd

APPENDICES

SOME OF THE ADMIRALTY CHARTS COVERING THE NORTH ATLANTIC

For more details of paper or electronic charts consult an Admiralty chart catalogue, available from a number of book shops and chandlers or go on line to website: www.catalogue.ukho.gov.uk/home_admiraltycharts.asp

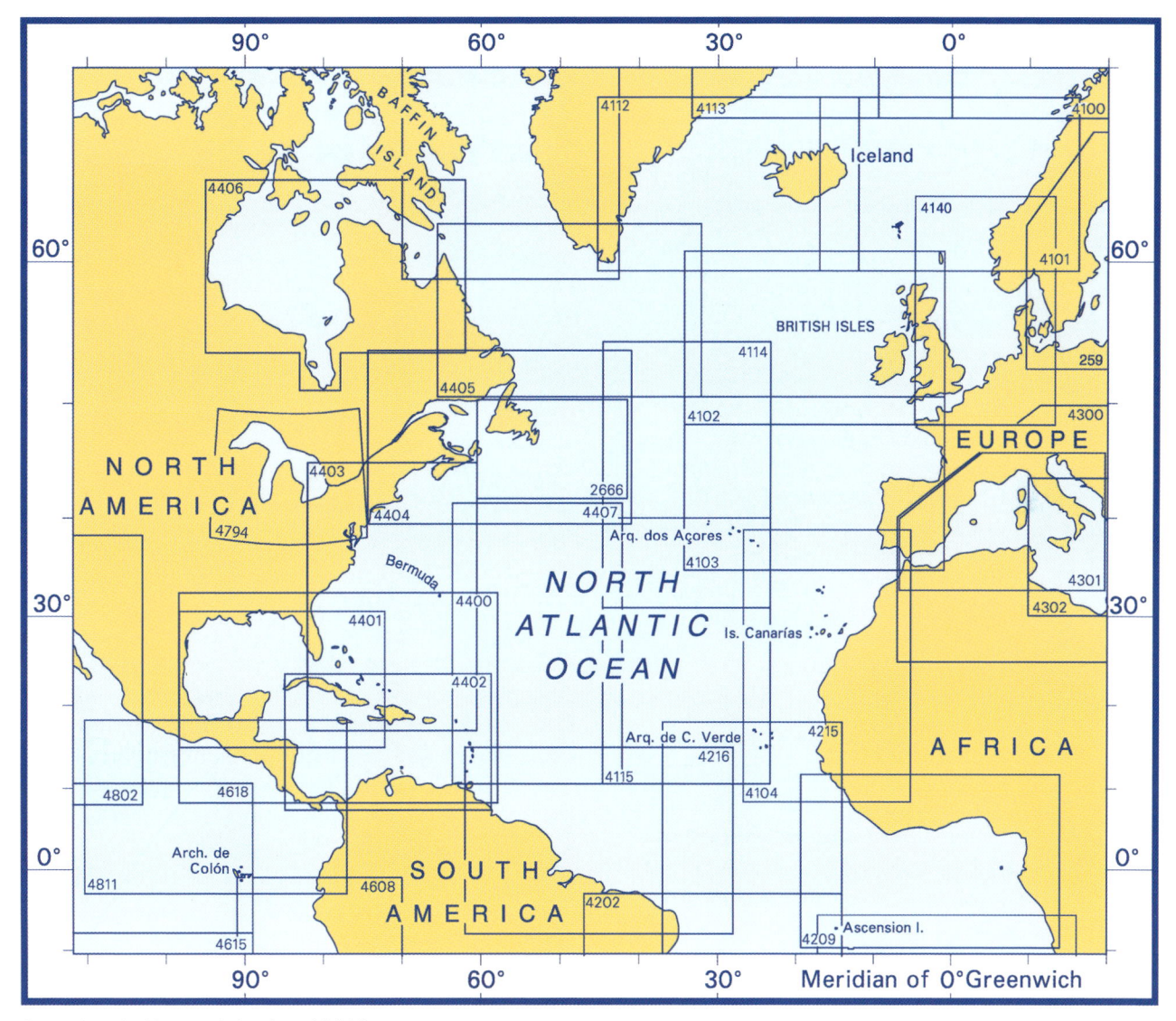

Reproduced with permission from UKHO

THE ATLANTIC CROSSING GUIDE

Appendix B

The Atlantic Hurricane Season

If you are unable to avoid remaining afloat in the Caribbean during hurricane season you need to think through the possible worst-case scenarios and prepare accordingly. Yachtsmen and women who have experienced the full force of a hurricane have reported finding it difficult to even breathe effectively on deck, let alone stand up. Such conditions should not be taken lightly.

> **Hurricane forecasts**
> The National Hurricane Centre is a part of the National Oceanic and Atmospheric Administration (NOAA). The NOAA is a US federal agency which focuses on the condition of the oceans and the atmosphere and produces excellent weather reports and forecasts, including hurricane forecasting and tracking. This is the most accurate and dependable source for tropical storm information. NOAA website: www.nhc.noaa.gov/
>
> Other useful sites are: www.stormcarib.com and www.crownweather.com

Forecasting of tropical storms is now so good that you should be aware of the possibility of a storm at least 2–3 days in advance. Be aware that the transition from 'tropical wave' to 'tropical depression' to 'named storm' to 'hurricane' may be very rapid.

Over recent years, the frequency and intensity of hurricanes has increased. Early and late season storms and less predictable storm tracks are further issues. NOAA has now extended the official hurricane season from 1 June until 30 November. Early season storms generally affect the eastern Caribbean and late season storms affect the western Caribbean. However, this is a generalisation and there may always be anomalies.

The boundaries of tropical depressions and hurricanes also continue to expand. Twelve degrees north was, for many years, considered to be a safe latitude. However, more recently, both tropical storms and hurricanes have moved along that latitude. In addition, tropical storms (called 'extra tropical') and even hurricanes have affected the east coast of Canada as far north as Nova Scotia. Many scientists see the Caribbean as being in an active part of a long-term cycle with tropical storms and hurricanes becoming more frequent, more intense and following trajectories previously unheard of.

FACTORS AFFECTING TROPICAL WEATHER PATTERNS IN THE NORTH ATLANTIC

by Denis Webster

Tropical weather systems are born from a large area of rising air along the equator where warm moist air rushes in from the northern and southern hemispheres. This is the area commonly called the doldrums or the Inter Tropical Convergence Zone (ITCZ). It is an area of thunderstorms, rain and no wind. The ITCZ is tracked on a daily basis in many bulletins and can be seen clearly on satellite pictures. It moves south in the dry season (the northern winter) to about approximately 10°S and back north to 10°N in the rainy season (the northern summer).

Air ascending from the ITCZ spreads out at high altitude and then begins to sink over an area of the North Atlantic around 30°N. This causes the semi-permanent feature called the Azores or Bermuda High. Clockwise circulation around this high helps to create the North Atlantic trade wind belt. The strength and direction of the trades varies from season to season and is dependent on the pressure gradient between the Azores High and the ITCZ. Colder, denser air in the northern winter creates a steeper gradient and stronger trade winds. Conversely, in the northern summer, the warmer air around the Azores High is less dense and the pressure gradient with the ITCZ is reduced, resulting in lighter winds. The following pressure gradients are an indication of wind speeds between 10° and 20°N:

4 mb	10–15 knots
5 mb	15–20 knots
6 mb	20–25 knots
7 mb or more	over 25 knots

The dry season

The dry season in the tropical North Atlantic is during the northern winter and begins with the formation of the first winter storm over the North American continent. An area of deep, low pressure moves across the continent and heads east into the North Atlantic. Behind this low pressure, cold dense air pushes south, displacing warm air. The dividing line is a cold front. As the low pressure moves east across the Atlantic it will trail a cold front to its south and south-west, out over the warmer water. Cold fronts frequently extend to the Bahamas, part way into the Caribbean basin or, occasionally, all the way to the South American coast. The tracks of low pressure systems slowly migrate south during the dry season. Cold fronts in the Caribbean basin frequently stall, creating a strong pressure gradient and moderate to fresh north-east winds.

Transition from dry season to rainy season

As spring arrives in North America, the ground begins to warm. Cold fronts extending into tropical areas become less intense and associated tropical winds become more moderate easterlies or south-easterlies. As the transition continues, troughs frequently establish themselves and remain in position for significant lengths of time. These are influenced by features in the upper atmosphere and may or may not appear as a feature on surface charts. These are frequent features of the Caribbean basin and are characterised by rain showers or thunderstorms.

In late May or early June, particularly off the coastline of Honduras and Belize, in the Gulf of Mexico and off the Florida coast, lows may form in association with upper level features. These may become tropical depressions or even early season hurricanes which move up the US East Coast and into the North Atlantic before dissipating.

The rainy (hurricane) season

The true rainy season arrives with the first appearance of tropical waves. These are travelling low pressure troughs which bring squalls, rain and thunderstorms and can develop into tropical depressions and hurricanes. Tropical waves first appear on charts and in bulletins around the end of May. They begin their march from Africa across the Atlantic in a uniform fashion, usually at a relatively constant speed. Also significant is the northern progression of the ITCZ which moves north from Brazil as far as the eastern Caribbean or Central America. The ITCZ is noted for its days of rain, thunderstorms and gusty winds in squalls.

As the rainy season progresses into October, tropical waves tend to be less frequent and intense, almost disappearing by mid November. In addition, the ITCZ starts to move south below 10°N, with only the occasional foray up into the Caribbean basin. In the western Caribbean, along the Central American coast, rain and thunderstorms often persist into December. Late season hurricanes may develop in the western Caribbean in late October and November, moving inland or up into the Gulf of Mexico.

As precipitation becomes less frequent and the air becomes drier, winds will begin to increase in speed and the wind direction will become more easterly. Typical winds would be easterly at 15 knots.

STEPS IN STORM DEVELOPMENT

by Denis Webster

1. North Atlantic hurricanes begin their lives as a tropical wave, although many tropical waves do not develop into hurricanes. During the hurricane season it is a good idea to monitor and track any tropical waves. These usually begin to form from early June and move at various speeds.

2. A tropical wave may be associated with an 'area of disturbed weather'. When they occur, these areas are reported in tropical weather bulletins. Such an area of disturbed weather may move, dissipate, or develop, depending upon weather conditions. When there is strong vertical wind shear at upper levels, the possibility of storm development decreases because stronger winds at higher altitudes tend to shear the tops of clouds and limit the vertical motion of air. When monitoring tropical waves, the first indication of development will be the inclusion of the word 'rotation' in a bulletin description. Circulation of air is not necessarily a concern unless it is associated with other factors. Hurricanes may develop where circulation of air occurs together with abundant moisture and no vertical wind shear. Storm bulletins give assessments of areas where development is expected and contain terms such as 'wind conditions are favourable for storm development'.

3. When conditions are favourable and observations confirm development, an advisory is issued for a tropical depression. Tropical depressions are the first stage of hurricane development where wind speeds are measured as 33 knots or less. Each tropical depression receives a number (for example TD1) and the location, development and forecast track is reported in bulletins. Some tropical depressions develop very rapidly and they should be monitored very closely.

4. When further development of a tropical depression occurs, wind speeds increase above 34 knots and air rotation becomes evident with a spiraling cloud formation. A central 'eye' may be observed. At this stage a tropical storm advisory is issued. Bulletins contain the forecast development and track for the following five days. Tropical storm watches or warnings will be issued for all coastal areas expected to be affected. Storm watches are valid for 36 hours, storm warnings for 24 hours. Your hurricane plans for you and your boat should be in place and executed by this stage.

5 Tropical storms become hurricanes when central wind speeds reach 64 knots. Bulletins and updates are issued at regular intervals and coastal areas will have watches and warnings posted. Hurricane trajectories (tracks) are predicted for a five-day period and include a 'cone of uncertainty'. Although forecast models and forecaster skills have improved dramatically over the past 15 to 20 years, there are factors which influence the development and track of storms and cannot be accounted for in the models. If you and your vessel are within this 'cone', you should be prepared for the worst.

6 Hurricanes can sometimes degenerate back into a tropical wave. This normally occurs if upper level wind shear is too strong. The storm can later re-intensify if the upper level shear abates.

7 Tropical storms and hurricanes are always accompanied by heavy rain and storm surges. Warnings may remain in effect for high water or high waves after the wind speeds have diminished below 64 knots and in areas peripheral to the path of the storm.

STORM SHELTERS

by John Franklin (with additional information by Richard Woods)

There are many traditional storm shelters and 'hurricane holes' in the Caribbean. However, the increasing number of boats has rendered many of these shelters so overcrowded that finding a safe position becomes impossible. Much of the damage incurred in anchorages is due to the 'loose cannon' effect when some boats drag, out of control, often causing other boats to drag or break free from their moorings. In his *Cruising Guides*, Don Street Jnr has advocated putting to sea to ride out a hurricane rather than being trapped with 'bareboat bombs' cannoning around. But this would seem extreme guidance if your own survival is valued more than the survival of your boat. However much your boat has become your life, if a hurricane tracks over you the safest place to be is on the shore.

If you are forced into finding a storm shelter it is important to try to predict where the storm will pass in relation to your planned location and what the likely wind directions will be. This will help you to decide where to anchor and in which directions to lay your anchors.

The following are some of the 'traditional' storm shelters. How safe they really are will depend on where the storm centre passes and how crowded they become with other boats.

Grenada: Port Egmont
This is the most protected harbour on the south coat of Grenada. Almost landlocked, it is surrounded by hills on all sides. However, during Hurricane Ivan, which occurred in 2004, the danger came from overcrowding and loose boats.

Many yachtsmen spend the hurricane season on the south coast of Grenada. At the first sign of an approaching tropical storm they sail southwards to Trinidad or Venezuela to be almost certain of escaping the direct path and the worst effects.

St Lucia: Marigot Bay
Marigot Bay is sheltered in all weathers, even in a hurricane, and has been a traditional shelter since the time of Nelson. However, it is now so crowded even in normal circumstances that it is useless as a storm shelter.

Martinique: Le Marin
You would probably be safe if you could pull your boat into the mangroves on the south side but otherwise there are just too many boats in Le Marin for it to be safe in a hurricane.

Martinique: Cohe de Lamentin
Draft in the approach channel is 6ft but otherwise it is described as an excellent hurricane shelter. However, due to the density of boats in Martinique, overcrowding would certainly be a problem.

Guadeloupe: Point a Pitre
There appears to be an excellent storm shelter in the Port du Plaisance de Bas du Fort just inside the harbour entrance. However, in practice overcrowding would be a problem.

Guadeloupe: Riviere Salee
The Riviere Salee has been described as 'not so much a river as a saltwater mangrove channel'. It is shallow and perfectly sheltered but access is controlled by two bridges at the southern end opening at 0500 Monday to Saturday.

Antigua: English Harbour
This has been a traditional hurricane shelter since the time of Nelson. The safest place is in the mangroves on the north side of Ordnance Bay but overcrowding would certainly be a problem.

Antigua: Jolly Harbour
This is a private resort marina on the west coast of the island. It is not a traditional storm shelter but is very protected.

St Martin
Good shelter may be found tucked up into the mangroves. Again, it is the volume of yachts crowding into any particular anchorage which can cause problems here.

St John: Coral Bay
There are a couple of hurricane holes at the extreme northern end of Coral Bay with good shelter except from the south. Technically this is within the Virgin Islands Coral

Reef National Monument and no anchoring is allowed. How this would apply during hurricane conditions is uncertain.

St Thomas: The Lagoon, Benner Bay
Draft is limited to 5ft. It is open to the east so doesn't provide very good shelter, but it is the best in St Thomas.

Culebra: Ensenada Honda
This is a huge, enclosed harbour with excellent holding but not a lot of protection from the wind. The best location is to the south-west of Cayo Pirata.

Vieques: Ensenada Honda
This is another large, deserted harbour offering complete shelter. The most sheltered location is in the extreme eastern end where it is possible to pull into the mangroves and into the mud.

Vieques: Puerto Ferro
The entrance is shallow (6–7ft) and narrow but once inside it is a small but perfect storm shelter.

Puerto Rico: Bahia de Jobos
On the northern side of Bahia de Jobos are many muddy creeks among the mangroves making it a perfect hurricane shelter. The marina at Fajardo is the largest marina in the Caribbean and has a good reputation for preparing boats effectively against hurricane damage. It is approved of by marine insurers.

Puerto Rico: Salinas
Salinas, just west of Bahia de Jobos, is very sheltered from all directions and offers excellent holding. The best shelter is on the east side among the mangroves.

Dominican Republic: Luperon
Luperon is perhaps the most famous hurricane hole in the Caribbean. It offers all-round protection, shallow water, good holding and mangroves on all sides. In these respects it is a perfect hurricane shelter. However, because of its narrow entrance, the water can become very stagnant and polluted.

Appendix C

Glossary of Meteorological Terms

by Denis Webster

Acceleration zone sometimes called 'squeeze zone' – wind speeds increase due to funneling between or around landmasses. Common acceleration zones include the areas between islands and along the northern coasts of Colombia and Honduras.

Air mass A large area of air, which has relatively uniform characteristics of temperature and moisture.

Anabatic wind Wind that blows up sloping terrain during the day as sunlight warms the land. Common in the Caribbean on the lee sides of islands during light trade winds.

Anticyclonic flow is the circulation of air in a clockwise direction around areas of high pressure in the Northern Hemisphere.

Azore's high sometimes referred to as the Bermuda High, is a large semi-permanent air mass of high pressure located along approximately 30°N.

Backing wind refers to an anti-clockwise change in wind direction over a period of time (eg west winds become south-west and then south).

Between season troughs Although not a technical term, it is sometimes used to describe troughs in the Caribbean which form either at the surface or aloft and persist for many days. They tend to have a presence during the transition from dry to rainy season, and rainy to dry season.

Buys Ballot Law states that, in the Northern Hemisphere, if you place your back to the wind, lower pressure systems are always to your left.

Easting or 'making easting' refers to vessels attempting to gain distance to windward against the prevailing easterly winds.

Easterly wave See tropical waves.

Front The boundary zone between cool or cold air and warmer air. Where the cold air is advancing, the boundary is called a *cold front*. Where the cold air is retreating, the boundary is called a *warm front*. Fronts with no movement are said to be *stationary* or to have *stalled*. Frontal boundaries that have become broad and cannot be identified are said to be *diffuse* or *dissipating*.

Gusts are sudden increases or rapid fluctuations of wind speed, usually of less than 20 seconds.

High pressure is an area where pressure is highest at a central point and is surrounded by lower pressure in all directions.

Inter Tropical Converence Zone (ITCZ) is the area on the Earth's surface where air from the Northern and Southern Hemispheres converges and is forced to rise. It is an area of light winds and thunderstorms sometimes called the doldrums.

Inversion A condition in the atmosphere, which causes temperatures to increase with height.

Inverted trough Troughs always extend from lower pressure toward higher pressure. In the tropics, the lowest pressure is the ITCZ. Troughs that extend north from the ITCZ are called 'inverted' as compared to those in the Atlantic which generally extend south from lows. Easterly (or tropical) waves are one form of inverted trough.

Isobar This is a line joining points of equal atmospheric pressure. Isobars are drawn on maps using pressure readings from surface observation stations corrected for altitude and temperature. They are drawn at 4-millibar intervals starting at 1000 mMb.

Katabatic winds are common features of large landmasses in the Caribbean, particularly along the mountainous coast of South America. After sunset, the land begins to cool. A layer of air close to the land surface also cools and becomes dense. It then slides down the mountain slope and blows from the land out over the water. These 'drainage winds' are light but, as the night progresses, they dominate over the tradewind flow. This phenomenon is beneficial to vessels which are trying to make easting.

Land breeze See katabatic winds.

Low pressure is an area where pressure is lowest at a central point and is surrounded by higher pressure in all directions.

Millibar A standard unit for measuring pressure, equivalent to 100 Newtons per square metre.

Pressure gradient The measurement of the change in atmospheric pressure over a fixed distance on the Earth's surface. This measurement will provide an estimate of wind speed.

Ridge An area of higher pressure extending from the centre of a high-pressure area. It is marked by a line such that pressures are lower on either side of the line.

Sea breeze With light winds during the day, land heats up and the air in contact with the land begins to rise. Air from the ocean moves in to take the place of the rising air, forming a breeze from the sea to the land. See also anabatic winds.

Squall A sudden onset of strong winds lasting at least one minute.

Tropical wave (also known as an easterly wave) This is an inverted trough (elongated area of relatively low air pressure extending northwards from the ITCZ) moving westwards across the tropics causing areas of cloudiness and thunderstorms. Tropical waves in the Atlantic basin develop over Africa and are influenced by the African Easterly Jetstream. Most Atlantic hurricanes develop from tropical waves, although many tropical waves do not develop into storms. Saharan dust blowing off the continent effects the development of tropical waves and may help to reduce the likelihood of hurricane formation. If a tropical wave is moving quickly, it can have strong winds of greater than tropical storm force, but it is not considered a tropical storm unless it has a closed circulation.

Trough A line of lower pressure extending out from a low pressure area. Pressures are higher on either side of the line.

Veer A clockwise change in wind direction (eg south winds become south-west and then west).

Vertical wind shear is the rate of change of wind speed with height. Strong vertical wind shear (a rapid increase in wind speed with altitude), is a deterrent to hurricane development.

Vorticity is a measure of small scale rotation at upper levels. It is used by forecasters to predict weather system development and intensity.

Wind direction The direction from which the wind blows.

Wind speed Wind speed is measured by various sets of units which include: metres per second (m/s), nautical miles per hour (knots or kts), and by the Beaufort scale.

Wind warnings Small craft warnings are issued by local weather services. The criteria may vary from country to country. A gale warning is issued for sustained winds between 34 and 47 knots. Note: terms such as 'near gale' and 'full gale', are sometimes used by weather services. A storm warning is issued for sustained winds between 48 and 55 knots.

Zulu time The letter Z is used in meteorological bulletins to denote GMT or UTC.

FRENCH METEOROLOGICAL TERMS USED BY METEO FRANCE

Force du Vent – wind strength
Vent faible – force 0 to 2
Vent modéré – force 3 to 5
Vent assez fort – force 6
Vent fort – force 7 and 8
Vent très fort – force 9
Vent violent – force 10 or greater

État de la mer – sea state
Calme calm – glassy
Ridée calm – rippled
Belle – smooth
Peu agitée – slight
Agitée – moderate
Forte – rough
Très forte – very rough
Grosse – high
Très grosse – very high
Énorme – phenomenal

Visibilité – visibility
Bonne – good (more than 5M)
Médiocre – moderate (2 to 5M)
Mauvaise – poor (0.5 to 2M).
Brouillard – fog (less than 0.5M visibility)

Anticyclone – high
Averses – showers
Avis ou BMS – warning
Avis de coup de vent (force 8) – gale warning
Dépression – low
Dorsale – ridge
Épars – at times
Grains – squalls
Grêle – hail
Houle – swell
Neige – snow
Occasionnels – occasional
Onde d'est ou onde tropicale – easterly wave or tropical wave
Orage – thunderstorm
Ouragan – hurricane
Pluie – rain
Se dissipant ou s'atténuant – dying out
SMDSM – GMDSS
Temporaires – *temporarily*
ZCIT – *ITCZ*

See also: Lexique at www.meteo.fr/meteonet_en/decouvr/guides/marine/mar2.htm#2

THE ATLANTIC CROSSING GUIDE

Appendix D

Weather Forecast Areas

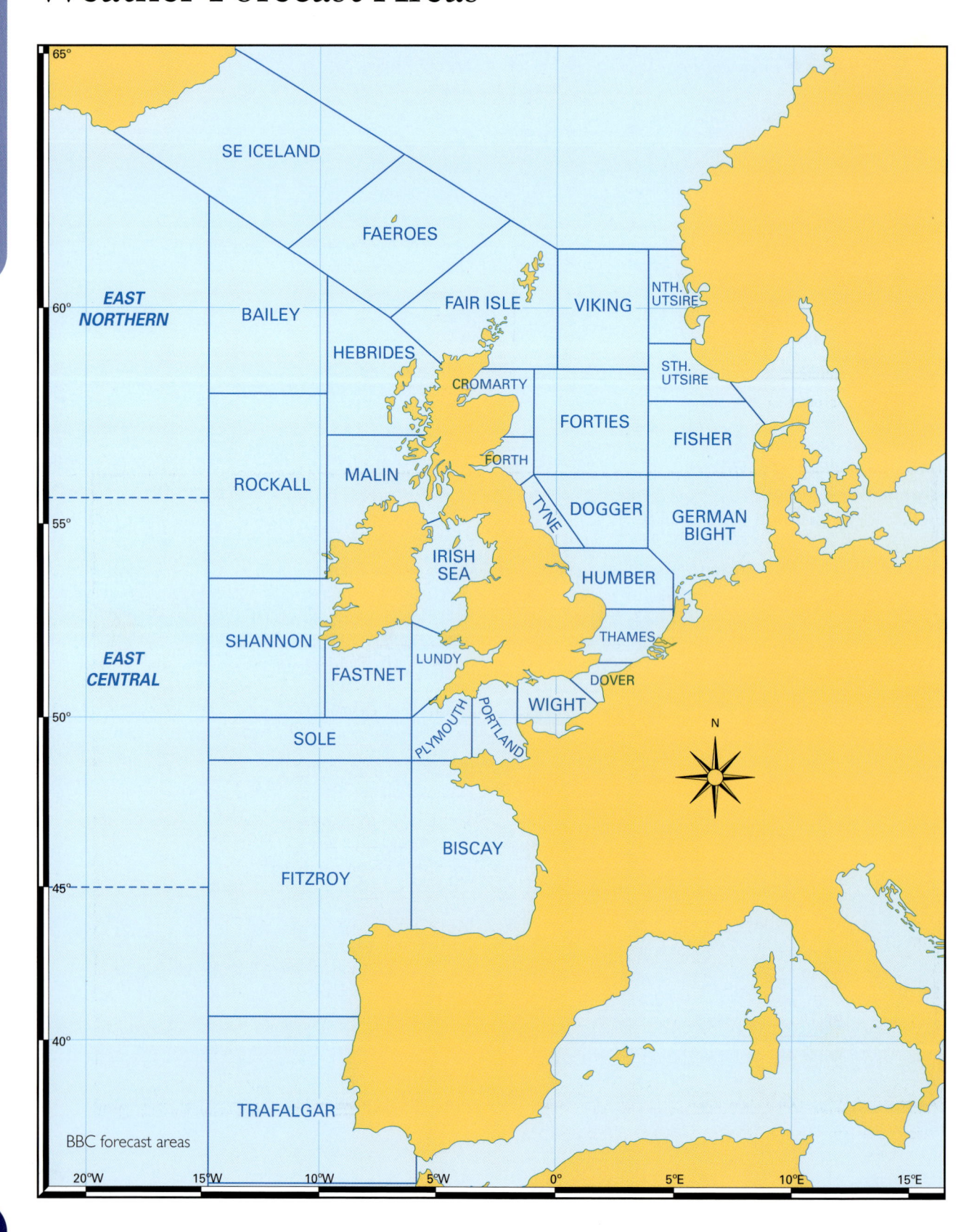

BBC forecast areas

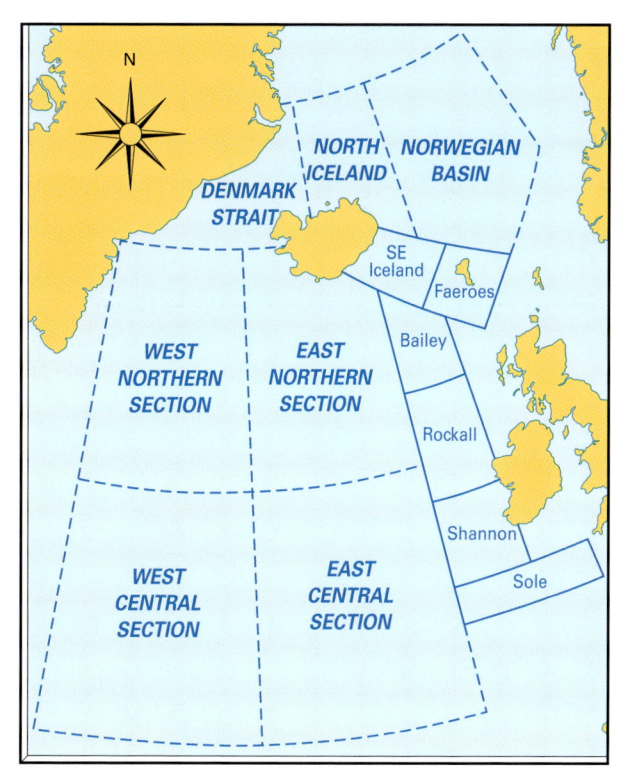

APPENDICES

BBC High seas forecast areas

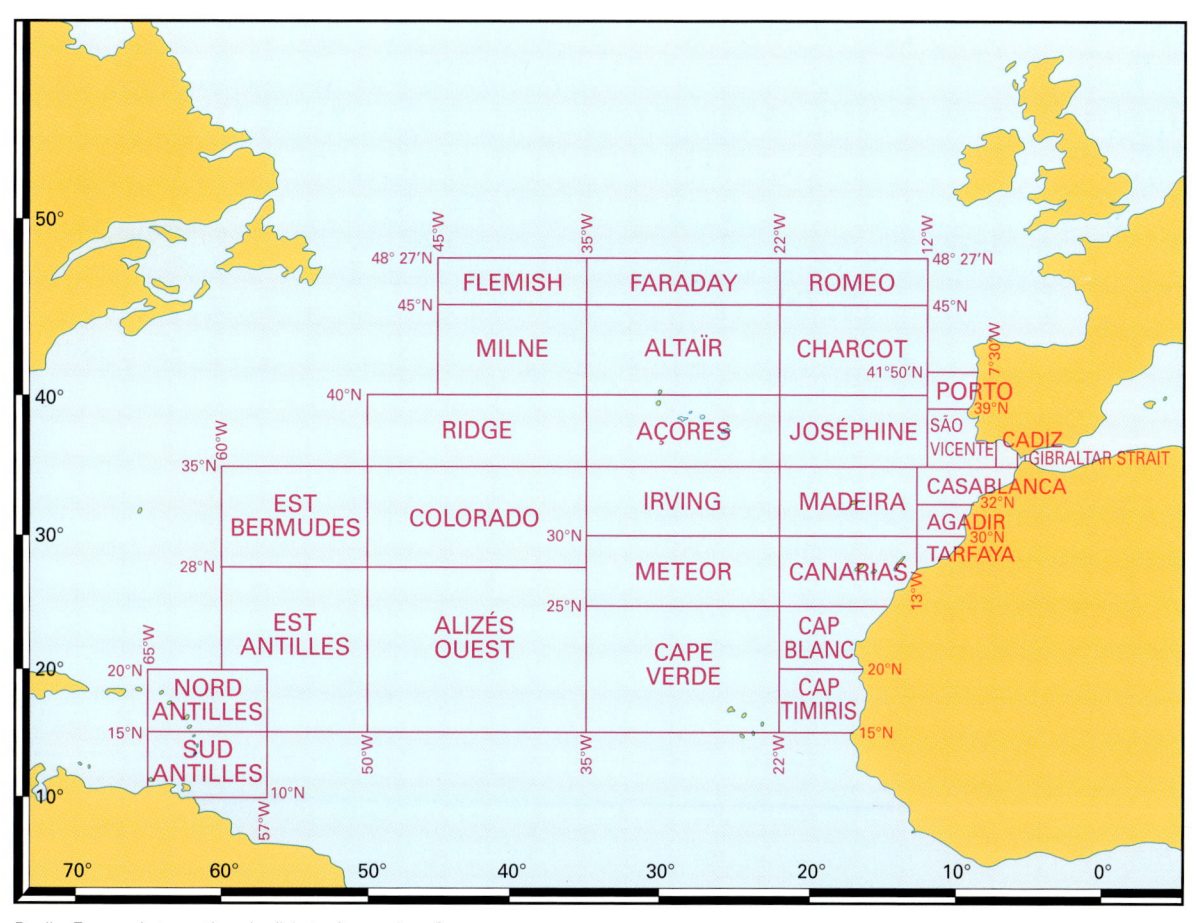

Radio France Internationale (Meteo) weather forecast areas

271

Appendix E

Weights, Measures and Conversions

The following are intended as outline reminders only – full conversion tables will be found in most almanacs and some cruising guides. Liquid measures are assumed to be of water.

British	American
(Long) ton = 2240 lb	(Short) ton = 2000 lb
Gallon = 160 fl oz	Gallon = 128 fl oz
Pint = 16 fl oz	Pint = 20 fl oz
	Cup = 8 fl oz

CONVERSION CHART		
To convert:	**Divide by:**	**To get:**
Centimetres	2.54	Inches
Gallons (Imp)	1.20094	Gallons (US)
Grams	28.349523	Ounces
Kilograms	0.4536	Pounds
Kilometres	1.609	Miles (statute)
Litres	4.54609	Gallons (Imp)
Litres	0.56826125	Pints
Litres	3.785412	Gallons (US)
Metres	1.828804	Fathoms
Metres	0.3048	Feet
Metres	1852	Miles (nautical)
Miles (nautical)	1.1516	Miles (statute)
Millimetres	25.4	Inches
Tonnes (metric)	0.9078	Tons (short)

Note: To do the above conversions in reverse, multiply instead of divide.

Celsius to Fahrenheit: ÷ 5 x 9 + 32
Fahrenheit to Celsius: −32 ÷ 9 x 5

Appendix F

Coping with Complete Electronic Failure

Before setting off across an ocean it is worth considering how to cope if the electrical system fails. Most modern cruising yachts are now heavily reliant on electronics, and therefore need a functioning electrical system in order to navigate safely. Some yachts carry a 'back-up' sextant on board, but relatively few have both the reliable skills and the necessary supporting information (such as Air Tables) to use one very effectively, least of all in a crisis. But skippers are responsible for doing all they can to ensure the safety of their crew. It is certainly worthwhile taking the trouble to gain a working knowledge of how to use a sextant to establish latitude at least by a noon site (or quantify the change in latitude from a previously logged position). This simple skill, which can be self taught with a little practice using books readily available from nautical bookshops, is likely to greatly reduce the level of uncertainty of an Estimated Position (EP).

It is advisable to keep a backup handheld GPS with spare batteries inside a waterproof bag and within a metal box (or the oven, but remember to remove before baking) for lightning protection. This is likely to resolve the vast majority of navigational equipment failures. Handhelds can be battery hungry but need only be switched on once a day for a position. Have a paper passage chart onboard and make sure that you keep a paper log of your daily position.

In the unlikely event that a backup GPS fails or the GPS system goes down for an extended period, it is worth remembering that people have successfully navigated across the Atlantic Ocean without electronics, mechanical logs or sextants for hundreds of years. The situation is far from disastrous. The primary concern is likely to be whether you are carrying sufficient water and food for a potentially longer time at sea. A worst case scenario in this respect would be if you encountered electrical wipe-out on route to Bermuda if you had planned to stop and re-provision there or, similarly, if you experience problems on route to the Cape Verdes.

The trade wind route – crossing to the Caribbean

Any vessel on the trade wind route is likely to arrive in the Caribbean sooner or later. This is proved almost every year when abandoned yachts turn up on the windward shores of Caribbean islands several weeks or months after being left at sea. As long as you have kept a paper copy of your passage log and have a paper passage chart, you should have some idea of your position and likely track. But even without these, if you continue in a westerly direction, away from the sunrise and towards the sunset, you will make landfall.

Crossing eastwards towards Europe

This is a trickier situation as the winds and currents are not so steadfast. You will wish to avoid Bermuda and may not arrive at the Azores. However, you are very likely to make landfall somewhere on the coast of Europe. Again, as long as you have kept a hand-written log and have a passage chart you should have some idea of your position and likely track.

Dead reckoning

Whichever direction you are heading, navigate by dead reckoning (DR). Use a compass (or the sunrise if there is nothing else) to maintain and record your direction. In the absence of a mechanical log, any small floating object can be used to check the speed of the boat through the water. Record the time (in seconds) it takes to travel 10 metres back after dropping it from the bow and then use the table (below).

You will have to estimate any effect of current from the information given on routeing charts and by comparing the record of boat log with GPS log prior to losing the electronics. The assistance given by the effects of current

Distance (metres)	10	10	10	10	10	10	10	10	10	10	10	10	10	10	10	10	10
Time (seconds)	1	2	3	4	5	6	7	8	9	10	11	12	13	14	15	16	17
Speed (knots)	19.4	9.7	6.5	4.9	3.9	3.2	2.8	2.4	2.2	1.9	1.8	1.6	1.5	1.4	1.3	1.2	1.1

may be considerable for both westward and eastward crossings and must be considered when estimating days to run before landfall.

Using a MW (AM) radio

A MW radio (perhaps a wind-up one kept in a grab bag for just such an emergency) can be very useful. Tuned to a local frequency and turned on from time to time you should start picking up stations at around 30 to 40 miles during daylight hours. This distance can be considerably increased or decreased by some atmospheric conditions – it tends to be increased at night. Once you have tuned in to a station, the aerial inside the set (not the telescopic one on top) will be surprisingly sensitive to the direction it is pointed in. The best signal will usually be when the flat front or back of the set is pointing directly at the transmitter (in other words you are likely to have good reception with the radio either facing the transmitter or with its back to the transmitter). Given that you should know the approximate direction of the nearest land, you should be able to work out the direction of the transmitting station. At one time a radio to be used in this way was a legal requirement for all Barbados fishing boats. They just followed the signal home.

Making landfall

The main concern will be making safe landfall. You should have some idea of your position from your dead reckoning, but it is a good idea to assume that you are one or more days closer, depending on how long you have been estimating position. The Caribbean islands and the European coast tend to be very well lit and it is likely that you will see the loom of lights from at least 40 miles in good visibility. Clouds tend to form over land and can be a good indicator during the daytime, particularly over the more mountainous islands. You are likely to see an increase in bird activity and may notice varieties of coastal birds. Off the whole of the coast of Europe you may notice a change in sea colour and you will encounter fishing fleets and commercial vessels in increasing numbers as you approach land. So you should have plenty of notice of your approach whether it is day or night. Modern equipment has led most of us into an impatient approach to making landfall. If you are in a less certain position it makes good sense to heave-to during the night. Aim to close the shore in daylight.

Gain confidence through practise

The normal availability of GPS makes it easy for a crew to practise emergency navigation by DR, EP and Sextant and then check the accuracy of their results. Doing so will make them familiar with the routine, help to mark the progress of the passage, and be one thing less to worry about if the electrics do fail. Some crew might relish turning their daily fixes into a competition with daily awards or 'booby-prizes'.

Index

AC power 19
Admiralty charts 263
Agadir, Morocco 111–12
air conditioning 25–6
AIS 48–9
alchohol 35
anchor cable 12–13
anchoring with two anchors 13
anchors 12
Annapolis, Maryland 209–12
Antigua 160–3
Atlantic coast
    Europe 75–96
      regional weather and passage
        timings 75–6
      coast of Morocco 97–100
      Trade Wind Routes 135–8
      coast of Morocco 97–100
automatic steering 15–16
autopilots 16
auxiliary generators 20
awnings 23–4
Azores 234–44
    to Northern Europe 229
    to Spain, Portugal or Gibraltar 229

backed anchors 13
Bahamas 177–8, 184–5, 186–7
Baiona, Spain 92–4
Barbados 149–52
barbecues 28
batteries 18–19
Bayona, Spain 92–4
Beaufort, North Carolina 202–4
Bermuda 229, 230–3
    to ports north of New York 226
    to the Azores 228
berths 25
bilge pumps 7
biminis 23
Brest, France 86–8
bridges on the ICW 197
Bridgetown, Barbados 149–52
British Virgin Islands 164–5
buoyage 74, 197
butane 27

Calor 27
Camping Gaz 27
Canary Current 137
Canary Islands 119–26
Cape Verdes Islands 127–32
Caribbean
    currency 141
    direct to the Azores 226–7
    Islands to Florida 176–90
    landfalls 139–67
    passage to Bermuda 225
    to Beaufort, North Carolina 226
carnivals 147
Cascais, Lisbon, Portugal 95–6
Ceuta, Spain 106–7
Chaguaramas Bay, Trinidad 153–6
chain, anchor 14
chart accuracy 46–7
chartplotter 47
children on board 42
ciguatera poisoning 37
CITES 53

clothing 29
Coast Guard (US) 195–6
cockpit drains 7
collisions 61
Cólon, Panama 173–5
communication 41, 46–5
computers 50, 51
conservation 64–5
contraception 45
cooking fuel 27–8
coral reefs 65
corrosion to engine 17
courtesy flags 56
crew 38–45
    recruitment 38
Crosshaven, Cork, Ireland 78–81
cruiser's radio nets 72
currency in the Caribbean 141
currents 68, 69
    and tides in the Eastern Caribbean 144
    in the Azores 235–6
cutless bearings 6

Dakar 133
deck fittings 5–7
decks, below 25–32
dengue fever 45
diarrhoea 43–4
dinghies 20–1
documents 53–7
dolphins and whales 64–5
Domincan Republic 179–81
dorado 37
downwind rig 10–11
DSC 50
duty-free imports 56

Eastern Caribbean 141–6
    anchorages 145
    currents and tides 144
    geology 146
    weather 143–4
    wind acceleration zones 144
echosounder 48
electrical system 17–18
electronic failure 273–4
emergency steering 60
engine 16–19
English Harbour, Antigua 160–3
entry procedures 53–7
EPIRBs 62
Europe to the USA or Canada via the
    Azores and Bermuda 229
Europe to US or Canada via northern
    route 247–8
eyeball navigation 49

Faial 239–41
Falmouth Harbour, Antigua 160–3
Falmouth, UK 82–5
Faroe 249
fendering 15
festivals, Caribbean 147–8
fire 81
firearms 63
fishing 35–6
flares 62
Flores 237–8
Florida 188–90, 198–200

flying fish 37
fog 70, 192
food 32–3
    pests 34
    storage 33
forked moor 13
formalities (USA) 53, 194–5
    in the Caribbean 141–3
    in the US Islands 142–3
Fort Lauderdale, Florida 188–90
freezers 28
French West Indies 141
fridges 28
fuel safety 28
furling gear 10

gales 59
galley 26
Gambia, The 134
gas cylinders 27
geology in the Caribbean 146
Georgetown, Great Exhuma,
    Bahamas 184–5
Georgia 200
Gibraltar 101–3
GMDSS 50
gnomonic charts 47
GPS 47
grab bags 61–2
Grand Banks shipping 194
Great Circle sailing 47
Greenland 249
GRIB files 51, 73
ground tackle 12–14
Gulf Stream 193

Halifax, Nova Scotia 250–3
harbour awnings 23
haul-out and repair facilities 147
health 43–5
heating systems 26
holding tanks 6–7
Horta, Faial 239–41
hull fittings 5–7
hurricanes 59, 68–70, 192, 264–6

ice reports 246
icebergs 71, 192–3
Iceland 249
Imray charts 260–2
INMARSAT 73
insulation 26, 54
insurance 56–7
Intracoastal Waterway 192, 197–201
inverters 19

keeping watch 40–1
kerosene 27

La Coruña, Spain 89–91
La Linea, Spain, 104–5
Labrador Current 193–4
Lamin, The Gambia 134
landfalls in the Caribbean 139–67
landfalls on the Atlantic Coast of the USA
    191–223
Lanzarote 120, 121
laptops 50
Las Palmas de Gran Canaria 122–4

THE ATLANTIC CROSSING GUIDE

laundry 30
liferafts 61
lightning 60
line squalls 59
living aboard 23–37
long range communication 52
Luperon, Dominican Republic 179–81

Madeira 113–14, 115–18
Maine 221–3
maintenance, yacht 21
malaria 44
man overboard 58–9
manchineel trees 147
Marina Atlantico, Santa Cruz de Tenerife 125–6
Marina Quinta do Lorde, Madeira 117–18
marine conservation 64–5
Marine SSB 51, 52
Marsh Harbour, Abacos, Bahamas 186–7
Maryland 209–12
mast and spars 7
medical cabinet 45
meteorological terms 267–9
Mindelo 130–2
Mohammedia, Morocco 109–10
money, obtaining 56
Morehead City, North Carolina 202–4
Moroccan coast 108, 109–10, 111–12
mosquito screens 24

Nantucket Shoals 194
navigation 46–52
　Caribbean 178
navigational equipment 46–50
NAVTEX 51, 73
New York 213–17
New York and Newport, approaches to 216–17
Newfoundland 249, 254–6
Newport, Rhode Island 218–20
Norfolk, Virginia 205–8
North Atlantic
　current 76–7
　overview 66–74
　passages and landfalls in the higher latitudes 245–59
　passages in the middle latitudes 224–44
　tides 77
North Carolina 201, 202
North Equatorial Current 137
Nova Scotia 250–3

ocean currents 137
OceansWatch 65
onboard entertainment 41
onboard routine 39
ORCA 64
outboard engines 20–1
overboard, falling 58–9

Panama 171, 172, 173–5
paraffin 27
passage timings 191
passages
　and landfalls in the higher latitudes of the North Atlantic 245–59
　in the middle latitudes of the North Atlantic 224–44
　westward 229
permits 54
pests 63
pilotage, Caribbean 178
Ponta Delgada, São Miguel 242–4

port entry procedures 53–7
port information 74
Port St Charles, Barbados 149–52
Portland, Maine 221–3
Porto das Lajes, Flores 237–8
Porto Grande, Mindelo, São Vicente, Cape Verdes 130–2
Porto Santo, Madeira 115–16
power consumption 18
power supply, alternative 19–20
preparation 2–4
preparing the boat 5–22
Prickly Bay, Grenada 139
propane 27
propeller shafts 6
protocol 53–6
Providenciales, Turks and Caicos Islands 182–3
provisioning 32–3, 146
Puerto de la Luz, Las Palmas de Gran Canaria 122–4

radar 48
radio 51–2
　amateur(ham) 51
　safety networks 51–2
　voice forecasts 73–4
rain catchers 35
rallies 3–4
Reef Check 65
reefing sails 10
Rhode Island 218–20
rigging 7–9
rigging, running 8–9
rigging, standing 7–8
risk, dealing with 58–63
Road Town, Tortola 166
Rodney Bay, St Lucia 157–9
route timing for Atlantic 67–71
Routes across the Caribbean 168–75
rum 146

safety equipment, personal and boat 58–9
safety, fuel 28
SafetyNET 73
sails 9–11
　chafe 9
　drives 6
　plan 9
　reefing 10
　storm 10
São Vicente 130–2
SARTs 63
satellite telephones 52
science, contribution to 64–5
Scottish coast 249
screens 23–4
scuba diving 57
seasickness 43
security 63, 148, 153
sextant 47
ship's log 46
ship's stamp 55
ship's time 41
shipping (USA) 194
shipping lanes 77
shore power 19
skin fittings 5–6
solar panels 20
South Carolina 200
spares and repairs 21–2
spear guns 37
squalls 59
St George's, Bermuda 230–3

St John's, Newfoundland 254–6
St Lucia 157–9
steering, automatic 15–16
stern glands 6
storm 264–6
　sails 10
　shelters 266
Stornaway, Isle of Lewis 257–9
stowage 27, 29
Strait of Gibraltar, harbours 97–107
sun protection and dangers 23, 44
swell 137

tax in the Azores 236
Tenerife 125–6
tides 74
　on the East coast of the USA 193–4
　North Atlantic 77
toilets, marine 6
tool boxes 22
Tortola 166
Trade Wind Routes 135–8
traffic separation schemes 57
Trinidad 153–6
Turks and Caicos Islands 177–8, 182–3
twin headsails 10–11

US charts 260
US Coast Guard 195–6
USA or Canada, routes to Europe 246–7
USA or Canada direct to the Azores 228
USA to Bermuda 227

vane steering gear 15–16
VAT 54
ventilation 25–6
VHF 50
Viking Route 248
Virgin Gorda Yacht Harbour, Virgin Gorda 167
Virginia 205–8

waste disposal 30–1
watch-keeping 40–1
water ingress and leaks 7
water supplies 34–5
water, plastic contamination 35
watermakers 34
water-powered generators 20
weather
　Azores 235
　Bermuda 229
　forecast areas 270–1
　forecast transmissions 71–4
　patterns in North Atlantic 224–5
　radio nets 72
　regional between Caribbean Islands and Florida 177
　regional for the Eastern Caribbean 143-4
　regional weather and passage timings 75–6
weights, measures and conversions 272
West Africa 133-4
whales and dolphins 64–5
wind acceleration zones in the Eastern Caribbean 144
wind generators 19-20
wind vanes 15–16
winds 67-8

yellow fever 44
Yellow Fever vaccination certificates 54

276